T0315950

The Who's Who of
LEEDS UNITED
1905-2008

The Who's Who of
LEEDS UNITED
1905-2008

DB
PUBLISHING

First published in Great Britain in 2008 by
The Breedon Books Publishing Company Limited
Breedon House, 3 The Parker Centre,
Derby, DE21 4SZ.

This paperback edition published in Great Britain in 2014
by DB Publishing, an imprint of JMD Media Ltd

© Martin Jarred and Malcolm Macdonald, 2008

All Rights Reserved. No part of this publication may be reproduced,
stored in a retrieval system, or transmitted in any form, or by any
means, electronic, mechanical, photocopying, recording or otherwise
without the prior permission in writing of the copyright holders, nor
be otherwise circulated in any form or binding or cover other than in
which it is published and without a similar condition being imposed
on the subsequent publisher.

A catalogue record for this book is available from the British Library.

ISBN 978-1-78091-434-3

Printed and bound in the UK by Copytech (UK) Ltd Peterborough

CONTENTS

PREFACE

FEW clubs in football history can have experienced the beautiful game's highs and lows like Leeds United in recent seasons. From a Champions League semi-final to the third tier of English football – it has been one of the most well-documented sporting falls from grace. The last five years has seen financial collapse, two relegations, points deductions and a conveyor belt of players through the revolving doors of Elland Road. The 2006 Championship Play-off Final at Cardiff's Millennium Stadium offered a false dawn – relegation and administration followed the next year. Despite a 15-point deduction, United showed great resolve to reach the League One Play-off Final at Wembley in 2008 when they lost 1–0 to Doncaster. Although they didn't quite go up, the signs are there that the club is finally pointing in the right direction.

Even at the club's lowest ebb, United's fans have kept the faith with huge crowds breaking League One records. But even the most ardent Leeds fan would have difficulty keeping track of the vast numbers of players who have pulled on the famous white shirt in recent years.

The Who's Who of Leeds United should help jolt a few memories. It includes details of every player to have made a senior appearance for United – and its predecessor Leeds City – up to the end of the 2007–08 season. According to our reckoning, that is 766 players, from the Revie era legends and Wilkinson's heroes to the lesser lights. They are all here.

This book is the outcome of decades of research in libraries around the country, particularly Leeds Library, the British Museum Newspaper Library in Colindale and the Football League archive, available when they were based in Lytham St Annes. More recently, the internet has proved an invaluable tool for unearthing information, particularly with the growing number of players from overseas.

We have taken material from other books, always trying to check it, and we are indebted to scores of other authors and members of the Association of Football Statisticians for their help. Dates of birth and death have been researched through the various national Registration Services. We are most grateful to The Press, York, for the use of many photographs, to Paul Dews and Don Warters of Leeds United's media department, our wives Jenny and Isobel, and to Breedon Books for their support.

Martin Jarred
Malcolm MacDonald
2008

FOREWORD

by Gary McAllister

THERE is no doubt I enjoyed my best years as a player with Leeds United. It is a fantastic club with a proud history, and to play for and manage Leeds United is a tremendous honour. When I returned to Elland Road in January 2008 I joined a select band of people who had done both, and to sit alongside legends like Don Revie, Billy Bremner, Eddie Gray and Allan Clarke is a great thrill.

Hopefully, the current squad will go on to create their own bit of history, as we all try to get Leeds United back in the top flight where they – and the fantastic supporters – should be.

My Leeds playing debut was certainly an eventful one. I was a summer signing from Leicester, and United were back in the old First Division for the first time in eight years, kicking-off at Everton. We took Goodison Park by storm, racing into a 3–0 lead, but Everton fought back to reduce it to a single goal and John Lukic had to make some great saves late on to ensure we took maximum points. But the message was loud and clear – Leeds United were back in the big time.

Under Howard Wilkinson's astute management, Leeds finished fourth that season and won the title the following year. We had a great squad, captained by the amazing Gordon Strachan, from whom I inherited the skipper's armband. John Lukic, Mel Sterland, Tony Dorigo, David Batty, Chris Whyte, Chris Fairclough, Rod Wallace, Lee Chapman and Gary Speed were all regulars in a talented Leeds squad that reached a pinnacle only Don Revie's superstars had achieved before – League champions.

All those players – and hundreds more – are included in this book. Some are true legends, and others played just minutes in the famous Leeds colours.

I wish every success to The Who's Who of Leeds United and hope it helps serve as an inspiration to the players of the future.

Gary McAllister,
Leeds
May 2008

LEEDS CITY PLAYERS

ACKERLEY George

Inside-forward

Born: West Derby, Liverpool, 21 May 1887.
Career: Liverpool amateur. LEEDS CITY March 1910.

■ Recruited in 1910 from Liverpool, where he was an amateur, by Frank Scott-Walford, George went straight into the side at Barnsley. He only figured in one more game, a 3–0 defeat, in the last away match of the season at Manchester City.

AFFLECK George

Full-back

Born: Auchendinney, Midlothian, 1 July 1888.
5ft 9in, 11st 6lb (1909).
Career: Pennicuik. LEEDS CITY June 1909. Grimsby Town October 1919. Coach in Rotterdam July 1925.

■ George provided 10 years' service at Elland Road, chalking up nearly 200 appearances. He was always one of the first names on the team sheet. Even when defender Alec Creighton joined Leeds, Affleck switched from left-back to right-back with ease. George's game was built on positional play rather than speed, and he consistently turned in a high level of performances. At the age of 31 he was forced to leave City when the club was disbanded, and he was sold in the historic auction of October 1919 to Grimsby Town for £500, joining the Mariners with colleague Arthur Wainwright. George stayed at Grimsby for six years, before going to Holland to take up a coaching appointment with a club in Rotterdam.

ALLAN John

Wing-half

Born: Newcastle upon Tyne, 11 May 1890
5ft 7½in, 11st 2lb (1910).
Career: Benwell St James. Bentwick Mission. Newcastle North End. Bedlington United. Carlisle United. Everton 1909. LEEDS CITY July 1912. Rochdale 1913. Coventry City May 1914. Walsall 1920.

■ Jack's best days were away from Elland Road. He made his Football League debut for Everton in the February 1910 Merseyside derby, a 1–0 win at Anfield. However, he was largely a reserve at Goodison, where he helped win the 1909–10 Lancashire Combination. He arrived at Leeds in summer 1912 but lost his place midway through the season and dropped out of the League to join Rochdale, then in the Second Division of the Lancashire Combination. He teamed up with his old Leeds manager, Frank Scott-Walford, at Southern League Coventry City. By this time he was a useful stand-in centre-forward and scored three hat-tricks in the final season before the Southern League closed down because of the war. When football resumed, he played in Coventry's first Football League game and was in the Coventry side which lost 4–0 to Leeds in their first away game.

ASTILL Thomas

Inside-left

Born: Brightside, Sheffield, 9 December 1889.
5ft 8in, 11st (1908).
Career: Sheffield Douglas. LEEDS CITY December 1908. Doncaster Rovers 1911. Mexborough Town 1913.

■ Tommy replaced Jimmy Gemmell for the West Riding derby defeat at Valley Parade in his only senior game for Leeds – on the same day Elland Road hosted the 1910 FA Cup semi-final between Everton and Barnsley. He joined Doncaster with Harry Bromage and the pair were in the Rovers side which won the Sheffield Challenge Cup in 1913.

BAINBRIDGE Simpson

Right-winger

Born: Silksworth, Co. Durham, 3 April 1895.
Died: Sunderland, 12 November 1988.
5ft 9in, 10st 2lb (1913).
Career: Seaton Delaval. LEEDS CITY November 1912. Preston North End October 1919. South Shields 1920. Aberdeen 1921–22. Wheatley Hill Alliance. Shildon Athletic.

■ Simpson represented England Schools against Wales at Aberdare in 1908. He eventually replaced Hugh Roberts on City's right-wing but, after the war, featured on the left. He was one of the more sought-after players at the Metropole Hotel auction, joining Preston North End, for whom he made his First Division debut against Newcastle United. However, he was not retained at the end of the season and joined South Shields, where his first goal for his new club was against the newly-formed Leeds United in a 3–0 Shields win on 8 September 1920. He then spent a season in Aberdeen, featuring in the side beaten 3–1 by Morton in the 1922 Scottish FA Cup Final.

BATES William Edric

Right-back

Born: Kirkheaton, nr Huddersfield, 5 May 1884.
Died: Belfast, 17 January 1957.
5ft 7½in, 11st 6lb (1907).
Career: Bolton Wanderers 1906. LEEDS CITY July 1907.

■ Billy did not really cut it as a footballer but instead made his mark in cricket, playing for both Yorkshire and Glamorgan. He certainly had a great sporting pedigree. His dad, Willie, was a cricket all-rounder who played for Yorkshire and England and also played rugby for his country. Billy started in football with Bolton Wanderers, where he played a couple of games at centre-forward. At Leeds, his winter career did not really take off and he proved far more adept at cricket, scoring nearly 16,000 first-class runs. At Headingley he was nicknamed 'The Marquis' because he was such a dapper dresser. He was a cricket professional at Briton Ferry and Broughton Hall (Cheshire) and coached in Ireland. He did leave a football legacy though: his son, Ted, was the well-known Southampton inside-forward and manager.

BEREN Hugh Gray

Right-half

Born: Leith, 9 October 1892.
Died: Leith, 1961.
5ft 8in, 12st 7lb (1909).

Career: Musselburgh, LEEDS CITY June 1909.

◼ Hugh arrived at Leeds from Scotland as a 16-year-old with a big reputation. He quickly got into the first team in place of Haydn Price but failed to impress. Sometimes, he was listed as Berens in football annuals of the day.

BLACKMAN Frederick Ernest

Right-back

Born: Kennington, Kent, 8 February 1884. 5ft 10in, 12st 7lb (1914).
Career: Woolwich Arsenal. Hastings & St Leonards May 1907. Brighton & Hove Albion May 1909. Huddersfield Town £300 May 1911. LEEDS CITY £1,000 February 1914. Fulham wartime guest. Queen's Park Rangers 1919.

◼ A carpenter and cabinet maker by trade, London-born Fred almost built himself an England career. He was a shade past his best when he joined Leeds but was still a class act. He started with Woolwich Arsenal before joining South Eastern League side Hastings & St Leonards for a couple of seasons – the second as skipper. He moved along the coast to Brighton and was an ever-present player in their 1910 Southern League Championship-winning team. He was at the peak of his powers that year and *Athletic News* described him as 'Wonderfully quick on his feet, sure kicker with either foot, fearless tackler.' He played in Brighton's 1–0 win over champions Aston Villa in the FA Charity Shield, represented the Southern League twice against the Football League, and in January 1911 had an England trial at

Tottenham. Although full national honours eluded him, Fred's reputation had soared and a big-money move took him to Huddersfield where he was appointed captain in the second of his three seasons with the Terriers. His transfer to Leeds was regarded as a big coup and he went straight into the team at right-back for Charlie Copeland.

BOWMAN Adam

Centre-forward

Born: Forfar, 4 August 1880. 5ft 11in, 12st (1908).
Career: St Johnstone. East Stirling. Everton December 1901. Blackburn Rovers March 1903. Brentford May 1907. LEEDS CITY May 1908. Portsmouth November 1909. Leith Athletic. Forfar 1910. Accrington Stanley March 1912.

◼ Adam forged a decent career, including a stop at Leeds, where he netted half a dozen goals in 15 League games. He came down from Scotland to launch his professional career in England with Everton. His best seasons were with Blackburn in 1904–05 and 1905–06 when he was top scorer and also enjoyed a productive time in the Southern League with Brentford, scoring 22 goals in 30 games.

BRIDGETT Harold

Left-winger

Born: Stoke-on-Trent, September 1886 or 1887.
Career: Stoke. LEEDS CITY May 1909.

◼ Harold hailed from Fegg Hayes, near Stoke, and spent four seasons at Leeds, mainly in the Midland League side. He may have been related to England's Arthur Bridgett, who played for Stoke and Sunderland.

BROMAGE Henry

Goalkeeper

Born: Derby, 17 May 1879. 5ft 10in, 12st 8lb (1905).
Career: Derby Constitutional. Derby County October 1898. Burton United 1901. LEEDS CITY August 1905. Doncaster Rovers 1911. Bentley Colliery 1913.

◼ Harry played more games in goal than

any other City player, making his debut in the club's first game in the Football League. He was a member of a well-known footballing family from Derby and made his debut for his home-town team on Boxing Day 1899 against Glossop. After a two-year spell at Burton he joined Leeds, eventually moving to Doncaster, where his brother, Billy, a former winger with Sheffield United and Gainsborough, was captain. Harry's uncle, Enos, also played in goal for Derby while Enos junior, possibly Harry's brother, also had a spell with the Rams.

BROUGHTON Thomas William

Right-half

Born: Clarence, Stockton, Co. Durham, 7 June 1888.
Career: Grangetown. LEEDS CITY October 1912.

◼ Local newspapers hailed Tom's City debut – a 3–0 win against Blackpool on New Year's Day 1912 – as 'excellent' but he only played three more times for the first team.

BURNETT James J.

Inside-forward
Born: Aberdeen.
5ft 10in, 12st (1904).

Career: Victoria United August 1895. Aberdeen July 1897. Portsmouth 1903. Dundee 1904. Grimsby Town May 1905. Brighton & Hove Albion May 1907. LEEDS CITY May 1908–10.

■ Jimmy was one of four Brighton players to follow manager Frank Scott-Walford to Elland Road in 1908. A decent player, the biggest criticism was his lack of pace, which saw the Scot eventually lose his place. He had a good strike rate at Portsmouth – nine goals in 15 Southern League games – but his best spell was his two years at Grimsby.

CAMPBELL Alexander

Full-back

Born: Inverness, 7 March 1883.
5ft 10in, 12st (1906).
Career: Inverness Clachnacuddin. Middlesbrough August 1906. LEEDS CITY December 1911.

■ Unlucky Alex broke his leg on his City debut – a 3–1 win against Nottingham Forest at Elland Road on 30 December 1911 and did not play again professionally. He was largely a reserve in his five years with Middlesbrough.

CLARK Andrew

Left-back

Born: Leith, 16 March 1880.
5ft 7in, 13st (1903).
Career: Hamilton Academical. Buckhaven United. Hearts August 1899. Stoke May 1901. Plymouth Argyle 1903. LEEDS CITY May 1906. Plymouth Argyle. Brentford. Southend United.

■ Scottish junior international Andy made his senior debut for Hearts against Rangers on 2 September 1899 but left the Edinburgh club after disciplinary problems. He moved about south of the border and was the first-choice left-back at Elland Road in 1906–07.

CLARKIN John

Inside-forward

Born: Ireland.
5ft 7in, 10st 5lb (1911).
Career: Shelbourne. LEEDS CITY May 1911. Belfast Celtic 1912.

■ John was one of many Irish players picked by Frank Scott-Walford on the cheap in 1911 – City had announced a loss of £1,000, preventing the manager from making any big-money signings. Clarkin's only game was at Gainsborough on Boxing Day 1911, City winning 2–1.

CLAY William Edward

Full-back

Born: Belfast, 31 October 1880.
5ft 7½in, 10st 3lb (1903).
Career: Belfast Celtic. Sheffield United 1903–04. Belfast Celtic. LEEDS CITY May 1911. Belfast Celtic 1912.

■ Despite a good pedigree in Irish football, Clay's only senior outing for City was an FA Cup second preliminary round replay against Mexborough. In the first of his three spells with Belfast Celtic, Clay had turned out for the Irish League against the Football League in Belfast, in 1902. The following season he was reserve to Sheffield United teammate Peter Boyle for the full internationals against Wales and Scotland.

COPELAND Charles William

Right-back

Born: Grangetown, Middlesbrough, 12 March 1892.
5ft 8½in, 12st 1lb (1912).
Career: South Bank. LEEDS CITY August 1912. Coventry City September 1919. Merthyr Town 1920.

■ Charlie is thought to have been the catalyst for the expulsion of City from the Football League. He served City throughout World War One but, after a row about wages, he reported the club to the football authorities, alleging they had made illegal payments to players during wartime football. This triggered a chain of events that eventually saw the club thrown out of the League.

COWEN Robert William

Inside-right

Born: Chester-le-Street, Co. Durham, 21 September 1886.
5ft 10½in, 11st 9lb (1914).
Career: Spen Black and White. LEEDS CITY April 1914. Spen Black and White 1918.

■ Bob played just twice in the first team in the four seasons he was registered as a City player and returned to Northern Alliance club, Spen Black and White, in summer 1918.

CREIGHTON Alexander

Left-back

Born: Greenock, 7 July 1885.
5ft 7in, 11st 6lb (1910).
Career: Distillery. LEEDS CITY August 1910. Glenavon 1912.

■ Although a Scot, Alec was one of seven players who came across the Irish Sea for the start of the 1910–11 season. He proved one of the successes, being ever present that season as City finished sixth in Division Two.

CROOT Frederick Richard

Right-winger

Born: Little Harrowden, Wellingborough, Northants, 30 November 1885.
Died: Rushden, Northants, 5 July 1958.
5ft 7in, 12st 2lb (1907)
Career: Wellingborough. Sheffield United 1905. LEEDS CITY May 1907. Clydebank 1919.

■ Fred was one of the most consistent of all City players, scoring 38 League goals in 213 appearances. He first caught Sheffield United's eye when playing for Wellingborough in the Southern League. Fred made his Division One debut in a 4–1 defeat at Nottingham Forest but did not quite cut it with the Blades. However, he settled well at Elland Road, where he was a trusted penalty taker – scoring 15 spot-kicks in all, including two in a game at Barnsley in April 1912.

CUBBERLEY Stanley Morris

Wing-half

Born: Edmonton, London, 18 July 1882.
5ft 8in, 11st 3lb (1906).
Career: Cheshunt. LEEDS CITY May 1906. Swansea Town 1913. Manchester United May 1914.

■ Stan was a versatile type who made his debut in a nightmare 5–0 defeat at West Brom, but kept his place and scored on his home debut against Lincoln. All three of his City goals, in seven years at Elland Road, came in that first season. He eventually settled at left-half for a long spell before moving to Swansea, then in the Southern League. He left Wales with teammate Arthur Allman for Manchester United but did not play in the senior team. Stan's brother, Archie, was an inside-forward with Tottenham Hotspur.

CUNNINGHAM George P.

Right-winger

Born: Belfast.
5ft 7in, 11st (1910).
Career: Shelbourne. LEEDS CITY May 1910. Crewe Alexandra 1913.

■ George joined City, with Shelbourne teammates Mick Foley and Joe Enright, with a glowing reference from the *Irish Sporting Illustrated*, describing his rise as 'meteoric' and claiming he was 'destined to attain greater fame'. The publication added: 'He is ideally set up for a winger. A good turn of speed, a fine command of the ball, a gentlemanly player as well, he proves adept in outwitting an opponent. But it is his deadly accuracy in placing the ball in the centre that has brought him so prominently as one of our best.' Three first-team appearances – all defeats – suggest George did not match his reputation. At Shelbourne he had played for the Irish League against the Football League and Scottish League in 1909.

CUNNINGHAM Thomas

Goalkeeper

Born: Sunderland, 9 September 1884.
Career: Sunderland Juniors. LEEDS CITY August 1908.

■ Tom was a reserve goalkeeper who was called in at the last minute for the trip to Derby on 23 January 1909. County won 5–1 in what was Cunningham's only League appearance.

DOUGAL David Wishart

Right-winger

Born: Dundee, 22 March 1882.
Died: Dundee, 5 March 1937.
5ft 8½in (1908).
Career: Dundee Hibernian August 1902. Dundee May 1903. Preston North End trial 1904. Grimsby Town trial 1904. Clapton Orient August 1905. Reading 1907. Brighton & Hove Albion February 1908. LEEDS CITY June 1908. Montrose November 1910.

■ Dave was one of several ex-Brighton men who made their way to Elland Road when former Seagulls manager Frank Scott-Walford was appointed City manager. He made his City debut in a goalless draw against one of his former clubs, Clapton Orient, on the opening day of the 1908–09 season. He returned to Scotland to join Montrose and later worked in the confectionery industry in the Dundee area.

DOUGHERTY Joseph

Centre-forward

Born: Cockerton, Darlington, 11 November 1894.
5ft 10in, 11st 7lb (1914).
Career: Darlington Forge. LEEDS CITY February 1914. Oldham Athletic £100 April 1919. Shildon Athletic. Hartlepools United March 1921. Lincoln City trial 1923.

■ Joe's only City game came when he replaced star centre-forward Billy McLeod for the home game against Clapton Orient on 14 April 1914 – a 0–0 draw. His best playing years were lost to World War One but he re-emerged with Oldham after impressing in trials. He started the following season as first-choice centre-forward at Boundary Park but eventually gave way to another former Leeds man, Billy Halligan. He later featured in Hartlepools' first-ever Football League game in 1921, a 2–0 win over Wrexham.

DRAIN Thomas

Centre-forward

Born: Eastwood, Pollokshaws, Glasgow, 26 June 1879.
Died: Edinburgh, 19 September 1952.
5ft 9in, 11st 7lb (1907).
Career: Drongan Juniors. Glasgow Celtic. Ayr United. Maybole. Bradford City October 1903. LEEDS CITY July 1905. Kilmarnock 1906. Aberdeen 1907–08.

Carlisle United 1908. Exeter City 1908. Woolwich Arsenal May 1909. Nithsdale Wanderers 1910. Galston 1911.

■ Tommy netted City's first-ever Football League goals in a 2–2 home draw against Lincoln City on 11 September 1905. But he was largely confined to the reserves and was selected for the Midland League XI to face champions Sheffield United at Bramall Lane, at the end of the season. Drain had been recruited from neighbours Bradford City, where he enjoyed a spectacular start, scoring on his Football League debut in a 3–1 win over Burnley at Valley Parade. He netted a hat-trick in his next match, when the Paraders were held 3–3 by Bolton at Valley Parade. Despite his flying start, he faded at Bradford and it was a similar tale at Elland Road. In later days he worked as a fireman in Fife.

EDMONDSON John

Centre-forward

Born: Carleton, Lancashire.
5ft 11in, 11st 8lb (1914).
Career: Leyland. LEEDS CITY April 1914. Sheffield Wednesday £800 October 1919. Swansea Town £500 May 1920. Exeter City September 1923.

■ John played for City either side of World War One and managed half a dozen goals in 11 appearances and averaged a goal every other game in his wartime matches. He fetched £800 when he was sold to Sheffield Wednesday in the Metropole Hotel auction. The promise he showed at Elland Road did not develop with the Owls but he was top scorer with Swansea in 1920–21.

ENRIGHT Joseph

Inside-left

Born: Belfast 1890.
5ft 7in, 10st 4lb (1910).
Career: Shelbourne. LEEDS CITY May 1910. Newport County £50 October 1913. Coventry City 1914. Athlone Town.

■ Joe and City teammate Joe Moran both played for Ireland in the 4–1 defeat against Scotland on 16 March 1912 – the first Irishmen to be capped at Leeds. Enright was already a seasoned performer when he arrived at Elland Road from Shelbourne with Mick Foley and George Cunningham. He had represented the Irish League against the Scottish League in 1909 and made a scoring debut for City in a 2–1 defeat at Blackpool. He finished the campaign with a dozen goals and hit 12 more in 1911–12 – just a couple behind leading marksman Billy McLeod. During World War One he served with the army in the RAOC until 1919, when he returned to Ireland.

FENWICK George

Left-winger

Born: Durham c.1892.
Career: Shildon Athletic. LEEDS CITY January 1913–May 1914.

■ George was recruited from North Eastern League club Shildon and, with Fred Croot injured, started a five-match run in the team the following month. He made a scoring debut in a 5–1 thumping of Leicester Fosse and then scored two more in a 5–1 victory over Preston a fortnight later. Despite this flurry of success, George was not on the retained list at the end of the season.

FERGUSON John

Left-back

Born: Dundee 1887.
5ft 8in, 11st 9lb (1912).
Career: Arbroath. St Johnstone. Dundee. LEEDS CITY June 1912. Bethlehem Steel (US). Philadelphia Field Club (US). J and P Coates (US). Bethlehem Steel (US).

■ Jock was City's first-choice left-back for the first half of the 1912–13 season after joining from Dundee. However, he was eventually ousted by George Affleck, who returned to the side as the regular full-back partner to Charlie Copeland. Jock later enjoyed a profitable spell in the United States, playing in Philadelphia and Rhode Island.

FOLEY Michael

Wing-half

Born: Dublin, 1892.
5ft 8in, 11st 10lb (1912).
Career: Shelbourne. LEEDS CITY May 1910. Shelbourne 1920.

■ Mick 'Boxer' Foley is regarded as one of the most successful of City's many Irish imports. He started out as a 'bits and pieces' player at Elland Road but settled down as a commanding left-half. He also turned out for the club in World War One, returning to Shelbourne after hostilities ceased. Back in the Emerald Isle he became an established player, winning an Irish Cup medal in his first season back with the Shels. He represented the League of Ireland five times between 1924 and 1927, and he captained Ireland in their first-ever international match – a 3–0 defeat by Italy in Turin on 21 March 1926. It was Mick's only full international appearance. Also in the team were two other ex-City men, Bob Fullam and John Joe Flood, the latter never making the Leeds first team.

FORTUNE James J.

Left-winger

Born: Dublin, c.1890.
Career: Shelbourne. Distillery 1910. LEEDS CITY 1911. Distillery 1912. Barrow. Queen's Park Rangers 1913. Bristol Rovers 1914.

Another of City's Irish contingent, Jimmy came in for Fred Croot, for his only Leeds outing, in the third game of the 1911–12 season – a 0–0 home draw with Chelsea. A second spell in England with Queen's Park Rangers proved more successful.

FREEBOROUGH James

Right-back

Born: Stockport, 13 February 1879.
Died: first quarter 1961.
6ft, 12st 7lb (1906).
Career: Stockport County 1902. Tottenham Hotspur 1904. LEEDS CITY April 1906. Bradford Park Avenue July 1908. Rochdale.

Jimmy was a tall, solid defender who went straight into the City team against Manchester United after joining from Tottenham in April 1906. He had started with his native Stockport, but when County failed to get re-elected in 1904 he went to Spurs, who were then in the Southern League. Jimmy was usually to be found in the reserves for the Western League but had more opportunities at Elland Road. He was City's first choice for much of 1906–07 but moved on to Bradford Park Avenue and featured in their first League season.

GEMMELL James

Inside-forward

Born: Glasgow 17 November 1880.
5ft 9in, 12st 7lb (1907).
Career: Duntocher Hibernian. Clyde August 1900. Sunderland November 1900. Stoke May 1907. LEEDS CITY November

1907. Sunderland May 1910. Third Lanark April 1912. West Stanley player-manager July 1913.

Jimmy was a class act who had been a fans' favourite at Sunderland, where he spent seven years in his first spell with the Rokerites. The highlight was when he won a League Championship medal in 1902, finishing joint top scorer with England international William Hogg. After a six-month stint at Stoke, Jimmy returned to the North for 'family reasons' and joined Leeds. A crisp and accurate shooter, he proved extremely consistent and popular in his three seasons at Leeds, before returning to Sunderland in 1910. His son, James junior, played left-back for Southport and for Bury, where he topped 250 games.

GEORGE John Spencer

Centre-half

Born: Irchester, Northants, 4 February 1884.
Died: Wellingborough, Northants, 29 October 1931.
5ft 10½in, 12st (1905).
Career: Kettering 1903. Tottenham Hotspur April 1904. LEEDS CITY April 1905. Croydon Common 1907. Hastings & St Leonards 1908.

John joined City after playing Southern League football with Kettering and Spurs. He started the 1906–07 season in the Leeds first team for a 1–1 draw against Bradford City but was dropped after the next match – a 5–0 drubbing at West Brom. He made only sporadic senior appearances after that and returned to London.

GIBSON Andrew

Inside-forward

Born: Glasgow.
5ft 8½in, 10st 10lb (1912).
Career: Strathclyde. Southampton May 1911. LEEDS CITY September 1912.

Southampton manager George Swift, the former Leeds City trainer, described Andy as 'the best forward I have seen' after he snapped up the Scot from under the noses of Celtic and Rangers. But 10 months later, Gibson and Saints' teammate Henry Hamilton were suspended *sine die* by the club for a

breach of discipline. Neither played for Southampton again and Gibson eventually moved to Leeds, making an inauspicious start in a 4–0 defeat at Fulham. He only played four more times for the City first team.

GILLESPIE William Ballintrae

Inside-forward

Born: Kerrykeel, Londonderry, 6 August 1891.
Died: Bexley, Kent, 2 July 1981.
5ft 10in, 11st (1910).
Career: Derry Celtic. LEEDS CITY May 1910. Sheffield United December 1912. Derry City manager 1932–48.

City erred by letting Irish star Billy slip away to neighbours Sheffield United, where he became one of the Blades' all-time greats. The son of a policeman, he was about to sign for Linfield from Derry when Leeds stepped in and persuaded him to turn professional. He went straight into the Leeds team at centre-forward and was averaging a goal a game. In 1911–12 he was switched to inside-left but lost his place and moved on to Sheffield in December. He was an instant hit at Bramall Lane and spent 17 seasons there, scoring 128 goals in 448 League appearances. His prematurely balding head contained a sharp football brain and he collected an FA Cup-winners' medal in 1925, as the Blades beat Cardiff 1–0 in the Final. He remains Sheffield United's most capped player with 25 appearances. He later returned to Ireland for a long spell as Derry's manager.

GOODWIN Ernest William

Left-winger

Born: Gateshead, 20 July 1894.
5ft 7in, 10st 5lb.
Career: Spennymoor United. LEEDS CITY May 1914. Spennymoor United 1918. Manchester City October 1919. Rochdale May 1921.

■ After City lost their opening four games of the 1914–15 season, they turned to Ernie for the home game with Blackpool and he responded with a debut goal in a 2–0 win. He remained on City's books during World War One and figured in City's last-ever match – a 4–2 win at Wolves – shortly before the club disbanded. He made a flying start with new employers Manchester City, scoring in a 4–2 win over Sheffield Wednesday on his First Division debut.

GREEN Joseph

Left-back

Career: LEEDS CITY April 1915.

■ Precious little is known about Joe, whose only City game was the last one before World War One – a 2–0 defeat against Barnsley, when he replaced George Affleck. He was not listed as a squad player at the start of that season and is thought to have been a local player.

GUY Richard William

Inside-forward

Born: Madeley, Shropshire, 4 August 1877.
5ft 8in, 11st 6lb (1908).
Career: Manchester City 1902. Bradford City June 1903. Hastings & St Leonards. LEEDS CITY May 1908. Portsmouth 1909. Hastings £25 1910.

■ Dickie proved an inconsistent player in his one season at Elland Road. His main claim to fame was scoring Bradford City's first-ever League goal in a 3–1 home defeat against Gainsborough Trinity on 5 September 1903.

HALLIGAN William

Inside-forward

Born: Athlone, 18 February 1886.
Died: 1950.
5ft 10in, 12st (1909).

Career: Belfast Distillery 1908. LEEDS CITY May 1909. Derby County £400 February 1910. Wolverhampton Wanderers £450 June 1911. Hull City £600 May 1913. Manchester United and Rochdale wartime guest. Preston North End July 1919. Oldham Athletic January 1920. Nelson £75 August 1921. Boston United 1922. Wisbech Town 1924–25.

■ Of all the players to cross the Irish Sea to join Leeds, Billy was certainly among the most successful – but spent little time in City colours. He first came to City's attention when playing for the Irish League against the Scottish League in February 1909. Within three months he became a Leeds player and enjoyed a two-goal debut in the 5–0 demolition of Lincoln City at Elland Road. He was called into the Irish squad to play England on 12 February 1910 after Airdrie's O'Hagan pulled out. However, Halligan rejected the chance to travel to Belfast to play in the international, which ended 1–1. He opted to play for Leeds against Birmingham instead, but it was to be the last time he pulled on a Leeds shirt. After 12 goals in 24 League games, he was transferred to Derby County. Capable of playing any role in the front line, he proved a player in demand, moving for big fees several times and notching more than 100 League goals in his career. He was capped twice – when at Derby and Wolves – and also figured in a couple of Victory internationals. His League career finished at Oldham after he broke his ankle against Bradford on Christmas Day 1920. He retired in 1925, aged 39, after playing non-League football.

HAMILTON Edward McDonald

Right-winger

Born: Paisley, 31 March 1886.
Career: Petershill. LEEDS CITY August 1909.

■ Signed from Scottish football in summer 1909, Ted's three games for City all ended in defeat – 2–1 against Oldham on his debut on 16 October, 7–0 at home to Barnsley the next week and 5–0 at Wolves the following month.

HAMILTON John

Centre-half

Born: Edinburgh.
5ft 11in, 12st 7lb (1907).
Career: Leith Athletic 1906. Brentford 1907. LEEDS CITY 1909. Brentford 1908. Swansea Town 1912.

■ Jock made his debut on the opening day of the 1908–09 campaign in a 1–0 win over Spurs at Elland Road. Despite playing in two-thirds of the games that season, he returned to Brentford in the summer.

HAMPSON John

Centre-half/Half-back

Born: Oswestry, Shropshire, 28 December 1887.
Died: Burslem, December 1960.
5ft 9½in, 11st 4lb (1910).
Career: Oswestry Town. Northampton Town 1910. LEEDS CITY August 1913. Aston Villa £1,000 October 1919. Port Vale £1,000 June 1921. Hanley Social Club, retiring in 1930.

■ John was rated by some observers as the best defender to play for City, figuring either side of World War One. He also played for the club nearly 100 times during hostilities – an appearance record at the club bettered only by Jack Peart and Arthur Price. In a wartime game at Nottingham Forest on 17 February 1917, he was loaned to the 10-man hosts, thus becoming the only registered Leeds player to have played against his own club. John fetched £1,000 at the City auction and enjoyed the best

part of two seasons with Aston Villa before moving to Port Vale. His Valiants debut was against the newly-formed Leeds United on 27 August 1921. A bad injury, sustained in April 1924, required several operations and effectively ended his professional career.

HARGRAVES J. Fred

Centre-forward/Wing-half

Born: Yorkshire.
Career: Burton United 1903–04. LEEDS CITY August 1905. Stoke 1909.

■ Fred was centre-forward in City's first-ever League game, a 1–0 defeat at Bradford City, but the following season switched to the half-back line. He arrived at Elland Road with Burton United teammate Henry Bromage and was sometimes mistakenly referred to in newspaper reports as Hargreaves, having played at Burton with another player of that name. He netted a dozen goals in his first Leeds League season plus seven more in the early stages of the FA Cup, including four in the 11–0 rout of Morley in the preliminary round.

HARKINS John Anderson

Right-half

Born: Milton, Glasgow, 10 April 1881.
Died: Amara, Iraq, 22 April 1916.
5ft 9in, 11st 6lb (1910).
Career: Black Watch Regiment. Middlesbrough September 1906. Broxburn Athletic 1908. Bathgate 1909. LEEDS CITY August 1910. Darlington 1912. Coventry 1914.

■ Middlesbrough bought John out of the army after watching him shine for his regiment against Celtic in a Scottish Cup tie. He made his Division One debut for Boro at centre-half, against Newcastle in October 1906, and missed only one more game that season. However, after switching to half-back he lost his place and moved to Leeds, where he proved extremely consistent. He later played at Coventry under his former City manager Frank Scott-Walford. John was killed in action with the Black Watch, aged 35.

HARWOOD Alfred

Centre-forward

Born: Bishop Auckland, 16 May 1881.
5ft 8in, 11st 6lb (1907).
Career: Crook Town 1900–01. Bishop Auckland 1901. Fulham 1903. LEEDS CITY May 1906. West Ham United 1907. Spennymoor United. Bishop Auckland.

■ One of the stars of the amateur game, Alf managed just one City appearance in a 2–1 win at Burnley on 2 March 1907. He won an FA Amateur Cup medal in 1901, when Crook beat King's Lynn 3–0 in the Final, and was also in the Bishop Auckland side that lost 1–0 to Old Malvernians at Leeds the following year. He also represented the Northern League before joining Fulham, a move which saw him lose his amateur status. He returned north with City and was a regular in the reserves, scoring both goals in the 1907 West Riding Challenge Cup Final when City beat Kippax Parish Church 2–0.

HEANEY Frank

Right-back

Born: Ireland.
6ft, 13st (1911).
Career: St James' Gate. LEEDS CITY May 1911.

■ After City were thrashed 5–1 at home by Burnley in December 1911, Irish import Frank was given his debut at Wolves. A 5–0 defeat saw him immediately out of the team and he made just one more appearance later in the season.

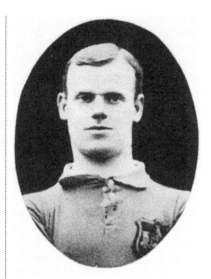

HENDERSON James Thomas

Left-half

Born: High Espley, Morpeth, Northumberland, 10 June 1877.
5ft 8in, 12st (1907).
Career: Morpeth Town. Reading 1903–04. Bradford City May 1904. LEEDS CITY July 1905. Preston North End July 1908. Clapton Orient May 1910. Rochdale June 1910, retiring December 1919. Rochdale trainer until July 1930.

■ A lightning-quick athlete, James enjoyed a long career in football lasting nearly 30 years. A sprinter with Morpeth Harriers in the summer, he reputedly clocked 11 seconds for the 100 yards in 1908. He moved to Leeds for their inaugural League season, joining from Bradford City with Tom Drain. Both men made their Leeds debuts against the Paraders. James moved on to Preston and then Clapton Orient, where he was joined by his younger brother, Bill, a right-back. James made nearly 200 appearances for Rochdale before retiring in December 1919. He then had a lengthy spell as trainer, working under one-time City wartime guest Jack Peart until July 1930.

HOGG Anthony

Goalkeeper

Born: Walker-on-Tyne, 9 January 1890.
5ft 10in, 11st 3lb (1909).
Career: Walton upon Tyne Church Lads. LEEDS CITY September 1909. Newcastle United 1920.

■ With Henry Bromage injured, Tony started the first three games of the 1910–11 season. After acting as understudy to Bromage, Leslie Murphy and Billy Scott, Tony finally became first choice in 1913 and went on to make 100 appearances for the club.

HOPKINS William

Centre-half

Born: Esh Winning, Co. Durham, 11 November 1888.
Died: Blackpool, 26 January 1938.
Career: Esh Winning Rangers. Crook Town 1907. Derby County trials. Esh Winning Rangers. Stanley United. Sunderland May 1912. LEEDS CITY £50 July 1919. South Shields £600 October 1919. Hartlepools United June 1921. Durham City August 1923, coach August 1924. Sheffield United assistant trainer. Charlton Athletic trainer. Grimsby Town trainer June 1931. Port Vale trainer 1935. Barnsley trainer 1936.

■ Leeds paid a rare fee to Sunderland – £50 – for Bill 'Pop' Hopkins, who had cut his football teeth in the non-League amateur game. He was auctioned to South Shields for £600 and later returned to the North East to feature in Hartlepools United's first-ever game in Division Three North. He was then in demand as a trainer but died suddenly, aged 49, at Blackpool while preparing Barnsley for an FA Cup fourth-round replay against Manchester United, in January 1938.

HORSLEY James Edward

Centre-half

Born: Newark, Nottinghamshire, 20 March 1890.
5ft 9in, 11st 6lb (1907).
Career: Newark. LEEDS CITY 1909.

■ James was signed from Midland League side Newark and initially shadowed Tom Morris before making his debut in a 1–0 win over Burnley at Elland Road on 6 November 1909.

HOWARD Gordon

Inside-forward

Born: Worsborough, Barnsley, 11 September 1886.
Career: Hoyland Town. LEEDS CITY June 1905.

■ Reserve inside-forward Gordon made just one City appearance – against Glossop just before Christmas 1905.

HYNDS Thomas

Centre-half

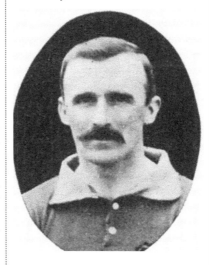

Born: Kilmaurs, Ayrshire, 5 November 1883.
5ft 10in, 11st (1907).
Career: Hurlford Thistle. Glasgow Celtic February 1898. Bolton Wanderers loan March 1899. Clyde loan October 1899. Manchester City loan October 1901, transfer September 1902. Arsenal December 1906. LEEDS CITY May 1907. Hearts May 1908. Ladysmith FC (Canada) 1910. Musselburgh January 1913. US football January 1914.

■ Experienced centre-half Tom was a major signing by Gilbert Gillies, having played for some of the best clubs in the country. At Manchester City he won a Division Two Championship medal in 1903, and the following year he played in the FA Cup Final, when Bolton were beaten 1–0 at Crystal Palace. Such successes pushed Tom to the brink of the Scottish team and he played for the Anglo Scots against the Home Scots, who won 2–0, in an international trial at Cathkin Park, Glasgow, in 1905. But his career hit the buffers when he was suspended for six months in June 1906 for his part in an illegal payments scandal at Manchester City. On completion of his suspension he joined Arsenal briefly before spending a year at Elland Road, where he proved a rock-solid defender. He returned to Scotland and later played

in British Colombia, Canada and the US before having to quit the game with sciatica. He returned to North America to coach and later coached in Italy.

JACKSON John Bertram

Inside-forward

Born: Dalry, Ayrshire, 21 June 1893.
Died: Glasgow, 1971.
5ft 6½in, 10st 2lb (1913).
Career: Ardeer Thistle. Clyde August 1908. Celtic loan January 1909 and October 1912. LEEDS CITY £1,000 December 1912. Ayr United loan December 1915. Clyde loan July 1916. Glasgow Rangers loan May 1917. Glasgow Celtic loan September 1917. Royal Scots Fusiliers May 1918. Clydebank loan January 1919. Motherwell October 1919. Dundee December 1919. Stevenston United loan 1920.

■ John was a tough, all-action, inside-forward who was better known for his exploits in Scotland. He did not quite justify the huge fee paid out to bring him to Elland Road but one of his best games came in the 4–2 FA Cup first-round victory over Gainsborough Trinity, when he scored twice. He initially made his name at Clyde, playing in the 1910 Scottish Cup Final against Dundee, who won 2–1 after a second replay. Jackson is reported to have put in so much effort to the first replay that he collapsed in extra-time. During the war he is also reported to have run from Edinburgh's Waverley Station to Hibernian's Easter Road ground, to play for Celtic because he could not get a taxi. It was his third loan spell with the Parkhead club.

JEFFERSON Robert William

Winger

Born: Sunderland 1882.
5ft 6½in (1908).
Career: Sunderland Royal Rovers. Bradford City November 1904. LEEDS CITY May 1906. Swindon Town 1908. Bath City 1922.

■ Elland Road was a port of call for former Navy deserter Bob. On leaving school in the North East, he joined the Navy but went AWOL after a couple of weeks and eventually bought his way out of the service. He worked in a foundry as an apprentice moulder and was playing

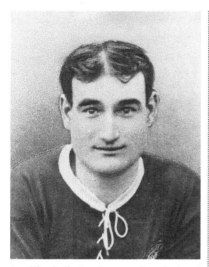

local football when he turned professional with Bradford City. Lack of first-team football saw him switch to Leeds, making a scoring debut in a 1–1 draw with Leicester Fosse on 16 September 1906. He was used at centre-forward, inside-forward and on the wing before moving to Swindon, where he became an instant success. His speed and powerful shooting were one of the features of Swindon's run to the 1912 FA Cup semi-final. Bob represented the Southern League 10 times – against the Football League (four times), Scottish League (four) and Irish League (two). He played in Swindon's first-ever Football League game – a 9–1 thrashing of Luton in 1920 – scoring one of the goals.

JOHNSON Garnet Joseph Wolsley

Left-winger

Born: Pudsey, 8 October 1882.
Career: Upper Armley Christ Church. LEEDS CITY November 1906.

■ Garnet's only City appearance came on 17 November – a 1–0 home defeat against Chelsea. He was among the leading players in the West Yorkshire League, playing for Upper Armley Christ Church, Leeds' best amateur side after Hunslet folded.

JOHNSON James Tennant

Right-winger

Born: Newcastle upon Tyne, 3 May 1892.
5ft 6in, 10st 2lb (1913).
Career: Bedlington. LEEDS CITY October 1910. North Leeds Athletic 1914.

■ Another one-game winger wonder,

James enjoyed a productive outing as a replacement for Simpson Bainbridge – a 4–1 thumping of Grimsby on 13 December 1913.

JOHNSON Samuel

Wing-half

Born: Colne, Lancashire, 1885.
5ft 7½in, 11st 4lb (1911).
Career: Newton Heath Albion. Colne 1904. Blackpool 1905. Colne 1907. Exeter City 1908. Coventry City 1909. LEEDS CITY 1911.

■ Sam's career never really lived up to its early promise. He scored on his Football League debut for Blackpool in 1905 in a 2–2 draw with Gainsborough Trinity, but returned to his local club, Colne, a Lancashire Combination outfit. He played in Exeter's first season in the Southern League and spent a year at Coventry but never fully established himself at Leeds; his highlight being a goal in a 2–1 win over Grimsby in January 1912.

JOYNES Richard Albert

Right-winger/Inside-forward

Born: Grantham, 16 August 1877.
5ft 10½in (1908).
Career: Newark. Notts County December 1901. Newark May 1903. Brighton & Hove Albion May 1905. LEEDS CITY May 1908.

■ After his appointment as Leeds manager, Frank Scott-Walford went for experience when he signed Dickie from his old club Brighton, where he had played more than 100 games. Despite his versatility he was used largely as cover at Leeds.

KAY Harry

Right-back

Born: Eccleston, Prescot, Lancashire, 10 February 1886.
5ft 9in, 11st 6lb (1907).
Career: Bolton Wanderers 1906–07. LEEDS CITY May 1907. Swindon 1908.

■ Leeds gave Harry his big break in League football and probably regretted letting him go. He began at Bolton but did not make the first team and joined City, who were in their third season under Gilbert Gillies. Utterly reliable, Harry played in 32 of City's 39 games in 1907–08 before moving to Swindon, where he amassed nearly 250 League games. He played in the Swindon teams that reached the FA Cup semi-finals of 1910 and 1912.

KELLY Christopher

Wing-half

Born: Tunstall, Staffordshire, 10 September 1887.
5ft 11in, 12st 6lb (1910).
Career: Goldenhill Wanderers. Stoke. Denaby United. LEEDS CITY 1910. Denaby United 1912.

■ Chris was a fringe player whose normal role was in the half-back line. However, for his League debut against Huddersfield in September 1910 he was drafted in at centre-half instead of Tom Morris. Despite the 3–2 defeat he kept his place when Morris returned, switching to his favoured half-back position.

KENNEDY James John

Wing-half

Born: Dundee 8 May 1883.
Died: Glasgow 20 July 1947.
6ft, 12st 4lb (1906).
Career: Glasgow Celtic. Brighton & Hove
Albion 1905. LEEDS CITY June 1906.
Stockport County August 1909. Tottenham
Hotspur March 1919. Swindon Town April
1912. Norwich City July 1913. Watford
£75 December 1913. Gillingham £25
December 1919–May 1920, later becoming
trainer. Partick Thistle trainer.

■ A former Celtic junior, Jimmy joined
City for their second League campaign,
missing just three League games. He fell
out of favour the following season and
left. Jimmy regularly moved around the
circuit, breaking a shoulder blade at
Spurs and skippering Watford to the
1914–15 Southern League title. He
finished at Gillingham, where he became
trainer for a couple of years before
returning to Scotland.

KIRK Gerald

Centre-half

Born: Bramley, Yorkshire, 14 July 1883.
Died: Ypres, Belgium, 24 April 1915.
Career: Pocklington School. Bradford City
April 1905. LEEDS CITY December 1906.
Bradford City September 1907–08.

■ Despite attending a rugby union-
playing school, Gerald was a good
enough footballer to be signed by
Bradford City. His games at Leeds were
limited and he returned to Bradford after
nine months. He was a second lieutenant

with the King's Own Royal Lancashire
Regiment at the time of his death on the
battlefields of Ypres, in Belgium, and is
buried in Poperinghe Old Military
Cemetery.

KIRTON William John

Centre-forward

Born: Newcastle upon Tyne, 2 December
1896.
Died: Sutton Coldfield, 27 September 1970.
5ft 6½in, 11st 11lb (1919).
Career: Todds Nook School, North Shields.
Pandon Temperance 1917. LEEDS CITY
May 1919. Aston Villa £500 October 1919.
Coventry City £1,700 September 1928.
Kidderminster Harriers 1930. Leamington
Town October 1930.

■ Leeds City followers could only guess
what might have been, had the the club
been able to hang on to young Billy
Kirton. He featured in City's last-ever
game – a 4–2 win at Wolves – but 13 days
later was sold as part of the infamous
auction at the Metropole Hotel. Kirton,
recently switched from full-back to the
forward line, went to Aston Villa for
£500. It proved a smart piece of business
by the Birmingham club as Kirton made
261 appearances for them, won an
England cap against Ireland in October
1921 – scoring in a 1–1 draw – and netted
the goal that beat Huddersfield in the
1920 FA Cup Final. In 1916 he collected a
runners'-up medal when Villa lost 2–0 to
Newcastle. He later ran a newsagents and
tobacconists in Birmingham and was
also a golfer of some distinction.

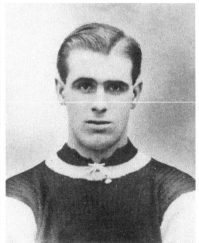

LAMPH Thomas

Right-half

Born: Gateshead, 16 November 1892.
Died: 24 February 1926.
5ft 9½in, 11st 2lb (1913).
Career: Pelaw United. Spennymoor
United. LEEDS CITY April 1914.
Manchester City £800 October 1919.
Derby County March 1920. LEEDS
UNITED February 1921, retired 1922.

■ Tom scored in City's last-ever game at
Wolves – his only goal for the club. He
and Ivan Sharpe are the only two players
to turn out for City and United. When at
Spennymoor he played for the North
Eastern League against the Southern and
Central Leagues (see Leeds United
Players).

LAVERY John

Inside-left

Born: Newcastle upon Tyne, 1 March 1882.
5ft 5½in, 10st 6lb (1908).
Career: Jarrow 1903–04. Barnsley
1903–04. Denaby United 1904–05. LEEDS
CITY March 1906. Swindon Town 1908.
South Shields.

■ Jack was a nippy little player with an
eye for goal, scoring a hat-trick in a 6–1
thumping of Stockport on 15 December
1906. An apprentice mason, he played
for Jarrow in the Northern Alliance
before joining Barnsley then Midland
League club Denaby before stepping
back into League football with City. He
left for Swindon with Harry Kay and
Bob Jefferson, playing in the Robins'
1910 FA Cup semi-final side against
Newcastle.

LAW George

Full-back/Right-half

Born: Arbroath, 13 December 1885.
5ft 9in, 12st 12lb (1912).
Career: Maxwelltown Volunteers. Sunderland 1906. Maxwelltown Volunteers. Arbroath. Glasgow Rangers March 1907. LEEDS CITY July 1912–August 1919. Arbroath 1921–22.

■ A fearless tackler, consistent George topped the 100-appearance mark for City. He had been a major defender with Rangers, playing in the 1909 Scottish Cup Final and replay against Glasgow rivals Celtic. Both matches were drawn at Hampden Park but the Cup was withheld after serious riots at the replay. George won three Scottish caps in 1910 against Wales, Ireland and England. The 2–0 victory over England in front of 110,000 at Hampden helped earn the Scots the Home Championship. When he retired, George went into an engineering partnership with his brother and briefly assisted his home-town club, Arbroath.

LAWRENCE Valentine

Wing-half

Born: Arbroath, 14 February 1890.
5ft 8in, 11st 8lb (1914).
Career: Dundee Violet. Newcastle United trial. Forfar Athletic 1910–11. Manchester City July 1911. Oldham Athletic £50 May 1912. LEEDS CITY May 1914. Darlington. Southend United August 1921. Abertillery.

■ Leeds was just one brief stop for defender Valentine in a much-travelled career. Oldham handed him his Football League debut but he mainly played in the Central League, as was the case at Elland Road.

LINTOTT Evelyn Henry

Centre-half

Born: Godalming, Surrey, 2 November 1883.
Died: Somme, France, 1 July 1916.
5ft 9in, 12st 4lb (1912).
Career: King Edward VI Grammar School, Guildford. St Luke's Training College, Exeter. Woking. Surrey County. Plymouth Argyle 1907. Queen's Park Rangers 1907. Bradford City November 1908. LEEDS CITY June 1912.

■ Evelyn was one of England's finest players of the pre-World War One era. He was one of the old school, an amateur combining his teaching career with playing. Revered in the Southern League with both Plymouth and Queen's Park Rangers, he won five England amateur caps. He made the first of his seven full England appearances against Ireland in 1908, becoming Queen's Park Rangers' first full England international (Rodney Marsh was the second in November 1971). Evelyn moved north to play with Bradford City and played in Division One alongside another famous City player, Jimmy Speirs. Evelyn, who also represented the Football League against the Irish League in 1909, joined Leeds in June 1912 and soon proved a class act. On the outbreak of war he joined up and was a member of the 15th Battalion West Yorkshire Regiment (Prince of Wales' Own) when he was cut down at the Somme, aged just 32.

LOUNDS Herbert Ernest

Right-winger

Born: Masborough, nr Rotherham, 30 May 1889.
Career: Silverwood Colliery. Gainsborough Trinity 1911–12. LEEDS CITY £50 August 1919. Rotherham

County October 1919. Halifax Town 1923.

■ Herbert spent only three months at City before the club's expulsion after joining from Gainsborough for £50. He figured on the right wing in all eight matches before City's closure in 1919 and was sold to Rotherham County.

McALLISTER Thomas

Right-half

Born: Scotland, 1884.
5ft 9in, 12st (1906).
Career: Castleford Town. Blackburn Rovers March 1904. Brentford 1906. LEEDS CITY May 1908. Castleford Town 1910. Halifax Town.

■ A contemporary of Adam Bowman at Blackburn, Tom was reported to have disciplinary problems at Ewood Park, where he made his League debut against Aston Villa in 1905. He played for Leeds for a couple of seasons before moving to Brentford, where he also played with Bowman.

McDANIEL Edward

Right-back

Born: Ireland.
6ft, 12st (1911).
Career: Belfast Celtic. LEEDS CITY May 1911.

■ Another of the Irish contingent who joined Leeds in the 1911 close season, Edward was one of the least successful, playing just once in a 2–1 win at Grimsby in January 1912.

McDONALD John

Right-back

Born: Ayr, 18 January 1883.
Died: 1915.
5ft 10in, 12st 6lb (1905).
Career: Arden Villa. Ayr United. Blackburn Rovers £90 May 1903. LEEDS CITY July 1905. Grimsby Town August 1906. Queen's Park Rangers 1907–13.

■ Jock established himself in the Football League at Leeds. He had played in the Scottish Second Division with his home-town club Ayr before joining Blackburn. At Elland Road, he established himself as a fine full-back, enhancing his reputation with Grimsby. But his best days were at Queen's Park Rangers, where he won Southern League Championship medals in 1907–08 and 1911–13. He played alongside Evelyn Lintott in three Charity Shield games for Rangers, against Manchester United (1908 and 1909) and Blackburn (1912).

McDONALD William

Wing-half

Born: Sanquhar, Dumfriesshire, 11 February 1874.
5ft 10in, 13st (1908).
Career: Nithsdale Wanderers. Kilmarnock April 1904. Lanemark loan. Nithsdale Wanderers April 1906. Brighton & Hove Albion May 1906. LEEDS CITY July 1908. Nithsdale Wanderers August 1909. Lanemark November 1909–15.

■ Willie made his name as a junior with Nithsdale Wanderers, based in Sanquhar, Dumfriesshire, and joined Kilmarnock, where his brother John also played. He made the long trip to join Brighton and was part of the exodus to Leeds, to join manager Frank Scott-Walford. The step up to the Second Division proved difficult in a poor City side and he returned to Nithsdale.

McLEOD William

Centre-forward

Born: Hebburn, Co. Durham, 4 June 1887.
5ft 9in, 11st 7lb (1910).
Career: Hebburn Argyle. Peebles Rovers. Lincoln City £25 June 1906. LEEDS CITY £350 November 1906. Bradford City loan World War One. Notts County £1,250 October 1919. Doncaster Rovers 1921.

■ Billy was the undisputed king of City, holding both club goals and appearance records. He netted 177 times in 301 games and was City's top scorer for a remarkable nine consecutive seasons. Equally remarkable was the English selectors' failure to award him a full cap. Born of Scottish parents, he hailed from the North East town of Hebburn, making his first big football impression with border club Peebles Rovers. Lincoln secretary-manager Jack Strawson bought Billy for £25 and stuck him straight in the first team. He scored in a 4–2 win on the opening day of the 1906–07 season and netted in both drawn games with Leeds City. Just 13 games and eight goals into the campaign, Lincoln netted a handsome profit as Gilbert Gillies persuaded the City directors to break the bank to get McLeod. It was a huge gamble on a 21-year-old but one that paid off handsomely. Billy had explosive shooting powers and bordered on the heroic when it came to getting his head on crosses. Success flowed, with his five-goal haul in a 6–2 win at Hull on 16 January 1915 a highlight. Leeds newspapers campaigned to get Billy honoured at international level, but the nearest he got was as a non-playing reserve for a 2–0 win over Wales in Cardiff, in 1914. He also suffered the same fate when the Football League played the Scottish League that year. He played a few City games in the war but predominantly worked at a Bradford engineering factory. He returned to Elland Road in peacetime and showed he had lost none of his old goalscoring magic. Fittingly, he scored a hat-trick in

City's final game at Wolves before being auctioned off with the rest of the squad. Not surprisingly, Billy had the highest price on his head and went to Notts County for £1,250. His goal return at Meadow Lane was modest as the Magpies were relegated and the old Leeds hero, now 34, dropped into the Midland League with Doncaster.

McQUILLAN John

Left-back

Born: Westoe, South Shields, 4 February 1888.
5ft 8½in, 11st 8lb (1912).
Career: Jarrow. Hull City October 1906. LEEDS CITY £100 July 1914. Fulham and Hull City wartime guest.

■ One of Hull City's finest early-era players, Jack joined Leeds and made his debut against Fulham on the first day of the 1914–15 season. Eventually he lost his place to George Affleck and was moved to right-back. Jack's playing career ended when a grinding machine in the Hull factory where he was working exploded, leaving him with head injuries and a broken collarbone. He continued to help the Tigers, for whom he had played more than 250 games, in a scouting capacity in the 1930s.

MILLERSHIP Harry

Right-back

Born: Chirk, nr Wrexham, 1889.
Died: Blackpool, 1959.
Career: Chirk. Goole Town. Blackpool

1912. LEEDS CITY August 1919. Rotherham County £1,000 October 1919. Barnsley September 1922. Castleford Town 1923.

■ Harry was looking forward to a bright future with Leeds when he arrived from Blackpool, but within a month the club was booted out of the Football League and the classy right-back was sold to Rotherham as part of the payments scandal auction. He was a star performer at Rotherham, where he won his six full Welsh caps. After giving up the game, he ran the Castle Inn in Castleford and then settled in Blackpool, where he was an attendant at the Winter Gardens before being employed by a building firm.

MORAN Joseph

Wing-half

Born: Dublin, 9 February, year not known.
5ft 9in, 12st (1911).
Career: Shelbourne 1910. LEEDS CITY May 1911.

■ Joe won a United Ireland Cup medal in 1911, when Shelbourne beat Bohemians 2–1, and joined Leeds a few weeks later. City had lost £1,000 the previous season so Frank Scott-Walford's limited budget saw him travel to Ireland to engage new recruits for a second successive summer. Wing-half Joe was among those he brought back and was a partial success at Elland Road. He won his only Irish cap in a 4–1 defeat at the hands of Scotland, at Windsor Park on 16 March 1912.

MORGAN Charles

Right-half

Born: Bootle, Lancashire.
5ft 8in, 11st 3lb.
Career: Everton. Tottenham Hotspur May 1904. LEEDS CITY April 1905. Bradford Park Avenue August 1909.

■ Charlie was one of City's most consistent players in their maiden Football League season. A Merseysider, he spent several seasons in the reserves of Everton and Spurs, breaking his jaw in a pre-season game for Tottenham. He featured in City's first-ever League game and, after four years, teamed up again with Gilbert Gillies at Bradford Park Avenue.

MORRIS John

Centre-half

Born: Leeds, 18 October 1887.
Career: Leeds Schools. LEEDS CITY October 1905.

■ John was a highly-rated schools player in Leeds but did not quite cut it at League level with his home club. He made his debut on New Year's Day 1906 – a 3–0 win at Blackpool.

MORRIS Richard

Inside-forward

Born: Newtown, Montgomeryshire, 25 April 1883.
Career: Llanidoes, Newtown RWW. Druids February 1902. Liverpool March 1902. LEEDS CITY July 1905. Grimsby Town June 1906. Plymouth Argyle 1907. Reading 1908. Huddersfield Town 1908–09.

■ Dickie was City's first-ever international, playing in Wales' 2–0 defeat against Scotland at Hearts' Tynecastle ground on 3 March 1906. Described as 'a tireless runner and top-speed dribbler', he fought in the Boer War and played for his home-town team, Newtown, before transferring to Druids, the Ruabon-based side. He was capped while at both clubs and added five more during a three-year spell at Liverpool. Although he was not a noted goalscorer at Elland Road, he did net four in the 11–0 FA Cup preliminary round thrashing of Morley. He was also Plymouth's first international.

MORRIS Thomas Henry

Centre-half

Born: Grimsby, Lincolnshire, 14 September 1884.
Died: Pozieres, France, 24 March 1918.
5ft 10in, 12st 10lb (1912).
Career: Haycroft Rovers. Grimsby Rovers. Grimsby Town February 1906. Brighton & Hove Albion May 1907. LEEDS CITY February 1909. Scunthorpe and Lindsay United player-coach May 1913. Coventry City May 1914.

■ Tom made more than 100 League and Cup appearances for City in just over four years at Elland Road. A thoughtful centre-half whom many thought was future management material, he had a year as Scunthorpe's player-coach before rejoining Frank Scott-Walford at Coventry. In March 1915 Tom joined the army and was killed in action, serving as a sergeant in the 2nd Battalion, Lincolnshire Regiment.

MULHOLLAND Tom S.

Inside-right

Born: Ireland c.1888.
5ft 8in, 11st (1909).
Career: Distillery. LEEDS CITY May 1909. Distillery 1912. Scunthorpe and Lindsay United 1913–14. Belfast Celtic 1919–20. Hartlepools United 1921.

■ Tom was one of the more successful of City's Irish imports. He arrived from Distillery as a 21-year-old and, after a slow start, developed into a goalscoring inside-right, reaching his peak in 1910–11 with a flurry of nine goals in 14 games. He hit double figures in the next campaign before returning to Ireland. After the war, he had a brief spell with Hartlepool and is credited with scoring their first-ever League goal in a 2–0 away win at Wrexham in Division Three North.

MURPHY Leslie A.

Goalkeeper

Born: Dunnamanagh, County Tyrone
5ft 10in, 12st (1911).
Career: Belfast Celtic 1910–11. LEEDS CITY May 1911. Glentoran 1913. Linfield. Wrexham August 1920. Bristol Rovers August 1922. Reading 1923.

■ Leslie started off as City's first-choice goalkeeper for the 1911–12 season but, by the end of the campaign, was sharing the job with Tony Hogg and Cecil Reinhardt. His decision to return to Ireland after a year proved a good one. He played in the Glentoran side which won the Irish title for the first time in 1912. Glentoran, Burnley and Celtic were then invited to Austria to play in the Vienna Cup, which Glentoran won by beating an Austrian Select XI. Leslie, who also represented the Irish League against the Football League and Scottish League that year, had another spell in English football in the 1920s. He was virtually an ever-present player for Wrexham in their final Birmingham and District League season, and was expected to be their number one on their election to the Football League. But on a summer visit home he contracted rheumatic fever, and after spending weeks in Downpatrick Infirmary, he lost his place.

MURRAY David Bruce

Full-back

Born: Cathcart, Glasgow, 4 December 1882.
Died: Loos, France, 10 December 1915.
5ft 8½in, 11st 12lb (1905).
Career: Glasgow Rangers. Everton 1903. Liverpool May 1904. LEEDS CITY £150 December 1905. Mexborough Town 1909. Burslem Port Vale.

■ Originally a Rangers reserve, David played a couple of League games for Everton before transferring across Stanley Park to Liverpool, where he won a Division Two Championship medal in 1904–05. He was one of the few players for whom City paid a decent fee, £150. The club was rewarded with four years' solid

service from the Scottish full-back, who proved a successful penalty-taker. Six years after leaving Elland Road he died, aged 28, while serving with the 11th Battalion Argyll and Sutherland Highlanders at Loos, France.

MURRAY William Brunton

Left-winger

Born: Forres, Morayshire, 15 November 1881.
Died: Kilmallie, 22 April 1929.
5ft 6in, 11st 7lb (1906).
Career: Forres Mechanics. Inverness Thistle. Sunderland August 1901. Northampton Town 1903. Tottenham Hotspur May 1904. LEEDS CITY May 1906.

■ Scottish Highlander Willie sprang to prominence at Sunderland, figuring in seven of the last eight games of their 1901–02 Division One Championship-winning season. He did so well that he was picked for the Scots against Anglo Scots 1902 international trial. He scored for the Rokerites on his League debut – a 3–1 win against Grimsby – when Jimmy Gemmell was a teammate. A typical dribble-loving winger, Willie did not fulfil that early promise and dropped into the Southern League before Leeds briefly resurrected his League career. He was asphyxiated aboard a ship while working as a labourer in 1929.

NAISBY Thomas Henry

Goalkeeper

Born: Sunderland, 12 March 1878.

5ft 8in, 13st (1907).
Career: Sunderland East End. Sunderland September 1889. Sunderland West End September 1901. Reading May 1903. Sunderland May 1905. LEEDS CITY October 1907. Luton Town 1910. South Shields March 1913. Darlington.

■ Tom emerged from local North East football to stand in a couple of times for the famous Scottish international Ned Doig at Sunderland. He enhanced his reputation with two years at Reading, which prompted a return to Roker. He contested the number-one spot at Leeds with Henry Bromage, coming into the City side after Bromage played in a 6–1 defeat against Derby in 1907–08.

PAGE George

Centre-forward

Born: London.
5ft 8in, 11st (1910).
Career: Cheshunt. Tottenham Hotspur guest April and September 1906. LEEDS CITY November 1906. Redhill 1907.

■ George got his chance after the tragic death of David 'Soldier' Wilson but did not hit the target in any of his four games – in all of which City were goalless – and returned South at the end of the 1906–07 campaign. Earlier, he had been a top performer with amateur club Cheshunt and played for Tottenham.

PARNELL Gresham Frederick

Right-winger

Born: Sutton-in-Ashfield, 1884.
5ft 8in, 11st (1908).
Career: Skegby United. Pinxton. Derby County 1903. LEEDS CITY August 1905. Exeter City 1908. Preston North End May 1909. Exeter City May 1910. Sutton Junction 1912. Mansfield Town November 1913.

■ Fred was a dashing wingman with a large dapper moustache that made him instantly recognisable. He was a City regular for three years, notching up more than a century of League appearances after joining from Derby County. He also did well in a couple of spells with Exeter, scoring twice in his home debut in the Southern League – a 3–3 draw with Bristol Rovers.

PEART Henry

Centre-half

Born: Newcastle upon Tyne, 3 October 1889.
5ft 11in, 10st (1912).
Career: Glasgow Strathside. Bradford City June 1909. LEEDS CITY September 1913. Blyth Spartans 1915.

■ Signed from neighbours Bradford City as a 20-year-old, Harry simply swapped reserve team football at one West Yorkshire club with another. At Elland Road he shadowed John Hampson but did manage to start the 1914–15 season in the first team, if only for a brief period.

PICKARD Herbert

Half-back

Born: c.1885.

5ft 9½in, 11st 6lb (1909).
Career: Upper Armley Christ Church. LEEDS CITY June 1905.

■ Bert was one of a clutch of local amateur players who joined City when the club entered the Football League. He turned out for Upper Armley Christ Church, who played at the Pasture Hill ground, then Park View, Stanningley.

PRICE Arthur

Inside-right

Born: Sheffield, 1886.
5ft 9in, 11st 8lb (1913).
Career: Worksop Town. LEEDS CITY December 1912. Sheffield Wednesday October 1919. Southend United 1922. Scunthorpe United 1924. Scarborough trainer November 1927. Barrow trainer 1934–35.

■ Arthur went straight into the Leeds team after joining from Midland League club Worksop, scoring on his debut – a 3–2 defeat against Fulham. He became a firm fixture in the side the following season when he, Billy McLeod and James Speirs all hit double figures to take City to the brink of promotion. Arthur's 11 goals in 1914–15 included a hat-trick in the 7–2 victory over Leicester Fosse. Loyal to City throughout the war, he played 120 times, scoring 59 goals – a wartime tally bettered only by guest Jack Peart (71 goals in 107 games), the Notts County centre-forward. Arthur fetched £750 when he was bought by Sheffield Wednesday at the infamous auction and was converted to a half-back by the Owls. He saw out his playing days

with Scarborough, winning the Midland League in 1930, and combining playing with being steward at Scarborough Conservative Club. With Boro's financial future uncertain, he left the Seasiders after eight years' service to be trainer at Barrow.

PRICE Ioan Hayden

Half-back

Born: Ystradyfodwg, Pontypridd, 1 March 1883.
Died: Portsmouth, 7 March 1964.
5ft 8in, 11st 6lb (1909).
Career: Maerdy Corinthians. Riverside. Aberdare 1902. Aston Villa December 1904. Burton United 1907. Wrexham 1908. LEEDS CITY May 1909. Shrewsbury Town June 1910. Walsall 1911, secretary-manager July 1912–15. Tottenham Hotspur wartime guest 1918. Mid-Rhondda United manager 1919–20. Grimsby Town manager July 1920–November 1920. Mid-Rhondda manager 1921–22.

■ Haydn already had five Welsh international caps by the time he arrived at Leeds – more than his total League appearances. Although a 'strong sprinter and good passer' he was soon out of the first team picture and returned closer to his roots in the Birmingham League with Shrewsbury. A teacher by profession, he played in the 1904 Welsh Cup Final for Aberdare against Druids. He moved up to join Aston Villa and was in their third team when he won his first Welsh cap against Scotland in 1907. His only game for Burton United was in their final match before being voted out of their League. He stuck with them in the Birmingham League before having a go with Wrexham and then Leeds. At Walsall, he became secretary-manager, recruiting centre-forward Arthur Campey, later to become City's trainer. His first venture into full management was at Welsh club Mid-Rhondda United but his spell in charge at Grimsby proved disastrous. Results were poor and he came in for criticism from the Mariners' directors. Price quit in a public letter to the *Grimsby Evening Telegraph* after just four months and was re-appointed manager of Mid-Rhondda. But further controversy followed, as players were not paid and other debts were not honoured, leading to the club's suspension by the FA of Wales.

RAY Richard

Full-back

Born: *Newcastle-under-Lyme, 4 January 1873.*
Died: *Leeds, 29 December 1952.*
Career: *Audley. Macclesfield Town 1893. Burslem Port Vale May 1894. Crewe Alexandra 1895. Manchester City May 1896. Macclesfield Town 1900. Manchester City September 1902. Stockport County 1903. Chesterfield 1904. LEEDS CITY July 1905. Non-League football 1908–12. LEEDS UNITED manager October 1919–February 1920. Doncaster Rovers manager 1923–July 1927. LEEDS UNITED manager July 1927–March 1935. Bradford City manager April 1935–February 1938. Millwall chief scout 1938.*

■ Richard was one of the most influential figures in the professional game in Leeds. He was City's first skipper and had two spells as manager of United (see Leeds City and United Managers). He made his League debut for Port Vale in a 1–0 win against Walsall Town Swifts on 1 September 1894. He was a first team regular until he arrived late for a match at Notts County the following February after misreading the train timetable. He was fined five shillings and left the club in the summer, eventually joining Leeds in 1905. Dick was a fine all-round sportsman, playing for Laisterdyke in the Bradford Cricket League and serving in the Royal Army Service Corps in World War One.

REINHARDT Dr Cecil Goodwin

Goalkeeper

Born: *Lewisham, London, 3 March 1888.*
6ft 1in, 12st 2lb (1912).
Career: *Leeds University. LEEDS CITY 1910.*

■ A doctor of chemistry at Leeds University, Cecil was a regular in the Central League side, stepping up to the first team after Leslie Murphy was on the receiving end of a 5–1 home defeat against Burnley in December 1911. He later changed his surname to Goodwin, his middle name.

RICHARDSON Webb F.

Right-winger

Born: *St Albans, Hertfordshire.*

5ft 7in, 11lb (1912).
Career: *Barnet and Alston. LEEDS CITY June 1913.*

■ Webb was a fleeting figure on the City scene, arriving from Athenian League club Barnet. The winger played just a couple of matches before leaving the club.

ROBERTS Hugh Pierce

Right-winger

Born: *Rhyl, Denbighshire, 14 October 1882.*
5ft 7in, 11st (1907).
Career: *Southport Central 1908–09. LEEDS CITY May 1909. Scunthorpe and Lindsay United 1913. Luton Town June 1914.*

■ Rhyl brothers Hugh and Dick were both on City's books in 1910–11. While Dick did not make the first team, Hugh amassed more than a century of games for Leeds. He was a dashing right winger with nifty footwork, a creator rather than taker of chances. He moved on to Luton with reserve right-back John Dunn in the summer of 1914.

ROBERTSON James

Inside-right

Born: *Glasgow 1880.*
5ft 8½in, 11st 4lb (1912).
Career: *Glasgow United. Crewe Alexandra 1901. Small Heath £25 April 1903. Chelsea £50 August 1905. Glossop North End 1907. Leyton. Partick Thistle. Ayr United. Barrow 1912. LEEDS CITY July 1912. Gateshead 1913.*

■ Much-travelled Scottish winger Jimmy marked his City home debut with a goal in a 2–0 win over Burnley. Quick and direct, with a deadly shot, Jimmy stayed at Elland Road just one season before seeing out his career at Gateshead. Earlier Small Heath (forerunners of Birmingham City) and Chelsea paid fees for his services.

RODGER Thomas

Inside-right

Born: *Dundee, 9 June 1882.*
5ft 8in, 12st (1908).
Career: *Dundee May 1903. Manchester United April 1904. Preston North End September 1904. Grimsby Town August 1906. Reading June 1907. Brighton & Hove Albion February 1908. LEEDS CITY May 1908. Scottish football.*

■ A month after manager Frank Scott-Walford joined City, he raided his old club Brighton to sign Tom, Dave Dougal and Dickie Joynes. Both Tom and fellow Dundonian Dougal played for Preston, Grimsby, Reading, Brighton and Leeds, in virtually parallel careers.

ROTHWELL Alfred

Right-winger

Career: *Accrington Stanley. LEEDS CITY May 1914.*

■ Alf's only appearance came in a 3–1 home defeat against Stockport County on 5 September 1914.

SCOTT William

Goalkeeper

Born: Belfast, 1 January 1883.
5ft 11½in, 12st 11lb (1912).
Career: Cliftonville. Linfield. Everton 1904. LEEDS CITY August 1912.

■ Billy won a total of 25 Irish caps between 1903 and 1913 – three of them with Leeds. He made his name at Linfield, where he played for the Irish League three times, but his best days were at Everton, winning an FA Cup-winners' medal in 1906 after beating Newcastle 1–0 in the Final at Crystal Palace. The Toffees also finished second in the Championship in 1905, 1909 and 1912 with Scott in goal. His younger brother, Elisha, won 31 Irish caps in 22 years with Liverpool.

SHARPE Ivan Gordon

Left-winger

Born: St Albans, Hertfordshire, 15 June 1889.
Died: Southport, 9 February 1968.
5ft 8in, 11st 2lb (1913).
Career: St Albans. Brighton guest February 1911. St Albans Abbey. Watford October 1907. Glossop August 1908–September 1911. Brighton & Hove Albion 1911. Derby County amateur October 1911. LEEDS CITY June 1913–November 1919. Glossop 1915. LEEDS UNITED November 1920–23. Yorkshire Amateurs.

■ A leading sports journalist and author, Ivan was an amateur left-winger throughout his distinguished career, winning an Olympic gold medal with the British football team at the 1912 Stockholm Games. The son of a St Albans cobbler, he was lightning-quick – a runner for Salford Harriers when he played at Glossop, where he won the first of his 12 amateur caps. He also had a full international trial at Derby in 1912, when he helped them to the Second Division title. The following year he joined Leeds after landing a job on the *Yorkshire Evening News*. He later returned to the city to play for United before retiring in 1923 (see Leeds United Players).

SHORT William

Inside-forward

Born: Gosforth, Northumberland.

5ft 11in, 11st 6lb (1919).
Career: Pandon Temperance. LEEDS CITY May 1914. Hartlepools United October 1919.

■ Billy was signed just before the ill-fated 1919–20 season and played in the opening five League games. He did not score and was dropped. Within weeks, the club folded and he returned to the North East with Hartlepools, where he featured in their first-ever Football League game in 1921.

SINGLETON Harry Bertram

Left-winger

Born: Widnes, Lancashire, 3 September 1877.
Died: Macclesfield, Cheshire, 5 July 1947.
5ft 9in, 12st 3lb (1905).
Career: Stockport County 1899. Bury 1900. Everton 1901. Grimsby Town 1902. New Brompton May 1903. Queen's Park Rangers May 1904. LEEDS CITY June 1905.

■ Harry found his form at Elland Road after struggling to make an impression on the circuit. His Football League debut, for Stockport, was a bitter experience – a 5–0 home defeat against New Brighton. It was his only senior outing for County and he did not get a chance at his next club, Bury, yet was signed by First Division Everton. Spells at Grimsby and in the Southern League followed before he arrived at Leeds, where he was a regular on the left wing in City's maiden season and netted the only goal of the game, at Leicester Fosse on 16 September 1905, to give the fledgling club their first-ever League victory.

SPEIRS James Hamilton

Inside-left

Born: Govan, Glasgow, 22 March 1886.
Died: Ypres, Belgium, 20 August 1917.
5ft 10½in, 12st 5lb (1913).
Career: Glasgow Annandale. Maryhill 1904. Glasgow Rangers August 1905. Clyde 1908. Bradford City September 1909. LEEDS CITY £1,400 1913.

■ War hero James Speirs ended his distinguished career with Leeds before serving in World War One. A Glasgow boilermaker by trade, he was a major hit at Ibrox, scoring 40 goals in 81 games. He

only won one Scottish cap though, in a 2–1 win over Wales at Dens Park in 1908. After a year at Clyde, he joined Bradford City and skippered them to 1911 FA Cup Final glory, when his header beat Newcastle 1–0 in a replay at Old Trafford. Leeds paid their neighbours an enormous fee for his services, and he continued to ooze class up to the outbreak of the war. He joined the 7th Cameron Highlanders in Perth and achieved the rank of sergeant, winning a Military Medal. He was killed in action in Belgium, aged 31, and is buried at Dochy Farm New British Cemetery at Zonnebeke.

STOCKTON Colin Moffat

Right-winger

Born: Ellesmere Port, Cheshire 19 July 1881.
5ft 9½in, 11st 6lb (1909).
Career: Carlisle 1908. LEEDS CITY 1909. Chester. Wrexham. Ellesmere Port Town.

■ Colin made a sparkling debut as City crushed Lincoln 5–0 on the opening day of the 1909–10 season. But competition for a wing berth was fierce, and he consequently made only a couple more appearances before vanishing from the Elland Road scene.

STRINGFELLOW Harold Twemlow

Centre-half

Born: Chorlton-on-Medlock, Lancashire, 27 May 1875.
5ft 8in, 11st (1905).
Career: Southport Central. Everton February 1898. Portsmouth 1899.

Swindon Town 1904. LEEDS CITY 1905. Preston North End September 1906. Wigan Borough.

■ City's first centre-half, Harry made up for his lack of defensive inches with speed, positioning and accurate passing. He first played for Southport Central and was transferred with Irish teammate Jackie Kirwan to big guns Everton for a combined fee of £130. He did not make the first team at Goodison but was an institution at Portsmouth, winning a Championship medal in 1901–02. He joined Leeds after a season as skipper at Swindon.

SWIFT George Harold

Full-back

Born: Oakengates, Shropshire, 3 February 1870.
Died: c.1942.
5ft 9in, 13st (1906)
Career: St George's School, Oakengates. St George's Swifts. Wellington Town 1885. Stoke trials 1886. Wellington St George's. Crewe Alexandra 1888. Wolverhampton Wanderers August 1891. Loughborough 1894. Leicester Fosse August 1896. Notts County June 1902. LEEDS CITY trainer 1904. Chesterfield secretary 1906–10. Southampton manager April 1911–April 1912.

■ George's sole Leeds appearance was as an emergency 36-year-old winger in an injury crisis, losing 4–0 at Chelsea in March 1906. George was City's trainer at the time, having ended a distinguished career as a full-back at Notts County. He was extremely well-known in the Midlands, winning an FA Cup-winners' medal with Wolves in 1893 when they beat Everton 1–0 at Fallowfield, Manchester. He was the only Loughborough player to win representative honours, playing for the Football League against the Irish League in 1895. He was captain at Leicester, where he was ever present in four of his six seasons. After Leeds, he was secretary-manager at Chesterfield for three years, during which they had to seek re-election twice and were voted out of the League in 1909. He was then Southampton's first-ever secretary-manager but resigned after a year, in April 1912, after his expensively-assembled team struggled near the foot of the Southern League.

THOMAS William

Inside-left

Born: Liverpool, c.1885.
5ft 8½in, 11st (1906).
Career: Newcastle Swifts. Burslem Port Vale June 1903. Everton 1906. LEEDS CITY 1906. Barnsley May 1908. Huddersfield Town August 1909–10.

■ Largely a reserve at all his clubs, Billy enjoyed a run in the Leeds team as a replacement for John Lavery in the middle of the 1907–08 season. The highlight was a two-goal performance against Chesterfield, but City went down 4–3 at Saltergate. At Huddersfield, his only goal for the Terriers came in a 5–1 win against City.

THORPE James

Wing-half/Full-back
Born: 1885.

5ft 8in, 11st (1907).
Career: Bolton Wanderers 1907. LEEDS CITY May 1907. Crystal Palace 1908.

■ Jimmy was a versatile member of City's 1907–08 squad. Although he featured in only nine games, he occupied four different positions – right-half (on his debut against Stoke), left-half, left-back and right-back.

TILDESLEY James

Full-back

Born: Halesowen, nr Birmingham, 7 October 1881.
Died: Newcastle, January 1963.
Career: Halesowen St John. Newcastle United February 1903. Middlesbrough £200 September 1906. LEEDS CITY £200 December 1909. Luton Town 1910.

■ City shelled out £200 for Middlesbrough reserve full-back Jim, midway through the 1909–10 season, but he only went on to play half a dozen League games. At Newcastle, he won two Northern League championships with their A team and stood in for internationals Jack Carr and Bill McCracken at Middlesbrough. He later scouted for Newcastle, discovering, among others, Bob Roxburgh, later to become Leeds United's trainer. Jim had a brother, Thomas Tildesley, who was also on Newcastle's books.

TOMPKINS Thomas

Right-half

Born: c.1884.
5ft 6in, 10st 11lb (1907).
Career: Doncaster Rovers 1904. Denaby United. LEEDS CITY May 1907. Mexborough 1908.

■ Tom, a well-known player in south Yorkshire, appeared in 11 of City's opening 13 games in 1907–08 before returning to the Midland League with Mexborough, in the summer.

TURNER Neil McDougall

Right-winger

Born: Govan, Glasgow, 7 October 1892. Career: Petershill. LEEDS CITY September 1913. Raith Rovers August 1914. Glasgow Benburb wartime guest. Vale of Leven August 1918. Kilmarnock September 1918. Sunderland August 1919. Aberdare Athletic May 1920. Dundee June 1922. Bethlehem Steel (US) August 1923. New Bedford Whalers (US). Springfield Babes (US).

■ Much-travelled Neil made an instant impact at Leeds, scoring on his debut in the 1–1 derby at Huddersfield on 8 November 1913, when he stood in for Simpson Bainbridge. Generally though, he received few opportunities and was on his way in the summer. After the war he featured in Aberdare's first Football League season and later played in the United States.

WAINWRIGHT Wilson

Left-half

Born: Morley, Leeds, 24 July 1892.
5ft 9in, 11st 7lb (1914).
Career: Morley. LEEDS CITY October 1914.

■ Described by *Athletic News* as 'fearless', local lad Wilson emerged from a testing 2–2 debut against Arsenal with much credit. He came in for Mick Foley but was selected for first-team action only once more by Herbert Chapman.

WALKER Frederick

Centre-half

5ft 10½in, 11st 8lb (1905).
Career: Barrow. LEEDS CITY June 1905. Huddersfield Town player-manager August 1908.

■ Fred was recruited from Barrow in time for City's first League campaign. At first he filled in for Harry Stringfellow but had a decent run in the side by the end of the campaign. In August 1908 he was appointed player-manager at neighbouring Huddersfield, who were just getting off the ground. He played for Town in their first two years in the North Eastern League and the Midland League before retiring in 1910.

WALKER Willis

Goalkeeper

Born: Gosforth, Northumberland, 24 November 1892.
Died: Keighley, 3 December 1991.
5ft 10in, 11st 4lb (1914).
Career: Sheffield United. Doncaster Rovers 1912. LEEDS CITY May 1914. South Shields £800 October 1919. Bradford Park Avenue 1925. Stockport County August 1926–27.

■ Sporting all-rounder Willis enjoyed a fine football and cricket career. In his early days he was a batsman with Sheffield United CC and played for the Blades in the winter. He did not make the first team at Bramall Lane so joined Doncaster, where he was understudy to Henry Bromage. Leeds handed him his League debut against Arsenal in 1915. Willis served with the Royal Navy during the war and was still the first-choice 'keeper when City fell from grace in 1919. He was sold for £800 at the Metropole Hotel auction to South Shields, where he made 195 appearances. In summer, Willis was a class batsman

with Nottinghamshire, scoring 1,000 runs in a season 10 times. He also played in the Bradford League for Keighley, where he ran a sports shop, but just missed out on his personal century, as he died, aged 99, in 1991.

WATSON John

Right-back

Born: Newarthill, Lanarkshire.
6ft, 14st (1908).
Career: Clyde. Newcastle United £200 November 1902. New Brompton. Brentford 1903. LEEDS CITY July 1908. Clyde 1910.

■ Jock was a powerfully-built defender who was ear-marked to take over the right-back spot after Harry Kay left Leeds. He certainly had a good pedigree, playing for a Glasgow Select XI before joining Newcastle. He went straight in to the Magpies' first team but did not live up to his £200 fee.

WATSON Robert

Inside-forward

Born: Middlesbrough, final quarter 1880 or 1881.
5ft 9in, 12st (1908).
Career: South Bank. Middlesbrough March 1902. Woolwich Arsenal June 1903. LEEDS CITY July 1905. Rochdale April 1908. Exeter City 1908. Stalybridge Celtic 1912.

■ Bob was virtually a permanent fixture in the City side for three seasons. A top-class acquisition, he was one of the most creative players to pull on a City shirt and weighed in with 21 League goals. He first gained attention at his home-town club, Middlesbrough, and in summer 1903 he joined Arsenal. Although not a first-team regular, he earnt a niche in the Gunners' history by scoring seven goals against a Paris XI – effectively the French national team – in a landslide 26–1 win at Plumstead on 5 December 1904. Bob was also Exeter's first professional captain.

WHITE Jabez W.

Full-back

Born: Droylesden, nr Manchester, 1879
5ft 10in, 12st 6lb (1908).
Career: Ollenshaw United. Grays Anchor. Swanscombe. Grays United. Queen's Park Rangers 1901. LEEDS CITY 1908. Merthyr Tydfil 1911.

■ Rock-solid full-back Jabez was always known as Jack at Leeds. He was a player who could perform on either flank with tenacity and skill. He had spent seven seasons at Queen's Park Rangers, winning the Southern League title in 1908. At Leeds, the perfect timing of his tackles became a trademark. He later helped Welsh side Merthyr to the Southern League Second Division title in 1911–12.

WHITLEY John

Goalkeeper

Born: Chorlton, Lancashire, 3 May 1872.
Died: London 1945.
5ft 11in, 13st (1908).
Career: Liskeard YMCA 1897. Darwen

1899. Aston Villa £50 May 1900. Everton 1902. Stoke August 1904. LEEDS CITY April 1906. Lincoln City. Chelsea August 1907–May 1914.

■ Jack was one of City's most popular players even though he did not command a regular place. He was back-up to number-one Henry Bromage in City's first two seasons. He played cricket for Leeds and was also a keen billiards player but it was at Chelsea where he found fame, spending 25 years there as a player and trainer. He helped the Pensioners win promotion to Division One in 1912 and retired two years later. He became trainer at Stamford Bridge until May 1939 and also helped prepare the England team.

WILSON David

Centre-forward

Born: Newcastle upon Tyne, 23 July 1883.
Died: Leeds, 27 October 1906.
5ft 8in, 12st 6lb (1905).
Career: Dundee. Heart of Midlothian £120 February 1905. Hull City £100 May 1905. LEEDS CITY £120 December 1905.

■ David was signed from Hull for £120 and made a great start with 13 goals in 15 League games, including four in the 6–1 thumping of Clapton Orient in March. Sadly, his great talent never reached fruition. He died at the age of 23, after collapsing during a City game against Burnley in October 1906. The free-scoring forward went off complaining of chest pains and, despite medical advice, returned to the pitch because two other City players – Jack Lavery and Harry Singleton – were hobbling. But he was clearly in distress, went off again and collapsed in the tunnel. He was carried to the treatment room but medics were unable to revive him. It was a tragic end for a fine player, nicknamed 'Soldier' because of his military service in the Boer War. The proceeds of an Elland Road friendly against Hull – a 3–3 draw watched by 3,000 spectators – were donated to David's widow. In a curious footnote to the sad affair, the Football League rapped City for their paperwork filed after the match. A League minute of 5 November 1906 stated: 'The secretary was instructed to write to the Leeds City chairman and point out that the word

"transferred" opposite D. Wilson's name in the result sheet for the match in which Wilson played and was injured, and his death took place before the close of play, was uncalled for and entirely out of place, as this was a national calamity.'

WILSON Thomas Carter

Left-winger

Born: Preston, 20 October 1877.
Died: Blackpool, 30 August 1940.
5ft 6in, 11st 6lb (1906).
Career: Fishwick Ramblers, Preston. Ashton-in-Makerfield. West Manchester. Ashton Town. Ashton North End. Oldham County 1896. Kendal Rise. Swindon Town May 1897. Blackburn Rovers May 1898. Swindon Town May 1899. Millwall May 1900. Aston Villa April 1901. London Caledonians January 1902. Queen's Park Rangers 1902. Old Fleet 1904. Bolton Wanderers May 1904. LEEDS CITY December 1906. Manchester United February 1908. Queen's Park Rangers 1909–10. Chorley manager 1912. Rochdale chairman October 1919, chairman-manager until February 1923.

■ Tommy was an amateur player, hence the vast number of clubs he served. He was not tied to any of his clubs, including Leeds, for any great length of time but his skilful wing play meant he was often in demand, and he featured in a 1901 England trial. He married the daughter of an Oldham licensee and was a publican himself, in Bolton, after ending his playing days. He remained a football man, though, managing Chorley and Rochdale.

ABEL Christopher Robert

Right-back

Born: Chorlton, Manchester, 28 April 1912.
Died: Manchester, September 1986.
Career: Manchester junior football.
LEEDS UNITED September 1931.
Bradford City July 1936. Stalybridge Celtic
May 1937.

■ Such was the consistency of Jack Milburn that young Bobby hardly got a look in at Leeds and his only appearance came the week before his 23rd birthday. Unable to make much headway, he switched to Bradford City, where he was not able to establish himself until Lawrie Scott was sold to Arsenal.

ADAMS Michael Richard

Left-back

Born: Sheffield, 8 November 1961.
5ft 7in, 10st 10lb (1987).
Career: Sheffield Boys. Sheffield United schoolboy forms. Gillingham apprentice, professional November 1979. Coventry City £75,000 July 1983. LEEDS UNITED £110,000 January 1987. Southampton £250,000 March 1989. Stoke City free March 1994. Fulham free August 1994, player-manager February 1997–September 1997. Swansea City manager October 1997. Brentford manager November 1997–July 1998. Brighton & Hove Albion manager February 1999–October 2001. Leicester City assistant manager, manager April 2002–October 2004. Coventry City manager January 2005–January 2007. Colchester United assistant manager July 2007–January 2008. Brighton manager May 2008.

■ Mickey's left foot helped fire United to their first FA Cup semi-final for 10 years. His long-range shot at windswept Wigan set up United's 2–0 win and a Hillsborough showdown with his old club, Coventry. Adams, a raiding left-back, had only joined United from the Sky Blues 10 weeks before that epic 1987

semi-final. The former England Youth international did not make the grade at Sheffield United but shone at Gillingham, prompting a step up to the First Division with Coventry before his switch to Elland Road. Two years later United more than doubled their money when Mickey moved on to Southampton. At 34 he became the youngest manager operating in the League when he combined playing for Fulham with running the team. He steered the Cottagers to promotion within a few months but chairman Mohamed Al Fayed, owner of Knightsbridge store Harrods, dumped Mickey a few weeks into the 1997–98 season and within hours former England superstar Kevin Keegan was installed as Fulham's Chief Operating Officer. Mickey took the job as Swansea manager, only to walk out 13 days later when he discovered that money promised for new players was not there. Brentford became his third club in six weeks, but he got the chop at the end of the season. Mickey then steered Brighton to the Division Three title in 2001 and has since managed Leicester and Coventry.

ADDY Michael

Wing-half

Born: Knottingley, Yorkshire, 20 February 1943.
5ft 10½in, 12st 2lb (1962).

Career: LEEDS UNITED apprentice, professional May 1962. Barnsley June 1964. Corby Town free 1967.

■ With Billy McAdams, United's new signing from Bolton, Cup-tied, Don Revie turned to 18-year-old England Youth international Mike for the first time to occupy the number-nine shirt in United's League Cup replay at Rotherham. Later in the year he featured in a couple of League games in his favoured position at wing-half. Unable to keep pace with the Revie revolution, he moved to Barnsley.

AGANA Patrick Anthony Olazinka

Winger

Born: Bromley, 2 October 1963.
5ft 11in, 12st 2lb (1992).
Career: Welling United 1981. Weymouth £4,500 March 1984. Watford £22,000 August 1987. Sheffield United valued at £35,000 in exchange deal involving Martin Kuhl and Peter Hetherston, February 1988. Notts County £750,000 November 1991. LEEDS UNITED loan February 1992. Hereford United free March 1997–May 1998. Cliftonville August 1998. Leek Town November 1998, player-manager March 1999. Guiseley 1999.

■ Howard Wilkinson added Tony to his squad as the 1991–92 title race with Manchester United started to gather pace. The experienced wing man came on loan from Notts County for a few weeks, coming on for Rod Wallace at Luton and starting the home game with Aston Villa, but he returned to the Magpies, who were relegated to Division Two at the end of the season. Tony was a relatively late starter in League football having had an excellent non-League career, winning an England semi-professional cap against the Republic of Ireland while at Weymouth before joining Watford. At Sheffield United he forged a powerful attacking partnership with Brian Deane that pushed the Blades all the way to the Second Division title. Notts County shattered their transfer record to recruit Tony but the Magpies did not really get the best out of him in terms of goals because of injuries. After more than 150 games for Notts – including three matches in charge as caretaker manager – he joined Hereford United but was unable to prevent them slipping out of the Football League.

AINSLEY George Edward

Centre-forward

Born: South Shields, 15 April, 1915.
Died: Seacroft, Leeds, April 1985.
6ft, 13st (1939).
Career: County Durham Schools. South Shields St Andrew's. Sunderland April 1932. Bolton Wanderers £2,500 August 1936. LEEDS UNITED December 1936. Blackpool, Southport, Liverpool, Manchester

United, Huddersfield Town, Birmingham, Crewe Alexandra and Bradford Park Avenue wartime guest. Bradford Park Avenue November 1947–May 1949. Cambridge University coach early 1950s. FA staff coach. US Armed Forces coach in Wiesbaden, Germany 1955. Pakistan national coach to autumn 1962. Highland Park of Johannesburg coach November 1962. Israel national coach late 1963–December 1964. Workington manager July 1965–November 1966.

■ George travelled the world plying his football skills, but Leeds was always close to his heart. He reached his peak in summer 1939 when he and Ken Gadsby toured South Africa with an FA squad. George arrived in Leeds just before Christmas 1936 and enjoyed a scoring debut, his first-ever League goal, in a 2–1 defeat at one of his former clubs, Sunderland. United only just managed to stay up and George, who was outstanding in the air, carved out many chances the following season for top scorer Gordon Hodgson. Just when George's career seemed to be on the up, war broke out and George, a warrant officer with the RAF, guested for a string of clubs as well as netting 35 goals in 64 wartime games for Leeds. After the war he was one of the few shining lights in the 1946–47 season. He joined Bradford and had the satisfaction of scoring his first League hat-trick in Park Avenue's 3–1 Division Two home win over United on 13 March 1948, aged 33. George became an FA staff coach, travelled extensively and had spells as the national team coach of Pakistan and Israel. From such exotic climes he arrived in Workington for his only stint of Football League management.

AIZLEWOOD Mark

Midfield

Born: Newport, Glamorgan, 1 October 1959.
6ft, 12st 8lb (1987).
Career: Hartridge School, Newport. Cromwell FC. Newport County apprentice 1975–76, professional October 1977. Luton Town £50,000 April 1978. Charlton Athletic £50,000 November 1982. LEEDS UNITED £200,000 February 1987. Bradford City £200,000 August 1989. Bristol City £125,000 August 1990. Cardiff City October 1993. Aberystwyth 1996–97.

Merthyr Town player and assistant manager. Camarthen Town player-coach 1997. Cwmbran Town player-coach 1999. Welsh Under-17 national manager. Welsh FA technical director 2002–04. Camarthen Town club coach December 2003. Chester assistant manager August 2004–April 2005.

■ Mark, a well-established Welsh international, saw his United career turn sour when he reacted to terrace boo-boys at Elland Road. He was skipper when the disappointing 1988–89 Division Two season was drifting to a close, and he was taking some stick from the sparse crowd in the penultimate home game of the season. After netting the only goal against Walsall, he thrust two fingers up to his tormentors. It was to prove his last game for Leeds as he was stripped of the captaincy by Howard Wilkinson. A Welsh Schools international and Youth team captain, Mark turned down the chance to join Arsenal in favour of his home-town club. At 16 years and 179 days he became Newport County's youngest player and had to get permission from his headmaster to make his debut against Darlington in March 1976. His elder brother, Steve, had also played for County at 16. Mark had broken into the Welsh Under-23 team by the time he moved to Luton, where he figured in midfield, central defence and at left-back. Four years on he switched to Charlton, making his debut against Leeds. After promotion with both the Hatters and the 'Addicks, Mark was recruited by Billy

Bremner as a midfield organiser, but was denied a third promotion when United lost to his former side, Charlton, in the last Play-off game of 1986–87. After a spell at Bradford, Mark was later player-coach under ex-Leeds man Terry Yorath at Cardiff, where he won the last of his 39 full caps. Since then he has played, coached and managed in the Welsh League, worked as a BBC Wales television pundit, run the Welsh Under-17 side and later had a spell as assistant to Ian Rush at Chester.

ALDERSON Thomas

Centre-forward

Born: Leasingthorne, Co Durham 8 December 1908
5ft 10½in, 12st 4lb (1930).
Career: West Auckland. Bradford City trials 1927. Cockfield. Huddersfield Town December 1929. LEEDS UNITED November 1930. Luton Town May 1932. Darlington June 1933. Chester June 1936. Darlington February 1938.

■ A two-goal Football League debut in a 3–0 win over West Ham promised big things, but they were to prove Tom's only goals in his short time at Leeds. As a kid, Tom enjoyed a fine amateur career before trying his luck with Huddersfield Town, where his Central League form prompted Dick Ray to sign him as cover for United forwards Charlie Keetley and Russell Wainscoat.

ALLAN James

Full-back

Born: Airdrie, Lanarkshire.
5ft 8in, 11st 3lb (1926).
Career: Ashfield. Airdrie. LEEDS UNITED June 1925. Third Lanark July 1928. Coventry City 1929.

■ According to one observer, Jimmy was 'speedy with a dashing style' when he joined Leeds from his home-town team of Airdrie. He was comfortable at either right or left-back and gave United three years' good service before returning to Scotland with Third Lanark.

ALLEN John William Alcroft

Left-winger

Born: Newburn, Northumberland, 31 January 1903.

Died: Burnopfield, Co. Durham, 19 November 1957.
5ft 10in, 12st 4lb (1926).
Career: Prudhoe Castle. LEEDS UNITED February 1922. Brentford August 1924. Sheffield Wednesday March 1927. Newcastle United £3,500 June 1931. Bristol Rovers £200 November 1932. Gateshead £100 August 1933.

■ One that definitely got away. Jack managed just two games in Leeds colours but carved out a memorable career elsewhere after being prematurely released by Arthur Fairclough. He established a goalscoring reputation with Brentford and won League Championship medals with Sheffield Wednesday in 1929 and 1930. After 85 goals in 114 games Jack was sold to Newcastle and scored both goals in their 2–1 FA Cup Final win over Arsenal in 1932. His equaliser at Wembley was highly controversial as newsreel footage showed that the ball had crossed the by-line before being centred for Jack to score. He became a publican and ran the Travellers' Rest at Burnopfield, County Durham, up to his death at the age of 54. His younger brother, Ralph, also played for Fulham, Brentford, Charlton, Reading, Northampton and Torquay.

AMEOBI Tomi

Forward

Born: Newcastle upon Tyne, 16 August 1988.
6ft 2in, 12st 2lb (2007).
Career: Walker Central. Newcastle United juniors. LEEDS UNITED juniors August

2007. Scunthorpe United loan November 2007.

■ Teenager Tomi followed older brother Shola by joining Newcastle but was not kept on and linked up with the Leeds Academy. He made his debut in the 2007 League Cup defeat at Portsmouth and was loaned to Scunthorpe three months later to gain more experience.

ANDREWS Ian Edmund

Goalkeeper

Born: Nottingham, 1 December 1964.
6ft 2in, 12st 2lb (1988).
Career: Nottingham Forest associate schoolboy. Mansfield Town apprentice 1980. Leicester City September 1981. Middlesbrough loan January 1984.

Swindon Town loan January 1984. Celtic £300,000 July 1988. LEEDS UNITED loan December 1988. Southampton £200,000 December 1989. Plymouth Argyle August 1994. Bournemouth £20,000 September 1994. Leicester City loan March 1997, Leicester City May 2001 physio.

■ Goalkeeper Ian did what was required in his only game on loan with United, keeping a clean sheet. He spent four weeks at Elland Road, coming from Celtic as cover for Mervyn Day, and distinguished himself with a solid performance at Crystal Palace while Day was temporarily out of action. Ian's best days were at Leicester, where he earned England Youth and Under-21 honours.

ANDREWS Wayne Michael Hill

Striker

Born: Paddington, London, 25 November 1977.
5ft 10in, 11st 12lb (1988).
Career: Watford trainee, professional July 1996. Cambridge United loan October 1998. Peterborough United loan February 1999. St Albans 1999. Chesham United. Oldham Athletic May 2002. Colchester United August 2003. Crystal Palace September 2004. Coventry City July 2006. Sheffield Wednesday loan November 2006. Bristol City loan January 2007. LEEDS UNITED loan October 2007. Bristol Rovers loan March 2008.

■ With main strikers Jermaine Beckford and Tresor Kandol suspended, Wayne was drafted in on loan and made his only start in the League for United in a 1–0 win at one of his former clubs, Oldham.

ANKERGREN Casper

Goalkeeper

Born: Koge, Denmark, 7 November 1979.
6ft 3in, 14st 7lb (2007).
Career: Koge BK (Denmark) July 1999. Brondby (Denmark) July 2001. LEEDS UNITED loan January 2007, free August 2007.

■ Former Danish Under-21 international Casper became the fourth man to play in goal for United in the troubled 2006–07 season, marking his second appearance with a penalty save in the 1–0 defeat at Cardiff. Prior to

arriving at Leeds on loan during the January 2007 transfer window, all his football had been played in his home country, where he won a League and Cup double in 2005 with parent club Brondby and kept a League record 18 clean sheets. After relegation he returned to Leeds on a three-year deal.

ARINS Anthony Francis

Defender

Born: Chesterfield, 26 October 1958.
5ft 11in, 12st 2lb (1988).
Career: Burnley apprentice, professional July 1976. LEEDS UNITED May 1980. Scunthorpe United loan November 1981, free February 1982–May 1982.

■ Tony had a brief Leeds career – just 30 minutes. He came on as substitute

for Brian Greenhoff in a 2–1 defeat at Ipswich in the 1981–82 relegation season and made his mark by being quickly booked. He began with Burnley as a junior and his main claim to fame was winning an Anglo–Scottish Cup medal after the Clarets defeated Oldham over both legs in the 1978 Final. Signed with fellow Turf Moorite and Scottish Youth international Marshall Burke by Jimmy Adamson, the pair struggled to adapt to life at Elland Road, Burke not even making a senior appearance. Tony quit League football in 1982 to join the Police Force, later managing the Nottinghamshire Police side.

ARMAND John Edward

Inside-forward

Born: Sabathu, India, 11 August 1898.
Died: Grimsby, summer 1974.
5ft 7in, 11st (1925).
Career: Army international. West Stanley August 1992. LEEDS UNITED December 1922. Swansea Town £500 May 1929. Ashton National June 1931. Newport County August 1932. Scarborough October 1933. Denaby United January 1934.

Armand

■ Jack was the first player born outside the British Isles to play for United. He had already played for the army when he joined Leeds from West Stanley with Albert Bell. 'Snowy' Armand made steady, if unspectacular, progress at Elland Road, and Leeds netted a £500 fee when he joined Swansea. He represented the Welsh League against the League of

Ireland in 1930, scoring twice in a 6–1 win. His most productive season was 1931–32, when he scored 48 goals for Ashton National in the Cheshire League.

ARMES Samuel

Winger

Born: New Seaham, Sunderland, 30 March 1908.
Died: Sunderland, 27 August 1958.
5ft 10in, 10st 4lb (1936).
Career: Howden FC. Dawdon Colliery. Carlisle May 1930. Chester June 1932. Blackpool January 1934. LEEDS UNITED

October 1935. Middlesbrough £2,000 February 1939–August 1946.

■ United actually made two payments to sign Sammy in October 1935. Although he was with non-League Wigan his League registration was held by Blackpool. It proved money well spent as Leeds boss Billy Hampson, who had been Sammy's manager at Carlisle earlier in his career, secured United £2,000 when he was sold to Middlesbrough four years later. Described as a 'sprinter marksman', Sammy flitted in and out of the Leeds team. His best scoring days were at Chester, where he scored nine goals in three successive home games in 1933–34.

ARMITAGE Leonard

Centre-forward

Born: Sheffield, 20 October 1899.
Died: Wortley, Sheffield, spring 1972.
5ft 9½in, 11st 7lb (1923).
Career: Sheffield Boys, Sheffield Forge and Rolling Mills. Walkley Amateurs. Wadsley Bridge. Sheffield Wednesday 1914. LEEDS UNITED June 1920. Wigan Borough 1923. Stoke March 1924. Rhyl 1931. Port Vale December 1932.

■ Len marked his Leeds debut by scoring United's first goal in the Football League – a 2–1 defeat at home to South Shields on 20 October 1920. He had been a bit of a boy star, winning an English Schools FA Shield medal while playing for Sheffield Boys in 1914. After shining in local football in his native city he played for Wednesday before joining United for their maiden League season. Noted as being deadly accurate from the penalty spot, his best years were at Stoke,

where he won a Division Three North Championship medal in 1926–27 and toured South Africa with the FA in 1929. Len's grandad, Tom, was a Yorkshire cricketer who was in the first-ever England touring party to Australia.

ASHALL James

Full-back

Born: Temple Normanton, nr Chesterfield, 13 December 1933.
5ft 10in, 11st 6lb (1956).
Career: Hasland Old Boys. Doe Lea Valley. LEEDS UNITED October 1951. Weymouth June 1961.

■ Spotted as a 17-year-old playing in the Chesterfield and District Youth League, Jimmy was given a month's trial at Elland Road before turning pro. But as soon as United got their man he was whisked away on national service with the Green Howards and did not make his League debut until four years later, a 1–1 draw at Swansea. Within three months of his appointment as player-manager Don Revie released Jimmy, who joined Southern League side Weymouth.

ASHURST John

Centre-half

Born: Coatbridge, Lanarkshire, 12 October 1954.
6ft, 12st 4lb (1987).
Career: Renton Juniors. Sunderland apprentice 1969, professional October 1971. Blackpool £110,000 October 1979. Carlisle United £40,000 August 1981. LEEDS UNITED £35,000 July 1986.

Doncaster Rovers £10,000 November 1988. Bridlington Town. Doncaster Rovers November 1990. Rochdale month's trial August 1992. Frickley Athletic. North Shields.

■ Experienced upright centre-back Jack was a surprise Billy Bremner signing from Carlisle for £35,000. It was a reasonably large sum for a cash-strapped club to invest in a 31-year-old. But Jack kept himself fit, rarely missed a game and used his defensive nous to good effect as United came within minutes of promotion and an FA Cup Final appearance in 1987. He followed Bremner to Doncaster (where he had two spells), having previously worked under Bob Stokoe at Sunderland, Blackpool and Carlisle. He was in Sunderland's squad for the 1973 FA Cup Final against Leeds but did not play. After quitting football he ran an electrical goods shop in Sunderland and is now a warehouse manager.

ASPIN Neil

Right-back/Centre-half

Born: Gateshead, 12 April 1965.
6ft, 12st 3lb (1987).
Career: Durham County Schools and England Schools trials. LEEDS UNITED from trainee October 1982. Port Vale £200,000 July 1989. Darlington free July 1999. Hartlepool January 2001. Harrogate Town player-coach June 2001, manager February 2005.

■ Neil was just 16 and preparing to face Doncaster juniors in the Northern Intermediate League on the morning of 20 February 1982 when he was told by manager Allan Clarke about a dramatic change on plan. The youngster was handed his senior debut against Ipswich at Elland Road. With Kenny Burns suspended, Trevor Cherry, Brian Greenhoff and Neil Firm injured, Clarke kept his plans under wraps until shortly

before the match. Aspin never gave less than 100 per cent for Leeds, even postponing his wedding as the date clashed with the 1987 FA Cup semi-final. After more than 200 games for the Whites he joined Port Vale, becoming a rock in the heart of the Valiants' defence. Hero-worshipped by the Vale faithful, he was a member of the side that beat Stockport 2–1 in the Autoglass Trophy Final in 1993. However, hopes of a Wembley double evaporated a few weeks later when Vale lost 3–0 in the Second Division Play-off Final to West Brom. Promotion was gained the following season and Neil was awarded a testimonial at Vale Park – a match that featured singer and huge Vale fan Robbie Williams. After spells at Darlington and Hartlepool, Neil hooked up with Harrogate Town, appointed manager by one-time Leeds chairman Bill Fotherby.

ATKINSON Joshua Whitehead

Wing-half

Born: Blackpool, 28 March 1902.
Died: Manchester 1983.
5ft 11in, 11st 4lb (1925).
Career: Blackpool. LEEDS UNITED May 1924. Barnsley July 1928. Chester £250 June 1930. Fleetwood Town.

■ Josh was the chief understudy to the brilliant Willis Edwards at Leeds. He kicked off his career with his home-town team Blackpool but moved to Leeds shortly after his boss at Bloomfield Road, Bill Norman, was appointed assistant manager at Leeds.

B

BAIRD Hugh

Centre-forward

Born: New Monkland, Lanarkshire, 14 March 1930.
Died: Aberdeen, 19 June 2006.
5ft 10½in (1962).
Career: Dalry Thistle. Airdrie March 1951. LEEDS UNITED £12,000 June 1957. Aberdeen £11,000 October 1958. Brechin City. Deveronvale. Rothes.

■ Scottish goal-poacher Hugh was bought to fill the boots of the incomparable John Charles. It was an impossible task, and although he averaged a goal every other game at Elland Road, he returned to Scotland after a year. Hugh first shot to prominence at Airdrie, where he scored 165 goals in six seasons, including 37 in 1954–55 when he was Scotland's top scorer as Airdrie stormed to the B Division Championship. He won his only cap in a 1–1 draw against Austria at Hampden Park on 2 May 1956. Hugh did his national service in the RAF and was stationed at Pitreavie. After his playing career he worked as a bricklayer in London before moving to Aberdeen.

BAIRD Ian John

Forward

Born: Rotherham, 1 April 1964.
6ft, 12st (1986).
Career: Bitterne Saints. St Mary's College, Southampton. Southampton, Hampshire and England Schools. Southampton apprentice July 1980, professional April 1982. Cardiff City loan November 1983. Newcastle United loan December 1984. LEEDS UNITED £75,000 March 1985. Portsmouth £285,000 June 1987. LEEDS UNITED £185,000 February 1988. Middlesbrough £500,000 January 1990. Hearts £400,000 July 1991. Bristol City £295,000 July 1993. Plymouth Argyle September 1995. Brighton £35,000 July 1996. Southampton youth academy manager 1996–97. Salisbury Town December 1997. Instant-Dict (Hong Kong) manager 1998. Hong Kong national coach 1999. Farnborough Town August 2000–May 2001. Stevenage Borough coach. Havant and Waterlooville manager November 2004. Eastleigh manager October 2007.

■ Fiery striker Ian never shirked a challenge in his two spells at Leeds, often getting himself into trouble with referees. His robust style endeared him to the Elland Road faithful, who boomed 'Bairdy's going to get you' when they smelled blood in the air. But he was more than a battering ram, piling in half a century of League goals for the Whites, and there were always clubs queuing up for his services. An England Schoolboy international, he arrived from Southampton but returned to Hampshire to play for newly-promoted Portsmouth. The fee was set by an FA Tribunal at £285,000 but hard-up Pompey sold him back to Leeds nine months later for £100,000 less. His second Elland Road spell was less successful, and he eventually lost his place to Lee Chapman. United netted a handsome profit when he moved on to Middlesbrough, scoring twice in Boro's 4–1 win over Newcastle on the final Saturday of the season. That result kept Boro up and helped Leeds beat off the challenge of the Magpies, enabling Ian to

collect a Second Division Championship medal, even though he was no longer a Leeds player. He had a successful time with Joe Jordan's Hearts and his goals for Brighton played a big part in keeping them in the Football League in 1996–97. He is now in charge of non-League Eastleigh and runs a vehicle leasing company.

BAKER Aaron

Right-half

Born: Basford Green, Staffordshire, 23 December 1904.
Died: Nottingham, 18 October 1963.
5ft 9in, 11st 4lb (1925).
Career: Ilkeston Town. LEEDS UNITED October 1927. Sheffield Wednesday December 1927. Luton Town 1929–30.

■ The least-known of a trio of brothers who played League football, Aaron made just a couple of League appearances for Leeds after joining from Ilkeston. His footballing brothers were Alf, who played for Arsenal and England, and Jim, the Leeds hero.

BAKER James William

Centre-half

Born: Basford Green, Staffordshire, 15 November 1891.
Died: Leeds, 13 December 1966.
5ft 8½in, 11st 8lb (1925).
Career: Ilkeston Town. Derby County. Portsmouth 1911–12. Hartlepool United 1912. Huddersfield Town May 1914. LEEDS UNITED May 1920. Nelson June 1926. Colne Valley.

■ Jim was a major figure at Elland Road, skippering United to promotion in 1923–24 and later becoming a director at the club. Arthur Fairclough was appointed Leeds manager in February 1920 and three months later went back to his old club, Huddersfield, to sign Baker. It was a cute bit of business as Baker became a cornerstone of the new United club. Although small for a central-defender, he was an inspirational leader whose tigerish tackling quickly made him a favourite with the fans, who dubbed him 'T'owd War Hoss'. Jim played 149 consecutive League and Cup games as United's skipper. His last appearance, a 1–1 home draw against Everton on 6 March 1926, was his 200th – and last – League game in a Leeds shirt. He was 34 when he joined Nelson but always kept close links with Leeds, running the Smyth's Arms in Whitehall Road, then the Mexborough Arms in Chapeltown. He scouted for the club and served on the board from 1959 to 1961.

BAKER Leonard Henry

Centre-half

Born: Sheffield, 18 November 1897.
Died: 1979.

5ft 10in, 12st (1920).
Career: Beighton. Blackpool 1919. LEEDS UNITED May 1923. Barnsley May 1925. Rochdale 1929. Nelson 1930.

■ Len was a peripheral figure during his two seasons at Leeds, making just 11 appearances. His manager at his first League club, Blackpool, was Bill Norman, and when Norman joined Leeds as assistant to Arthur Fairclough, he persuaded the United manager to sign Len. He fared better at Barnsley, where he played for five years.

BAKKE Eirik

Midfield

Born: Sogndal, Norway, 13 September 1977.
6ft 2in, 12st 9lb (2003).
Career: Sogndal (Norway). LEEDS UNITED £1.25 million July 1999. Aston Villa loan 2005. Brann Bergen (Norway) August 2006.

■ Eirik proved one of David O'Leary's most astute signings for Leeds. The

Norwegian Under-21 captain was snapped up from his home-town club and broke into the United first team sooner than expected. He was a key player in the squad that reached the Champions League and UEFA Cup semi-finals, a member of Norway's Euro 2000 and World Cup 2002 squads and totalled 25 full caps. A forceful, box-to-box midfielder, Eirik's strength in the air earned him a few games as an emergency striker under Terry Venables. But an injury while on national duty saw his Leeds career hit a brick wall. He managed only sporadic starts in his last three years and by that time United had financially imploded. The club were keen to offload Eirik as he was a high wage-earner but a deal that would have seen him rejoin O'Leary at Villa on a permanent basis fell through and he eventually returned to Norway.

BALCOMBE Stephen William

Forward

Born: Bangor, Wales, 2 September 1961.
6ft 1in, 11st (1981).
Career: Republic of Ireland Schools. Home Farm. LEEDS UNITED June 1978, professional October 1979. Home Farm September 1982. Dundalk August 1983. Shamrock Rovers December 1983. Oaklands player-coach. Whitby Town. Collingham. Tadcaster Albion.

■ Steve scored a brilliant solo goal on his debut to salvage a home point against Aston Villa in the 1981–82 relegation season. But that was as good as it got for the young forward who was born in Wales but raised in Ireland. After leaving Leeds, where he was capped by Wales at Under-21 level, Steve went back to the Republic and featured for several clubs, including Dublin-based Home Farm where United first spotted his potential. He combined his football with selling insurance before returning to Yorkshire, where he played non-League football and carved out a successful career as a pub landlord.

BANNISTER Edward

Full-back

Born: Leyland, Lancashire, 2 June 1920.
Died: Preston, October 1991.
5ft 10in, 12st 8lb (1948).

Career: Leyland and Oaks Fold. LEEDS UNITED May 1946. Barnsley July 1950.

■ Eddie was one of the few men to play League football in spectacles. As an amateur, he had trials with his local club, Preston, but was not taken on. He was a regular soldier in the Irish Guards and signed for Leeds when he was demobbed. He later dispensed with his famous spectacles for contact lenses but is reported to have lost one during a match and accidentally tackled Liverpool referee Bill Evans. Eddie's dad, Ernest, was on the books of Manchester City and Preston before World War One.

BARMBY Nicholas Jonathan

Midfield

Born: Hull, 11 February 1974.
5ft 7in, 11st 3lb (2003).
Career: Tottenham Hotspur from trainee April 1991. Middlesbrough £5.25 million August 1995. Everton £5.75 million November 1996. Liverpool £6 million July 2000. LEEDS UNITED £2.75 million August 2002. Nottingham Forest loan February 2004. Hull City free July 2004.

■ Nicky was Terry Venables's first signing for United in summer 2002 and made an instant impact with an early goal in the opening day 3–0 win over Manchester City. But his career with Leeds turned sour when he injured himself in the warm-up prior to a game at one of his old clubs, Spurs. He hardly got a kick under the stewardship of Peter Reid or Eddie Gray, and was loaned to Forest. Nicky was one of several high-profile names to leave Elland Road when the Whites lost their Premiership status,

and he dropped into League One with his home-town club, Hull. He helped the Tigers to two promotions, even scoring the club's fastest-ever goal after seven seconds against Walsall. A product of the FA National School at Lilleshall, Nicky shot to fame at Tottenham and figured in big-money moves to Middlesbrough, Everton and Liverpool. He gained the last of his 23 England caps just 10 months before his move to Elland Road.

BARNES Peter Simon

Outside-left

Born: Rugeley, Manchester, 10 June 1957.
5ft 10in, 11st (1981).
Career: Chorlton Juniors. Chorlton Grammar School. Whitehall. Gatley Rangers. Mane and Orst Boug. Manchester City July 1972, professional August 1974. West Bromwich Albion £650,000 July 1979. LEEDS UNITED £930,000 August 1981. Real Betis (Spain) loan August 1982. Melbourne JUST (Australia) loan April 1984. Manchester United loan May 1984. Coventry City £65,000 October 1984. Manchester United £50,000 July 1985. Manchester City £30,000 January 1987. Bolton Wanderers loan October 1987. Port Vale loan December 1987. Hull City March 1988. Drogheda United 1988. Sporting Farense (Portugal) August–September 1988. Bolton Wanderers November 1988. Sunderland February 1989. Stockport County player-coach March 1989, Hamrun Spartans (Malta) 1989. Tampa Bay Rowdies (US) April–August 1990. Northwich Victoria August–October 1990. Wrexham 1991. Radcliffe Borough 1991. Mossley 1991–October 1991. Cliftonville November 1992. Runcorn manager January–March 1996. Coaching in Norway 1996.

■ At £930,000 Peter was United's record signing when he joined the club in summer 1981. After dazzling as a youngster at Manchester City and West Brom, he was seen by Allan Clarke as the man to create chances with his wing wizardry. But it simply did not work out for him at Elland Road, and he proved to be an expensive flop as Leeds spiralled to relegation. He was loaned out to Spanish club Real Betis for a season before returning to Second Division United and being sold for a cut-price £65,000 to

Coventry. His early career saw him named Young Player of the Year in 1976, just months after scoring in Manchester City's League Cup Final win over West Brom. The following year he won the first of his 22 England caps – the last two coming as a substitute when he was a Leeds player. He certainly clocked up some miles, playing in England, US, Australia, Spain, Portugal, Malta, Norway, Ireland and Wales. Peter worked as a summariser on local radio in Manchester, helped run the Manchester City social club at Maine Road and coached the youngsters at City's Platt Lane training complex. He also had a stint selling insurance and, latterly, artificial turf. Peter's dad, Ken, also played for Manchester City.

BARRITT Ronald

Centre-forward

Born: Huddersfield, 15 April 1919.
Died: Huddersfield, June 2004.
5ft 9in, 12st (1951).
Career: Wombwell. Doncaster Rovers January 1949. Frickley Colliery 1950. LEEDS UNITED £500 April 1951. York City July 1952.

■ Ron, an engineer who made cutting tools, was given a second chance at League football by United as a part-timer. He had netted six goals for Doncaster Rovers in 13 League games before dropping back into the Midland League with Frickley, where United recruited him as cover for their regular attack.

BATES Michael John

Midfield

Born: Doncaster, 19 September 1947.
5ft 7in, 10st 7lb (1975).
Career: Yorkshire Schools. LEEDS UNITED apprentice, professional September 1964. Walsall £25,000 June 1976. Bradford City £20,000 June 1978. Doncaster Rovers June 1980. Bentley Victoria.

■ Midfielder Mick showed immense loyalty to United during Don Revie's golden era. He was often used to fill in when Billy Bremner and Johnny Giles were unavailable and several clubs, notably Southampton with a £100,000 bid, tried to lure him from Elland Road. Mick, a Yorkshire Schools player who trialled for England, stayed at Leeds 12 years and was a vital cog in the footballing machine that Revie had pieced together. The personal high point for Mick was a goal in the 2–2 draw with Juventus in the first leg of the 1971 Inter-Cities Fairs Cup Final which proved priceless as United went on to lift the trophy on away goals. He lost a couple of years to injuries before moving on to the lower divisions. At non-League Bentley, he played alongside old Leeds teammate Rod Belfitt. Mick recently retired from his own insurance business.

BATEY Norman Robert

Wing-half

Born: Haltwhistle, Northumberland, 18 October 1912.
Died: Chorley, 29 November 1988.
5ft 9in, 11st 2lb (1946).
Career: Greenhead South Tyne Rangers. Carlisle United amateur September 1931, professional September 1932. Preston North End March 1934. LEEDS UNITED April 1946. Southport free June 1947. Annfield Plain player-coach May 1948. Leyland Motors 1949. Chorley player-coach September 1952.

■ Bob started the disastrous 1946–47 season at left-half for United after being demobbed from the RAF. He had guested for Leeds in wartime when he was still a Preston player. At Deepdale he figured in North End's 1938 FA Cup-winning side and made more than a century of League appearances.

BATTY David

Midfield

Born: Leeds, 2 December 1968.
5ft 8in, 12st (2002).
Career: Allerton Grange School, Leeds and West Yorkshire Schools. Tingley Athletic. LEEDS UNITED from trainee August 1987. Blackburn Rovers £2.75 million September 1993. Newcastle United £3.75 million March 1996. LEEDS UNITED £4.4 million December 1998–May 2004.

■ Local hero David was idolised by the Leeds fans in his two spells with the club. A superb ball-winner and passer, he became an established central midfield player with England under Graham Taylor after a series of magnificent displays for United. He made his debut at 18 against Swindon in November 1987 and rapidly achieved international status at Under-21 level. He progressed during United's 1989–90 Second Division

David Batty

Championship campaign to win England B honours and won the first of his 42 senior caps against the USSR. His midfield partnership with Gordon Strachan, Gary McAllister and Gary Speed was at the heart of United's 1991–92 Division One title success. But the United faithful were stunned by his shock £2.75 million move to Blackburn Rovers. It proved a highly successful switch for David, as he finished the season as Rovers' Player of the Year and the following campaign collected a Premiership Championship medal. A £4.5 million move took him to Newcastle and he featured in the 1998 World Cup, missing the crucial spot-kick against Argentina which saw England eliminated in a penalty shoot-out. Life came full circle and he re-joined Leeds in December that year as a 30-year-old. He sustained a rib injury on his second Leeds debut against Coventry, which ruled him out for 15 games. He then needed pain-killers for a heart problem which was brought on by the injury. When fit he proved an inspiration to the younger members of David O'Leary's burgeoning team but an achilles problem ruled him out for more than a year. He bounced back to prime form in 2001–02, but United slid into financial decline and he retired at the end of the 2003–04 relegation season. David is one of United's modern-day legends and was under par in only a handful of his 350-plus games in a Leeds shirt – the only thing missing from his armoury was goalscoring. He is a vice-president of Harrogate Town.

BAYLY Robert

Midfield

Born: Dublin, 22 February 1988.
5ft 8in, 11st 1lb (2006).
Career: Cherry Orchard. Shelbourne.
LEEDS UNITED August 2006.

■ Republic of Ireland Youth international Robert made his debut at 18 as a substitute in the 3–1 League Cup defeat against Southend, on the day Dennis Wise was made United manager. 'Bocca' was sent off on his full debut – the 2–0 defeat at Derby in the final game of the Championship season – a result which confirmed United's relegation to

the third tier of English football for the first time in their history.

BECKFORD Jermaine Paul

Forward

Born: Ealing, 9 December 1983.
6ft 1in, 13st 2lb (2006).
Career: Wealdstone. Uxbridge loan.
LEEDS UNITED March 2006. Carlisle United loan October–November 2006. Scunthorpe United loan January–May 2007.

■ Hot property Jermaine was a surprise capture from Ryman League side Wealdstone, where he had scored 35 goals in 40 appearances. United beat the likes of Chelsea, Crystal Palace and Watford for his signature and quickly gave him a taste of Championship action from the subs' bench. He was loaned out to gain more experience and

found scoring form at Scunthorpe as the Iron won promotion to the Championship, passing United on the way up. He began the following campaign in fine style and earned an extension to his contract. He finished as the club's top scorer with 20 goals and was named Player of the Season.

BEENEY Mark Raymond

Goalkeeper

Born: Pembury, Kent, 30 December 1967.
6ft 4in, 14st 7lb (1995).
Career: Ringlestone Colts. Gillingham from apprentice August 1985. Maidstone United free January 1987. Aldershot loan March 1990. Brighton & Hove Albion £30,000 March 1991. LEEDS UNITED £350,000 April 1993. Doncaster Rovers 1999. Chelsea Under-21 goalkeeping coach 2000. Dover 2001. Sittingbourne manager 2002–November 2004, becoming full-time Chelsea goalkeeping coach.

■ United gained special permission from the FA for Mark to make his debut in the final match of the 1992–93 season. Signed from Brighton for £350,000 the previous month, he was ineligible to play until the start of the following season, but with nothing at stake for either Coventry or United the FA agreed he could play instead of John Lukic. The transfer money effectively rescued the Seagulls from financial ruin. Mark took up goalkeeping at the age of 14 when he was an apprentice with Gillingham. He joined non-League Maidstone United and was ever present as they won the Conference title and promotion to the

Football League. While a Stones player he played for the England semi-professional team against Italy. Mark retired from the full-time game in 1999 as a result of rupturing an achilles in a reserve game at Stoke. He ran a successful executive chauffeur's business, managed Kent side Sittingbourne and joined Chelsea's goalkeeping coaching staff.

BEESLEY Paul

Central-defender

Born Liverpool, 21 July 1965.
6ft 1in, 11st 5lb (1995).
Career: Marine. Wigan Athletic September 1984. Leyton Orient £175,000 September 1989. Sheffield United £300,000 July 1990. LEEDS UNITED £250,000 August 1995. Manchester City £500,000 February 1997. Port Vale loan December 1997. West Bromwich Albion loan March 1998. Port Vale August 1998. Blackpool May 1999. Chester assistant manager July 2000. Stalybridge Celtic October 2001. Worksop Town September 2002. Stockport County kit man. Nottingham Forest Under-14 coach. LEEDS UNITED Under-18 coach February 2007. Notts County kit man and scout August 2007.

■ Howard Wilkinson's only signing in summer 1995, the experienced Paul was recruited from Sheffield United as cover for United's central defence, although he also had a handful of games at full-back. The Merseysider's stay at Leeds was blighted by injury and the club did well to double their money when he moved on to Manchester City for £500,000. He was always a player in demand in the lower divisions earlier in his career, with both Wigan and Leyton Orient breaking their transfer records for him. After giving up the game he had a spell as Stockport's kit man when former Leeds teammate Carlton Palmer was in charge at Edgeley Park and also had a stint as a Youth team coach back at Leeds.

BEGLIN James Martin

Left-back

Born: Waterford, 29 July 1963.
5ft 11in, 11st (1989).
Career: Shamrock Rovers. Liverpool £25,000 May 1983. LEEDS UNITED free July 1989. Plymouth Argyle loan December 1989. Blackburn Rovers loan October 1990.

■ United manager Howard Wilkinson resurrected Jim's career after it was cruelly shattered in his Liverpool days when he broke a leg in the January 1987 Merseyside derby. His United debut was his first senior game in two and a half years since that incident. Signing Jim was always a risk but a month's loan spell at Plymouth helped him back to something like full fitness, and at the end of the Division Two Championship campaign, he was in possession of the number-three shirt. He was then loaned to Blackburn before a troublesome knee injury ended his professional career. At Liverpool Jim featured in the 1986 double-winning side and the ill-fated European Cup Final against Juventus at the Heysel Stadium in 1985. His 15 Irish caps were all won while at Anfield. In retirement he worked as a radio summariser and reporter with the BBC and RTE.

BELFITT Roderick Michael

Forward

Born: Doncaster, 30 October 1945.
5ft 10½in, 11st 6lb (1970).
Career: Doncaster United. Retford Town. LEEDS UNITED July 1963. Ipswich Town £55,000 November 1971. Everton £80,000 November 1972. Sunderland £70,000 October 1973. Fulham loan November 1974. Huddersfield Town February 1975. Worksop Town June 1976. Frickley Athletic. Bentley Victoria.

■ Rod's highlight during his 11-year stay at Elland Road was a hat-trick in the 1967 Inter-Cities Fairs Cup semi-final first leg against Kilmarnock. He provided excellent cover – mainly for Mick Jones – as Don Revie's side battled on several fronts. A strapping, hard-working front-runner, Rod came on as a substitute at Wembley in the 1968 League Cup Final win over Arsenal, having scored twice in the semi-final second leg against Derby. He also appeared in the Fairs Cup Final first-leg win against Ferencvaros the following year. Later in his career he had a spell at centre-back with Sunderland. After his professional career he returned to his original work as a draughtsman, before becoming a financial advisor.

BELL Albert

Right-back

Born: Sunderland, 8 February 1898.
Died: Annfield Plain, autumn 1973.
5ft 10in, 11st 12lb (1922).
Career: Annfield Plain. West Stanley.
LEEDS UNITED December 1922.
Accrington Stanley May 1925. Durham
City August 1927.

■ Albert arrived at Elland Road with John Armand from West Stanley. While Armand was fairly successful, Albert only made one appearance – a 1–0 win at Southampton – when Bert Duffield missed a rare match.

BELL Thomas Gilbert

Left-back

Born: Usworth, nr Gateshead, 11 April 1899.
5ft 7in, 11st 2lb (1922).
Career: Birtley. LEEDS UNITED March
1922. Southend United June 1925.
Portsmouth March 1928. Carlisle United
May 1930. Burton Town August 1931.
Usworth Colliery October 1931.

■ Tom was another defender from the North East called Bell who made just one outing in a Leeds shirt. His only match was a 1–1 Christmas Day draw at Bury in 1922. He did better at Southend, where he was made captain and was also in the Portsmouth side that lost 2–0 to Bolton in the 1929 FA Cup Final.

BELL William John

Left-back

Born: Johnstone, Lanarkshire,
3 September 1937.
5ft 10in, 11st 8lb (1963).
Career: Neilston Juniors. Queens Park
1957. LEEDS UNITED July 1960.
Leicester City £45,000 September 1967.
Brighton & Hove Albion July 1969.
Birmingham City coach May 1970,
manager September 1975–September
1977. Lincoln City manager October
1977–October 1978.

■ Don Revie converted Willie from a run-of-the-mill centre-half into a quality international left-back. He completed an engineering apprenticeship while with Queen's Park and won two Scottish amateur caps before signing as a professional with United. After an initial

struggle he proved a reliable left-back as United won the Second Division title, and he also played in the 1965 FA Cup Final defeat against Liverpool at Wembley. The following year he earned Scottish caps against Portugal and Brazil. The emergence of Terry Cooper saw Willie move on to Leicester after nearly 250 games for Leeds. He completed his playing career at Brighton before becoming coach at Birmingham under old Leeds teammate Freddie Goodwin, who has been his manager at Brighton. When Goodwin was dismissed in 1975, Willie was installed as manager at St Andrews, where he remained for two years. After a 10-month spell as Lincoln manager he went to Colorado in the US to join a religious group called the Campus Crusade for Christ. He coached at Liberty Baptist College, Virginia, before returning to England to work for the Within The Walls organisation.

BENNETT Ian Michael

Goalkeeper

Born: Worksop, 10 October 1971.
6ft, 12st 10lb (2005).
Career: Queen's Park Rangers trainee.
Newcastle United March 1989.
Peterborough United free March 1993.
Birmingham City £325,000 December
1993. Sheffield United loan December

2004. Coventry City loan February 2005.
LEEDS UNITED June 2005. Sheffield
United £100,000 July 2006.

■ Experienced goalkeeper Ian was brought in by Kevin Blackwell as cover for Neil Sullivan at the start of the 2005–06 season. He kept clean sheets in his opening three Championship games but lost his place to Sullivan after a 3–3 home draw with Brighton. Ian first came to prominence at Peterborough, earning a big-money move to Birmingham, where he made more than 300 appearances.

BENNETT William

Inside-forward

Born: Manchester, 16 May 1906.
5ft 8in, 10st (1930).
Career: Winsford United. LEEDS
UNITED November 1928. Southport July
1933. Rossendale August 1934. Upton
Colliery September 1933.

■ Bill made a contribution to United's 1930–31 promotion season with four goals in 10 games, the highlight being a double in the 4–3 win at Stoke in March. United finished two points ahead of the Potters at the end of the season. He was a consistent scorer in the reserves but did not get a look-in after United were promoted.

BEST Jeremiah

Outside-left

Born: Mickley, Northumberland, 23 January 1901.
Died: Darlington 1975.
5ft 10in, 10st 7lb (1920).
Career: Mickley Colliery Welfare. Newcastle United December 1919. LEEDS UNITED £100 July 1920. Northern League football 1921. Providence Clamdiggers (US) September 1924. New Bedford Whalers (US) September 1926. River Fall Marksman (US) November 1929. Pawtucket Rangers (US) December 1929. New Bedford Whalers (US) September 1930. Clapton Orient August 1931. Darlington 1933. Hull City October 1936. Hexham 1937.

■ A member of a big Northumberland footballing family, Jerry appeared in United's first-ever Football League game at Port Vale. He came from Newcastle United but was unable to nail down a regular Leeds place and was eventually ousted from the left-wing berth by Basil Wood. Jerry also played for several clubs in the United States before re-entering the Football League with Clapton Orient. He was a big hit at Darlington, scoring 68 goals in 109 games for the Quakers. His brother, Robert, played for Sunderland and Wolves.

BLAKE Nathan Alexander

Forward

Born: Cardiff, 27 January 1972.
5ft 11in, 13st 2lb (2005).
Career: Newport County. Chelsea trainee. Cardiff City August 1990. Sheffield United £300,000 February 1994. Bolton Wanderers £1.5 million December 1995. Blackburn Rovers £4.25 million October 1998. Wolverhampton Wanderers £1.4 million September 2001. Leicester City free August 2004–July 2005. LEEDS UNITED loan December 2004. Stoke City trial July 2006. Newport County August–October 2006.

■ Powerful Welsh international striker Nathan's stay at United was all-too brief. He arrived on loan from Leicester and netted in his second game – a 2–1 victory at Coventry. But in his next game, a third round FA Cup tie at Birmingham, he ruptured a hamstring, an injury which ended his pro career. Nathan's strength

and eye for goal earned him large transfer fees for moves to Bolton, Blackpool and Wolves. He runs his own property management company in Wales.

BLAKE Noel Lloyd George

Centre-half

Born: Kingston, Jamaica, 12 January 1962.
6ft 1in, 13st 5lb (1988).
Career: Sutton Coldfield Town. Walsall non-contract. Aston Villa August 1979. Shrewsbury Town loan March 1982. Birmingham City £55,000 September 1982. Portsmouth £150,000 April 1984. LEEDS UNITED free July 1988. Stoke City £175,000 February 1990. Bradford City free July 1992. Dundee December 1993. Exeter City August 1995, becoming player-assistant manager, then manager January 2000–September 2001. Retired as a player June 2001. Notts County coach 2003. Barnsley assistant manager. Stoke City Academy manager. England Under-16 and Under-19 assistant coach February 2007.

■ Noel was the first West Indian to play for United. The Jamaica-born centre-half was popular in his 18 months at Elland Road, where the fans dubbed him Bruno. He led the side on several occasions after being snapped up on a free transfer from Portsmouth, where he had been Player of the Year in successive seasons. United netted a tidy profit when Howard Wilkinson sold him to Stoke for £175,000. He later entered management

at Exeter, and after a period as a geography and PE teacher he re-entered football as first-team coach at Notts County. He then ran Stoke's academy before becoming an England FA coach.

BLAKE Robert James

Forward

Born: Middlesbrough, 4 March 1976.
5ft 9in, 12st 6lb (2005).
Career: Darlington trainee, professional July 1994. Bradford City £300,000 March 1997. Nottingham Forest loan August 2000. Burnley £1 million January 2002. Birmingham City £1.25 million January 2005. LEEDS UNITED £800,000 July 2005. Burnley £250,000 July 2007.

■ It took Robbie a few months to get into his stride with United after a big-money move from Birmingham City. A clever link-up player with good close control, he also proved a dangerous customer at free-kicks, from which he netted some spectacular goals. At neighbouring Bradford he helped the Bantams into the top flight and earned a

£1 million move to Burnley, where he scored 51 goals to spark a transfer into the Premiership with Birmingham City. After relegation in 2007 with Leeds he returned for a second spell with Burnley.

BLUNT Jason John

Midfield

Born: Penzance, 16 August 1977.
5ft 8in, 10st 10lb (1996).
Career: LEEDS UNITED apprentice, professional January 1995. Raith Rovers trial April 1998. Blackpool free July 1998. Castelneta (Italy) July 1999–December 2000. Grottaglio (Italy). Scarborough March 2001. Yeovil Town February 2003. Doncaster Rovers February 2003. Tamworth October 2003. Halifax Town

September 2004. Alfreton Town April 2005. Scarborough 2005. Sutton Town August 2006, player-manager February 2007. Goole September 2007.

■ Jason was among a batch of youngsters blooded by Howard Wilkinson the week after the 1996 Coca-Cola Cup Final debacle against Aston Villa. The 18-year-old Cornishman found himself on the bench against Middlesbrough, coming on at half-time when Lucas Radebe went in goal because of an injury to John Lukic. United's young team went 1–0 down. After a spell in Italy he helped Doncaster regain their League status in 2003. He works as a PE teacher at a Wakefield school.

BOARDMAN William

Centre-forward

Born: Urmston, Manchester, 14 October 1895.
Died: Manchester 1968.
5ft 10in, 11st 4lb (1920).
Career: Eccles. LEEDS UNITED October 1920. Doncaster Rovers January 1922. Crewe Alexandra August 1927. Chester.

■ Billy was a free-scoring reserve recruited from Eccles, where he had done well enough to represent the Manchester League against the Irish League. He did not score in any of his four senior outings with Leeds, but it was a different story at Doncaster where he netted more than 50 goals, the bulk of them in the Midland League.

BOWMAN Robert

Full-back

Born: Durham, 31 November 1975.
6ft 1in, 11st 12lb (1995).
Career: Durham City juniors and Durham County. Manchester United School of Excellence. Newcastle United juniors. LEEDS UNITED trainee December 1989, professional November 1992. Rotherham United February 1997. Carlisle United August 1997–May 2000. Bohemians 2000. Gateshead December 2000. Brandon United 2002. Coxhoe Athletic 2004. Shildon August 2005.

■ Rob emerged from nowhere to make his Premiership debut at just 17 years and 77 days after hardly any reserve-team football, coming off the bench at

Wimbledon to replace David Rocastle. Two days later he made his full debut against leaders Manchester United at Elland Road, taming England winger Lee Sharpe, a future Leeds player, in a 0–0 draw. He made his mark against the Red Devils again at the end of the season, playing in both legs of the FA Youth Cup Final, which saw Leeds' young tyros gain a 4–1 aggregate victory. To cap a super season, Rob also featured in the England Under-18 side that won the 1994 European Youth Championship. He did not play for the senior side again until he received a surprise call-up to face PSV Eindhoven in the UEFA Cup two years later. Before signing for Leeds he captained Durham District Under-16s and represented the city at the triple jump.

BOWYER Lee David

Midfield

Born: Canning Town, London, 3 January 1977.
5ft 9in, 10st 6lb (1999).
Career: Charlton Athletic from trainee April 1994. LEEDS UNITED £2.6 million July 1996. West Ham United £100,000 January 2003. Newcastle United free July 2003. West Ham United July 2006.

■ Lee was rarely out of the headlines during his seven-and-a-half years with United. He became the country's most expensive teenager when he was signed by Howard Wilkinson from Charlton in summer 1996. He arrived with a reputation of being a firebrand and did little to shake off that tag. He scored on his debut at Derby and quickly became a driving force in midfield with bags of energy, plenty of skill and a thirst for victory. His biting tackles and fiery temperament landed him in plenty of trouble on the pitch, but his performances saw him skipper England Under-21s. However, his international career was put on hold by the FA as Bowyer became embroiled in a protracted court case after being charged with attacking a student in Leeds city centre. Rather than collapse in the glare of the media spotlight, Lee's performances, particularly in Europe, went from strength to strength, being the club's Player of the Year in 1999 and 2001. Eventually, he was found not guilty of grievous bodily harm but was then transfer-listed after a disagreement with chairman Peter Ridsdale over his contract. Although the issue was resolved and he finally earned his sole England cap against Portugal, he never consistently hit his best form again and was allowed to leave for West Ham for a cut-price £100,000 in January 2003. In between periods of injury, he slowly began to look like the old Bowyer, being sent off three times for Newcastle in 2004–05, including a well-publicised bust-up involving teammate Kieron Dyer.

BOYLE Wesley Samuel

Striker

Born: Portadown, Northern Ireland, 30 March 1979.
5ft 8in, 10st 1lb (1999).
Career: Career: Portadown junior. LEEDS UNITED from trainee April 1996. Portadown March 2002. Doncaster Rovers trials. Loughgal 2006. Portadown.

■ Wes was a member of the 1997 Youth Cup-winning side and was given his chance as a 17-year-old by George Graham in the post-Wilkinson rebuilding era. Injuries then ruled him out for the best part of two years and an ankle injury suffered when playing for Northern Ireland Under-21s effectively finished his career at Leeds in March 2002. Wes returned home to play for his native Portadown, winning an Irish Cup medal in a 5–1 Final win over Larne at Windsor Park in 2005.

BRAVO Raul Senfelix

Left-back

Born: Gandia, Spain, 14 April 1981.
5ft 9in, 11st 5lb (2003).
Career: Real Madrid juniors (Spain) 1996. LEEDS UNITED loan February–May 2003. Olympiakos (Greece) £1.2 million July 2007.

■ Terry Venables used his continental contacts to obtain Raul Bravo on loan from Spanish giants Real Madrid in an effort to halt United's slide down the Premiership. Although he could not dislodge Brazilian star Roberto Carlos at

the Bernabeu Stadium he was still a Spanish international when he turned up at Leeds and added to his tally of caps during his brief stay at Elland Road. Venables left Leeds a few weeks after Bravo arrived and caretaker boss Peter Reid eased the defender out of the starting line-up. He returned to Spain in the summer and managed more games for Real, often at centre-back, before leaving after 11 years in Madrid for Greek side Olympiakos.

BREMNER William 'Billy' John

Midfield

Born: Stirling, 9 December 1942.
Died: Doncaster, 7 December 1997.
5ft 5½in, 9st 13lb (1974).
Career: St Modan's High School, Stirling. Gowanhill Juniors. LEEDS UNITED December 1959. Hull City £30,000 September 1976. Doncaster Rovers manager November 1978. LEEDS UNITED manager October 1985–September 1988. Doncaster Rovers manager July 1989–November 1991.

■ Legend Billy was the driving force behind Don Revie's great United sides. At his peak he was one of the world's greatest midfield players and possessed an almost telepathic understanding with clubmate Johnny Giles. Billy's marvellous range of passing, eye for goal,

endless depths of energy and an iron will to win made him a Leeds hero. Arsenal, Chelsea and Celtic all gave him trials as a kid but the straightforward manner of Leeds chairman Harry Reynolds impressed young Bremner, who was one of the stars of the Scottish Boys team. Billy made his senior debut for United as a 17-year-old in a 3–1 win at Chelsea on 23 January 1960. He played on the right wing that day with former England international Don Revie as his inside partner – a combination which was to thrive as manager and captain in future years. Despite Billy's eye-catching start, Leeds were relegated and his continued homesickness prompted him to request a transfer. Hibernian offered £25,000 for the flame-haired tiger, but United wanted a minimum of £30,000 so Bremner was obliged to stay. By this time, Revie was installed as manager and within a couple of seasons turned the club round, with Billy a key player in the squad that won the Second Division title in 1964. The following year United missed out on the Championship on goal difference and lost to Liverpool in extra-time in the FA Cup Final, but for Billy there was the compensation of the first of his 54 Scottish caps. The Revie machine was up and running with Billy in the engine room before becoming the club's most successful skipper, leading United to two League Championships, an FA Cup Final win, two Inter-Cities

Fairs Cup triumphs and the League Cup. He won the 1970 Footballer of the Year award and went on to lead the Scots in the 1974 World Cup, but his international career ended prematurely after a 1–0 European Championship victory over Denmark in September 1975 when he was one of five Scots players banned for life by the Scottish FA for an alleged nightclub brawl. It was the second high-profile incident involving Billy in just more than a year. After Revie left to take up the England job, Billy was sent off with Kevin Keegan in the FA Charity Shield at Wembley on 10 August 1974. Both players were hit with a £500 fine and banned until the end of September. By the time Bremner returned to action – after suspension and injury – the Leeds board had sacked Brian Clough. But Billy's return saw an upturn in United's fortunes and they reached the European Cup Final under Jimmy Armfield. The 2–0 defeat to Bayern Munich was to be a watershed in United's history and, after one more full season at Leeds, Billy moved on after 587 League appearances to join Hull City. He then entered management with Doncaster Rovers, winning a couple of promotions before being tempted back to Elland Road as manager in October 1985 (see Leeds City and United Managers). The football world was stunned when Billy died of pneumonia on 7 December 1997, just two days short of his 55th birthday. But his legend lives on at Elland Road in the form of a statue created by Frances Siegelman, which was unveiled outside the ground on 9 August 1999.

BRIDGES Michael

Forward

Born: Whitley Bay, 5 August 1978.
6ft 1in, 10st 11lb (2000).
Career: Mardon Bridge Middle School. Monkseaton High School. Northumberland Schools. Sunderland trainee May 1995, professional November 1995. LEEDS UNITED £5.6 million July 1999. Newcastle United loan February 2004. Bolton Wanderers free July 2004. Sunderland free September 2004. Bristol City July 2005. Carlisle United January 2006 after loan. Hull City £350,000 September 2006. Sydney FC (Australia) loan October 2007–March 2008.

■ Michael looked to be heading for full international status when his United career was cruelly cut short. He rose to prominence at Sunderland, where he won England Schools, Youth and Under-21 honours and Division One winners' medals in 1996 and 1999. After that second promotion he switched to Leeds and scored a hat-trick in his second appearance – a 3–0 win at Southampton. He proved to be worth the £5.6 million fee with a 19-goal League campaign as United made it to the Champions

League. But it was in Europe that Michael's dreams were shattered when he damaged ankle ligaments against Besiktas in Turkey, putting him out for nearly two years. He then snapped his left achilles against Malaga in the UEFA Cup in 2002 and made just one League start the following season. He attempted to resurrect his career with Newcastle, Bolton and Sunderland, making a contribution to the Black Cats' 2004–05 Championship title-winning season and scoring his first League goals for more than four years.

BROCK John Robert Eadie

Winger

Born: Cargill, Perthshire, 4 October 1897.
5ft 9in, 11st 6lb (1920).
Career: Edinburgh City. LEEDS UNITED October 1920–May 1921.

■ John opted to join Leeds rather than Hearts after both clubs sought his services from Edinburgh City. He only managed half a dozen League games at Elland Road, being largely confined to the Midland League side, and was released at the end of the season.

BROCKIE Vincent

Right-back

Born: Greenock, 2 February 1969.
5ft 8in, 10st (1988).
Career: Linworth High School, Paisley. Paisley and District Schools. Greenock Morton schoolboy forms. LEEDS UNITED apprentice July 1985, professional July 1987. Doncaster Rovers loan January 1989, £15,000 March 1989. Goole Town 1991. Guiseley. Hyde United. North Ferriby. Guiseley. Eastwood Town December 1998. Garforth 1999. Glasshoughton Welfare 2001–02. Horsforth St Margaret's manager. Harrogate Railway assistant manager August 2005, manager February 2007–April 2008.

■ Fiesty young right-back Vince was given his chance by Billy Bremner in the final two games of the 1987–88 season but was released the following year by Howard Wilkinson. He was signed by Joe Kinnear at Doncaster and thrived at Rovers under Billy Bremner until he dropped into non-League football, playing at Wembley in the 1992 FA Vase Final for Guiseley.

BROLIN Per Tomas

Forward

Born: Hudiksvall, Sweden, 29 November 1969.
5ft 8in, 12st 7lb (1996).
Career: FinnFlo Flyers (Sweden). Nasvikens IK (Sweden) 1984. GIF Sundsvall (Sweden) 1986. LFK Norrkoping (Sweden) 1989. Parma (Italy) £1.2 million 1990. LEEDS UNITED November 1995–October 1997. FC Zurich (Switzerland) loan September 1996. Parma (Italy) loan December 1996–June 1997. Crystal Palace January–May 1998. Hudiksvallas ABK (Sweden) August 1998.

■ Tomas is regarded by many as the costliest flop in United's history. At £4.5 million, the Swedish striker was the most expensive player ever to pull on a United shirt when he signed in November 1995. His pedigree on the international stage could not be questioned but he struggled to adapt to the rigours of the English game and recover from an ankle injury sustained the previous season with Italian club Parma. He failed to make the starting line-up in the 1996 League Cup Final and soon fell out with Howard Wilkinson's successor, George Graham. Loaned out to FC Zurich, his career was in limbo, with Graham not considering him for the first team, and Tomas agreed a financial settlement in October 1997 after a loan spell back in Italy with Parma. He later re-emerged with Crystal Palace but finished at the age of 29,

although he did a bit of coaching in America before returning to Sweden where he played one game for his local club in the Swedish Third Division – as a goalkeeper. He moved into the property business, co-owned a restaurant and marketed his own brand of footwear. Despite his miserable time in England he remains revered in his homeland, shooting to prominence as a youngster by scoring a debut hat-trick for IFK Norrkoping and netting twice on his full international debut against Wales. Tomas was one of the leading lights of the 1990 World Cup and soon established himself among the top echelons of the Italian game with Parma.

BROOK Harold

Forward

Born: Sheffield, 15 October 1921.
Died: Sheffield, November 1998.
5ft 9½in, 10st 12lb (1947).
Career: Sheffield Schools. Woodburn Alliance. Hallam. Fulwood. Sheffield United September 1940, turning professional in 1943. LEEDS UNITED £600 July 1954. Lincoln City March 1958–May 1958. Sheffield FC coach.

■ Veteran forward Harold scored nearly half a century of goals for United and led the Division Two promotion-winning attack of 1955–56. Leeds spent £600 on the 33-year-old former Sheffield United skipper and it proved money well spent. The Blades thought his best days were

gone after 89 goals in 229 League appearances, but his departure from Bramall Lane was premature, as he was as sharp as a tack at Leeds. He marked the club's return to the First Division with a 21-minute hat-trick against Everton on the opening day of the 1956–57 season but moved on during the following campaign to finish his career at Lincoln. He later ran a newsagent's in Meadowcroft, Sheffield, and had a stint coaching Sheffield FC.

BROWN Anthony James

Centre-half

Born: Bradford, 17 September 1958.
6ft 2in, 12st 10lb (1984).
Career: Thackley. LEEDS UNITED March 1983. Doncaster Rovers loan March 1985, transfer May 1985. Scunthorpe United August 1987. Rochdale August 1989–93. Bradford Park Avenue. Eccleshill United manager 2002–04.

■ Big Tony was plucked from non-League football as a 24-year-old and developed into a centre-back of some standing in the lower divisions. He was recruited from Northern Counties East League club Thackley after United's relegation from the top flight and within a few weeks made his United debut. He played a fair chunk of the following season but when United brought in Andy Linighan, Tony moved on to Doncaster and became captain. He made more than a century of appearances for Rochdale and later worked in sales for an insurance company and a power tools firm.

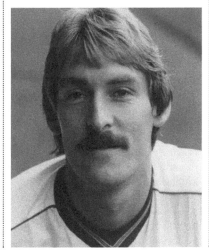

BROWN George

Centre-forward

Born: Mickley, Northumberland, 22 June 1903.
Died: Birmingham, 10 June 1948.
5ft 9in, 10st 7lb (1935).
Career: Mickley. Huddersfield Town May 1921. Aston Villa £5,000 August 1929. Burnley October 1934. LEEDS UNITED September 1935. Darlington player-manager October 1936–October 1938.

■ Former England international George proved a big hit in his only full season at Elland Road, being top scorer with 18 goals in 1935–36. 'Mickley' Brown's illustrious career may have been coming to a close at 32, but he was an astute capture by Leeds boss Billy Hampson. George made his name with the Huddersfield side which dominated the 1920s. He was a pit boy on strike when Herbert Chapman signed him for the Terriers in 1921, going on to score 142 League goals in eight years to set a Huddersfield aggregate record which he shares with Jimmy Glazzard. His 35 League goals in 1925–26 – Town's third successive Championship-winning season – equalled their club record for a season. George led their attack in the 1928 FA Cup Final before moving to

Aston Villa the following season. At Villa Park he added another England cap to the eight he collected at Huddersfield and switched to Leeds after a short spell at Burnley. His cousin, Joe Spence, played for Manchester United and England. George later ran a pub in Aston after giving up football.

BROWN Victor Charles

Right-back

Born: Bedford, 26 July 1903.
Died: 1971.
5ft 11in, 12st (1928).
Career: Bedford Town. LEEDS UNITED August 1929. Coventry City June 1933. Chester June 1939. New Brighton and Wrexham wartime guest. Haarlem (Holland). Coventry City coaching staff.

■ After signing from Bedford, Vic was confined to the reserves at United because of the remarkable consistency of brothers George and Jack Milburn. He made just one appearance – a 3–1 home defeat against Leicester – but later prospered at Coventry, where he captained them to the Division Three South Championship.

BROWNE Robert James

Wing-half

Born: Londonderry, 9 February 1932.
Died: 1994.
5ft 8in, 10st 10lb (1935).
Career: Maleven. Clooney Rovers. Derry City. LEEDS UNITED £1,500 October 1935. Watford wartime guest. York City August 1947. Thorne Colliery player-manager 1949. Halifax Town coach 1954, caretaker manager October–November 1954.

■ Former Leeds City, Sheffield United and Irish international star Billy Gillespie did much to further Bobby's career. Initially Bobby combined his job as a joiner with part-time football in Ireland, where he played under Gillespie's management at Derry City. He caught the eye when the Irish League beat the Football League 2–1 at Blackpool in September 1935 and joined United the following month. He won six Northern Ireland caps during his time at Elland Road before a wartime posting took him back to Ulster. An army PT staff sergeant,

Bobby guested for Watford when he was stationed at Colchester.

BROWNING Leonard James

Centre-forward

Born: Leeds, 30 March 1928.
6ft 2½in, 11st 8lb (1948).
Career: Quarry Brae and Leeds Secondary Modern Schools. England Youth Clubs. Headingley Rangers. LEEDS UNITED August 1946. Sheffield United £12,000 November 1951. East End Park.

■ Len established a reputation as a teenage whizz-kid when he joined the United ranks. The Leeds-born youngster had represented England Youth Clubs against Wales and against the Air Training Corps at Wembley before joining United's nursery side, Headingley Rangers. Len's stock continued to rise with a hat-trick in the reserves shortly before his League debut as an 18-year-old – a 5–0 defeat at Charlton on 25 September 1946. It was almost two years before Len's name was back on the senior team sheet. But with plenty of Central League experience under his belt he showed he had learned well and was leading scorer in 1948–49 and 1950–51. His height made him an aerial threat, but he showed good groundwork too, and it was a surprise when he was sold to Sheffield United, with whom he won a

Second Division Championship medal in 1952–53. Tuberculosis cut short his League career in October 1953 at the age of 25, but Len did play amateur Yorkshire League football before a broken leg forced him to call it a day. He and his wife, Mollie, were also excellent table tennis players, both representing the Leeds Victoria club. Outside football, Len worked as a technician at All Saints' College, Horsforth.

BUCK Teddy

Wing-half

Born: Dipton, Co. Durham, 29 October 1904.
Died: Grimsby, 3 August 1993.
5ft 9½in, 12st (1928).
Career: West Stanley. LEEDS UNITED May 1927. Grimsby Town £2,000 December 1929, coaching staff 1945.

■ All of Teddy's eight League appearances for United came in 1928–29 as cover for Willis Edwards and George Reed. He had arrived from North East League club West Stanley but did not make his mark as a League player until he joined Grimsby, where he made 354 appearances. He won a Second Division Championship medal with the Mariners in 1933–34 and joined their coaching staff as the war was ending.

BUCKLEY Arthur

Left-winger

Born: Oldham, 13 April 1913.
5ft 10in, 11st 4lb (1936).
Career: Greenfield. Oldham Athletic amateur March 1932, professional October 1932. LEEDS UNITED £2,500 October 1936. Oldham Athletic war-time guest. Mossley 1947.

■ For two seasons in the late 1930s Arthur was a goalscoring winger – and goal provider – for United. He was first spotted by his local club Oldham in amateur football and spent four years at Boundary Park before his move to Leeds. He chipped in with a goal about every four games and provided a string of accurate crosses for centre-forward Gordon Hodgson. He shared the left-wing berth with Jack Hargreaves in the final season before the war and guested for Oldham during hostilities before a highly successful 1946–47 season at Mossley where he was top scorer.

BUCKLEY John William

Winger

Born: East Kilbride, Lanarkshire, 10 May 1962.
5ft 9in, 10st 7lb (1986).
Career: Queen's Park. Celtic May 1978. Partick Thistle March 1983. Doncaster Rovers July 1984. LEEDS UNITED £35,000 June 1986. Leicester City loan March 1987. Doncaster Rovers loan October 1987. Rotherham United £30,000 November 1987. Partick Thistle £45,000 October 1990. Scunthorpe United £40,000 August 1991. Rotherham United £20,000 February 1993.

Buxton December 1994. Hatfield Main 1995. Rotherham United football in the community officer 1995. LEEDS UNITED Academy part-time role. Scunthorpe United Under-16s coach 1999. Hull City youth coach. Doncaster Belles manager 2003.

■ Tricky winger John followed manager Billy Bremner from Doncaster to Elland Road. Although he was blessed with slippery dribbling skills he could not make an impact at Elland Road. He was an old-fashioned ball player who thrived in his native Scotland with Partick Thistle. After leaving Leeds, John helped Rotherham to the Division Four Championship but his second spell with the Millers almost ended in tragedy. He fractured his skull against Plymouth and was in a coma for several days before having a blood clot removed from his brain. He made a full recovery but announced his retirement in July 1993. John played in a few non-League games but finally called it a day after collapsing in a Northern Counties East League game for Hatfield Main. He remained in football, coaching youngsters at various clubs, including Leeds, before becoming manager of ladies team Doncaster Belles.

BULLIONS James Law

Right-half

Born: Dennyloanhead, Stirlingshire, 12 March 1924.
5ft 11in, 11st 10lb (1945).
Career: Chesterfield amateur. Clowne.

Derby County October 1944. LEEDS UNITED November 1947. Shrewsbury Town September 1950. Worksop Town. Matlock Town. Gresley Rovers. Sutton Town. Alfreton Town manager September 1960.

■ Jim, the youngest member of Derby County's 1946 FA Cup-winning side, served United as a ball-winning wing-half. He went straight into the team after joining from the Rams and stayed there for the rest of the season. After that he spent most of his time in the Central League team before going to Shrewsbury. He embarked on a lengthy spell on the non-League circuit, including nine years as manager of Alfreton Town.

BURBANKS William Edwin

Winger

Born: Doncaster, 1 April 1913.
Died: Hull, 26 July 1983.
5ft 8in, 10st 7lb (1953).
Career: Doncaster Grammar School. Doncaster YMCA. Thorne. Denaby United. Sunderland £750 February 1935. Doncaster Rovers, Chesterfield and Blackpool wartime guest. Hull City June 1948. LEEDS UNITED July 1953–May 1954.

■ Eddie earned his niche in United history by being the oldest man to play for the club. His last game for Leeds was as captain against Hull City – one of his former sides – on 24 April 1954, just three weeks after his 41st birthday. Eddie was a top-notch winger and a natural left-footer, but he played on the right,

having a penchant for cutting in and letting fly with his powerful shooting. He scored in Sunderland's 1937 FA Cup Final victory over Preston and, after losing a big slice of his career to the war, played a key role in Hull City's Division Three North title-winning campaign in 1948–49 under the leadership of his pal Raich Carter. When Carter became manager at Elland Road he brought Eddie with him. After Eddie gave up the game he ran a sweet shop with his wife, Joyce, in Holderness Road, Hull, until his retirement in November 1979.

BURDEN Thomas David

Wing-half

Born: Andover, Buckinghamshire, 21 February 1924.
Died: Taunton, October 2001.
5ft 8½in, 11st 5lb (1951).
Career: Somerset County Boys. Wolverhampton Wanderers August 1941. Chester November 1945. LEEDS UNITED July 1948. Bristol City £1,500, plus £500 a year for three years, October 1954.

■ Natural leader Tommy skippered United for four seasons in the early 1950s. The West Country boy was recommended to Wolves manager Major Frank Buckley by his headmaster and was only 16 when he played for Wolves in wartime. Tommy served with the Rifle Brigade and Royal Fusiliers and was wounded in the D-Day landings but went on to complete a physical training

course at Loughborough College. He had been playing for Chester when Major Buckley, now installed at Elland Road, persuaded him to come to Leeds, even though Tommy was still based in Somerset. Despite the geographical difficulties, his commitment to United never wavered until the travelling finally took its toll after more than 250 games in a United shirt. He asked to move nearer home and went with United's blessing to Bristol City, where he won a Third Division South Championship medal in 1955. He continued to give City sterling service before retiring in 1960 and later worked as a senior executive with Clark's Shoes in Street, Somerset.

BURGIN Edward

Goalkeeper

Born: Stannington, Sheffield, 29 April 1927.
5ft 9in, 11st 7lb (1959).
Career: Alford Town. Sheffield United March 1949. Doncaster Rovers December 1957. LEEDS UNITED March 1958. Rochdale January 1962. Glossop player-manager July 1966. Oswestry. Wellington Town. Burton Albion.

■ A member of England's 1954 World Cup squad, goalkeeper Ted took over from Roy Wood in the late 1950s at Elland Road. An acrobat and athlete, he wrote to Sheffield United for a trial and his talent was recognised when he went to Australia in 1951 as a member of the FA tour party. Three years later he was deputy to Birmingham City's Gil Merrick at the World Cup in Switzerland. Although Ted won England B honours the call to the highest honour eluded him. He enjoyed another FA tour in 1956, this time to South Africa, but with future England 'keeper Alan Hodgkinson emerging at Bramall Lane, Ted moved on briefly to Doncaster Rovers before alighting at Leeds. He was 33 when he moved on to Rochdale, where he figured in the 1962 two-legged Football League Cup Final defeat against Norwich when Dale were a Fourth Division club. Ted, who worked for Rochdale Council before retiring to the Fylde coast, was the younger brother of former Yorkshire cricketer, Edwin Burgin.

BURNS Jacob Geoffrey

Midfield

Born: Sydney, Australia, 21 January 1978.
5ft 9in, 11st 12lb (2003).
Career: Sydney United (Australia), Paramatta Power (Australia) August 1999. LEEDS UNITED £250,000 August 2000. Feyenoord (Holland) January 2003. Barnsley free October 2003. Wisla Kracow (Poland) February 2006. Unirea Urziceni (Romania) free February 2008.

■ United invested £250,000 in Australian defensive midfielder Jacob's potential, but he did not turn out to be the next Harry Kewell. Although he won two full and 19 Under-21 caps for his country, he was never more than a squad player at Elland Road and after trials with Dutch club Feyenoord joined Barnsley, where he partnered former Leeds teammate Stephen McPhail in midfield.

BURNS Kenneth

Defender

Born: Glasgow, 23 September 1953.
5ft 10½in, 11st (1981).
Career: Rangers schoolboy. Birmingham City apprentice June 1970, professional July 1971. Nottingham Forest £150,000 July 1977. LEEDS UNITED £400,000 October 1981. Derby County loan March 1983 and February 1984, transfer March 1984. Notts County loan February 1985. Barnsley August 1985. IF Elsborg (Sweden) March 1986. Sutton Town August 1986, player-manager March 1987. Stafford Rangers July

1987. Grantham Town player-coach 1988–89. Gainsborough Trinity player-coach 1989. Ilkeston Town player coach 1990–93. Oakham United player-coach. Telford United assistant manager July 1993–94. Later Nottingham Forest corporate department.

■ Even a player with Kenny's pedigree could not stop United sliding out of the top flight of English football. As hard as nails and a born winner, the former Scottish international accepted a lucrative contract to move from Nottingham Forest, where he had won a stack of silverware. He was deployed in Leeds' midfield by Allan Clarke, but injury meant Leeds fans rarely saw the best of him. Originally he was a defender but shot to stardom as a striker with Birmingham City, where he won Scottish Youth and Under-21 caps before making the first of his 20 appearances for the national side. But it was at Forest that he excelled as an outstanding defender under Brian Clough. Kenny was named Footballer of the Year in 1978 before flying to Argentina for the World Cup Finals. While at the City Ground he gained two European Cup-winners' medals, a First Division Championship medal, two Football League Cup-winners' medals and a European Super Cup prize. He had a pretty short fuse that led to a few suspensions, but he still made more than 500 appearances as a professional before combining work in a variety of businesses with playing, coaching and managing

non-League clubs. He ran a fashion shop with his wife, worked as a salesman, ran pubs in Uttoxeter and Ilkeston, helped with corporate match-day entertainment at Forest and did some radio work and after-dinner speaking.

BUTLER Paul John

Defender

Born: Manchester, 2 November 1972. 6ft 2in, 13st (2005).
Career: Moston Brooks High School. Manchester Schools. Bradford City trainee 1989. Rochdale trainee August 1990, professional July 1991. Bury £100,000 July 1996. Sunderland £600,000 July 1998. Wolverhampton Wanderers loan November 2000, £1 million January 2001. LEEDS UNITED free July 2004. Milton Keynes Dons loan November 2006, transfer January–March 2007. Chester City July 2007.

■ After United crashed out of the Premiership, Kevin Blackwell hastily put together a makeshift squad to get them through the 2004–05 Championship season. Paul proved to be his most important capture, the centre-back rejecting a new contract at Wolves to go to Elland Road, where he was installed as skipper. In a season that saw no less than 37 players pull on a first-team shirt, Paul was a model of consistency, although his campaign almost ended in tragedy when he swallowed his tongue in a collision with goalkeeper Neil Sullivan. He returned the following season, as committed as ever, to lead United to the

Play-offs. At Sunderland he won his one and only cap for the Republic of Ireland – through the family line – against the Czech Republic. That came after helping Sunderland win the 1999 Division One Championship, two years after assisting Bury to the Second Division title.

BUTLER Walter John

Forward

Born: Skirlaugh, nr Hull, 19 October 1902. Career: Leeds Steelworks. LEEDS UNITED August 1920. Doncaster Rovers 1921. Goole Town 1922. Darlington 1922.

■ Walter was a well-known local Leeds amateur who won a host of medals before joining newly formed United from Leeds Steelworks. He netted a hat-trick against his old club the following month in an FA Cup preliminary-round game when United fielded a reserve side. Walter's only senior outing for Leeds came in a 2–0 defeat at Stockport in February 1921.

BUTTERWORTH Aiden James

Forward

Born: Leeds, 7 November 1961. 5ft 8in, 11st (1982).
Career: Tadcaster Grammar School. England Schools. LEEDS UNITED May 1980. Doncaster Rovers August 1984. Guiseley.

■ Aiden was a little terrier-like forward who did not give defenders a moment's

rest. He was quick and for a little guy did not do badly in the air, as he could spring quite high. He joined United after completing his A-levels at Tadcaster Grammar School, where he had played for the England Schools side. He scored in his first full United appearance in a 3–1 defeat at Nottingham Forest on 31 October 1981 and netted the only goal against Notts County the following week at Elland Road. With United sliding down the table, Allan Clarke brought in Frank Worthington and Aiden was temporarily out of the picture. He gave up football to go to college and pursue a different career but spent a couple of seasons with Doncaster Rovers while taking a degree in Human Movement Studies at Carnegie College, Leeds. After a spell selling and buying non-ferrous metals he spent 10 years with Adidas' marketing department before setting up his own sports consultancy business.

BUTTERWORTH Frank Cyril

Centre-half

Born: Wokingham, nr Reading, 19 April 1913.
Died: Wokingham, nr Reading, July 1999.

6ft, 12st (1946).
Career: Barnet. LEEDS UNITED 1942. Watford wartime guest.

■ In 1945–46 the FA Cup competition was reinstated after it had been suspended during the war years. Matches were played over two legs, and Frank played in both games against Middlesbrough, which saw United draw 4–4 at home and lose 7–2 away. A former player with Isthmian League club Barnet, Frank had played more than 100 times, chiefly at centre-half, for United during the war but did not play any League football.

C

CADAMARTERI Daniel Leon

Forward

Born: Cleckheaton, Yorkshire, 12 October 1979.

5ft 7in, 11st 12lb (2005).

Career: Everton trainee April 1995, professional October 1996. Fulham loan November 1999. Bradford City free February 2002. LEEDS UNITED free July 2004. Sheffield United £50,000 September 2004. Bradford City June 2005. Barnsley trial November 2006. Oldham trial December 2006. Grays Athletic December 2006. Leicester City January 2007. Doncaster Rovers loan March 2007. Huddersfield Town June 2007.

■ Danny had a 10-week stint at Elland Road in which he was restricted to a 20-minute substitute appearance in a League Cup tie against Swindon. Cash-strapped Leeds picked him up on a free from Bradford City, but nine days after his Swindon outing was sold to Sheffield United for £50,000. An England Youth player, he burst on to the Premiership scene as a 17-year-old at Everton, where he won a Youth Cup-winners' medal and Under-21 honours.

CALDWELL Stephen

Central-defender

Born: Stirling, 12 September 1979.

6ft, 11st 5lb (2004).

Career: Newcastle United from trainee October 1997. Blackpool loan October 2001. Bradford City loan December 2001.

LEEDS UNITED loan February 2004. Sunderland free July 2004. Burnley £200,000 January 2007.

■ With United's defence urgently needing some stability, Stephen was drafted in on loan from Newcastle and played alongside Dominic Matteo. However, once United's relegation from the Premiership was virtually confirmed he was recalled by the Magpies. During his time at Leeds he was capped by Scotland and in summer 2004 joined Sunderland, whom he helped to the Championship title in his first season. Stephen also represented his country at B, Under-21 and Youth level – as did his brother Gary, the former Coventry, Derby and Hibs defender, now with Celtic and Scotland.

CALDWELL Terence

Full-back

Born: Sharlston, nr Wakefield, 5 December 1938.

5ft 8in, 11st 13½lb (1960).

Career: Huddersfield Town amateur March 1956. LEEDS UNITED December 1959. Carlisle United July 1961. Barrow July 1970.

■ England Youth international Terry was a teenage prodigy on Huddersfield Town's groundstaff before making the switch to Elland Road. He only played four times for the Terriers and found his opportunities at Leeds limited by the

consistent form of first-choice right-back Grenville Hair. Terry made 340 League appearances for Carlisle, winning a Third Division Championship medal.

CAMARA Zoumana

Defender

Born: Paris, France, 3 April 1979.

5ft 10in, 12st 10lb (2004).

Career: St Etienne (France) August 1996. Inter Milan (Italy) July 1998. Empoli (Italy) loan January 1999. Bastia (France) August 1999. Marseilles (France) August 2000. Lens (France) January 2002. LEEDS UNITED loan August 2003. St Etienne (France) August 2004. Paris St Germain (France) July 2007.

■ French defender Zoumana was one of several players to join United on loan for

the 2003–04 season. He netted in a 3–2 win at Middlesbrough but found himself out of favour when Eddie Gray took over as manager from Peter Reid. With Leeds in financial difficulties, Camara was offered the chance to end his loan spell early but he declined and stayed until the summer when he joined St Etienne for a second spell. He won a French cap against Australia in 2001.

CAMERON Robert

Inside-forward/Right-half

Born: Greenock, 23 November 1932.
5ft 7in, 11st 11lb (1960).
Career: Port Glasgow. Queen's Park Rangers June 1950. LEEDS UNITED July 1959. Gravesend & Northfleet July 1962. Southend United October 1963. Adamstown Rosebuds (Australia).

■ Scottish Schools international Bobby spent three seasons in a struggling United side. He made his debut in the 1959–60 relegation season but fared much better the next term with eight goals in 30 appearances. He had made his name at Queen's Park Rangers where he gave seven years' service to the Hoops.

CANTONA Eric Daniel Pierre

Forward

Born: Paris, France, 24 May 1966.
6ft 2in, 13st 11lb (1992).
Career: Grande Bastide Secondary School,

Mazargue. Caillos. Nice juniors. Auxerre juniors May 1981, professional June 1986. Martigues loan September 1985. Marseille £2.2 million June 1987. Bordeaux loan. Montpellier July 1989. Nîmes £1 million 1991. Sheffield Wednesday trials January 1992. LEEDS UNITED loan February 1992, transfer £900,000 May 1992. Manchester United £1.2 million November 1992–May 1997.

■ Fiery French star Eric Cantona's shock departure to arch-rivals Manchester United stunned Leeds fans. Overnight he went from hero to zero in the eyes of many of the Whites' followers. Eric spent just nine months at Elland Road, arriving in time to add impetus to the charge to the Championship. He started the following campaign in grand style with a hat-trick in the 4–3 Charity Shield success over Liverpool. Another treble against Tottenham soon followed in the League, and the 'Ooh-ah Cantona' love affair with Leeds looked likely to blossom. The relationship turned sour when Eric and manager Howard Wilkinson failed to see eye to eye and the mercurial Gallic star crossed the Pennines for a bargain £1. 2 million. Eric had joined Auxerre as a 15-year-old before playing for the French Army XI. Youth and Under-21 international honours quickly followed before he made his full international debut for *Les Bleus* against West Germany. When at Marseille a verbal blast at national team manager Henri Michel earned Eric a year's ban from international football. After winning a French Cup-winners' medal with Montpellier in 1990, a dressing room scuffle heralded his departure to Nîmes, where he ran into more trouble after throwing a ball at a referee and storming off the pitch. After his disciplinary hearing he announced his retirement from football but surfaced at Sheffield Wednesday in January 1992 for trials. Wilkinson stepped in to snatch him away, and Eric was a revelation at Leeds. After the title was wrapped up, Wilkinson concluded a £900,000 deal with Nîmes. But his nine months at Elland Road ended in acrimony as he was sold to Manchester United, whom Leeds had pipped to the title three months earlier. While the Whites started to fade, Eric blossomed at Old Trafford and was

elevated to cult-hero status, winning a stack of honours. Always controversial, he attacked a spectator with a 'kung-fu' style kick after being ordered off at Crystal Palace, but an initial two-week jail sentence was reduced on appeal to community service. After a worldwide playing ban he returned in triumph as Alex Ferguson's side stormed to another League and Cup double that saw Eric named as 1996 Footballer of the Year. On retirement from football he pursued a career as a writer and film actor.

CARLING Terrence Patrick

Goalkeeper

Born: Otley, Yorkshire, 26 February 1939.
5ft 9in, 12st (1956).
Career: Dawsons PE, Otley. LEEDS UNITED November 1956. Lincoln City July 1962. Walsall June 1964. Chester December 1966. Macclesfield Town 1971.

■ Goalkeeper Terry was signed as a teenager from local amateur club Dawsons PE and spent most of his six years in the juniors and reserves at Elland Road. He made more than 400 appearances in the lower divisions and later worked as a milkman in Chester.

CARLISLE Clarke James

Centre-back

Born: Preston, 14 October 1979.
6ft 1in, 12st 10lb (2005).

Career: Blackpool from trainee August 1997. Queen's Park Rangers £250,000 May 2000. LEEDS UNITED free July 2004. Watford £100,000 August 2005. Luton Town loan March 2007. Burnley £250,000 August 2007.

■ Former England Under-21 international Clarke made a useful contribution to the new-look United following relegation from the Premiership in 2004. He joined Kevin Blackwell's rebuilding programme after helping Queen's Park Rangers win promotion to the Championship. Centre-back Clarke weighed in with some useful goals – notably in both matches against Watford, the club he was to join on a three-year deal in summer 2005. All three of his Under-21 caps came as a substitute when he was at Loftus Road.

CAROLE Sebastien

Winger

Born: Pontoise, France, 8 September 1982.
5ft 6in, 11st 4lb (2006).
Career: Monaco (France). West Ham United loan January 2004. Brighton & Hove Albion August 2005. LEEDS UNITED July 2006.

■ Former French Youth international Seb's sizzling display for Brighton in a 3–3 draw at Elland Road left a lasting impression on manager Kevin Blackwell. Less than a year later, the former Monaco man became a Leeds player, adding

speed and skill to the flanks on the rare occasions he was called upon. He got more of a run under Dennis Wise.

CARR James Proctor

Centre-forward

Born: Ferryhill, Co. Durham, 27 December 1912.
5ft 9in, 11st 6lb (1935).
Career: Spennymoor United. Ferryhill Athletic. Arsenal January 1934. Spennymoor United free May 1935. LEEDS UNITED September 1935. York City January 1938. Spennymoor United May 1938.

■ Leeds manager Billy Hampson snatched Jimmy from under the noses of West Ham. As a Hammers representative was rushing to the North East to sign the Spennymoor player, Hampson arranged to meet Jimmy at Darlington, where the deal to join Leeds was struck. In his first spell with Spennymoor, Jimmy had signed for Arsenal on a railway station platform in January 1934 as he waited for a train to Norwich. After failing to crack it at Highbury he returned to Spennymoor on a free before having another go at League football with Leeds.

CARSON Scott Paul

Goalkeeper

Born: Whitehaven, Cumbria, 3 September 1985.
6ft 3in, 13st 7lb (2005).
Career: Cleator Moor Celtic. LEEDS UNITED from apprentice September 2002. Liverpool £750,000 January 2005. Sheffield Wednesday loan March 2006. Charlton Athletic loan August 2006. Aston Villa loan August 2007.

■ Scott stepped up from the junior ranks to shadow Paul Robinson after Nigel Martyn's departure to Everton. The England Youth international made his Leeds debut as an 18-year-old against Manchester United at Old Trafford and won his first Under-21 cap, against Holland, in the same week. Scott had been recommended to Leeds by Workington manager Peter Hampton, the former Leeds full-back. The young Cumbrian was on bench-warming duty for most of his time at Elland Road – even after Robinson went to Spurs – and

his big-money sale to Liverpool helped ease the club's cash problems. At Anfield he won an England B cap against Belarus in April 2006 when he came on for the injured Robert Green, the man he was to replace in that year's World Cup squad. He was Charlton's Player of the Year in 2006–07 and made his full England debut the following season.

CASEY Terence David

Half-back

Born: Abergwynfi, Swansea, 5 September 1943.
5ft 7in, 11st 3lb (1961).
Career: LEEDS UNITED October 1960. Worcester City.

■ Rising young Welsh star Terry's career was cut short while still in his teens. He had joined United's groundstaff and made his debut aged 17 in a League Cup match at Rotherham. But he was badly injured in a car crash, which also involved Norman Hunter and a few other younger players, and doctors had to remove his spleen. He was forced to quit at 19 and moved back to South Wales.

CASEY Thomas

Wing-half

Born: Comber, Bangor, Northern Ireland, 11 March 1930.
5ft 8½in, 11st 4lb (1950).
Career: Comber School. Argyle Second School, Belfast. Clara Park. Belfast YMCA. East Belfast. LEEDS UNITED May 1949. Bournemouth August 1950. Newcastle United £7,500 August 1952. Portsmouth £8,500 July 1958. Bristol City £6,000

March 1959. Gloucester City player-manager 1963. Inter Roma (Canada). Swansea Town trainer-coach October 1966. Distillery manager 1967. Everton trainer-coach July 1972. Coventry City chief coach 1974. Grimsby Town manager February 1975–November 1976. Later coached in Iceland and Norway and managed the Northern Ireland Youth side.

■ Tom was one of three young players from Irish club Bangor who joined Leeds in May 1949. A Northern Ireland Youth international, Tom did not get many opportunities with United but blossomed at Bournemouth and moved to Newcastle, where he won the first of his 12 full caps and played in the Magpies' 1955 FA Cup-winning side. A hard-tackling dynamo of a player, he also featured in the 1958 World Cup Finals and later worked as a trainer and coach – although he was sacked as Grimsby's manager on the day he moved into his newly purchased house. He later worked as a fishmonger at Portbury, near Bristol.

CASWELL Brian Leonard

Left-back

Born: Wednesbury, Birmingham, 14 February 1956.
5ft 10in, 10st 7lb (1987).
Career: Wood Green School, Walsall. Walsall apprentice June 1971, professional September 1973. Doncaster Rovers £20,000 August 1985. LEEDS UNITED £10,000 November 1985–March 1988. Wolverhampton Wanderers loan January 1987. Birmingham City football in the community coach 1990, then youth coach.

Stoke City youth coach 1992. Telford United assistant manager. Northampton Town youth coach. Shrewsbury Town youth coach.

■ Brian arrived at Elland Road with a reputation as one of the best full-backs in the lower divisions, but a succession of injuries meant Leeds fans never saw him at his best. He played more than 450 times in 14 years for Walsall and turned out under Billy Bremner's management at both Doncaster and Leeds. Bremner loaned him to Wolves, where he was promptly injured in his first match and returned to Elland Road. He quit in March 1988 and worked as a youth coach for several clubs before moving out of football in 2002 to become a car salesman.

CHADWICK Wilfred

Inside-forward

Born: Bury, 7 October 1900.
Died: Bury, 14 February 1973.
5ft 10in, 11st 7lb (1926).
Career: Bury May 1917, professional October 1918. Nelson November 1920. Rossendale United August 1921. Everton February 1922. LEEDS UNITED November 1925. Wolverhampton Wanderers August 1926. Stoke City £250 May 1929. Halifax Town £100 October 1930–May 1932.

■ After averaging a goal every other game with Everton, great things were expected of Wilf at Leeds. But he did not recapture the form that brought him 55 goals in 109 appearances with the Toffees in his short spell at Elland Road. Wilf had piled in the goals early on in his non-League career – 35 in only 23 games for Rossendale – prompting a step up to Everton. He packed a powerful right-foot shot and was the First Division's leading goalscorer in 1923–24 with 28 League goals. His move to Leeds caused quite a stir, but he simply did not click and after a sparkling display for the reserves against Wolves, the Midlands club made their move for him. He was soon in his stride at Molineux, hitting 44 goals to go beyond the century mark in his career.

CHANDLER Jeffrey George

Midfielder/Winger

Born: Hammersmith, London, 19 June 1959.
5ft 7in, 10st 1lb (1979).

Career: Blackpool apprentice 1975, professional August 1976. LEEDS UNITED £100,000 September 1979. Bolton Wanderers £40,000 October 1981. Derby County £38,000 July 1985. Mansfield Town loan November 1986. Bolton Wanderers August 1987. Cardiff City £15,000 November 1989–90.

■ Jeff's spell at Elland Road coincided with a time of great upheaval under the management of Jimmy Adamson. Bought from Blackpool, he put in some effective displays on the left side of midfield and earned himself a couple of appearances for the Republic of Ireland against Czechoslovakia and the US, qualifying through his Irish parentage. At club level he was more successful at Bolton and Derby, figuring in successive promotions as the Rams went from Division Three to Division One. Knee ligament damage curtailed Jeff's career and after a stint as a salesman he became a youth justice worker.

CHAPMAN Lee Roy

Forward

Born: Lincoln, 5 December 1959.
6ft 3in, 13st (1989).
Career: Stoke Schools. Stoke City junior June 1976, professional June 1978. Plymouth Argyle loan December 1978. Arsenal £500,000 August 1982. Sunderland £200,000 December 1983. Sheffield Wednesday £100,000 August 1984. Niort (France) £350,000 June 1988. Nottingham Forest £350,000 October 1988. LEEDS UNITED £400,000 January 1990. Portsmouth £250,000 August 1993. West Ham United £250,000 September 1993. Southend United loan January 1995. Ipswich Town £70,000 January 1995.

LEEDS UNITED loan January 1996. Swansea City free/non-contract March–May 1996.

■ Big, blond and brave, Lee headed United back into the top flight with the only goal at Bournemouth, which clinched the 1990 Second Division title. He had arrived in January that year from Sheffield Wednesday to link up with former boss Howard Wilkinson. Lee took over from the popular Ian Baird and added impetus to United's promotion push. He was adept at feeding off great crosses from the right by overlapping full-back Mel Sterland, and his goal tally continued to mount. Two goals against his old club, Nottingham Forest, in the final game of 1990–91 took his seasonal tally to 31 – the best in Division One – and his career total to 200. Lee was never the quickest player around but led the line like an old fashioned centre-forward. He scored 80 times for Leeds, and struck up an excellent partnership with Rod Wallace. Brian Deane's arrival at Elland Road signalled Lee's departure to Portsmouth and the start of a succession of short spells at various clubs. He popped up at Elland Road again on loan in January 1996, at the age of 37, when Wilkinson found himself short of strikers, but Lee was sent off on his second Leeds debut against West Ham. Lee kicked off his career at Stoke, netting a hat-trick for the Potters in a 3–1 win at Leeds in February 1981. England Under-21 honours and a

big-money move to Arsenal followed, but it was not until he joined Wilkinson at Wednesday that he hit scoring form with 69 goals in 149 appearances. That rich vein continued at Forest after a short spell in France. Lee played in both Forest's League Cup and Zenith Data Systems Cup Final wins at Wembley. The son of Roy Chapman, the former Aston Villa and Port Vale player, Lee is married to actress Leslie Ash and after retiring from football in 1996 entered the wine bar and restaurant business in London.

CHAPUIS Cyril Sylvain Thierry

Forward

Born: Lyon, France, 21 March 1979.
6ft, 12st 4lb (2003).
Career: Ales (France). Niort July 1998. Stade Rennes (France) July 2000. Olympique Marseille (France) January 2002. LEEDS UNITED loan August 2003–January 2004. Strasbourg (France) loan January 2004. Ajaccio (France) August 2004. FC Bruxelles (Belgium). Glasgow Rangers trial June 2006. Grenoble (France) July 2006. FC Metz (France) January 2008.

■ Cyril was signed on a 12-month loan deal with Marseille teammates Lamine Sakho and Zoumana Camara by Peter Reid at the start of 2003–04. The French forward's only United start came in the League Cup against Swindon, as his loan deal was cut short as part of the club's cost-cutting when Eddie Gray took over as boss.

CHARLES William John

Centre-half/Centre-forward

Born: Cwmbwrla, Swansea, 27 December 1931.
Died: Wakefield, 21 February 2004.
6ft 1½in, 13st 12lb (1957).
Career: Cwymdu Junior School, Manselton Senior School, Swansea. Swansea Boys. Swansea Town groundstaff. LEEDS UNITED January 1949. Juventus (Italy) £65,000 May 1957. LEEDS UNITED £53,000 August 1962. Roma (Italy) £70,000 October 1962. Cardiff City £25,000 August 1963. Hereford United player-manager 1966–71. Merthyr Tydfil manager. Swansea City youth coach 1973.

■ Many regard the legendary John Charles as United's greatest-ever player – a player in a relatively modest Leeds team who made a massive impact. He was on the groundstaff of his home-town club Swansea when United's scout in South Wales, Jack Pickard, alerted United manager Major Frank Buckley about the talented teenager. Pickard persuaded John and his Swansea teammates, Bobby Hennings and Harry Griffiths, to go for trials at Leeds. His two mates returned to Swansea but John was taken on. As he grew, John was switched to centre-half and got his senior chance in a friendly against Queen of the South as a 17-year-old towards the end of the 1949–50 season. He kept his place for the final two League games of the season; after that there was no turning back. Charles was awesome in the air, powerful in the tackle, had a vast array of passes and could thump the ball as hard as anyone. In 1950 he became Wales's youngest international at 18 years 71 days when he won the first of his 38 caps. By this time John was doing his national service with the 12th Lancers and skippered his side to victory in the 1952 Army Cup. He was still playing for Leeds – but in a new role as centre-forward – although he missed a big portion of the 1951–52 season because of knee surgery. The following campaign, Major Buckley started with John in defence before finally settling on using him at number-nine with devastating effect. John smashed in 26 goals in 28 League games as a forward, including hat-tricks against Hull and Brentford. In that period he scored 10

successive goals without any of his teammates getting on the scoresheet – no wonder Leeds were dubbed 'Charles United'. In 1953–54 he was unstoppable, with a club record 42 League goals in a season, yet United only finished 10th in the Second Division. John, who was on the maximum wage of £15 a week, was hankering to play in the First Division, but a transfer request was turned down, and he was used to plug a leaky defence in 1954–55 as United rose to fourth place. The emergence of Jack Charlton the following season enabled United to deploy their star asset up front again. He did not disappoint and United grabbed promotion on a tidal wave of John's goals. He scored almost a goal per game in his first season in the top flight. That, and a string of superb displays for Wales, prompted Italian giants Juventus to make a British record bid of £65,000 for Big John. It was an offer the Leeds board could not afford to turn down and John, at the peak of his powers, became a massive star in Italian football. He led Wales to the quarter-finals of the World Cup in 1958 and was named Italian Footballer of the Year. Even rough-house

Italian tactics failed to ruffle John, who was dubbed *Il Gigante Buono* – the Gentle Giant. After five years, 108 Juventus goals, three Italian Championships and two Italian Cup medals, John returned to Leeds. He was not the same player, so United banked a £17,000 profit when he went back to Serie A with Roma after only 11 matches. He then played in defence for Cardiff and prolonged his career as player-manager at Southern League Hereford, where he scored 130 goals in 243 appearances before retiring just before his 40th birthday. John then ran a pub, a toy shop and a clothes shop before hitting financial problems. In 1988 United organised a joint testimonial for John and Bobby Collins – two players hero-worshipped by United's faithful. John, never sent off or even booked in his career, was from strong sporting stock. His son, Terry, is a former Cardiff and Wales B rugby union forward, his brother Mel played for Swansea, Arsenal and Wales and his nephew Jeremy (Swansea, Queen's Park Rangers and Oxford) also played for Wales. A true sportsman, John died in 2004, aged 73,

and after his funeral at Leeds Parish Church the procession headed to Elland Road where thousands gathered inside the ground to say their final goodbyes to a genuine hero. A bronze bust of the 'Gentle Giant', commissioned by Suzannah Bates, wife of the club chairman, was unveiled at Elland Road in December 2006.

CHARLTON John 'Jack'

Centre-half

Born: Ashington, Northumberland, 8 May 1935.

6ft 1½in, 12st 13lb (1971).

Career: Hurst Park Modern School, Ashington. East Northumberland Schools. Ashington YMCA. Ashington Welfare. LEEDS UNITED amateur 1950, professional May 1952. Middlesbrough manager May 1973–April 1977. Sheffield Wednesday manager October 1977–May 1983. Newcastle United manager June 1984–August 1985. Middlesbrough caretaker manager March 1984. Republic of Ireland manager February 1986–January 1996.

■ World Cup winner 'Big Jack' is the daddy of them all at Elland Road. He made more than 770 first-team appearances for the club – 629 of them in the League – in 21 years. It is a long-playing record that is likely to stand forever. Jack may not have been the most elegant footballer but developed from a run-of-the-mill centre-half into one of the world's best defenders. Brother Bobby hit more headlines with Manchester United and England, but Jack forged a much longer career in football, following his playing days with success at club and international level as a manager. Jack's uncles, George, Jim and Jack Milburn, all starred with United and it was Jim who recommended the skinny teenager to Leeds. After completing his national service with the Royal Horse Guards he gradually cemented his place and in October 1957 represented the

Football League against the League of Ireland. He had a spell as captain but gave up the job because of his superstition of coming out of the tunnel last. It was only when Don Revie took over as player-manager that Jack's game really started to develop. As Leeds moved into the top flight, Jack maintained his consistency. He proved an excellent tackler, was near unbeatable in the air and perfected the tactic of standing in front of the goalkeeper at Leeds corners. He weighed in 70 League goals – the vast majority with his head – and won his first cap at the age of 29 in a 2–2 draw against Scotland. Brother Bobby was in the team that day, and the brothers played key roles in England's 1966 World Cup triumph. In total, Jack won 34 full caps, represented the Football League six

times and was named Footballer of the Year in 1967. Jack featured in all United's early successes under Revie – the League Cup, first League title and Fairs Cup honours before winning an FA Cup-winners' medal in 1972, two days before his 37th birthday. The following year he was appointed Middlesbrough manager and was named Manager of the Year in his first season as Boro powered to the Second Division title by a record points margin. He stood down in 1977 and took over at struggling Sheffield Wednesday, guiding them to promotion to Division Two. After a brief stint as caretaker boss back at Middlesbrough, he took over as boss at Newcastle United but quit after a season after being booed during a pre-season friendly in 1985. The following year he was appointed manager of the Republic of Ireland international team and pulled off a famous 1–0 win over England in the 1988 European Championships. He led Eire to the 1990 World Cup quarter-finals and into round two of the US Finals four years later. A hero in the Emerald Isle, he earned the Freedom of Dublin and retired in January 1996 after the Irish just failed to qualify for that year's European Championships in England.

CHERRY Trevor John

Defender/Midfielder

Born: Huddersfield, 23 February 1948. 5ft 10in, 11st 6lb (1977).
Career: Newsham County Secondary Modern School, Huddersfield. Huddersfield YMCA. Huddersfield Town July 1965. LEEDS UNITED £100,000 June 1972. Bradford City player-manager December 1982–January 1987, retiring as a player 1985.

■ When Trevor joined Don Revie's multi-talented squad he was the only non-international first-teamer. By the time he moved on 10 years later he had won 27 England caps and had the honour of captaining his country. Trevor had formed an excellent defensive partnership with Roy Ellam at Huddersfield and led the Terriers from left-half when they won the Second Division title in 1970. Two years later United shelled out £100,000 for Trevor's services and proved highly versatile in a

number of defensive roles and as an adept anchor man in midfield. In his second season he won a League Championship medal and once Trevor became a Leeds regular, England appearances followed over a four-year period, his first cap coming against Wales in 1976 at the age of 28. As Revie's famous squad broke up, Trevor was appointed skipper and also captained England against Australia in 1980. After United slipped into Division Two, Trevor joined Bradford City as player-manager and led them into Division Two. Trevor was in charge during City's spell in receivership and at the time of the horrific Valley Parade fire disaster. Shortly after City moved back into their revamped £3.6 million modern stadium Trevor was surprisingly sacked. Since then he has been a director of a sports promotions firm, worked on local radio, been an associate director at Huddersfield Town and is a regular visitor to Elland Road.

CHISHOLM Kenneth McTaggart

Inside-forward

Born: Glasgow, 12 April 1925.
Died: Chester-le-Street, Co. Durham, 30 April 1990.
5ft 11in, 12st (1949).

Career: Queen's Park February 1941. Leicester City, Chelsea, Portsmouth and Bradford Park Avenue wartime guest. Partick Thistle 1946. LEEDS UNITED £8,000 January 1948. Leicester City player-exchange deal December 1948. Coventry City player-exchange deal March 1950. Cardiff City March 1952. Sunderland £15,000 December 1953. Workington £6,000 August 1956. Glentoran player-manager January 1958. Spennymoor United June 1958. Los Angeles Kickers (US) 1959.

■ Former RAF bomber pilot Ken touched down briefly at Elland Road in his nomadic career. A bull of an inside-forward with a thumping shot, his football career took off with Scottish club Queen's Park, winning a Victory cap against Ireland in 1945. He was a qualified physical training instructor by the time he joined Leeds from Partick Thistle but within 11 months moved to Leicester, with United receiving £11,000 and Ray Iggleden in return. Ken netted 17 goals in 40 games for Leeds and had a similar return at Leicester, with whom he figured in the 1949 FA Cup Final. Ken later became embroiled in an illegal payments scandal which came to light when he was a Sunderland player. He was suspended *sine die* for refusing to answer the investigating committee's questions.

CLAPHAM James Richard

Left-back

Born: Lincoln, 7 December 1975.
5ft 9in, 10st 11lb (2007).

Career: Tottenham Hotspur trainee, professional July 1994. Leyton Orient loan January 1997. Bristol Rovers loan March 1997. Ipswich Town £300,000 January 1998. Birmingham City £1 million January 2003. Wolverhampton Wanderers free August 2006. LEEDS UNITED loan August 2007. Leicester City January 2008. Leicester City free January 2008.

■ Experienced Wolves left-back Jamie tasted defeat just once in his 15 appearances for United during a three-month loan spell. His father, Graham, played for Shrewsbury and Chester.

CLARK James Robinson

Winger

Born: Bensham, Gateshead, 20 October 1895.
Died: Gateshead, September 1947.
5ft 9in, 11st (1924).
Career: Annfield Plain. Jarrow. Newcastle United £350 January 1921. LEEDS UNITED £300 May 1924. Swindon Town June 1925. Greenock Morton December 1926. Ashington March 1927–28. Shelbourne.

■ James did not live up to the relatively large fee Leeds paid for his talents. He sparkled in the reserves, where his speed tore defences apart. He was a fringe player at Newcastle, winning the North Eastern League title with their reserves in 1923. After his playing days were over he returned to the North East to work at the Wright-Anderson steelworks.

CLARK Wallace

Winger

*Born: Jarrow, Co. Durham, 14 July 1896.
Died: Jarrow, Co. Durham, 20 November 1975.
5ft 7in, 11st 10lb (1922).
Career: Durham City. Middlesbrough May 1919. LEEDS UNITED May 1921. Birmingham City March 1923. Coventry City £600 October 1924. Boston United August 1925. Barrow June 1926. Torquay United July 1927. Connah's Quay. Shotton January 1930.*

■ Winger Wally was another capture from the North East who failed to live up to expectations in United's early days. He had few opportunities at Middlesbrough and did not get many more at Elland Road despite his ability to play on either flank.

CLARKE Allan John

Forward

*Born: Short Heath, nr Willenhall, 31 July 1946.
6ft, 11st 1lb (1972).
Career: Birmingham Schools. South East Staffordshire Boys. Walsall apprentice 1961, professional August 1963. Fulham £35,000 March 1966. Leicester City £150,000 June 1968. LEEDS UNITED £165,000 July 1969. Barnsley player-manager May 1978. LEEDS UNITED manager October 1980–June 1982. Scunthorpe United manager February 1983–August 1984. Barnsley manager July 1985–November 1989. Lincoln City manager June–November 1990.*

■ 'Sniffer' Clarke ferreted out scores of important goals for United – including the stunning diving header that won the 1972 FA Cup. His nose for goals brought him 110 League goals in 270 starts and 43 goals in other competitions in a Leeds shirt. Allan was a deadly penalty box predator and his partnership with Mick Jones was one of the most fruitful in the club's history. Allan came from a footballing family – brothers Wayne, Frank, Derek and Kelvin all played League football. He first started knocking in goals for Walsall to earn a move to First Division Fulham, where he netted 45 goals in 85 League games. The slimline striker headed to Leicester for a record fee for both clubs and stayed at Filbert Street a year. He was Man of the Match in their 1–0 FA Cup Final defeat against Manchester City in 1969. The following month Leeds paid out a British record fee to take him to Elland Road, where he quickly clicked into scoring action. Already an England Under-23 and Football League representative, he was elevated to full international status in the 1970 World Cup, scoring the only goal of the game – a penalty against Czechoslovakia – on his debut. He finished with 19 caps and 10 goals and was the spearhead as United won the FA Cup, 1974 League Championship and the 1971 Fairs Cup. He continued to find the net as player-manager at Barnsley, steering the Tykes to promotion from Division Four in his first season. With Leeds in freefall during Jimmy Adamson's ill-fated reign, the Whites appointed Allan as boss, but the move did not work out (see Leeds City and United Managers). After quitting the game, he worked for a company selling industrial flue extractors to construction firms and is a regular visitor to Elland Road.

CLARKE James Henry

Centre-forward

*Born: Broomhall, Northumberland, 27 March 1921.
5ft 6½in, 10st 2lb (1946).
Career: Goole Town. Rotherham United May 1937. Darlington April 1946. LEEDS UNITED £4,000 February 1947. Darlington November 1947. Hartlepools United November 1949. Stockton 1950. Darlington September 1952.*

■ Harry was a regular goal scorer in the lower divisions but could not transform his statistics to a higher level at Elland Road. Bought to boost a feeble 1946–47 Leeds attack, he scored just once in 14 games – none of which were won. He soon returned to Darlington, where he scored half a century of goals in 73 games spread over three spells.

COATES Walter Albert

Right-winger

*Born: Kyo, Co. Durham, 4 April 1895.
5ft 8in, 11st 6lb (1921).
Career: Burnhope. Craghead United. Sacriston United. Army football. Fulham August 1919. Leadgate Park July 1920. LEEDS UNITED May 1921. Newport County July 1925. Hartlepools United August 1928–29. Chester-le-Street. Newport (Isle of Wight). Burnhope Institute. Consett.*

■ Winger Walter scored the goal that secured the 1923–24 title for United. He netted the winner against Nelson in the penultimate game of that season, which secured First Division status for the Peacocks for the first time in their history. Walter became a victim of that success as he did not cut it at the higher level and moved on to Newport. He first came to prominence playing for the army in Italy and earned himself a chance at Fulham, playing a couple of games before returning to County Durham, where his displays for North Eastern League side Leadgate Park attracted Leeds' attention. A knee injury curtailed his career at Hartlepool.

COCHRANE David Andrew

Right-winger

*Born: Portadown, Northern Ireland, 14 August 1920.
Died: Leeds, June 2000.
5ft 4in, 10st (1938).
Career: Portadown. LEEDS UNITED £2,000 August 1937–October 1950. Portadown. Shamrock Rovers, Linfield, Shamrock Rovers wartime.*

■ Teenage starlet David, one of Northern Ireland's youngest-ever professionals, was the first Leeds winger to win full international honours. Diminutive Dave was a box-of-tricks winger with blistering speed in the mould of his father, who had played as an inside-right for Linfield. Cochrane junior was playing in Portadown's reserve team at 15 and turned professional five days after his 16th birthday. He was still only 17 when he scored 14 Irish League and Cup goals in 13 games, but it was a stunning display in Portadown's Gold Cup semi-final replay with Derry City that prompted United to sign him. Dave was gradually eased into the first team, but that did not stop the Irish selectors from giving him his full debut against England at Old Trafford when he was only 18 years and three months old. What looked like being a long and productive international career did not materialise, as the war left him with just a dozen caps. During hostilities he returned to Ireland and played as a guest for Portadown, Shamrock Rovers and Linfield, winning an Irish Cup-winners' medal with the latter in 1945. He went back to Elland Road after the war and turned out a string of consistent displays on the right wing for four seasons before retiring in October 1950. He ran a newsagent's in Beeston, close to Elland Road, for many years.

COCHRANE Thomas

Outside-left

Born: Newcastle upon Tyne, 7 October 1908.
Died: Cleveland 1976.
5ft 8½in, 11st 4lb (1933).
Career: St Peter's Albion. Hull City trials. Sheffield Wednesday trials. LEEDS UNITED August 1928. Middlesbrough £2,500 October 1936. Bradford Park Avenue £1,100 May 1939.

■ Patience proved a virtue for both Tom and United's fans as he took time to win over the Elland Road faithful. He was signed from Tyneside League club St Peter's Albion by Dick Ray, who first spotted Tom in trials matches with Sheffield Wednesday and Hull City when he was Doncaster's manager. After taking charge at Leeds, Ray remembered Tom's displays in those trials and persuaded him to sign pro at Elland Road. He had a bit of a rough start as the supporters preferred to see Tom Mitchell flying down the left wing, and the new player's

inconsistent early form led to some barracking from the terraces. But Ray stuck by his man and was rewarded with more than 250 games in eight years. Tom's partnership with Billy Furness was one of the vital components of United's Division Two promotion success in 1932. He later had three good years with Middlesbrough, scoring four goals in a 6–1 rout of Manchester City at Maine Road in March 1938.

COLLINS Robert Young

Inside-forward

Born: Govanhill, Glasgow, 16 February 1931.
5ft 4in, 10st 3lb (1963).
Career: Polmadie Street School and Calder Street Schools, Glasgow. Polmadie Hawthorns. Pollok Juniors. Celtic August 1948. Everton £25,000 September 1958. LEEDS UNITED £25,000 March 1962. Bury February 1967. Morton August 1969 after trial. Ringwood City (Australia) player-coach August 1971. Hakoah (Australia) player-coach October 1971. Wilhelmina (Australia) player-coach. Oldham Athletic player-coach October 1972. Shamrock Rovers loan April 1972. Oldham Athletic assistant manager April 1973. Huddersfield Town manager July 1974–December 1975. LEEDS UNITED coach July 1976. Hull City coach July 1977 manager (after two weeks as caretaker manager) October 1977–February 1978. Blackpool coach March–May 1978. Barnsley coach October 1980, caretaker manager February 1984, manager June 1984–July 1985. Guiseley manager September 1987–September 1988.

■ Small in stature but a huge figure in Elland Road's history, Bobby was the midfield rock on which Don Revie built the Leeds United dynasty. United, then a struggling Second Division club, paid Everton £25,000 for the 31-year-old former Scottish international. It seemed a curious piece of business all round – a large fee for a player seemingly past his best and prepared to drop out of the top level to join a moribund club. But Bobby, a former Celtic great, reeled off a series of superb midfield displays while Revie skilfully slotted in an array of talent around his little talisman. Bobby skippered Leeds to the Second Division title in 1963–64 and was voted Footballer

of the Year in 1965. He was recalled to the Scottish national team after an absence of six years and added three more caps to the 38 he had won with Celtic and Everton. His great revival was brought to a shattering halt when he broke a thigh bone in the second leg of United's first-ever European tie against Torino. Bobby managed a comeback before leaving on a free transfer to Bury and embarking on a football journey that took him to Australia and Ireland before several coaching and managerial jobs in the Yorkshire area. Bobby, an apprentice cobbler, was dubbed 'The Wee Barra' at Celtic, where he won a Scottish Cup-winners' medal in 1951, scored a hat-trick of penalties against Aberdeen in 1953 and was an integral part of the Hoops squad that did the double in 1954 and enjoyed League Cup glory in 1957 and 1958. His international debut came against Wales in October 1950, and he was in the squad that reached the 1958 World Cup Finals. He proved a class act at Goodison, but it was only when he joined Leeds that commentators truly recognised his influence in English football. After his Elland Road days he helped Bury to promotion in 1968 and was 42 when he made his final League appearance.

Despite his greatness as a player he could not transfer his skills to management, although he was always in demand as a coach. He eventually left the game to work in the wholesale fashion business and then worked as a chauffeur at Leeds University garage. Still revered at Elland Road, where he remains a regular visitor, he and John Charles shared a testimonial in April 1988.

CONNOR Terence Fitzroy

Forward

Born: Leeds, 9 November 1962.
5ft 7in, 10st (1982).
Career: Foxwood School and Leeds City Schools. LEEDS UNITED apprentice May 1979, professional November 1979. Brighton & Hove Albion player exchange March 1983. Portsmouth £200,000 July 1987. Swansea City £150,000 August 1990. Bristol City £192,000 September 1991. Swansea City loan November 1992. Yeovil Town 1994. Calne Town player-manager January 1994. Swindon Town football in the community department. Bristol Rovers football in the community officer, reserve-team manager 1995. Bristol City coach 1997. Wolverhampton Wanderers coach August 1999.

■ Terry's debut for United was straight out of a boy's adventure comic. The local lad was only 17 when he came on as substitute against West Brom on 17 November 1979 and scored the only goal of the game. England Youth international Terry won a European Youth Championship-winners' medal in 1980, but as United began to struggle Terry lost

form and after a spell in midfield was traded for Brighton's Andy Ritchie. It was a good move for both clubs; Terry was the Seagulls' top scorer for three seasons and earned an Under-21 cap as an over-age player in a 1–1 draw with Yugoslavia in November 1986 when he scored the England goal. At Bristol City a broken leg virtually ended his pro career, but he has been highly regarded as a coach and assistant at several clubs.

CONSTANTINE Leon

Forward

Born: Hackney, London, 24 February 1978.
6ft 2in, 11st 10lb (2007).
Career: Edgware Town August 1999. Millwall August 2000. Leyton Orient loan August 2001. Partick Thistle loan January 2002. Brentford free August 2002. Southend United free August 2003. Peterborough United free July 2004. Torquay United loan October 2004, £75,000 December 2004. Port Vale £20,000 November 2005. LEEDS UNITED August 2007. Oldham Athletic loan March 2008.

■ Much-travelled lower-League striker Leon's Leeds debut was delayed for three months after he was injured in pre-season. He had scored 40 goals in two seasons while at Port Vale and netted within seven minutes of his first full start for United against Bury. After damaging a shoulder when scoring against Oldham on New Year's Day, he didn't play for Leeds again but spent some time on loan with the Latics.

COOPE Dick

Right-back

Born: Pudsey, 20 February 1893.
5ft 9in, 11st 10lb (1920).
Career: Laisterdyke. LEEDS UNITED July 1920. Denaby United. Frickley Colliery 1924.

■ Dick was one of the first men to join the newly formed Leeds United but did not make the first team. His only senior appearances came in the FA Cup qualifying rounds, when United's reserves beat Halifax junior club Boothtown and Leeds Steelworks. Those games clashed with Second Division fixtures, hence United fielding their second string.

COOPER George Frederick

Half-back

6ft, 11st 10lb (1920).
Career: Kimberworth Old Boys. LEEDS UNITED August 1920.

■ Research has unearthed very little about George, who did not play in the Football League. It is thought he was born in either Stockton-on-Tees or Wharfedale and later lived in the Rotherham area. Like Dick Coope, his only outings for United were in both FA Cup qualifying round ties against Boothtown and Leeds Steelworks, which were won 5–2 and 7–0 respectively.

COOPER Terence

Left-back

Born: Brotherton, nr Castleford, 12 July 1944.
5ft 8in, 10st 9lb (1970).
Career: Brotherton School. Wath Wanderers. Wolverhampton Wanderers trial. Ferrybridge Amateurs 1960. LEEDS UNITED apprentice May 1961, professional July 1962. Middlesbrough £50,000 March 1975. Bristol City £20,000 July 1978. Bristol Rovers player-coach August 1979, manager April 1980–October 1981. Doncaster Rovers November 1981. Bristol City player-manager May 1982–March 1988. Exeter City May 1988. Birmingham City manager August 1991–November 1993. Exeter City manager January 1994–June 1995. Southampton assistant manager and overseas scout.

to the Fourth Division title in 1989–90. After a stint at Birmingham City, where he was also a director, he returned to manage Exeter but ill health forced him to quit. He re-entered the game as assistant to Graeme Souness at Southampton and was later based in Tenerife as the Saints' foreign scout. His son Mark, who played at Bristol City, Exeter, Birmingham, Fulham, Huddersfield (loan) and Wycombe, also managed Conference outfit Tamworth.

COPPING Wilfred

Half-back

Born: Barnsley, 17 August 1909.
Died: Southend, June 1980.
5ft 7in, 10st 3lb (1934).
Career: Houghton Council School, Dearne Valley Old Boys. Middlecliffe Rovers. LEEDS UNITED March 1929. Arsenal £6,000 June 1934. LEEDS UNITED March 1939–42. Royal Beerschot (Belgium) and Belgian national team coach. Southend United trainer 1946. Bristol City trainer July 1954. Coventry City trainer November 1956–May 1959.

■ Rock-hard Wilf was the 'Iron Man' of England inter-war football. His reputation as an uncompromising half-back struck fear into opponents before

■ Terry brought a new dimension to the role of full-back. In addition to his defensive duties he became a masterly exponent of the art of the attacking overlap, providing another option on the left for Don Revie. The sight of Terry in his white boots dribbling down the left flank became one of the most feared sights in football, and at his pomp he was regarded as one of the world's best players. He had started at Leeds as a pacy left-winger and made his debut with a clutch of other up-and-coming young players in a famous 3–0 win at Swansea towards the end of the 1963–64 season. Terry was converted to left-back, and although he regularly supplemented the Leeds attack his goals were relatively rare, but he did score against Arsenal in the 1968 League Cup Final at Wembley to give United their first major trophy. Two years later he won the first of his 20 England caps and played in the 1970 World Cup. Terry broke a leg at Stoke in 1972 but fought his way back to fitness and even earned an England recall from Revie in November 1974, although he limped off early on – his last performance on the international stage. The following March, Terry's 14-year association with United ended and he joined Middlesbrough. At Bristol City he linked up with Norman Hunter, and then took up coaching before entering management, taking the Ashton Gate club to victory in the 1986 Freight Rover Trophy. He made his final League appearance as a 40-year-old and became the country's first player-director. Terry lost his job in March 1988 when he was replaced by his assistant, another Leeds legend, Joe Jordan. Terry, who also played local amateur football, bounced back as manager of Exeter, steering the Grecians

he even set foot on the pitch. Legend has it that he once broke his nose in a League game, reset it himself, and played on. He added to his menacing aura by rarely shaving before a match, leaving the stubble round his 'Desperate Dan' chin. Wilf was an astute passer of the ball, possessed a torpedo of a throw-in and was an ever present in his first season at Elland Road. He became an integral part of the United team, which boasted an all-England half-back line of Willis Edwards, Ernie Hart and Wilf. It took a £6,000 transfer to Arsenal to prise Wilf away from Leeds in June 1934. Arsenal were the big guns of the First Division and Wilf won two League Championship medals and an FA Cup-winners' medal with the Highbury team before returning to Elland Road just before the war. Wilf won 20 England caps – seven of them with United, the first coming in May 1933 against Italy – and also represented the Football League twice. During the war he served as a Company Sergeant-Major Instructor in North Africa, playing a handful of games for Leeds when on leave. He was trainer to the Army XI in Dusseldorf in 1945 and when based in Belgium had a stint training the national team and Antwerp club Royal Beerschot. Wilf settled in Southend and worked at Ford's car plant in Dagenham. A keen wireless enthusiast, he later lived at Prittlewell, near Southend.

COUTTS Thomas

Right-back

Born: Gateshead, 10 May 1902.
Died: 1968.
5ft 8in, 11st 4lb (1928).
Career: Saltwell Villa. Ashington 1923. Dunstan Atlas Villa. LEEDS UNITED January 1927. Southampton August 1928. Newport (Isle of Wight) £100 1929.

■ Fiery Tom was mild-mannered off the pitch but had a reputation for being wild on it. He was sent off a few times, once reportedly after leaving the pitch to punch a spectator. He played in the North East before Leeds took a gamble on him in January 1927 but he played only one senior game – a 3–2 defeat at Grimsby that October.

COUZENS Andrew

Midfield/Defender

Born: Shipley, 4 June 1975.
5ft 9in, 11st 6lb (1995).
Career: LEEDS UNITED from trainee March 1993. Carlisle United £100,000 July 1997. Blackpool March 1999–May 2000. Barnet trials. Hartlepool United trials. Harrogate Town.

■ A member of the 1993 FA Youth Cup-winning squad, Andy made his debut as a substitute for Lucas Radebe in a Premiership victory over Coventry. His breakthrough was quickly followed by a call-up to the England Under-21s for the annual Toulon summer tournament in France. His versatility gave manager Howard Wilkinson more options during the fragmented 1995–96 campaign as the youngster was used in midfield and defence. Despite scoring the first goal of George Graham's reign, Andy fell out of favour and moved on to Carlisle before a year at Blackpool, where he ended his professional career at the age of 25 and became a full-time fitness instructor. As a teenager Andy represented Yorkshire at badminton and was also Bradford Under-16 and Under-18 tennis champion.

COYNE Cyril

Wing-half

Born: Barnsley, 2 May 1924.
Died: December 1981.
5ft 8in, 10st 8lb (1946).
Career: Barnsley Main. LEEDS UNITED October 1944. Stalybridge Celtic. Halifax Town June 1951.

■ Cyril made more than 50 wartime appearances for United – and some as a York City guest – but did not play League football for Leeds. His senior experience was limited to both legs of the 1945–46 FA Cup tie against Middlesbrough – the only season in which matches were played on a home and away basis. He later played at Halifax under Gerry Henry, with whom he played wartime football for Leeds.

CRAINEY Stephen Daniel

Left-back

Born: Glasgow, 22 June 1981.
5ft 9in, 9st 11lb (2005).
Career: Glasgow Celtic from juniors July 1997. Southampton £500,000 January 2004. LEEDS UNITED £200,000 August 2004 after brief loan. Blackpool July 2007.

■ Stephen became United's first cash signing for two years after the club's financial meltdown which saw them tumble out of the Premiership. The former Celtic left-back had six full Scottish caps to his name, plus a B international appearance and seven Under-21 games under his belt when he arrived at Elland Road from

Southampton. But the switch from the SPL to the South Coast had not worked out. He suffered knee ligament damage in his first Leeds season but recovered the following campaign to help United reach the Championship Play-off Final at Cardiff. However, he missed that game against Watford after being sent off in the semi-final victory over Preston.

CRESSWELL Richard Paul Wesley

Forward

Born: Bridlington, 20 September 1977.
6ft, 11st 8lb (2006).
Career: Bridlington Rangers. York City from trainee November 1995. Mansfield Town loan March 1997. Sheffield Wednesday £750,000 March 1999. Leicester City £750,000 September 2000. Preston North End £500,000 March 2001. LEEDS UNITED £1 million August 2005. Stoke City August 2007.

■ Striker Richard was recruited just three games into the 2005–06 season to add power and variety to United's attack. The previous season he had scored 21 goals for Preston, bagging more than half a century of goals. He had suffered two Play-off disappointments with the Lilywhites and endured another with United. Richard had just battled back to fitness in time to face his old club in the Championship semi-finals when he was

sent off in the second leg at Deepdale and so missed the Final against Watford at the Millennium Stadium. Relegation followed 12 months later after another injury-hit season and he moved on to Stoke after an initial move to Hull fell through. For helping Stoke to the Premiership in 2008, United banked £200,000 as part of his original transfer. Richard was developed at York City, where he won the first of his four England Under-21 caps before a big-money move to Sheffield Wednesday.

CROWE Christopher

Winger/Inside-forward

Born: Newcastle upon Tyne, 11 June 1939.
Died: Bristol, May 2003.
5ft 7½in, 11st 11lb (1957).
Career: St John's School, Edinburgh. Scotland Schools. LEEDS UNITED juniors July 1954, professional June 1956. Blackburn Rovers £25,000 March 1960. Wolverhampton Wanderers £30,000 February 1962. Nottingham Forest £30,000 August 1964. Bristol City £15,000 January 1967. Walsall £1,000 September 1969. Auburn FC (Australia) May 1970. Bath City February–May 1971.

■ With his mop of blond hair, winger Chris was a striking figure. His early days were certainly unusual, having the distinction of playing for Scotland Schools when his family moved to Edinburgh, and shortly afterwards he won the first of his eight England Youth caps when he was on United's books. He fell just short of a century of appearances

for Leeds and won a couple of Under-23 caps against France and Scotland. With relegation looming, United sold Chris to Blackburn, where he gained two more Under-23 caps, but did not reach his peak until he joined Wolves, winning his solitary full cap against France in October 1963. After leaving the game he ran a pub and also worked as a shoe shop manager and taxi driver.

CURRIE Anthony William

Midfield

Born: Edgware, London, 1 January 1950.
5ft 11in, 12st 9lb (1977).
Career: Childs Hill Junior School. Whitefield Secondary Modern School, Cricklewood. Hendon Boys. Queen's Park Rangers amateur November 1964. Chelsea youth team. Watford May 1967. Sheffield United £26,500 May 1967. LEEDS UNITED £240,000 June 1976. Queen's Park Rangers £400,000 August 1979. Toronto Nationals (Canada) £60,000 May–June 1983. Chesham United August 1983. Southend United September 1983. Chesham United November 1983. Torquay United non-contract March 1984. Dunstable Town. Hendon. Goole Town player-coach September 1987. Sheffield United football in the community officer February 1988.

■ Flamboyant Tony was one of the greatest entertainers ever seen at Elland Road. After the departure of Billy Bremner and Johnny Giles, Leeds boss Jimmy Armfield turned to the skills of Currie to fill the vacuum. Tony actually played a handful of games with Bremner

before forging his own midfield partnership with Bryan Flynn. Tony had a wonderful range of passing, intricate ball skills and a booming shot, winning 11 of his 17 England caps while at Elland Road. He won England Youth honours with Watford before joining Sheffield United, where he was worshipped by the fans. He played for the Football League and England Under-23s before winning his first full cap against Northern Ireland in 1972. Leeds were constantly trying to get Tony to Elland Road and he eventually moved up the M1 after a successful £240,00 bid. He added consistency to his game at Leeds but after three years with the Whites returned to his native London because his wife was unsettled. He helped Queen's Park Rangers to the 1982 FA Cup Final against Tottenham. Eventually he rejoined Sheffield United as their full-time football in the community officer – a role he still holds.

CURTIS Alan Thomas

Forward

Born: Ton Pentre, nr Pontypridd, 16 April 1954.
5ft 11in, 12st 7½lb (1979).
Career: Porth Grammar School. Swansea City July 1972. LEEDS UNITED £400,000 May 1979. Swansea City £165,000 December 1980. Southampton £85,000 November 1983. Stoke City loan February 1986. Cardiff City March 1986. Swansea City October 1989. Barry Town player-coach 1990. Haverfordwest July 1991. Swansea City football in the community officer, then youth-team coach 1996, assistant manager 1999–2001 and head of youth development 2002.

■ Alan made a dream start to his United career with both goals in an opening day 2–2 draw at Bristol City in August 1979. Sadly for the Welsh international striker that was as good as it got during his disappointing time at Elland Road. He had arrived from Swansea for £400,000 – a record for a Third Division player – but a bad knee injury and a lack of form saw

him stay in Yorkshire for just 17 months. He went back to the Swans, where he enjoyed hero status, for a cut-price fee. Alan did, however, score a stunning last-gasp solo goal at Southampton three months after joining Leeds, which earned United their first away win in six months. A nephew of Roy Paul, the former Manchester City and Wales star, he joined the Swans as a 16-year-old and earned the first of his 35 Welsh caps in 1976, scoring in a 2–1 defeat against England. In his second spell at Vetch Field he helped the Swans to the First Division for the first time in their history and was among the scorers as the Welsh side hammered United 5–1 on the opening day of the 1981–82 season. He retired in summer 1990, played a bit of Welsh League football and worked as a financial consultant before rejoining his beloved Swansea on the coaching staff and acting as assistant manager to various managers.

CUSH Wilbur

Half-back/Inside-forward

Born: Lurgan, Northern Ireland, 10 June 1928.
Died: Lurgan, July 1981.

5ft 5in, 11st 7lb (1957).
Career: Carrisk School, Lurgan. Lurgan Boys' Club. Shankhill YMCA. Glenavon 1947. LEEDS UNITED £7,000 November 1957. Portadown June 1960. Glenavon November 1966, later player-coach.

■ Small in stature, Wilbur was massive in heart and a major figure in Northern Ireland football. He shot to prominence with Glenavon just after the war. With Wilbur in the engine room, the Lurgan-based club won their first-ever Irish League title in 1952 and the Irish Cup double in 1957. They also won the Irish Gold Cup in 1954 and 1956 and the Ulster Cup in 1955. At the end of the season Wilbur, Ulster's Footballer of the Year, became a Leeds player and quickly took to the English game. He was appointed United's captain by Raich Carter and was a member of the 1958 Northern Ireland World Cup squad. A stocky, barrel-chested player, he possessed a bone-jarring tackle – Sir Stanley Matthews once said a Cush tackle was like being hit by a tank. Wilbur, also known as Billy, spent nearly three years at Elland Road and stood aside as captain in preference to Don Revie before returning to Ireland, where he won the last of his 26 caps in 1962. After retiring from the game he became a butcher.

D

DA COSTA Gui Paradela Maciel (Filipe)

Midfield

Born: Lisbon, Portugal, 30 August 1984
5ft 11in, 11st 5lb (2007).
Career: Benfica (Portugal) trainee. Amora (Portugal) 2001. Sporting Braga (Portugal) 2002. Reggiana (Italy) 2003. Ionikos Pireaus (Greece) 2005. Larissa (Greece) loan 2006. LEEDS UNITED August 2007–April 2008. Falkirk trial January 2008.

■ Filipe's Leeds debut was delayed as United became embroiled in a contractual dispute between the Portuguese winger and his former club, Greek side Ionikos. He was sent off in his only start for Leeds – a 2–1 Johnstone's Paint Trophy home defeat against Bury – and was released in April 2008.

DACOURT Olivier Nicolas Andre

Midfield

Born: Montreuil-sous-Bois, France, 25 September 1974
5ft 9in, 11st 12lb (2001).
Career: Aulnay sous Bois (France) 1989. Thorvars (France) 1991. Racing Club Strasbourg (France) August 1992. Everton £4 million August 1998. Lens (France) £6.5 million June 1999. LEEDS UNITED £7.2 million July 2000. AS Roma (Italy) loan January 2003, £3.5 million May 2003. Inter Milan (Italy) May 2006.

■ Olivier added steel, energy and guile to a youthful United midfield in the Elland

Road reign of David O'Leary. The French Under-21 international improved his game in Yorkshire and was elevated to full international status. A £7.2 million signing, he was in the Leeds side that reached the semi-finals of the UEFA Champions League. Financial worries prompted United to offload the midfielder, and he moved to Roma, helping them reach the Italian Cup Final in 2003. Olivier, a French title winner with Strasbourg, had Premiership experience with Everton before joining Leeds. His only red card for Leeds came against Everton, against whom he also scored one of his only three United goals.

DANIELS John Francis Charles

Goalkeeper

Born: Prestwich, nr Manchester, 6 October 1913.
Died: 1970.
5ft 10in, 11st 10lb (1935).
Career: Stockport County amateur August 1932. Manchester North End. Ashton National. LEEDS UNITED amateur October 1933, professional April 1934. Stockport County June 1935. Accrington Stanley July 1938. Tranmere Rovers June 1939. LEEDS UNITED December 1940. York City wartime guest.

■ Although John's only peacetime appearance for Leeds was a disaster – they lost 7–1 at Stamford Bridge, Joe Bambrick scoring four – he gave United distinguished service during the war,

making 121 appearances as a guest. Within three months of the Chelsea debacle he rejoined his old club, Stockport, and forged a decent career in the lower divisions. An excellent cricketer, he was also a qualified FA coach and in the 1950s he was games master at Boston Spa Special School before moving to Canada. He was also known as Jack.

DANSKIN Robert

Centre-half

Born: Scotswood, Newcastle upon Tyne, 28 May 1908.
Died: Newcastle upon Tyne, September 1985.
5ft 8in, 11st 7lb (1938).
Career: Throckley. Wallsend United. LEEDS UNITED May 1929. Bradford Park Avenue £2,000 December 1932–May 1947.

■ Bob was signed from Newcastle side Wallsend as cover for Ernie Hart but found it near-impossible to dislodge the England man. He made his debut in the final game of the 1930–31 season, a 3–1 home win against Derby. He was a key man at Bradford Park Avenue, where he made 506 League and wartime appearances and also featured on Bradford's coaching staff. A regular Methodist church-goer who liked a round of golf, he bred pigs and cattle after his playing days.

DARK Alfred James

Half-back/Centre-half

Born: Keynsham, nr Bristol, 21 August 1893.
Died: St George's, Bristol, 3 August 1964.
6ft, 12st (1922).
Career: Wallsend United. Newcastle United. LEEDS UNITED May 1921. Port Vale June 1923. Halifax Town 1924. Barrow 1928. Sittingbourne. North Shields.

■ Alf was among United's earliest signings, joining them from Newcastle in May 1921. Originally an inside-forward, he did not make the Magpies first team and only managed three outings with Leeds, making his debut at the age of 29 in a 2–1 defeat at Leicester in October 1922.

DAWSON Robert

Right-back

Born: South Shields, 31 January 1935.
5ft 10in, 11st 4lb (1957).
Career: Bolden School, South Shields. Manchester City trial. South Shields. LEEDS UNITED November 1953. Gateshead November 1955.

■ Bobby worked as an electrician at Harton Colliery, represented the Durham County Amateur League and had a trial as a 16-year-old with Manchester City. He joined Leeds from South Shields but because of Jimmy Dunn's consistency made only one appearance – at Hull in the final game of the 1953–54 season. He had more success at Gateshead, where he played more than 100 games.

DAVEY Nigel Geoffrey

Full-back

Born: Garforth, nr Leeds, 20 June 1946.
5ft 9in, 10st 10lb (1970).
Career: Great Preston Juniors. LEEDS UNITED February 1964. Rotherham United July 1974.

■ Fate did not deal a good hand to Nigel during his 10 years at Elland Road. He served a long apprenticeship but when the chance of an extended run in Don Revie's star-studded team arrived he was unable to take it. On the same day Terry Cooper broke his leg at Stoke in April 1972, Nigel, Cooper's natural replacement, fractured his leg in a reserve game against West Bromwich Albion.

DAVIES Byron

Half-back

Born: Llanelli, Glamorgan, 5 February 1932.
5ft 11in, 12st 10lb (1956).
Career: Llanelli 1951. LEEDS UNITED May 1952. Newport County June 1956.

■ Byron, a black belt at judo, was a product of Camarthenshire League football and joined Llanelli at the start of 1951–52. He soon attracted United's attention, but despite looking good in the reserves he could not bridge the gap to the Football League. He made just one senior appearance and after completing his national service moved to Newport County.

DAVISON Robert

Forward

Born: South Shields, 17 July 1959.
5ft 8in, 11st 8lb (1987).
Career: Brinkburn Comprehensive School. Red Duster. Seaham Colliery Welfare. Huddersfield Town July 1980. Halifax Town £20,000 August 1981. Derby County £80,000 December 1982. LEEDS UNITED £350,000 November 1987. Derby County loan September 1991. Sheffield United loan March 1992. Leicester City £50,000 August 1992. Sheffield United September 1993. Rotherham United October 1994. Hull City loan November 1995. Halifax Town 1996. Guiseley player-manager 1998–October 2000. Bradford City youth coach, assistant manager June 2004. Sheffield United coaching staff. Ferencvaros (Hungary) advisory coach February 2008, coach April 2008.

■ Proven goalscorer Bobby was signed from Derby for a big fee to add firepower to United's understrength attack. He had been the top scorer in four successive years at the Baseball Ground as the Rams rose from the Third to the First Division. The former shipyard worker netted 31 goals in 91 League appearances for Leeds and made a significant contribution to the 1989–90 Second Division Championship-winning campaign. He found goals harder to come by and after loans to his old club, Derby, and Sheffield United, he joined Leicester. After moving out of League football he was player-manager at Northern Counties East League side Guiseley, where he was assisted by Neil Parsley, who had also been on United's books.

DAY Mervyn Richard

Goalkeeper

Born: Chelmsford, 26 June 1955.
6ft 2in, 15st 1lb (1987).
Career: King Edward VI Grammar School, Chelmsford. Chelmsford and Essex Schools. West Ham United apprentice July 1971, professional March 1973. Leyton Orient £100,000 July 1979. Aston Villa £25,000 May 1983. LEEDS UNITED £30,000 February 1985. Coventry City loan March 1991. Luton Town loan March 1992. Sheffield United loan May 1992. Carlisle United free player-coach July 1993, manager February 1996–September 1997. Everton goalkeeping coach 1997. Charlton Athletic first-team coach May 1998, then assistant manager to June 2006. West Ham United assistant manager December 2006.

■ Leeds have had some outstanding goalkeepers over the years and Mervyn is

in that category. He made a rapid climb to the top at his first club, West Ham, holding down a first team place as a teenager. He won an FA Cup-winners' medal when he just turned 20 in 1975 and was named Young Footballer of the Year the same year. He featured in the Hammers side beaten by Anderlecht in the European Cup-Winners' Cup the following year and won a clutch of Youth and Under-23 caps. Mervyn lost form, precipitating a move to Leyton Orient, where he won a place on the bench for England B against New Zealand. But that full cap, which looked such a certainty in his teens, eluded him. Eddie Gray brought him to Leeds and it proved a smart piece of business. Cool, calm and collected, Mervyn was unspectacular in his work but highly reliable. He passed his 600th League appearance on his way to a Second Division Championship medal in 1989–90 but John Lukic's £1 million return saw Mervyn pushed to the sidelines. He spent his last season at Elland Road helping with coaching and joined Carlisle as player-coach. The Cumbrians stormed to the Division Three title in 1994–95 but were beaten 1–0 from a sudden-death goal by Birmingham City in the Auto Windscreens Final at Wembley the same season. Day stepped up as manager but could not stop Carlisle falling back into Division Three. However, the following year Mervyn got them back up again and steered the club to Auto Windscreens glory in a penalty shoot-out against Colchester at Wembley. Within a month of the new season he was controversially

sacked by Michael Knighton and after a time as goalkeeping coach at Everton joined his old West Ham teammate Alan Curbishley as coach at Charlton. He later became assistant manager and spent eight years at the Valley before following Curbishley back to West Ham.

De MANGE Kenneth John Philip Petit

Midfield

Born: Dublin, 3 September 1964.
5ft 9in, 11st 10lb (1987).
Career: Sacred Heart and St Kevin's Schools, Dublin. Dublin Schools. Stella Maris. Home Farm. Limerick. Liverpool August 1983. Scunthorpe United loan December 1986. LEEDS UNITED £65,000 September 1987. Hull City £65,000 March 1988. Cardiff City loan November 1990 and loan March 1991. Limerick 1992. Ards 1993. Bohemians November 1993. Dundalk October 1993.

■ Ken made a great start to his career at Leeds with an eighth-minute goal in a 2–0 win against Manchester City at Elland Road. That proved to be the Republic of Ireland midfielder's only United goal in a disappointing six-month stay. A former Irish Young Player of the Year as a 17-year-old with Home Farm, Johnny Giles's old club, Ken earned a three-year contract with Liverpool. Although he did not make the Reds' first team, the Under-21 international did gain a full cap as a substitute against Brazil in Dublin in May 1987. He later worked as a baggage handler at Heathrow airport.

DEANE Brian Christopher

Forward

Born: Leeds, 7 February 1968.
6ft 3in, 12st 7lb (1996).
Career: Leeds City Boys. LEEDS UNITED youth team 1984. Doncaster Rovers apprentice December 1985. Sheffield United £30,000 July 1988. LEEDS UNITED £2.9 million July 1993. Sheffield United £1.5 million July 1997. Benfica (Portugal) £1 million January 1998. Middlesbrough £3 million October 1998. Leicester City £150,000 November 2001. West Ham United free October 2003. LEEDS UNITED free July 2004. Sunderland free March 2005. Perth Glory (Australia) July 2005. Sheffield United December 2005–06.

■ Although a club record signing when he arrived at Elland Road for £2.7 million, Brian had played for Leeds' youth team in 1984 after starring with Leeds City Boys. He was not taken on, but joined Doncaster Rovers as an apprentice instead. A traditional target-man striker, his powerful displays took him to Sheffield United, where he struck up a devastating partnership with Tony Agana, netting 46 goals between them as the Blades earned promotion to Division Two. He was top scorer the following season when the Blades finished runners-up to Leeds in the Division Two Championship and went on the England tour of Australasia, earning two caps against New Zealand. A third followed against Spain, adding to his three B international caps. It was only when Tony Yeboah arrived that he really found a new lease of life at Leeds, playing on the left side of the attack. He rejoined the Blades and played for several other clubs before returning to Elland Road at the age of 37 after Leeds' relegation from the Premiership. He enjoyed a great personal highlight in 2004–05, scoring four times in the 6–1 home win against Queen's Park Rangers before joining Sunderland.

DELPH Fabian

Forward

Born: Bradford, 21 November 1989.
5ft 7in, 9st 7lb (2007).
Career: Tong Secondary School. LEEDS UNITED trainee July 2006.

■ Promising teenager Fabian came on at half-time in the final match of the 2006–07 relegation season at Derby, making him the 44th player to be used by United in the ill-fated Championship campaign. He has represented England at Under-19 level.

DEPEAR Ernest Roland

Centre-half

Born: Spalding, Lincolnshire, 10 December 1923.
Died: Boston, Lincolnshire, January 2001.
6ft 3in, 14st (1996).
Career: Boston United. LEEDS UNITED £500 May 1948. Newport County player exchange June 1949. Shrewsbury Town July 1950. Bangor City player-manager July 1952–55.

■ Roly was Major Frank Buckley's first signing for Leeds, recruited from Midland League side Boston United. The Major arranged to pay £500 for the defender, plus a further £300 if he made 10 or more appearances. They also agreed to meet Boston in the Mather Cup, a Lincolnshire charity competition. In the event, Leeds did not have to find the extra cash as Roly, who had served as a Royal Marine commando in World War Two, was transferred to Newport County in an exchange deal involving Harold Williams. Roly was valued at £8,000 and Williams at £12,000. Roly later skippered Shrewsbury Town.

DERRY Shaun Peter

Midfield

Born: Nottingham, 6 November 1977.
5ft 10in, 10st 3lb (2005).

Career: Notts County from trainee April 1996. Sheffield United £700,000 January 1998. Portsmouth £300,000 March 2000. Crystal Palace £400,000 August 2002. Nottingham Forest loan December 2004. LEEDS UNITED February 2004. Crystal Palace loan November 2007, signed January 2008.

■ All-action midfielder Shaun was a throwback to the 1970s, with his headband and long hair making him a stand-out character in his first season under Kevin Blackwell's reign. His ball-winning tackles and driving runs did much to propel United to the Play-off Final in 2006. Shaun kicked off his career as a full-back with Notts County but was soon snapped up by Sheffield United, where Blackwell was Neil Warnock's second-in-command. He featured in a Nationwide Under-21 side that played their Italian counterparts while on the Blades' books. After Shaun gained promotion with Crystal Palace via the Play-offs he found himself on the fringe of the Premiership action at Selhurst Park. A deal to take him to Elland Road fell through in Christmas 2004 but went ahead the following February after a loan spell with Nottingham Forest. Shaun signed a three-year deal with Leeds and scored the winner in a 2–1 home win against West Ham on his debut. After Blackwell's departure, he found he did not figure in Dennis Wise's plans and eventually rejoined Crystal Palace.

De VRIES Mark

Striker

Born: Paramaribo, Surinam, 24 August 1975.
6ft 3in, 12st 1lb (2007).
Career: Den Helder (Holland). Hollandia (Holland). Volendam (Holland). Chamois Niortais (France) 1998. Dordrecht (Holland) August 2000. Hearts July 2002. Leicester City January 2005. Heerenveen (Holland) loan January–May 2006 and August 2006–May 2007. LEEDS UNITED loan October and November 2007. Dundee United loan January 2008.

■ Giant striker Mark netted a last-minute winner against Yeovil on his home Leeds debut after coming on as substitute. He had arrived on loan but went back to the Foxes before his loan period was up because of a broken toe, returning to Leeds the following month. Born in Surinam, his family moved to Holland when he was six months old. He showed early potential at several Dutch clubs before making his name in Scotland with Hearts, scoring four times on his debut in the Edinburgh derby against Hibernian. He played in the 2008 Scottish League Cup Final against Rangers.

DICKINSON Martin John

Defender/Midfield

Born: Leeds, 14 March 1963.
5ft 10in, 11st (1985).
Career: Wykebeck and Foxwood Schools, Leeds, Leeds City and Yorkshire Boys. Leeds Celtic. Yorkshire Amateurs. West Bromwich Albion trial July 1978. LEEDS UNITED apprentice July 1979, professional May 1980. West Bromwich Albion £40,000 February 1986. Sheffield United free July 1988–June 1989.

Local lad Martin became the 500th United player to figure in League football when he made his debut in a 2–0 home win against Middlesbrough towards the end of the 1989–90 season, less than three weeks after his 17th birthday. He was mainly a central-defender but was also used as a ball-winning midfielder. After more than a century of Leeds appearances he was transferred to West Brom on the same day Brendan Ormsby arrived at Elland Road from Aston Villa. Martin, a noted pigeon-fancier and breeder, returned to Yorkshire with Sheffield United but made just one appearance for the Blades, as a motorway accident left him with whiplash injuries, forcing him to retire at the age of 26. He then operated a laundry before starting a window-cleaning business.

DOIG Russell

Winger

Born: Millport, Isle of Cumbrae, 17 January 1964.
5ft 8in, 10st 9lb (1986).
Career: Scottish Schools. St Mirren. East Stirlingshire 1983. LEEDS UNITED £15,000 July 1986. Peterborough United loan October 1986. Hartlepool United £10,000 March 1988–90. Halifax Town. Harrogate Town. Nuneaton Borough. Farsley Celtic.

Scottish Schools international Russell was spotted by St Mirren scout Jack Gilmour but did not make the Buddies

first team and joined East Stirling, where he made 109 appearances before signing for Billy Bremner's Leeds. Russell's chances were few and far between in his two years at Leeds before a move to Hartlepool. He later worked as a taxi driver in Leeds.

DOMI Didier

Left-back

Born: Sarcelles, Paris, France, 12 May 1978.
5ft 10in, 11st 4lb (2003).
Career: Paris St Germain (France). Newcastle United £3.25 million January 1999. Paris St Germain (France) £4 million January 2001. LEEDS UNITED loan August 2003–May 2004. Espanyol (Spain) July 2004. Olympiakos (Greece) July 2006.

Left-back Didier arrived at Elland Road on a season-long loan from French side Paris St Germain at the start of the ill-fated 2003–04 season. Despite his previous Premiership experience with Newcastle and his obvious pedigree, he was used sparingly at Leeds before returning to his parent club.

DONNELLY John

Midfield

Born: Glasgow, 8 March 1961.
5ft 10½in, 11st 6lb (2003).
Career: Notts County apprentice. Motherwell. Dumbarton. LEEDS UNITED £10,000 March 1983. Partick Thistle loan November 1984, transfer March 1985. Dunfermline June 1986.

John became Eddie Gray's first signing when he arrived from Dumbarton for £10,000 plus £5,000 for each League appearance, so Leeds ended up forking out £85,000. It was his second stab at English football after being rejected as an apprentice by Notts County. At his best John was as good as any midfielder in the old Second Division but lacked consistency and returned to Scotland where he went on to help Dunfermline win promotion to the Premier Division in 1987. John was always a bit of a maverick and Dunfermline announced in April 1988 that they had sacked him for breach of contract after he failed to turn up to play or train. He then worked as a coach for the Scottish FA, working with youngsters in Glasgow.

DORIGO Anthony Robert

Left-back

Born: Melbourne, Australia, 31 December 1965.
5ft 10in, 10st 10lb (1996).
Career: Birmingham Schools. Aston Villa apprentice 1981, professional January 1982. Chelsea £475,000 July 1987. LEEDS UNITED £1.3 million May 1991. Torino (Italy) June 1997. Derby County October 1998. Stoke City June 2000–June 2001.

■ Class act Tony was United's left-back and the club's Player of the Year in the 1991–92 Championship season. He probably ranks as United's best post-war left-back after Terry Cooper, with his instant control, acceleration and magic wand of a left-foot marking him out as a player of international standard. Born in Australia of Italian parents, Tony got his first break at Aston Villa, where he won seven England Under-21 caps and England B honours before a big-money move took him to Chelsea and then full England status. He helped the Blues win the Second Division Championship in 1988–89, was a member of England's 1990 World Cup squad and scored the winning goal in Chelsea's Zenith Data Systems Final victory over Middlesbrough at Wembley. He made a scoring return to Wembley with Leeds in the 4–3 victory against Liverpool in the 1992 Charity Shield. Nine of his 15 England caps were won at Leeds, but his last couple of seasons were blighted by injury. He spent a year in Italy with Torino and returned to England as a full-back and sweeper with Derby and Stoke. He then entered business with a vehicle leasing firm, a property development company in Portugal and a lifestyle management company for footballers.

DOWN William

Goalkeeper

Born: Ryhope, nr Sunderland, 22 January 1898.
Died: Northumberland, spring 1977.
5ft 9in, 11st 7lb (1920).
Career: Ashington. LEEDS UNITED July 1920. Doncaster Rovers September 1925. Burnley September 1927–November 1929. Torquay United. Wigan Borough December 1930.

■ Billy kept goal in United's first Football League fixture – a 2–0 defeat at Port Vale on 28 August 1920. He was an ever present in that maiden season, and despite losing his place to Fred Whalley in 1921–22 the recruit from Ashington recaptured the number-one position for the majority of the 1923–24 Division Two Championship-winning campaign. When he played for Burnley he suffered a haemorrhage of the left kidney after a collision in a game against Blackburn Rovers. He collapsed on his way home and was taken to hospital where he was seriously ill and did not play for the Clarets again. Billy served in the minesweeping service during World War One.

DOUGLAS Jonathan

Midfield

Born: Monaghan, Ireland, 22 November 1981.

5ft 10in, 12st 12lb (2005).
Career: Blackburn Rovers trainee, professional February 2000. Chesterfield loan March 2003. Blackpool loan August 2003. Gillingham loan March 2005. LEEDS UNITED loan September 2005, free August 2006.

■ Hard-working Jonathan, a full Republic of Ireland international, joined United on a 12-month loan from Blackburn in United's 2005–06 Play-off Final season. He played the bulk of that campaign alongside fellow loanee and fellow Irish international Liam Miller. Both went back to their respective clubs at the end of the season but Jonathan was signed on deadline day August 2006 and went on to skipper United.

DUBERRY Michael Wayne

Central-defender

Born: Enfield, London, 14 October 1975.
6ft 1in, 13st 6lb (2004).
Career: Enfield Grammar School. Chelsea trainee, professional June 1993. Bournemouth loan September 1995. LEEDS UNITED £4 million July 1999. Stoke City loan October 2004, free March 2005. Reading £800,000 January 2007.

■ Muscular centre-back Michael never really cemented a regular place in his five years at Elland Road, A £4 million David O'Leary purchase from Chelsea, the England Under-21 international

replaced David Wetherall in the heart of the Leeds defence. His career was not helped by the notorious Bowyer-Woodgate court case – in which he gave evidence – and he eventually moved on a free transfer to Stoke, where he was appointed captain. He had enjoyed early success in 1998 as Chelsea won the European Cup-Winners' Cup, League Cup and European Super Cup.

DUDLEY Frank Ernest

Inside-forward

Born: Southend, 9 May 1925.
5ft 11in, 10st 12lb (1950).
Career: Southend United amateur September 1945, professional October 1945. LEEDS UNITED August 1949. Southampton February 1951. Cardiff City October 1953. Brentford December 1953. Folkestone July 1958–July 1960. Southend United youth manager 1961–65.

■ Frank was top scorer in his first full season with Leeds in 1949–50 when he filled all the forward positions. United's gamble on the Southend forward paid dividends, and explosive shooting was a feature of his game. He was then involved in a player swap with Southampton's Ernie Stevenson – Frank signed the Saints forms on a Leeds-to-London train. He went on to break through the 100 League career goals barrier at his final club, Brentford, before moving into coaching at Southend. He worked as a local government officer after leaving football until his retirement in 1985.

DUFFIELD Albert

Right-back

Born: Owston Ferry, Lincolnshire, 3 March 1894.
Died: Beeston, Leeds, 27 September 1981.
5ft 7½in, 11st 10lb (1922).
Career: Gainsborough Trinity. Castleford Town. LEEDS UNITED July 1920. Bradford Park Avenue November 1925–May 1928.

■ An ever present in United's first Football League season, Bert was one of the club's unsung heroes in the Peacocks' early years. He made his name in the Midland League with Gainsborough Trinity and Castleford Town, once scoring four goals as a stand-in centre-forward for the latter against Notts County Reserves. United were impressed

by his defensive work and signed him from Cas, and he rewarded them with 203 League appearances and barely a bad performance. Bert, who had served as a bombardier in France during World War One when he was wounded, helped United win their first promotion to Division One. His displays with full-back partner Jimmy Frew were a key factor. Bert moved on to Bradford PA before retiring after the end of Avenue's 1927–28 Division Three North Championship season. Bert then went into the pub business before working as a greengrocer near the Elland Road Greyhound Stadium. He then ran a poultry farm near Goole, where he also coached Rawcliffe.

DUGGAN Harry Anthony

Right-winger

Born: Dublin, 8 June 1903.
Died: Leeds, September 1968.
5ft 7in, 9st 13lb (1928).
Career: Richmond United. LEEDS UNITED May 1925. Newport County £1,500 October 1936–40.

■ Apprentice stonemason Harry chiseled out an excellent career with United in the inter-war years. The young Dubliner took up the trade after leaving school and played part-time with junior club Richmond United, scoring 49 goals in 1924–25. Leeds signed the talented 19-year-old and groomed him as Bobby Turnbull's understudy. In 10 years at Elland Road Harry scored 45 League goals in 187 games, captaining the 1932 promotion side. Right-

winger Harry's work was rewarded with eight caps for Northern Ireland and four for the Republic between 1926 and 1935. He made his Eire debut against Italy B in April 1927 and his first NI game was a 3–0 defeat at the hands of England in October 1929. Harry skippered Newport County to the Third Division South title in 1938–39, and during World War Two he was an air raid warden before returning to Leeds to work for a firm of glass merchants.

DUNDERDALE William Leonard

Right-winger

Born: Willingham-by-Stow, Lincolnshire, 6 February 1915.
Died: Saxilby, Lincolnshire, 11 January 1989.
6ft 1in, 13st 6lb (1938).
Career: Goole Town 1933. Sheffield Wednesday amateur March 1934, professional May 1934. Walsall March 1936. Watford £1,000 May 1938. LEEDS UNITED £3,750 March 1939. LEEDS UNITED, Grimsby Town, Lincoln City, Watford and Mansfield Town wartime guest. Watford April 1946. Margate August 1948. Sittingbourne 1949. Berkhamsted Town coach 1949–February 1954. Sun Sports coach. Watford scout February 1954. Berkhamsted Town coach 1956–57, and from June 1960.

■ Free-scoring Len was a transfer gamble that did not pay off. Watford banked a club record £3,750 when he joined Leeds in March 1939, but the

Peacocks got little return for their investment as he managed just four scoreless games before peace-time football closed down. He returned to Watford after the war and later worked as a scout for the Hornets. Len once scored seven goals in a game for Walsall Reserves.

DUNN James

Right-back

Born: Rutherglen, 23 October 1922.
Died: Leeds, 24 January 2005.
5ft 8in, 11st 9lb (1951).
Career: Rutherglen Glencairn. LEEDS UNITED June 1947. Darlington July 1959. Scarborough 1960.

■ Jimmy was 'Mr Consistency' and undoubtedly unlucky not to win a full Scotland cap. In 11 years at Elland Road he barely put a foot wrong and was often

tipped for full honours but ignored by the Scottish selectors. He served with the Royal Marines in World War Two and played in the Services Cup Final at Home Park, Plymouth. Jimmy then took a labouring job and played for Scottish junior club Rutherglen Glencairn. Several clubs were on his trail and although Arbroath were favourites to sign him, they were pipped by Leeds. Jimmy became a permanent fixture at right-back, including four ever-present seasons, and he played a major role in United's 1955–56 promotion season. He left for Darlington but a knee injury cut short his career, and after a handful of Midland League games with Scarborough in 1960–61 he called it a day. Jimmy then worked as a driver's mate and for the Post Office before retiring in 1987.

DUTHOIT John

Full-back

Born: Beeston, Leeds, 4 November 1918.
Died: Boston, Lincolnshire, November 2001.
5ft 10in, 11st 10lb (1949).
Career: Carlton United. LEEDS UNTED April 1945. York City May 1946. Boston United June 1950.

■ Signed from West Riding League club Carlton United, Jack made 21 wartime appearances for Leeds and played in both legs of the 1945–46 FA Cup against Middlesbrough. An electrical engineer, he played as an amateur at Elland Road.

DUXBURY Thomas

Wing-half

Born: Accrington
5ft 8in, 11st 9lb (1922).
Career: Accrington. Preston North End December 1919. LEEDS UNITED £300 June 1924. Fleetwood 1926.

■ Tom had already played in an FA Cup Final when he joined United from Preston. He was in the Lilywhites side beaten 1–0 by Huddersfield Town at Wembley in 1924. The wing-half was in and out of the side at Deepdale and hoped his transfer to Leeds would give him more first-team opportunities. The move was a flop, with Tom making just three starts at right-half, all of them defeats.

E

EDWARDS Keith

Wing-half

Born: Stockton-on-Tees, 16 July 1957.
5ft 8in, 10st 3lb (1987).
Career: Roseworth School and Stockton
Boys. LEEDS UNITED, Wolverhampton
Wanderers and Leyton Orient trials.
Middlesbrough youth team. Sheffield
United October 1975 after three-month
trial. Hull City £55,000 August 1978.
Sheffield United £75,000 September 1981.
LEEDS UNITED £125,000 July 1986.
Aberdeen £60,000 September 1987. Hull
City £50,000 March 1988. Stockport
County £60,000 September 1989.
Huddersfield Town loan April 1990,
£25,000 August 1990. Plymouth Argyle
loan December 1990.

■ Keith was one of the best penalty-box
predators in the lower divisions but was
hit-and-miss in his stay at Elland Road.
He had scored buckets of goals for
Sheffield United and Hull, but his
partnership with Ian Baird did not really
fire at Leeds. However, he came off the
bench to score vital goals in both Play-off
legs against Oldham to take them
through to the Final against Charlton
and netted in the FA Cup semi-final
thriller against Coventry. His scoring
record meant he was always in demand,
and he netted the last of his 256 League
goals with Huddersfield. Of that total 143
were scored in two spells with Sheffield
United. After packing in playing he
became a lorry driver and did football
analysis work for local radio in Sheffield.

EDWARDS Malcolm Keith

Defender

Born: Neath, 26 September 1952.
5ft 11in, 12st 3lb (1971).
Career: LEEDS UNITED apprentice,
professional October 1969. Swansea City
July 1972. Cork City.

■ Welsh Schools and Youth international
defender Keith's only taste of action for
United lasted just 19 minutes when he
came on for Paul Reaney in the 2–1 defeat
at Huddersfield on 25 September 1971.

EDWARDS Neil Ryan

Goalkeeper

Born: Aberdare, 5 December 1970.
5ft 9in, 11st 2lb (1989).
Career: Mid-Glamorgan Schools. LEEDS
UNITED trainee, professional March
1989. Huddersfield Town loan August
1990 and January 1991. Shelbourne loan.
Stockport County £10,000 September
1991. Rochdale £25,000 November 1997.
Bury July 2005–June 2006. Carlisle United
goalkeeping coach 2006. Bolton Wanderers
assistant goalkeeping coach. Carlisle
United goalkeeping coach. Bolton
Wanderers assistant goalkeeping coach.

■ A rare injury to Mervyn Day gave
reserve goalkeeper Neil his only first-
team action for United in a Zenith Data
Systems Cup victory at Barnsley on 28
November 1989. The Welsh Youth,

Under-15 and Under-18 international
had loans with Huddersfield Town and
Irish club Shelbourne, before forging an
excellent career in lower division
football. He played at Wembley three
times in 12 months for Stockport,
finishing on the losing side each time.
County lost 1–0 to Stoke in the 1992
Autoglass Cup Final, then the side were
beaten 2–1 by Peterborough in the
Division Three Play-off Final eight days
later. In 1993 Neil featured in another
Autoglass Cup Final defeat when
Stockport were beaten 2–1 by Port Vale.

EDWARDS Walter

Winger

Born: Mansfield, 26 June 1924.
5ft 9½in, 12st 3lb (1951).
Career: Woodhouse Amateurs. Mansfield
Town amateur July 1947, professional
November 1947. LEEDS UNITED March
1949. Leicester City August 1949. Rochdale
September 1950.

■ Walter was a dashing right-winger who
played army representative football when
he served with the Royal Electrical and
Mechanical Engineers in Palestine. He
represented Nottinghamshire in the
Northern Counties Amateur
Championship and enhanced his
reputation at Mansfield Town from whom
he joined United, who put him straight
into the side at Grimsby as a replacement
for right-winger David Cochrane. United
lost 5–1 and Walter managed only one
more senior Leeds game.

EDWARDS Willis

Half-back

Born: Newton, nr Alfreton, 28 April 1903.
Died: Leeds, 27 September 1988.
5ft 8in, 11st 9lb (1930).
Career: Newton Rangers, Chesterfield £10
1922. LEEDS UNITED £1,500 March
1925–46, assistant trainer 1946, manager
April 1947–April 1948, reverting to
assistant trainer until 1960.

■ Willis is one of the Elland Road all-
time greats, with a 35-year association as
a player, manager and trainer. His
marvellous career stretched into World

War Two and saw him play 444 times for Leeds and 16 times for England, five as captain. Although quite short for a wing-half, he had supreme heading skills, wonderful ball control and a wide range of crisp passing. As a teenager Willis was working the mines of Derbyshire and starring for his local club Newton Rangers when he was offered a trial by Blackburn. However, Chesterfield, much closer to his home, intercepted Willis as he was about to go to the Lancashire club and he joined the Spireites on a wage of 30 shillings (£1.50) a week. On 1 March 1926 Willis won the first of his England caps in a 3–1 defeat against Wales, at the age of 22. He was the best wing-half of his day, even keeping his place in the national team when United were relegated. Willis also represented the Football League 11 times and continued to play for United in emergencies during World War Two. He became assistant to trainer Bob Roxburgh with responsibility for the reserves, and in April 1947 he replaced Billy Hampson as manager after a disastrous season (see Leeds City and United managers). He later worked briefly in a jam factory until his retirement.

EHIOGU Ugochuku

Centre-back

Born: Hackney, London, 3 November 1972.
6ft 2in, 14st 2lb (2006).
Career: West Bromwich Albion trainee,

professional July 1989. Aston Villa £40,000 July 1991. Middlesbrough £8 million October 2000. LEEDS UNITED loan November 2006–January 2007. Glasgow Rangers January 2007. Sheffield United January 2008.

■ With United leaking goals left, right and centre, Dennis Wise turned to the experienced former England international Ugo to stop the rot. Despite showing his undoubted class and scoring on his home debut – a 2–2 draw with Barnsley – Ugo was not fully fit and United's defensive fortunes did not really improve. He played four times for England and won an England B cap and 15 caps at Under-21 level. He was in the Villa side that beat Leeds in the 1996 League Cup Final and collected a winners' medal in the 2004 Final with Middlesbrough.

EINARSSON Gylfi

Midfielder

Born: Reykjavik, Iceland, 27 October 1978.
6ft, 12st 8lb (2005).
Career: Fylkir (Iceland). FR Reykjavik (Iceland) July 2000. Lillestroem (Norway) July 2001. Cardiff City trial October 2004. LEEDS UNITED January 2005–June 2007. Barnsley trial October 2007. SK Brann (Norway) January 2008.

■ Gylfi, an established Icelandic international midfielder, signed for United at the end of 2004, although he arrived at Elland Road two months earlier and was unable to complete his move from Norwegian club Lillestroem

until the transfer window opened. He had a reputation as a goalscoring midfielder and was particularly good in the air. He netted 16 goals in his last season in Norway and was also on target for his country in a famous 2–0 friendly win over Italy in August 2004. His Leeds career never really took off as a hip injury took its toll.

ELDING, Anthony Lee

Forward

Born: Boston, Lincolnshire, 16 April 1982.
6ft 1in, 13st 10lb (2008).
Career: Boston United August 1999. Gainsborough Trinity loan February 2003. Stevenage Borough February 2003. Kettering Town January 2006. Boston United February 2006. Stockport County January 2007. LEEDS UNITED January 2008.

■ Striker Anthony was signed in the immediate aftermath of manager Dennis Wise's departure to Newcastle and plunged straight into the Leeds first team by new boss Gary McAllister days later. The former non-League England international had been prolific with Stockport and had been tracked by Wise for some time.

ELI Roger

Midfielder

Born: Bradford, 11 September 1965.
5ft 11in, 11st 3lb (1985).
Career: Upper Hanson and Bradford Schools. Yorkshire County Schools.

England Schools trials. Nottingham Forest associate schoolboy. LEEDS UNITED apprentice June 1982, professional September 1983. Wolverhampton Wanderers January 1986. Cambridge United non-contract August 1987. Crewe Alexandra non-contract September 1987–May 1988. Pontefract Collieries August 1988. York City non-contract November 1988. Bury non-contract December 1988. Northwich Victoria. Burnley July 1989–June 1994. Scarborough trial June 1994. Fushan (China) 1994. Scunthorpe United February 1995. Partick Thistle April 1995. Farsley Celtic. Otley Town player-manager.

■ If at first you don't succeed…That could be Roger's motto. The leggy, young midfielder made just a couple of outings for Leeds – the first as a sub in a 5–2 win over Wimbledon in December 1984. After his release he played on non-contract terms with a host of clubs before finally making his mark at one of them – Burnley. His enthusiastic displays brought him plenty of goals, including 10 in the Clarets' Fourth Division Championship season. Knee injuries checked his progress and he resumed his travels again, even having a spell in China. Latterly he has worked exporting textiles and selling corporate gifts.

ELLAM Roy

Centre-half

Born: Hemsworth, 13 January 1943.
6ft, 12st 6lb (1973).
Career: South Elmsall Boys. Queen's Park Rangers trials. Robin Hood Athletic.

Bradford City amateur August 1959, professional May 1960. Huddersfield Town January 1966. LEEDS UNITED £35,000 August 1972. Huddersfield Town July 1974. Philadelphia Atoms (US) May 1975. Washington Diplomats (US) May 1976. Gainsborough Trinity player-manager.

■ Roy was signed by Don Revie as a possible replacement for Jack Charlton, but a return to form by the veteran World Cup hero and the emergence of Gordon McQueen left Roy on the fringes. He had earlier given grand service to Bradford City and Huddersfield Town, winning a Second Division Championship medal with the Terriers when he played alongside Trevor Cherry in defence. Cherry joined Leeds in June 1972 and Roy followed him the following month. Outside of football he worked for a horticulture firm before moving into the licensed trade.

ELLIOTT Robert James

Defender

Born: Gosforth, 25 December 1973.
5ft 10in, 10st 6lb (2006).
Career: Wallsend Boys Club. Newcastle United schoolboy 1989, professional April 1991. Bolton Wanderers £2.5 million July 1997. Newcastle United July 2001. Sunderland August 2006. LEEDS UNITED January 2007. Hartlepool United July 2007.

■ Struggling at the back, United moved in for experienced Robbie to shore up their defence. He had actually been on trial with Leeds before the start of the 2006–07 season but was not taken on and joined Sunderland. He played just two Championship games before suffering injury but did return before the end of the campaign. Robbie, who had trials at Manchester United before joining his local club, Newcastle, won a couple of England Under-21 caps in his first spell with the Magpies.

ELLIOTT Thomas

Forward

Born: Leeds, 9 September 1989.
6ft 3in, 11st 2lb (2006).
Career: Mount St Mary's School, Leeds. LEEDS UNITED from trainee July 2006.

■ Leeds-born England Under-17 forward Tom made his first-team debut when he came on in the 2–1 defeat at Norwich in February 2007. At the time he was just a 16-year-old studying for his GCSEs at Mount St Mary's School.

ELLSON Merton Frederick

Inside-right

Born: Thrapston, Northants, 10 July 1893.
5ft 10in, 11st 6lb (1922).
Career: Frickley Colliery. LEEDS UNITED July 1920. Frickley Colliery May 1922. Halifax Town 1922 –24.

■ Merton, known as Matt by his colleagues, doubled up as a footballer and schoolmaster at Leeds. He soon established himself in United's first

Football League season, scoring twice in the club's first-ever victory – a 3–1 home win over Port Vale. An ankle injury and the arrival of Jim Moore put Merton out of the picture and he rejoined Frickley. He served in the Middlesex Regiment in World War One.

ENTWISTLE Wayne Peter

Centre-forward

Born: Bury, 6 August 1958.
5ft 11in, 11st 5lb (1982).
Career: Bury apprentice, professional August 1976. Sunderland £30,000 November 1977. LEEDS UNITED £80,000 October 1979. Blackpool free November 1980. Crewe Alexandra loan March 1982. Wimbledon free July 1982. Grays Athletic February 1983. Bury August 1983. Carlisle United July 1985. Bolton Wanderers October 1985. Burnley loan August 1986–September 1986. Stockport County October 1986. Bury non-contract August 1988. Wigan Athletic October 1988. Hartlepool non-contract September 1989. Altrincham. Curzon Ashton.

■ Wayne endured a torrid time at Elland Road under his old mentor Jimmy Adamson. The England Youth international shone with his home-town club Bury, prompting a move to Sunderland where Adamson was in charge. The fair-haired Wayne managed just two goals in 13 months at Leeds and was released on a free to Blackpool. He then trawled around the lower divisions, with his best season coming at Bury when he scored 21 goals in their 1984–85 Division Four promotion side. After giving up the game in 1990 he went into the cold meat distribution business, having had a farming background before becoming a professional footballer.

EVANS Gareth Joseph

Left-back

Born: Leeds, 15 February 1981.
6ft, 11st 12lb (2001).
Career: Rothwell School. LEEDS UNITED trainee, professional March 1998.
Huddersfield Town free August 2001. Blackpool free August 2003–February 2006.

■ Leeds-born England Youth international Gareth was a tidy left-back who saw some action at Elland Road at the start of the 2000–01 season when the squad was hit by injuries. He made his debut as a 70th-minute substitute in the Champions League qualifier at 1860 Munich and also came on in the 2–1 Premiership defeat at home to Manchester City 13 days later. Gareth could not establish himself and moved to Huddersfield in summer 2001. A knee injury brought his career to an end at the age of 25.

F

FAIRCLOUGH Courtney Huw

Central-defender

Born: Nottingham, 12 April 1964.
5ft 11in, 11st 2lb (1989).
Career: Parkhead Academicals. Nottingham Forest apprentice June 1980, professional October 1981. Tottenham Hotspur £385,000 June 1987. LEEDS UNITED loan March 1989, £500,000 April 1989. Bolton Wanderers £500,000 July 1995. Notts County free July 1998. York City loan March 1999, retired February 2001. Nottingham Forest youth coach 2001.

■ Chris was one of the stars of the 1991–92 Championship-winning side, forming a superb central defensive barrier with Chris Whyte. He arrived from Spurs, initially on loan, and made his debut on the same day as Gordon Strachan – a 1–0 home win against Portsmouth on 25 March 1989. A deal was hammered out with Tottenham at the end of the season and Chris was United's Player of the Year in the Second Division title-winning side. He was also deployed as a defensive midfielder after David Batty's departure to Blackburn before signing for Premiership newcomers Bolton. Although christened Courtney, he was always known as Chris and after retiring through injury at his last club, York, became a youth coach at his first club, Nottingham Forest. It was at Forest that he won the first of his seven England Under-21 caps in 1985, and he played for England B against Malta in October 1987 while at Spurs.

FAULKNER John Gilbert

Central-defender

Born: St Mary Cray, Orpington, Surrey, 10 March 1948.
6ft, 12st 3lb (1971).
Career: Cray Wanderers. Sutton United 1969. LEEDS UNITED £10,000 March 1970. Luton Town £6,000 March 1972–March 1978. Memphis Rogues (US) April 1978. California Surf (US) July 1980–82. Luton Town youth coach 1982–87, first-team coach 1987–89. Barton Rovers manager 1984. Everton scout. Norwich City reserve-team coach July 1992, Under-21 coach 1995–January 1996, assistant manager January 1996, caretaker manager April 1978. Sheffield Wednesday coach and scout.

■ John played centre-half in the Sutton United team walloped 6–0 by United in the FA Cup fourth round in 1970. Although the Isthmian League amateurs were outclassed, Don Revie liked the look of the trainee surveyor and within a few weeks persuaded him to turn professional with United. His luck was not in at Elland Road; he scored an own-

goal on his debut against Burnley a week before the 1970 Cup Final and fractured his kneecap a fortnight later against Manchester City. He made more than 200 appearances for Luton, where he also had a spell on the coaching staff after playing in America. John was influential behind the scenes in two spells at Norwich, including as assistant to Mike Walker, taking temporary charge of the team for a game when Walker moved on to become Everton's boss.

FEARNLEY Harrison Lochheed

Goalkeeper

Born: Morley, Leeds, 27 May 1923.
5ft 9in, 10st 6lb (1941).
Career: Bradford Park Avenue amateur. LEEDS UNITED November 1941. Halifax Town January 1949. Newport County July 1949. Selby Town 1953. Rochdale July 1955. Winsford United September 1955.

■ Harry joined United as a 17-year-old during the war but was restricted to 10 wartime games, as he was required by the Services. He was a commando and represented the Royal Navy against the Army before linking up with United again after the war. Generally Harry played second fiddle to Jim Twomey and Harry Searson at Elland Road. He supplemented his income at Newport with a window-cleaning round.

FELL John Wilson

Left-winger

Born: Quebec, Co. Durham, 14 May 1902.
Died: Hartlepool, 14 January 1979.
5ft 6in, 10st 9lb (1925).
Career: Durham Schools. Tow Law Town. Durham City July 1921. Crook Town 1924. LEEDS UNITED amateur May 1925, professional September 1925. Southend United July 1927. Hartlepools United May 1928. Connah's Quay. Shotton July 1929. Southport July 1930. Connah's Quay. Shotton November 1930. West Stanley.

■ United gave Jackie his second break in professional football. The former Durham Schools player worked at Hamsteels

Colliery in his home village of Quebec and played with Tow Law before having a few Football League games with Durham City. He returned to the Northern League with Crook, but it was not long before Leeds took a chance on him. Jackie shadowed Billy Jackson and Tom Mitchell at Southend, where he broke a leg. On his return to the North East he resumed his life at the pit, working at Blackhall Colliery, where he was secretary of the football team for 12 years and later trained the side.

FERDINAND Rio Gavin

Central-defender

Born: Peckham, London, 8 November 1978.
6ft 2in, 12st 1lb (2000).
Career: West Ham United from trainee November 1995. Bournemouth loan November 1996. LEEDS UNITED £18 million November 2000. Manchester United £29.1 million July 2002.

■ Classy Rio became the world's most expensive defender when David O'Leary signed him from West Ham for £18 million. A superb reader of the game, he became captain at Elland Road and was the defensive pillar on which United built their Champions League challenge. He was regarded as the best ball-playing centre-back in the Premiership and maintained high standards at Leeds, where his work improved under the guidance of former international defender O'Leary. Rio became an England regular under Sven-

Goran Eriksson, featuring in the 2002 and 2006 World Cups. However, it emerged that United had overstretched themselves financially, and just 20 months after joining Leeds he was sold to Manchester United for a British record £29.1 million, who went on to win the Premiership in 2003. His career was put on hold when he was banned for eight months in December 2003 after failing to provide a sample for a routine drugs test. He came back for club and country as strong as ever and won his 50th England cap against Sweden in the 2006 World Cup. Rio had an excellent grounding at West Ham, where he won England Youth and Under-21 honours, earned his full international debut against Cameroon and received a call-up as a 19-year-old to the 1998 World Cup squad. His younger brother, Anton, is a central-defender at West Ham, and his cousin Les was a prolific scorer with Queen's Park Rangers, Tottenham, Newcastle, West Ham and England.

FIDLER Frank

Forward

Born: Middleton, nr Manchester, 16 August 1924.
6ft 1in, 12st 12lb (1951).
Career: Windermere GS. Manchester United amateur World War Two. Witton Albion. Wrexham May 1950. LEEDS UNITED October 1951. Bournemouth December 1952–May 1955. Yeovil Town 1955. Hereford United 1957–60.

■ Frank was thrown in at the deep end, making his Leeds debut at Blackburn in October 1951, just 12 hours after signing for the Peacocks. The new centre-forward from Wrexham responded with a goal in a 3–2 victory and netted four goals in his first five games, but the goals dried up and his time at Elland Road was curtailed when the incomparable John Charles took the number-nine jersey. In his early days, Frank had piled in 179 goals for Witton Albion in three seasons, triggering a move to Wrexham after winning the Cheshire League title.

FINLAY John

Right-winger

Born: Glasgow, 1 July 1925.
5ft 8½in, 10st 10lb (1951).

Career: Clyde. New Brighton March 1951. LEEDS UNITED £6,000 with Bill Heggie. Yeovil Town 1952. Walsall August 1953–June 1954.

■ Jock played in five divisions in three Leagues in a two-and-a-half-year spell. His whistlestop career included a brief stop at Leeds, arriving from New Brighton for £6,000 with Bill Heggie. Jock had been New Brighton's last signed professional, but he played just three games for Leeds, while full-back Heggie did not manage a game.

FIRM Neil John

Centre-half

Born: Bradford, 12 January 1958.
6ft 3in, 13st 9lb (1982).
Career: Yorkshire Schools. England Schools trials. LEEDS UNITED apprentice July 1964, professional January 1976. Oldham Athletic loan March 1982. Peterborough United August 1982. Diss Town January 1986. Ramsey Town.

■ Big Neil came up through United's junior ranks and was given his debut in a 1–1 draw at Manchester City by Jimmy Adamson in the 1979–80 season. Excellent in the air, he was used as cover for Paul Hart but found the First Division forwards too sharp on the ground for him. Neil did well at Peterborough, where he played in front of former Leeds junior goalkeeper David Seaman. An achilles injury forced Neil out of the full-time game and after running a pub in Diss, Norfolk, he joined the police in 1988 and went on to become a Detective Inspector with Thetford CID.

FIRTH Joseph

Half-back/Inside-forward

Born: Glasshoughton, nr Pontefract, 27 March 1909.
Died: 1983.
5ft 9in, 10st 12lb (1930).
Career: Glasshoughton. LEEDS UNITED July 1927. Southend United June 1935. York City June 1938. Rochdale December 1938. Retired during World War Two.

■ South Yorkshire miner Joe gained promotion to Division One with Leeds in 1931–32 as a regular in the inside-right berth. His personal highlight came in United's record 8–0 League win over Leicester City when he scored twice. Despite his useful goalscoring record he struggled to retain his place in the top division.

FITZGERALD Peter Joseph

Centre-forward

Born: Waterford, Ireland, 17 June 1937.
5ft 10in, 11st 7lb (1960).
Career: Waterford. St Patrick's Athletic. Sparta Rotterdam (Holland) May 1959. LEEDS UNITED £7,000 August 1960. Chester July 1961. Waterford 1963.

■ Although he did not make much of an impression for United, Peter won all five of his full Republic of Ireland caps during a 13-month stay at Elland Road, scoring twice in his second game – a 3–1 win over Norway. He was a bright prospect in his native Ireland, making four appearances for the League of Ireland XI. Peter won an FA of Ireland Cup runners'-up medal with Waterford in 1959 and had a brief spell in Holland with Sparta Rotterdam before arriving at Leeds, who had just been relegated. He won a League of Ireland Championship medal with Waterford in 1966.

FLO Tore Andre

Forward

Born: Stryn, Norway, 15 June 1973.
6ft 4in, 13st 8lb (2007).
Career: Stryn (Norway) August 1992. Sogndal (Norway) January 1994. Tromso (Norway) January 1995. Brann (Norway) January 1996. Chelsea £300,000 August 1997. Glasgow Rangers £12 million November 2000. Sunderland £6.75 million August 2002. Siena (Italy) August 2003.

Valarenga (Norway) August 2005. LEEDS UNITED January 2007–March 2008.

■ With Leeds struggling near the foot of the Championship, Dennis Wise dived through the January transfer window to recruit his former Chelsea teammate Tore Andre. The big Norwegian striker was 33 but scored just minutes into his full debut for United – a 3–2 home defeat to West Brom – only to pick up an injury that ruled him out for the rest of the season. The following season he weighed in with several crucial goals after coming off the bench before announcing his retirement inMarch 2008. He had been a major success at Stamford Bridge, figuring in their triple Cup-winning year of 1998 that included the FA Cup, European Cup-Winners' Cup and European Super Cup. His £12 million transfer to Rangers was a record for both clubs, and at full international level he netted 23 goals in 76 matches. His brothers Jostein and Jarle and cousin Harvard were all professional players.

FLYNN Brian

Midfield

Born: Port Talbot, 12 October 1955.
5ft 3½in, 9st (1978).
Career: Sandfields Comprehensive School, Neath and Wales Schools. Afon Lido. Burnley apprentice 1970, professional October 1972. LEEDS UNITED £175,000 November 1977. Burnley loan March 1982, £60,000 November 1982. Cardiff City £15,000 November 1984. Doncaster Rovers November 1985. Bury July 1986. Limerick player-coach January 1987, Doncaster Rovers August 1987. Burnley

football in the community officer. Wrexham February 1988, caretaker manager October 1989, manager November 1989–October 2001. Swansea City manager September 2002–April 2004. Wales Under-21 and Youth coach.

■ Little Brian may have been small in stature, but the midfielder had a huge appetite for work. His partnership with Tony Currie was among the best of the post-Revie era, with busy Brian the fetcher and carrier for his skilful sidekick. Capped 66 times for Wales, Brian won half of them with Leeds and the other half at Burnley, who signed him as a youngster. The Welsh Youth and Under-23 international was never a great goalscorer at Turf Moor, but he netted his first Wales goal – against Scotland – in only his third appearance before opening his account for the Clarets. After Burnley's relegation to Division Two, Brian became a Leeds player and made more than 150 League appearances. His accurate, incisive passing and non-stop running made him popular with the fans. He returned to Burnley in 1982 and played out the twilight of his career at a variety of clubs, his last appearance coming at Wrexham as a 37-year-old player-manager. He steered the North Wales side to a famous FA Cup victory over League champions Arsenal and was in charge at the Racecourse Ground for more than 10 years, making him Wrexham's longest-serving boss. He has since managed Swansea and the Welsh Under-21 side.

FLYNN Peter

Inside-right

Born: Glasgow, 11 October 1936.
5ft 7in, 9st 9lb (1953).
Career: Petershill. LEEDS UNITED October 1953. Bradford Park Avenue June 1957.

■ Peter joined United as a 17-year-old from Scottish club Petershill. Although a highly rated member of the Leeds junior squad, he made just one appearance – a 2–1 home defeat against Fulham in January 1954. He served Bradford Park Avenue for seven years, helping them to promotion in 1960–61.

FORD Mark Stuart

Midfield

Born: Pontefract, 10 October 1975.
5ft 8in, 10st 8lb (1995).
Career: York and North Yorkshire Schools. LEEDS UNITED apprentice, professional March 1993. Burnley £250,000 July 1997. Lommelse (Belgium) 1999. Torquay United July 2000. Darlington £15,000 February 2001–May 2002. Leigh RMI loan January 2002. Garforth Town. Marcia. Tadcaster Albion.

■ Hard-tackling England Youth international midfielder Mark was skipper of United's successful 1993 FA Youth Cup-winning side. A ball-winner in the David Batty mould, he made his full debut as a substitute in the final game of the 1993–94 season – a 5–0 romp at relegated Swindon. Mark made a solid contribution to United's run to the Coca-Cola Cup Final, earning a place in the starting line-up against Aston Villa

at Wembley. He gained three England Under-21 caps but his Leeds career was not helped by suspensions, a trait that continued at Burnley. After a season in Belgium Mark played lower League football but quit the full-time game in 2002, aged 28. He then operated in the Northern Counties East League, as well as playing Sunday League football in York when his work as a railway guard allowed.

FORREST John Robert

Inside-forward

Born: Rossington, nr Doncaster, 13 May 1931.
Died: Weymouth, 3 May 2005.
5ft 10in, 10st 5lb (1957).
Career: Rossington Modern School. Rossington Youth Club. Rossington Colliery. Retford Town. LEEDS UNITED £500 December 1952. Notts County February 1957. Weymouth July 1962.

■ Bobby was a bargain signing from Midland League club Retford Town, whom he had joined almost by accident. He went to Retford with a friend to see a game and the two youngsters were asked to play. Bobby did well and signed just before Christmas 1952. His non-stop running made him popular at Elland Road, and he scored on his home debut – a 2–0 victory over Everton on 11 April 1953. He did not feature in any of the first 12 games of the following season but returned with a bang, scoring a hat-trick in a 3–3 draw against Bristol Rovers. It was still not enough to nail a regular place and he moved on to Notts County, skippering to promotion to Division Three in 1959–60.

FORRESTER Jamie Mark

Striker

Born: Bradford, 1 November 1974.
5ft 7in, 10st (1995).
Career: Blackpool Rangers. Poulton le Fylde. Auxerre (France). LEEDS UNITED £60,000 October 1992. Southend United loan September 1994. Grimsby Town loan March–May 1995, free October 1995. Scunthorpe United March 1997. FC Utrecht (Holland) June 1999. Walsall loan December 1999. Northampton Town £150,000 March 2000. Hull City January

2003. Bristol Rovers free July 2004. Lincoln City loan March–May 2006, free July 2006. Notts County June 2008. Notts County May 2008.

■ A spectacular overhead-kick goal, in front of 31,037 fans at Elland Road in the 1993 FA Youth Cup Final second leg against Manchester United, earmarked razor-sharp striker Jamie as a star of the future. But the diminutive front man, who also featured in the England side that won the Under-18 European Championship the same year, couldn't establish himself in the Premiership. He and Kevin Sharp had attended the FA National School of Excellence before spending some time as teenagers with French club Auxerre. He was regularly in demand with lower division clubs, taking his career goals beyond the 100 barrier. Jamie played in the Scunthorpe side that beat Leyton Orient in the 1999 Division Three Play-off at Wembley.

FOWLER Alan

Centre-forward

Born: Rothwell, nr Leeds, 20 November 1911.
Died: nr Caen, France, 10 July 1944.
5ft 6in, 10st 6lb (1928).
Career: Rothwell and England Schools. Whitehall Printers. LEEDS UNITED November 1927. Whitehall Printers loan. Brodsworth Main. Swindon Town May 1934.

■ England Schools international forward Alan was a boy star who did not quite twinkle with Leeds. In 15 games he scored eight goals but was generally behind Tom Jennings, Charlie Keetley and Arthur Hydes in the pecking order. He took the chance to join Swindon, where his tricky dribbling and accurate shooting brought him 67 goals in 173 appearances up to the war. He served as a sergeant with the Dorset Regiment and was killed in action just after the Normandy Landings in 1944. There is a plaque dedicated to him on the North Stand at Swindon's County Ground.

FOWLER Robert Bernard

Forward

Born: Liverpool, 9 April 1975.
5ft 11in, 11st 10lb (2002).
Career: Liverpool trainee, professional April 1992. LEEDS UNITED £11 million November 2001. Manchester City £3 million January 2003. Liverpool March 2006. Cardiff City July 2007.

■ Goal-poacher Robbie was seen as the final piece in David O'Leary's jigsaw when the ace marksman joined Leeds in an £11 million deal. Unfortunately, it turned out to be money United could not afford and the sharpshooter's stay at Elland Road came to a premature end. He had taken on the scoring mantle of Ian Rush at Liverpool, with 120 goals in just under 250 League games. A master of the scoring arts, he had an uncanny knack of being in the right place at the right time, winning a stack of honours

with the Reds – a Football League Cup-winners' medal in 1995 and four trophies in 2001 – UEFA Cup, European Super Cup, FA Cup and the Football League Cup (again). Youth and Under-21 appearances were quickly followed by full England honours. Leeds fans soon appreciated Robbie's finishing skills, which included a hat-trick at Bolton on Boxing Day in his sixth start in a Leeds shirt. However, he suffered a back injury in the penultimate game of the season and missed the first five months of the following campaign through injury, although he was a member of the 2002 World Cup squad, making his 26th and final England appearance as a substitute in a 3–0 win over Denmark. As United's financial crisis unravelled they were forced to sell Robbie to Manchester City for a cut-price £3 million and also continued to make a sizeable contribution to his wages. He went on to become only the third player in the history of the Premiership to score 150 goals before briefly rejoining his beloved Liverpool and then moving to Cardiff, where he formed an attacking spearhead with Jimmy Floyd Hasslebaink.

FOXE Hayden Vernon

Centre-back

Born: Sydney, Australia, 23 June 1977.
6ft 4in, 13st 5lb (2006).
Career: Blacktown City (Australia). Ajax Amsterdam (Holland) 1995. Arminia Bielefeld (Germany). Sanfrecce Hiroshima (Japan) August 1999. West Ham United March 2001. Mechelen (Belgium) loan March 2001. Portsmouth £400,000 June

2002. LEEDS UNITED September 2006–May 2007. Perth Glory (Australia) July 2007.

■ Big defender Hayden's two-year injury nightmare was ended by Leeds. After missing two seasons with a stress fracture of the foot, the former West Ham and Portsmouth man signed a six-month deal with Leeds. His first start was a disastrous 5–1 defeat, but he did have the satisfaction of netting the United goal. He was capped 14 times by Australia, returning there after Leeds went into administration.

FRANCIS Clifford Thomas

Inside-left

Born: Merthyr Tydfil, 28 December 1915.
Died: 1961.
5ft 6in, 10st 6lb (1928).
Career: Aberaman Athletic. LEEDS UNITED October 1935. Swindon Town June 1938–45.

■ Welsh inside-forward Cliff made just one appearance – a 1–0 home defeat at the hands of Arsenal in Division One on 9 April 1938 – when he stepped in for Eric Stephenson, who was playing for England against Scotland at Wembley that day.

FRANCIS Gerald

Right-winger

Born: Johannesburg, South Africa, 6 December 1933.
5ft 8in, 10st 7lb (1959).
Career: City and Suburban (South Africa).

LEEDS UNITED amateur, professional July 1957. York City October 1961. Tonbridge 1962.

■ South African-born Gerry became the first black player to turn out for United when he made his debut against Everton in a 3–3 home draw in October 1959, scoring a week later in another 3–3 draw at Blackpool. The former shoe repairer had come to England hoping to make a name for himself as a professional player, but found himself at Leeds during a period of upheaval and joined York City. He studied accountancy while at Bootham Crescent, but went on to become a postman when he joined Southern League side Tonbridge.

FREEDMAN Douglas Alan

Striker

Born: Glasgow, 21 January 1974.
5ft 9in, 11st 2lb (2008).
Career: Queen's Park Rangers trainee, professional May 1992. Barnet free July 1994. Crystal Palace £800,000 September 1995. Wolverhampton Wanderers £800,000 October 1997. Nottingham Forest £950,000 August 1998. Crystal Palace £600,000 October 2000. LEEDS UNITED loan March 2008.

■ Former Scottish international Dougie's delicate skills helped propel United to the League One Play-offs at Wembley. He scored some vital goals after arriving on loan from Crystal Palace, including the winner at Yeovil as United reached the Play-offs despite being docked 15 points at the start of the season. His 96th-minute goal which

trimmed Carlisle's 2–0 advantage at Elland Road in the Play-off semi-finals also proved crucial as United overturned the deficit at Brunton Park. Dougie had topped well over 100 goals in two spells with Palace.

FREW James Hearty

Left-back

Born: Kinghorn, Fife, 12 May 1892.
Died: Leeds, April 1967.
5ft 9in, 11st 4lb (1920).
Career: Newcastle City. Hearts May 1913. LEEDS UNITED £200 June 1920. Bradford City June 1924–December 1926.

■ Jimmy formed a superb full-back partnership with Bert Duffield in United's early years after arriving at the new-look Leeds with excellent credentials. He came to prominence at Hearts, making his Scottish League debut against Celtic in 1914. When war broke out, Jimmy enlisted as a farrier in the 1st Lowland Edinburgh Royal Garrison Artillery, rising to the rank of sergeant. He continued to play football and was in the Scotland side which lost 4–3 in a Military International at Goodison Park in May 1916. He played 99 times for Leeds in four seasons before joining Bradford City, where injury cut short his career. Jimmy became chief coach to the West Riding FA and ran a sports outfitters in the Harehills area of Leeds, which was the official supplier to Leeds United. His firm's advertisements appeared in the club programme for many years.

FROST Desmond

Centre-forward

Born: Congleton, Cheshire, 3 August 1931.
5ft 10½in, 12st (1950).
Career: Civil Service Defence Messengers. Congleton Town. LEEDS UNITED April 1949. Halifax Town January 1951. Rochdale November 1953. Crewe Alexandra September 1954.

■ Des could not quite make it at Second Division level after joining United from Congleton. He had served with the Northamptonshire Regiment and the RASC, representing England against Scotland in a Services international in Singapore. After demob he played up front

Official Programme 3d.
DESMOND FROST

for his home-town club and Leeds took him on towards the end of the 1948–49 season, the fee going towards ground improvements at Congleton. A hat-trick for the reserves against Blackpool in January 1951 prompted Halifax Town officials to sign him. They were well rewarded, as Des finished top scorer in three successive seasons at The Shay.

FULLAM Robert

Inside-left

Born: Ringsend, Dublin, 17 September 1895.
Died: London 1974.
5ft 9in, 12st (1923).
Career: St Brendan's North End. Olympic. Shelbourne 1917–18. Shamrock Rovers 1921. LEEDS UNITED May 1923. Shamrock Rovers 1924. Philadelphia Celtic (US). Holly Carburettors (US) 1927–28. Shamrock Rovers 1929.

■ Bob is credited with scoring the Republic of Ireland's first-ever international goal in a 2–1 defeat to Italy at Landsdowne Road, Dublin, in April 1927. Although he spent only a year at Leeds, he is regarded as one of his country's best inside-forwards of the inter-war years. He worked as a Dublin docker and won an Irish FA Cup medal with Shelbourne in 1920 before becoming skipper of Shamrock Rovers, as they won the Irish Championship in 1922–23. He came to Leeds with teammate John Joe Flood, but neither made a significant impact. Bob scored twice in seven games while Flood did not make the first team. They both returned to Ireland, Flood winning five full caps and Bob two to add to his six League of Ireland appearances. Bob won further Championship honours with Shamrock, sandwiched between a stint in the United States playing for clubs in Philadelphia and Detroit.

FURNESS William Isaac

Inside-left

Born: New Washington, Co. Durham, 8 June 1909.
Died: Norwich, 29 August 1980.
5ft 6in, 10st 6lb (1930).
Career: Washington Colliery. Usworth Colliery. LEEDS UNITED £50 August 1928. Norwich City £2,700 June 1937–47, then assistant trainer, trainer and physiotherapist.

■ Billy represents one of United's best buys of all time. He was plucked from non-League football and developed into an England player. A busy and skilful inside-forward, former colliery clerk Billy quickly stamped his mark at Leeds, where he formed a dangerous left-sided partnership with his Geordie pal, Tom Cochrane. As United won promotion to Division One in 1931–32, Billy had a golden autumn, scoring in eight successive League games. His consistent brilliance earned Billy his only cap, against Italy in May 1933 when he was still only 23. He went on to score 62 goals in 243 League appearances for Leeds before joining Norwich, against whom he had fractured a collar bone in an FA Cup defeat in 1935, for a big fee. He did well at Norwich and settled in the Norfolk city, qualifying as a coach for the County FA in 1939 and going into business as an electrical masseur. Billy became physiotherapist and trainer at Carrow Road until his retirement in June 1970.

G

GADSBY Kenneth John

Left-back

Born: Chesterfield, 3 July 1916.
Died: Downham Market, Norfolk, 13 June 2003.
5ft 9in, 11st 10lb (1938).
Career: Middlecliffe Rovers. LEEDS UNITED October 1934. Sheffield United and Yeovil Town wartime guest. King's Lynn 1948.

■ Ken bounced back from a dreadful debut in Leeds' colours to push himself to the brink of the full England team. His first appearance was a 7–1 First Division thumping at Everton on 3 March 1937, but within a year Ken was being tipped as a future international. That never materialised but he toured South Africa with the FA in 1939 and played fairly regularly for United during the war. Ken settled in Norfolk and was a PE teacher at Smithdon High School, Hunstanton. His father, Ernest, was centre-forward in the Barnsley side beaten by Newcastle after a replay in the 1910 FA Cup Final.

GALVIN Christopher

Winger

Born: Huddersfield, 24 November 1951.
5ft 10in, 10st 7lb (1972).

Career: LEEDS UNITED apprentice, professional November 1968. Hull City £25,000 July 1973. York City loan December 1976–April 1977. Stockport County April 1979 –May 1981. Taun Wan (Hong Kong) player-manager 1981.

■ Chris was a talented reserve winger during the Don Revie era, his first break coming as a substitute in a 3–0 European Cup win at Ferencvaros in 1969. The England Youth international possessed plenty of tricks but spent the best part of five years covering the all-star attack at Elland Road before moving to Hull City. After finishing his League career, Chris had a stab at player-management in Hong Kong before working as a players' agent. His brother, Tony, a Republic of Ireland international, won FA Cup-winners' medals with Tottenham in 1981 and 1982. Chris also represented Yorkshire Schools at cricket.

GARDNER Scott

Full-back

Born: Luxembourg, 1 April 1988.
5ft 10in, 11st (2008).
Career: LEEDS UNITED apprentice, professional August 2007. Farsley Celtic loan January 2008.

■ England Under-16 and Under-18 full-back Scott made his full debut in a League Cup victory at Macclesfield, a week after signing his first pro contract.

GASCOIGNE Thomas Clinton

Right-half

Born: Scotswood, Newcastle upon Tyne, 4 November 1899.
Died: Watford, April 1991.
5ft 9in, 11st (1922).
Career: Scotswood. LEEDS UNITED May 1921. Doncaster Rovers 1924. Bradford City March 1926, Tranmere Rovers September 1927.

■ Tom provided effective cover for Harry Sherwin during United's formative years. He skippered Doncaster Rovers and also played for Bradford City while he ran a business in Bradford.

GAVIN Mark Wilson

Left-winger

Born: Baillieston, Glasgow, 10 December 1963.
5ft 8in, 10st 7lb (1985).
Career: High Tunstall School, Hartlepool. Cleveland and Durham Boys. Scottish Youth trials. LEEDS UNITED schoolboy May 1979, apprentice May 1980, professional December 1981. Hartlepool United loan March 1985. Carlisle United free July 1985. Bolton Wanderers £10,000 March 1986. Rochdale £20,000 August

1987. Hearts £35,000 January 1988. Bristol City £25,000 September 1988. Watford £250,000, including player exchange, July 1990. Bristol City £65,000 December 1991. Exeter City February 1994–May 1996. Scunthorpe United August 1996. Hartlepool United September 1997.

■ Speed-merchant winger Mark was one of many young players used by Eddie Gray after United's relegation from the top flight in 1982. He was actually released by Allan Clarke that summer but re-signed when Gray took charge. He made his debut as a sub in a 2–1 win at Cambridge in October, and his next appearance came in December when he scored the only goal at Rotherham in his first senior start. Early promise gave way to inconsistency and Mark moved around several clubs, including some time at Rochdale under his old mentor, Gray.

GIBSON Archibald

Right-half

Born: Dailly, nr Girvan, Ayrshire, 30 December 1933.
5ft 8in, 10st (1956).
Career: Girvan High School. Coylston Juveniles. LEEDS UNITED May 1951. Scunthorpe United July 1960. Barnsley September 1964.

■ Archie was working as an apprentice joiner and playing for Ayrshire junior club Coylston Juveniles when he first came to United's attention. His outstanding performance in a Scottish Juvenile Cup semi-final at Falkirk sealed his move to Elland Road, where his

tackling and non-stop running served Leeds well. During his national service with the RASC, Archie was based at Catterick in North Yorkshire and played for Northern Command. Initially an inside-forward, he was switched to a more defensive wing-half role with great success and spent the best part of five years as a United regular, moving on after relegation in 1960.

GILES Michael John

Midfield

Born: Cabra, Dublin, 6 January 1940.
5ft 7in, 10st (1973).
Career: Brunswick Street School, Dublin. St Columbus FC, Dublin, and Republic of Ireland Schools. Dublin City (later Munster Victoria). The Leprechauns. Stella Maris. Home Farm. Manchester United amateur July 1956, professional November 1957. LEEDS UNITED £33,000 August 1963. West Bromwich Albion £48,000 player-manager June 1975–May 1977. Shamrock Rovers player-manager and executive director July 1977–February 1983. Philadelphia Fury (US) January–June 1978. Vancouver Whitecaps (Canada) coach November 1980–December 1983. West Bromwich Albion manager February 1984–September 1985. Republic of Ireland player-manager October 1973–April 1980.

■ No Leeds player has passed a football better than Johnny. He could coax the ball any length, pace and angle to a teammate during his time in the midfield cockpit with Billy Bremner. The brilliant Irishman was a £33,000 steal from Manchester United, where he had recovered from a broken leg in his early days at Old Trafford to feature on the right wing in the 1963 FA Cup Final victory over Leicester City – his final competitive game for the Red Devils. He was persuaded by Don Revie to drop down a division and that started a 12-year love affair with Leeds as he succeeded Bobby Collins as the midfield string-puller alongside the driving force of Bremner. Johnny figured in all of United's triumphs in the Revie glory years. When he played in the 1973 FA Cup Final against Sunderland, Johnny equalled the pre-war mark of Arsenal and Huddersfield forward Joe Hulme of appearing in five Finals. Allied to his

acute football brain was a degree of steel and mental toughness, making him the complete midfielder. He also weighed in with 88 goals for Leeds – many coming from the penalty spot. Johnny's last game in a Leeds shirt was the ill-fated European Cup Final against Bayern Munich. He was recommended by Revie to succeed him as manager, but the Leeds board opted for Brian Clough and Johnny moved on to West Brom as player-manager, steering the Baggies back to the First Division in his first season. Johnny is hailed as one of Ireland's all-time greats, with 60 caps in a 19-year career, many of them as player-manager. He became his country's youngest international when he made his debut against Sweden aged 18 years 361 days, scoring Ireland's opening goal in a 3–2 win in Dublin. He is the brother-in-law of World Cup winner Nobby Stiles, with whom he played at Old Trafford, and uncle of former Leeds player John Stiles. Johnny's father and his son, Michael, also played for Shamrock.

GOLDBERG Leslie

Right-back

Born: Leeds, 3 January 1918.
5ft 9in, 11st (1946).
Career: England Schools. LEEDS UNITED groundstaff 1934, professional May 1935. Arsenal and Reading wartime guest. Reading trial July 1946, signed March 1947. Newbury Town manager 1955. Reading coaching staff 1969–71.

■ Big things were expected of Les when he played twice for England Schools and signed professional forms with United after a year on the club's groundstaff. He broke into the side just before Christmas 1937 and looked the natural successor to Jack Milburn at right-back until war was declared. Les played several wartime games for Leeds, saw military service in India and was later stationed near Reading. In summer 1948 he changed his surname from Goldberg to Gaunt, but it did not bring him much luck at Reading. He lost his place through injury then fractured a leg at Norwich, ending his playing career. He later ran a menswear business and scouted for Reading and Oxford before spending a couple of years as an administrative and technical assistant to manager Jack Mansell at Reading.

GOLDTHORPE Ernest Holroyd

Centre-forward

Born: Middleton, Leeds, 8 June 1898.
Died: Leeds, 5 November 1929.
5ft 9½in, 11st 7lb (1920).
Career: Yorkshire Schools. Tottenham Hotspur 1918–19. Bradford City June 1919. LEEDS UNITED June 1920. Bradford City March 1922. Manchester United free September 1922. Rotherham United October 1925.

■ Ernie was a member of a famous Leeds sporting family from the Hunslet area. He was the son of Walter Goldthorpe, a well-known Northern Rugby player, but Ernie excelled at the round ball game, playing for Yorkshire Schools against Lancashire at Bury. He joined the army as a teenager and served as a lance corporal with the Pay Corps of the Coldstream Guards. When stationed in London he played wartime games with Spurs before returning North to sign for Bradford City, then Leeds. Ernie was in United's first Football League line up, but a knee injury restricted him to just six games in which he scored twice – in a 3–1 win against Leicester when he became United's first-ever penalty scorer. Eventually he drifted out of the game, worked in a bank and had farming interests. He died at the age of 31 after collapsing in the street 150 yards from his home following a game of badminton in Hunslet. Ernie's brother

Walter had 21 years in the rugby league game, while Albert played for Hunslet rugby league and captained Hunslet CC. James played rugby for Hunslet and was secretary of Leeds Cricket, Football and Athletic Club. John had a brief career at Hunslet, and William played in the first-ever Hunslet game at Parkside.

GOODWIN Frederick

Right-half/Centre-half

Born: Heywood, Lancashire, 28 June 1933. 6ft 2in, 13st 4lb (1960).
Career: Chorlton County Secondary School. Stockport and Cheshire Schools. Manchester United October 1953. LEEDS UNITED £10,000 March 1960. Scunthorpe United player-manager December 1964. New York Generals (US) manager October 1966. Brighton & Hove Albion manager October 1968. Birmingham City manager May 1970–September 1975. Minnesota Kicks (US) manager 1976.

■ Freddie's career with Leeds came to an abrupt end with a triple fracture of his leg in an FA Cup victory over Cardiff in January 1964. United went on to win the Second Division Championship but Freddie did not get a medal as he was only able to play in a dozen League games. The multiple break was the worst of a succession of injuries that defender Freddie suffered at Elland Road, but he still topped the century mark of appearances, and Scunthorpe made him their player-manager after he received a glowing reference from Don Revie. Freddie began at Manchester United, breaking into the team after the Munich

air disaster and appearing in the 1958 FA Cup Final defeat against Bolton Wanderers. Sandwiched between two managerial spells in America, Freddie was boss at Brighton and Birmingham, guiding the Blues to promotion to Division One. After giving up football he continued to live in the States, recruited players for the American Indoor League and set up a travel business. Freddie was also a fast–medium pace bowler with Lancashire, taking 27 wickets in 11 first-class games between 1955 and 1956.

GRAHAM Arthur

Left-winger

Born: Castlemilk, Glasgow, 26 October 1952.
5ft 8in, 11st 10lb (1980).
Career: Cambuslang Rangers. Aberdeen 1969–70. LEEDS UNITED £125,000 July 1977. Manchester United £45,000 August 1983. Bradford City June 1985, reserve and junior coach February 1987, caretaker manager January–February 1989, assistant manager and first-team coach February 1990. Halifax Town coach. LEEDS UNITED Academy coach.

■ Arthur was one of Jimmy Armfield's best-ever buys for Leeds. Fast and direct, he was a creator and scorer of goals. Arthur shot to prominence as a 17-year-old when he won a Scottish Cup medal with Aberdeen in 1970 in a 3–1 win over Celtic – after playing just four Scottish League matches. The Will o' the Wisp winger was soon scaling the international ladder, with Youth and

Under-23 appearances followed by the first of his 10 full Scottish caps. He also represented the Scottish League and won a Scottish League Cup-winners' medal with the Dons before arriving at Elland Road. Arthur scored hat-tricks against Valetta in the UEFA Cup, Wolves and Birmingham City – the latter coming in six minutes at St Andrews in 1978. After United were relegated he stayed on for one more season before a surprise move to Manchester United. Arthur joined Trevor Cherry at Bradford City and took up coaching at Valley Parade, where he also worked under Terry Yorath. He then coached at Halifax, where he had a physiotherapy business, and worked at the Leeds Academy at Thorp Arch. Arthur's brothers were also footballers. Tommy played for Motherwell, Aston Villa, Barnsley, Halifax Town, Doncaster Rovers and Scarborough, Jimmy turned out for Bradford City and Rochdale, and David had games with Queen's Park.

GRAHAM Daniel Anthony William

Forward

Born: Gateshead,12 August 1985.
5ft 11in, 12st 5lb (2005).
Career: Chester-le-Street. Middlesbrough June 2004. Darlington loan March 2004. Derby County loan November 2005. LEEDS UNITED loan March 2006. Blackpool loan August 2006. Carlisle United loan January–May 2007, free June 2007.

■ With Richard Cresswell injured, Leeds drafted in teenage striker Danny Graham on loan from Middlesbrough to act as cover for Rob Hulse and keep United on course for the Championship Play-offs. Danny made just one start – a 1–0 home win over Crewe, but limped off with a groin problem.

GRAINGER Colin

Left-winger

Born: Ryehill, Wakefield,10 June 1933.
5ft 9in, 10st 12lb (1959).
Career: Ryehill Junior and South Hindley Secondary School. Ryehill and Haverscroft. South Elmsall. Wrexham October 1950. Sheffield United £3,000 June 1953. Sunderland £7,000 and player-exchange February 1957. LEEDS UNITED £15,000 July 1960. Port Vale £6,000 October 1961. Doncaster Rovers August 1964. Macclesfield Town 1966–October 1966. Huddersfield Town scout.

■ Few English players can boast being on a winning England side against Brazil – but Colin can. Not only that, he scored twice on his international debut in the first meeting between the two countries at Wembley in a 4–2 win in May 1956. Four years later Colin became United's record signing when he moved from Sunderland for £15,000. But he did not have the happiest of times at Leeds, undergoing a cartilage operation towards the end of the disappointing 1960–61 season, and he moved on to Port Vale after 14 months. Colin got into professional football via his cousin, Dennis Grainger, who was playing for Wrexham. Dennis persuaded the Welsh club to check him out and he made his League debut as a 17-year-old. After two years' national service with the RAF, Colin returned to Yorkshire with Sheffield United, where he earned international honours and a Football League appearance against the Irish League. Colin was known as 'the singing winger' and took up singing professionally when he packed in playing, bringing out a disc called *Are You*. He later worked as a director of a wine and spirits company before retiring in 1995.

GRAINGER Dennis

Left-winger

Born: Royston, Barnsley, 5 March 1920.
Died: Duckmanton, Derbyshire, 6 May 1986.
5ft 7in, 11st (1920).
Career: South Kirby. Southport amateur August 1937, professional October 1938. Doncaster Rovers, Millwall, Walsall, Rotherham United, Lincoln City and Sheffield United wartime guest. LEEDS UNITED £1,000 October 1945. Wrexham December 1947. Oldham Athletic player-exchange June 1951. Bangor City August 1952. Flint Town August 1953.

■ Dennis and cousin Colin belong to a real football clan. Colin played for England, while Dennis's brother, Jack, played for Southport and Barnsley and guested for Leeds during World War Two. Another brother, Horace, was on Chesterfield's books, and their nephew,

Eddie Holliday, played for Middlesbrough, Sheffield Wednesday and England. Colin's brother-in-law was England Under-23 player Jim Iley of Newcastle United. Dennis was working in the mines looking after pit ponies before joining older brother Jack at Southport. He was a decent winger with pace and power who spent two seasons at Leeds. Towards the end of his career he got involved in the pub business as well as working in the drilling and boring industry in Southport.

GRANVILLE Daniel Patrick

Left-back

Born: Islington, London, 19 January 1975.
5ft 11in, 12st 6lb (1998).
Career: Cambridge United from trainee May 1993. Chelsea £300,000 March 1997. LEEDS UNITED £1.6 million July 1998. Manchester City £1 million August 1999. Norwich City loan October 2000. Crystal Palace £500,000 December 2001. Colchester United July 2007–May 2008. Leyton Orient June 2008.

■ Just seven Premiership starts was a poor return for George Graham's £1.7 million investment in Danny. The left-back arrived on the crest of a wave after helping Chelsea to European Cup-Winners' Cup and Football League Cup success. Ian Harte's resurgent form meant Danny's path to first-team football was largely blocked but he had an eventful year at Elland Road. A thigh strain in pre-season 1998 did not help and his first touch of the ball for Leeds

came when he scored in the penalty shoot-out victory over Maritimo in Madeira. After Graham left for Spurs, David O'Leary handed Danny his first start against Nottingham Forest, but he was sent off after receiving two yellow cards. The England Under-21 international remained in the squad but was sold to Manchester City the following summer.

GRAVER Frederick

Inside-right

Born: Craghead, Co. Durham, 8 September 1897.
Died: 1950.
5ft 9in, 12st (1922).
Career: Burnhope Institute. Darlington 1920–21. Shildon August 1921. Grimsby Town May 1922. West Stanley May 1924. LEEDS UNITED May 1924. Southend United May 1925. Wallsend 1926.

■ Fred had scored 41 goals in a season for North Eastern League side West Stanley to earn a move to United at the end of the 1923–24 season, but he did not really make the grade. His sons, Andy and Alf, both joined Lincoln but had contrasting fortunes. Andy is the Imps' record scorer with 144 goals in two spells, but Alf did not make the first team.

GRAY Andrew David

Left-winger

Born: Harrogate, 15 November 1977.
5ft 11in, 11st (1996).
Career: St John Fisher School, Harrogate and North Yorkshire Schools. LEEDS UNITED associate schoolboy April 1993, professional July 1995. Bury loan December 1997. Nottingham Forest £175,000 September 1998. Preston North End loan February 1999. Oldham Athletic March 1999. Bradford City free August 2002. Sheffield United February 2004. Sunderland £1.1 million August 2005. Burnley loan March –May 2006, £750,000 June 2006. Charlton Athletic £1.5m January 2008.

■ Andy's fourth start for Leeds came as an 18-year-old in the 1996 League Cup Final against Aston Villa, where he was a rare shining light in a poor team display. The son of Frank and nephew of Eddie, the Scottish Youth international did not

build on that early impact and moved on to another of his dad's old clubs, Nottingham Forest. His career took off at Bradford, where he won full Scottish caps against Lithuania and New Zealand and became a player in demand.

GRAY Edwin

Left-winger/Left-back

Born: Holyrood, Glasgow, 17 January 1948.
5ft 11in, 12st 7lb (1979).
Career: Glasgow and Scotland Schools. LEEDS UNITED amateur 1972, professional January 1965, player-manager May 1984–October 1985, retiring as a player May 1984. Whitby

Town November 1985. Middlesbrough 1986 reserve and youth-team coach, Rochdale manager December 1986. Hull City manager June 1988–May 1989. Whitby Town manager September 1989–May 1990. LEEDS UNITED coaching staff March 1995, assistant manager May 2003, manager November 2003–May 2004, consultancy role.

■ Worshipped as a player and respected as a manager, Eddie's association with United spanned 30 years. Eddie scored on his debut as a 17-year-old in a 3–0 win over Sheffield Wednesday on New Year's Day 1966. His career took off rapidly with two Under-23 caps followed by his full Scottish debut against England in 1969. The following year he scored one of the greatest solo goals ever seen at Elland road. A series of drag-backs, feints and ball trickery scattered a series of Burnley defenders before he fired home from just inside the box. The following week he gave a man-of-the-match performance at Wembley in the drawn FA Cup Final against Chelsea. Eddie could send his marker the wrong way simply by dropping one of his hunched shoulders, making to go one way and dribbling off in the opposite direction. The football world was at Eddie's feet but a series of bad injuries restricted him to just a dozen full Scottish internationals, and he seemed bound for the departure gate when Brian Clough arrived for his torrid 44 days in charge. Clough's

successor, Jimmy Armfield, helped get Eddie back to full fitness by arranging for him to assist with coaching the junior players. Eddie made a triumphant comeback in January 1975 and continued to sparkle on the left flank, even though United were no longer the power that saw Eddie win League Championship, FA Cup, League Cup and Fairs Cup medals. His career was prolonged at left-back, and he continued in that role when he took over as player-manager following Allan Clarke's sacking in July 1982 – the first of two spells in charge of the club (see Leeds City and United Managers). Despite injury, he notched more than 550 appearances for Leeds, was never booked or sent off and was made an MBE in 1985. His son, Stuart, has played for Celtic, Morton, Reading and Rushden, and son Nick was also on Leeds' books. Eddie played alongside brother Frank many times at Leeds and is also uncle to Frank's son, Andy.

GRAY Francis Tierney

Left-back/Midfield

Born: Castlemilk, Glasgow, 27 October 1954.
5ft 9½in, 11st 10lb (1978).
Career: Glasgow Schools. LEEDS UNITED apprentice May 1970, professional November 1971. Nottingham Forest £475,000 July 1979. LEEDS UNITED £300,000 May 1981. Sunderland £100,000 July 1985. Darlington player-coach 1989, retiring as a player 1991, manager June 1991–February 1992. Blackburn Rovers and Sheffield Wednesday scout. Harrogate Town manager December 1993–June

1994. Al Mananmah (Bahrain) manager June 1994–97. Southampton academy coach. Farnborough Town manager May 2005. Grays Athletic manager May 2006–October 2006. Woking manager May 2007–April 2008. Basingstoke Town manager May 2008..

■ Frank followed elder brother Eddie on the path from Glasgow to Leeds and international stardom. Although not as skilful as Eddie, he won 32 caps for Scotland and a European Cup-winners' medal with Nottingham Forest. Frank trained with Celtic as a kid and was a ballboy at Parkhead but signed for United, who beat off about 30 clubs for his signature. Frank emulated Eddie by scoring on his full debut – a 4–0 thumping of Crystal Palace on 21 April 1973. He starred in five Under-23 games and was equally at home on the left side of midfield or at left-back. But it was not until he joined Brian Clough's Nottingham Forest that he hit peak form, playing in the 1980 Forest side that beat Hamburg in the European Cup Final and Barcelona in the European Super Cup. Frank had cost Forest a record fee but after two seasons at the City Ground he returned to Leeds for four more years, playing under his elder brother's management. Frank figured in the 1982 World Cup in Spain, but after topping 400 appearances for Leeds he moved on to Sunderland, where he won a Third Division Championship medal. He then helped Darlington to the Conference Championship in 1990.

GRAY Michael

Left-back

Born: Sunderland, 3 August 1974.
5ft 7in, 10st 10lb (2005).
Career: Castle View School, Sunderland. Sunderland and Durham County Schools. Manchester United associated schoolboy October 1988. Sunderland trainee July 1990, professional July 1992. Celtic loan August 2003. Blackburn Rovers free January 2004. LEEDS UNITED loan February 2005–May 2006 and March–May 2007. Wolverhampton Wanderers July 2007.

■ Former England international Michael spent three months on loan with Leeds as the Whites slid out of the Premiership.

Although he looked the part at left-back he was red-carded in his sixth game against Gillingham, got injured later in the season and then returned to Blackburn, where he recaptured his first-team spot in 2005–06. He had a second, shorter loan spell at Elland Road the following season. Michael starred for his native Sunderland, scoring in the first minute of his full debut against Barnsley in December 1992. He enjoyed Division One Championship successes with the Black Cats in 1996 and 1999 and won his England caps in 1999 against Hungary, Bulgaria and Sweden.

GRAYSON Simon Nicholas

Midfield/Full-back

Born: Ripon, North Yorkshire, 16 December 1969.
5ft 11in, 11st 7lb (1987).
Career: Bedale School. North Yorkshire Schools. LEEDS UNITED apprentice 1986, professional June 1988. Leicester City £50,000 March 1992. Aston Villa £1.35 million July 1997. Blackburn Rovers £750,000 July 1999. Sheffield Wednesday loan August 2000. Stockport County loan January 2001. Notts County loan September 2001. Bradford City loan February 2002. Blackpool free August 2002, reserve-team coach August 2005, caretaker manager January 2006, manager February 2006.

■ Simon made his League debut in a 0–0 draw at Huddersfield in September 1987 when United were hit by a crop of injuries. Although he could play at either full-back or in midfield, Simon took the chance to get more regular football by joining Leicester and skippered the Foxes at Wembley, leading his side to Play-off

glory against Derby. After subsequent big-money moves to Aston Villa and Blackburn he joined Blackpool, where he was appointed the managerial successor to former Scottish international Colin Hendry. Simon's cricketing brother, Paul, played for Essex, and also had trials at Elland Road.

GREEN Harold

Right-winger

Born: Sheffield, 8 October 1909.
5ft 5in, 10st 4lb (1934).
Career: Sheffield amateur football. Oldham Athletic November 1928. Mexborough 1929. LEEDS UNITED April 1930. Bristol City May 1934. York City June 1935–June 1936. Frickley Colliery March 1937.

■ The presence of internationals Bobby Turnbull and Harry Duggan meant opportunities at Leeds were slim for little winger Harry. The former Sheffield steelworker had previously had a go at the League with Oldham but dropped back into the Midland League with Mexborough, from whom Leeds picked him up.

GREENHOFF Brian

Full-back/Midfield

Born: Barnsley, 24 April 1953.
5ft 10in, 12st 2lb (1979).
Career: Barnsley and Yorkshire Schools. Manchester United apprentice August 1968, professional June 1970. LEEDS UNITED £350,000 August 1979–82. Hong Kong football. Rochdale December 1983–March 1984.

■ Brian was a ball-boy at Wembley when he saw older brother Jimmy win a 1968

League Cup medal with Leeds. Brian was later to tread the Twin Towers turf with Manchester United and England. He won an FA Cup medal with the Red Devils in 1977, four Under-23 caps and an England B honour, and he went on to gain his first full cap against Wales in 1976. His versatility at Old Trafford was invaluable, but his time at Leeds was punctured by a succession of injuries. He seemed to alternate between midfield and full-back at Leeds and managed one more England appearance – as a sub against Australia – to take his total of full internationals to 18. Outside football he ran a pub in Rochdale and helped coach local side Chadderton. He then took charge of a snooker hall in Manchester, worked as a rep for a sports goods wholesaler and later ran a restaurant in Menorca.

GREENHOFF James

Forward

Born: Barnsley, 19 June 1946.
5ft 10in, 11st 2lb (1968).
Career: Barnsley and Yorkshire Schools. LEEDS UNITED apprentice June 1961, professional August 1963. Birmingham City £70,000 August 1968. Stoke City £100,000 August 1969. Manchester United £120,000 November 1976. Crewe Alexandra December 1980. Toronto Blizzard (Canada) player-coach March 1981. Port Vale August 1981. Rochdale player-manager March 1983–March 1984. Port Vale coach March 1984, assistant manager April–May 1984.

■ Jimmy had the unusual experience of being transferred in the middle of a Cup Final. He played in the first leg of the Fairs Cup Final against Ferencvaros in August 1968 when he came on as a sub, but by the time the return leg came around Jimmy was a Birmingham player. The blond forward, who was in the Barnsley side that won the 1961 English Schools Trophy, was a highly rated member of the Elland Road squad, scoring valuable goals at home and abroad. He continued the trend at St Andrews, scoring 11 times in his first 10 games, including four against Fulham when he also missed a penalty. Such stats earned him an England Under-23 call-up and a further move to Stoke with whom he won a League Cup medal in 1972, four years after gaining one with Leeds. He was called up by Don Revie for the England squad but pulled out because of club commitments and did not get another chance to add to his England B and Football League representative honours. He joined Manchester United, aged 30, and scored the FA Cup Final winner against Liverpool in 1977. Jimmy had a brief stab at management and coaching before setting up his own insurance business in the Stoke area.

GREGAN Sean Matthew

Midfield/Central-defender

Born: Guisborough, 29 March 1974.
6ft 2in, 14st 2lb (2005).
Career: Darlington from trainee January 1991. Preston North End £350,000 November 1996. West Bromwich Albion

£1.5 million August 2002. LEEDS UNITED £500,000 September 2004. Oldham Athletic loan November 2006, free January 2007.

■ Kevin Blackwell tried for months to sign Sean from West Brom but was forced to play a waiting game because of the Whites' precarious finances. He eventually got the powerful midfielder, whose rugged, combative style earned him a crop of cards. He also weighed in with several appearances as a central-defender – his original position at Darlington – as United reached the 2006 Play-offs. Sean won the Division Two Championship with Preston, where he was captain.

GRIBBEN William Howatt

Centre-half

Born: Glasgow, 28 October 1906.
Died: 1969.
5ft 11in, 12st (1928).
Career: Beeston Parish Church. LEEDS UNITED August 1928. Harrogate Town 1929.

■ Bill was plucked from local Leeds amateur football and four months later made a successful First Division debut for the Peacocks as a replacement for Ernie Hart in a 1–0 win at FA Cup holders Blackburn. He played just twice more for Leeds before joining Harrogate, where he was captain and played for the Yorkshire League XI against United.

GRIFFIT Leandre

Winger

Born: Maubeuge, France, 21 May 1984.
5ft 8in, 11st 4lb (2005).
Career: Amiens (France) August 2002. Southampton free July 2003. LEEDS UNITED loan January–February 2005. Rotherham United loan March 2005. Elsborg (Sweden) March 2006. Norkopping (Sweden) loan 2007.

■ Blink and you would have missed French winger Leandre's contribution to Leeds. On loan from Southampton, he made a cameo appearance as a substitute at Derby during United's rebuilding phase under Kevin Blackwell.

GRIFFITHS Joel Michael

Winger

Born: Sydney, Australia, 21 August 1979.
6ft, 11st 11lb (2006).
Career: Sydney United (Australia) 1998. Paramatta Power (Australia) 1999. Newcastle Breakers (Australia) 2001. Neuchatel Xamax (Switzerland) 2003. Hearts trial January 2006. LEEDS UNITED February 2006. Newcastle United Jets (Australia) July 2006. Avispa Fukuoka (Japan) loan March 2008.

■ Aussie winger Joel's move to Leeds from Swiss club Neuchatel Xamax was supposed to open the door to selection for the Australian squad for the 2006 World Cup Finals. Instead he spent a miserable four months at Elland Road, initially in limbo because of problems getting international clearance for the transfer. The former Youth international had one full cap – scoring against Jamaica in a 5–0 win – but managed just two substitute appearances for Leeds. He returned home to Newcastle Jets where his twin brother, Adam, who had spells at Watford and Bournemouth, also plays.

GUPPY Stephen Andrew

Left-winger

Born: Winchester, Hampshire, 29 March 1969.
5ft 11in, 12st (2004).
Career: Southampton trialist. Coldon Common. Wycombe Wanderers September 1989. Newcastle United £150,000 August 1994. Port Vale £225,000 November 1994. Leicester City £950,000 February 1997. Celtic £350,000 August 2001. Leicester City free January 2004. LEEDS UNITED free August 2004. Stoke City free September 2004. Wycombe Wanderers free November 2004. DC United (US) March 2006. Stevenage Borough August 2006. Rochester Rhinos (US) player-assistant coach March 2008.

■ Former England winger Steve spent a few weeks on trial at Leeds after the club's relegation from the Premiership. He had mixed fortunes during his only start – scoring against Nottingham Forest but giving away a penalty that enabled the visitors to snatch a late point. He lacked the fitness required for Championship football and was released.

H

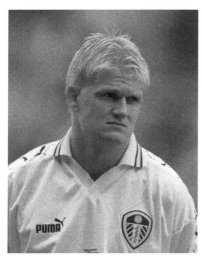

HAALAND Alf-Inge Rasdal

Midfield/Central-defender/Full-back

Born: Stavanger, Norway, 23 November 1972.
5ft 10in, 12st 12lb (2001).
Career: Bryne (Norway). Nottingham Forest January 1994. LEEDS UNITED £1.6 million July 1997. Manchester City £2.5 million June 2000–August 2003.

■ Strong-tackling, versatile Norwegian international Alfie never shirked a challenge in his three years at Leeds. He had a cracking first season at Elland Road but was surprisingly omitted from Norway's 1998 World Cup squad. United banked a handsome profit when David O'Leary sold him to Manchester City, where he endured a nightmare time with injuries. Two knee cartilage operations prompted him to call it a day in 2003 at the age of 30. Alfie, who aided Nottingham Forest to Premiership promotion in 1994, won 34 full caps and 29 at Under-21 level.

HACKWORTH Anthony

Forward

Born: Durham, 19 May 1980.
6ft 1in, 13st 7lb (2000).
Career: LEEDS UNITED trainee, professional May 1997. Sogndal (Norway) loan May 2000. Notts County £150,000 July 2001. Scarborough loan March–April 2004, free July 2004. Whitby Town 2007. Harrogate Town November 2007.

■ Twenty-year-old Tony was handed the most testing of debuts by David O'Leary in front of 85,000 fans in Barcelona's Nou Camp stadium, coming on in United's 4–0 drubbing on their Champions League debut. The powerful forward was regarded as one of the brightest stars of the 1998 FA Youth Cup-winning team but missed the Final with a broken ankle, then suffered a cruciate ligament injury. He was embroiled in the Bowyer–Woodgate attack saga but was quickly cleared of any involvement. The England Youth international moved to Notts County but struggled for goals and dropped into the Conference with Scarborough.

HADDOCK Peter Murray

Defender/Midfield

Born: Newcastle upon Tyne, 9 December 1961.
5ft 11in, 11st 5lb (1986).
Career: Cramlington High School. South Northumberland Boys. Cramlington Juniors. Newcastle United apprentice June 1978, professional December 1979. Dunedin City (New Zealand) loan 1985. Burnley loan March–April 1986. LEEDS UNITED £45,000 July 1986–July 1992.

■ Peter was an undervalued member of the Leeds squad during the 1990 Second Division title success. 'Fish' took time to

win over the fans after his move from Newcastle, but an ability to play in a variety of positions saw him pass the century mark in League games for Leeds. He looked most at home in central defence but a knee injury sustained in the League Cup semi-final second leg against Manchester United ended his career. His League debut for Newcastle as a 19-year-old came in dramatic circumstances. The Geordies' regular left-back was taken ill in London as the squad prepared for their game at Queen's Park Rangers and Peter had to be rushed down to the capital on the morning of the game to fill in. After giving up the game through injury he sold insurance, ran a bakery, was a postman and worked as a courier.

HAIR Kenneth Grenville Arthur

Left-back

Born: Burton upon Trent, Derbyshire, 16 November 1931.
Died: Bradford, 7 March 1968.
5ft 9in, 11st 2lb (1962).
Career: Burton Technical High School. Newhall United. LEEDS UNITED November 1948. Wellington Town player-manager May 1964. Bradford City trainer February 1967, manager January 1968.

■ Had Grenville been with a more fashionable club in the 1950s, he could have been a contender for an England cap. He was a wonderful Leeds servant, notching up 443 League games after being signed from Burton and District League club Newhall United. A schools' athletics champion, Grenville also excelled at tennis and basketball, was super-fit, sharp in the tackle and a great distributor of the ball. He did his national service alongside John Charles with the 12th Royal Lancers at Barnard Castle in North Yorkshire, when they won the Northern Command trophy. A fine club ambassador, he gained FA recognition on tours to the West Indies in 1955, Nigeria and Ghana in 1958 and New Zealand in 1960. After learning the ropes as player-manager at Wellington Town he was trainer at Bradford City

before taking over as boss at Valley Parade in 1968. Grenville had only been in the hot seat a matter of weeks when he collapsed and died, aged just 36, while supervising a City training session.

HALLE Gunnar

Midfield/Full-back

Born: Larvik, Norway, 11 August 1965.
5ft 11in, 11st 2lb (1996).
Career: Larvik Gurn (Norway). Lillestrom (Norway). Oldham Athletic £280,000 February 1991. LEEDS UNITED £400,000 December 1996. Bradford City £200,000 June 1999. Wolverhampton Wanderers loan March 2002. Lillestrom (Norway) 2002, youth coach 2003. Aurskog Finstdbru (Norway) player-coach 2004. Lillestrom assistant coach 2004–November 2006. Viking Stavanger (Norway) assistant manager 2007.

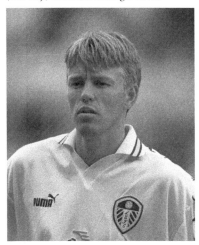

■ Howard Wilkinson wanted to sign Gunnar for Leeds but the deal fell through. It was revived by his successor George Graham, who made Gunnar his first signing. Capped 64 times by Norway, he was a surprise choice ahead of teammate Alfie Haaland for the 1998 World Cup squad. Gunnar was given a new two-year deal by David O'Leary but the dependable squad man did not see it out and was transferred to Bradford City before returning to Norway.

HALLETT Thomas

Half-back

Born: Glenneath, nr Swansea, 10 April 1939.
5ft 11in, 12st 10lb (1962).
Career: Glenneath Secondary Modern and Neath Grammar Schools. Welsh Schools. LEEDS UNITED groundstaff June 1954, professional April 1956. Swindon Town July 1963. Bradford City £1,200 June 1966–June 1971.

■ Welsh Schools star Tom made just one Leeds appearance, in a 4–0 defeat at Blackburn when the League Cup competition was in its infancy. After a spell at Swindon he played 200 times for Bradford City, being skipper in 1968–69. He later worked as a prison officer.

HAMPSON Thomas

Wing-half

Born: Salford, 10 August 1916.
Died: 18 October 1947.
5ft 8½in, 10st 12lb (1938).
Career: Droylsden. LEEDS UNITED November 1934. Oldham Athletic August 1939.

■ Signed as a teenager from Manchester amateur side Droylsden, Tom made two appearances in 1938–39, at Chelsea and Wolves. He did not play for Oldham in the truncated 1939–40 season but turned out regularly for the Latics during the war. After demob he suffered a bad knee injury and gave up the game. He became a plumber but died, aged just 31, after fracturing his skull in a fall.

HAMPTON Peter John

Full-back

Born: Oldham, 12 September 1954.
5ft 7½in, 10st 12lb (1978).

Career: Etherley Lane Junior School, Bishop Auckland. Bishop Auckland Grammar School and Durham County Schools. LEEDS UNITED September 1971. Stoke City £175,000 August 1980. Burnley May 1984. Rochdale free August 1987. Carlisle United player-physiotherapist December 1987, later coach and assistant manager. Bury physiotherapist. Workington manager 1998–October 2002.

■ Compact full-back Peter played alongside Ray Hankin in the England Youth team in 1973, making his Leeds debut at Southampton the same year. He did not feature in the 1973–74 Championship side but had more chances when Frank Gray switched from left-back to midfield. He figured in the 1977 FA Cup semi-final against Manchester United and the League Cup semi against Nottingham Forest the following year before four productive seasons at Stoke and nearly 150 games for Burnley. A physio, he had a successful time as manager of Workington, and has worked in a variety of roles with Carlisle United.

HAMSON Gary

Midfield/Full-back

Born: Nottingham, 24 August 1959.
5ft 8in, 10st 11lb (1986).
Career: Derby County trials. Sheffield United November 1976. LEEDS UNITED £140,000 July 1979. Bristol City July 1986. Port Vale £5,000 December 1986–March 1988, youth coach August 1988–July 1989.

■ Aggressive midfield enforcer Gary had more than his fair share of brushes with referees. He received a nine-match ban in February 1981 – a record under the penalty points system at the time. But he was also a talented player and would have easily surpassed his 150-odd games for United but for a bad knee injury sustained in the 2–0 defeat at West Brom, in the final game of 1981–82 season, which condemned Leeds to relegation. Bad luck was never in short supply for Gary. At Sheffield United he was picked for an England Youth match against Wales but the game was called off, and he was never given another international call. His career was cut short by a recurring ankle injury at Port Vale, and after working as a builder and insurance salesman he became a financial advisor.

HANKIN Raymond

Forward

Born: Wallsend, nr Newcastle upon Tyne, 2 February 1956.
6ft 2in, 14st (1979).
Career: Wallsend and Northumberland Schools. Wallsend Boys Club. Burnley apprentice, professional February 1973. LEEDS UNITED £172,000 September 1976. Vancouver Whitecaps (Canada) March 1980. Arsenal non-contract November 1981–January 1982. Shamrock Rovers 1982. Vancouver Whitecaps (Canada) March 1982. Middlesbrough £80,000 September 1982. Peterborough United £7,000 September 1983.

Wolverhampton Wanderers March–August 1985. Whitby Town March 1986. Blue Star December 1986. Guisborough Town July 1987. Hamrun Spartans (Malta). Northallerton Town manager March 1989. Newcastle United football in the community officer. Darlington manager March–July 1992. Newcastle United Football in the Community manager 2001.

■ Former shipyard worker's son Ray could cut his way through the iron defences of the First Division when he was in his prime at Leeds. Jimmy Armfield paired former Burnley man Ray with Joe Jordan at the start of 1977–78 to form a frightening twin spearhead. Even though Jordan moved to Manchester United midway through the season, Ray finished with 20 League goals. The England Youth and Under-23 international was a hefty old-fashioned centre-forward on the up, but left Leeds for Canada when he was 24 and never really got his career back on track. Long-standing knee injuries and discipline proved a problem – he was sent off on his Middlesbrough debut at Grimsby, sacked by Peterborough after being dismissed five times in a season and even received a red card for refusing to wear the Guisborough captain's armband in an FA Cup tie against Bury. Ray later worked at a mental hospital near Middlesbrough before becoming Newcastle's Football in the Community officer.

HARDING Daniel Andrew

Left-back

Born: Gloucester, 23 December 1983.
6ft, 11st 11lb (2005).
Career: Brighton & Hove Albion trainee, professional July 2003. LEEDS UNITED £850,000 July 2005. Ipswich Town player-exchange August 2006.

■ Kevin Blackwell invested £850,000 – a fee set by a tribunal – in England Under-21 international Dan, but midway through the 2005–06 season the blond-haired youngster had lost his left-back slot to the more experienced Stephen Crainey. Dan moved on to Ipswich after 12 months in a swap deal with midfielder Ian Westlake. He played in Brighton's Division Two Play-off Final triumph against Bristol City in Cardiff.

HARGREAVES John

Left-winger

Born: Rotherham, 1 May 1915.
Died: Bristol, 22 December 1978.
5ft 9in, 10st 2lb (1938).
Career: Sheffield junior football. LEEDS UNITED August 1934. Bristol City wartime guest August 1945. Reading April 1947. Yeovil 1948.

■ Jack lost his best footballing years to the war after competing with Arthur Buckley for the Leeds left-wing berth. He was a key member of the United team that won the Central League in 1937 before the RAF sent him to work in Bristol at an aircraft factory. Jack was a member of the famous non-League Yeovil side that knocked mighty Sunderland out of the FA Cup in 1949.

HARLE David

Midfield

Born: Denaby, nr Doncaster, 15 August 1963.
5ft 9in, 10st 7lb (1986).
Career: Doncaster Rovers apprentice, professional November 1980. Exeter City free July 1982. Doncaster Rovers September 1983. LEEDS UNITED £5,000 December 1985. Bristol City loan March–May 1986, £10,000 June 1986. Scunthorpe United November 1986. Peterborough United £15,000 March 1989. Doncaster Rovers £13,000 March 1990. Stafford Rangers 1992 loan. Armthorpe Welfare assistant manager to February 2002.

97

■ Former England Youth international David was certainly rated by manager Billy Bremner, who signed him three times – twice for Doncaster and once for Leeds. The move to Elland Road proved a step too far, although David was in demand in the lower divisions, having his best games at Scunthorpe.

HARRIS Carl Stephen

Right-winger

Born: Neath, 3 November 1956.
5ft 9in, 11st 1lb (1979).
Career: Hengwert Primary and Cwrtsart Secondary Schools. Neath and Wales Schools. Briton Ferry. Burnley trial. LEEDS UNITED November 1973. Charlton Athletic £100,000 July 1982. Bury December 1985. Swansea City and Cardiff City trials July 1987. Airdrie trials August 1987. Rochdale January 1988. Exeter City December 1988. Briton Ferry player-manager 1992, later general manager to 1994.

■ Persistence paid off in United's pursuit of teenager Carl. The 16-year-old had been rejected by Burnley but Leeds took him on, although within days he was homesick and returned home to Wales to work in a factory. United persuaded the blazingly fast winger to return though, and he zipped through the Youth and Under-23 ranks and made his Leeds debut in the European Cup against Ujpest Doza in 1974. His League debut came five months later, and he scored after coming on in a 2–1 home win over Ipswich. Eleven months later Carl won the first of his 24 caps but despite being a fairly regular performer for his country, he spent a lot of time on the subs' bench for Leeds. United's top scorer in 1980–81, he was transferred to Charlton after Leeds were relegated the following season. His patchy form with the London club was not helped by injuries, and he was not re-signed after a trial back at Leeds. After football he ran a removals business in Neath.

HARRIS Joseph

Outside-left

Born: Glasgow, 5 November 1891.

Died: Summer 1966.
5ft 10in, 11st 10lb (1922).
Career: Vale of Clyde. Ashfield. Burnley September 1910. Bristol City 1912. LEEDS UNITED July 1922. Fulham October 1925–28.

■ Joe was a mainstay of the 1923–24 Division Two Championship-winning side, providing numerous goals for Jack Swan and Joe Richmond from the left flank. An ever present in United's first-ever Division One campaign, he spent three productive years at Elland Road. A product of Scottish junior football, Joe made more than 200 appearances for Bristol City and played a lot of army representative football. At Bristol he was suspended for a year and fined £50 for being paid while on amateur terms, but that did not stop the Robins from awarding him a £600 benefit before his move to Leeds. Joe's brother, Neil, played for Newcastle United and Scotland, while nephew John played for Chelsea and later managed Sheffield United.

HARRISON Peter

Left-winger

Born: Sleaford, Lincolnshire, 25 October 1927.
Died: Llandough, Mid-Glamorgan, 25 July 2006.
5ft 6in, 9st 2lb (1951).
Career: Aveling and Barford. Notts County amateur March 1944. Peterborough United amateur. LEEDS UNITED amateur August 1948, professional January 1949. Bournemouth August 1952. Reading June 1957. Southport free July 1959. Macclesfield Town 1962. Runcorn

1963–64. Cardiff City trainer and youth coach to 1984.

■ Peter was signed from amateur works team Aveling and Barford by Notts County boss Major Frank Buckley, and when the Major took over at Leeds he recruited the winger again. Peter became good friends with John Charles and each was best man at the other's wedding. Peter played army representative football while serving in the RAOC in Germany. After leaving Leeds he was never short of work, making more than 400 career appearances.

HARRISON Ralph

Left-winger

Born: Clayton-le-Moors, Lancashire, 18 December 1926.
5ft 11½in, 11st 8lb (1949).
Career: Harwood St Hubert's. Great Harwood. LEEDS UNITED January 1949.

■ During the late 1940s, United had two left-wingers called Harrison on their books, but Ralph was not related to his namesake Peter. Ralph saw service with the Royal Navy in Ceylon during World War Two. After his demob he worked for the National Coal Board and played amateur Lancashire football before joining Leeds. To add to the confusion of football statisticians he only played twice for United, his only League club, in 1949–50 before his place on the wing was taken by Peter Harrison.

HART Ernest Arthur

Centre-half

Born: Overseal, Staffordshire, 3 January 1902.
Died: Adwick le Street, nr Doncaster, 21 July 1954.
5ft 11in, 13st (1933).
Career: Overseal School. Overseal Juniors. Woodlands Wesleyans. LEEDS UNITED 1920. Mansfield Town £350 August 1936–March 1937. Tunbridge Wells Rangers manager July 1938.

■ Ernie was one of United's all-time greats in the inter-war years, winning eight England caps. The solidly built former miner was signed by Arthur Fairclough from Doncaster junior club Woodlands Wesleyans shortly after United's formation, and some storming displays in the reserves saw Ernie quickly elevated to the first team at the age of 19. He spent 16 years at Elland Road, amassing 472 League and Cup appearances, many as captain. Hard but fair in defence, he was a better passer than many of his defensive peers. A member of United's 1924 Second Division Championship-winning side, he was also in the promotion teams of 1928 and 1932. Ernie twice represented the Football League and toured South Africa with the FA in 1929. Ernie's cap tally could have been greater but for a lengthy ban after being sent off in the 1933 West Riding Cup Final against Huddersfield. He served a month's suspension, lost £32 in wages and was axed by the FA from the England tour to Italy and Switzerland.

HART Paul Anthony

Centre-half

Born: Golborne, nr Manchester, 4 May 1953.
6ft 2in, 12st 8lb (1983).
Career: Manchester Boys. Stockport County apprentice June 1969, professional September 1970. Blackpool £25,000 June 1973. LEEDS UNITED £300,000 March 1978. Nottingham Forest May 1983. Sheffield Wednesday August 1985. Birmingham City December 1986. Notts County £15,000 player-coach June 1987. Chesterfield manager November 1988–January 1991. Grantham 1991. Nottingham Forest coach June 1991. Sheffield Wednesday coach 1994. LEEDS UNITED youth coach, acting as caretaker manager September 1996. Nottingham Forest coach and Youth Academy Director, manager July 2001–February 2004. Barnsley manager March 2004–March 2005. Rushden & Diamonds manager May–October 2006. Portsmouth director of youth operations March 2007.

■ When Gordon McQueen moved to Manchester United, Leeds brought in big Paul to fill his boots at centre-half. Although his early days were bedevilled by errors he settled in the core of the Leeds defence to become an excellent, powerful stopper tipped for England honours. Paul, son of Manchester City inside-forward Johnny Hart, had an excellent club career but his only game for Birmingham saw him break a leg. Paul built a reputation as a fine coach and returned to Leeds to run the Youth Academy at Thorp Arch, enjoying a superb first year as his youngsters won the FA Youth Cup for the first time in the club's history. He even held the managerial fort for a few days after Howard Wilkinson left United, and although Paul's name was linked with managerial vacancies at Leeds he did not get the call.

HARTE Ian Patrick

Left-back

Born: Drogheda, Ireland, 31 August 1977.
5ft 10in, 11st 8lb (1999).
Career: St Kevin's Boys, Drogheda. LEEDS UNITED apprentice, professional December 1995. Levante (Spain) July 2004. Sunderland August 2007–May 2008.

■ When 18-year-old Ian came on for his Leeds debut in the Coca-Cola Cup against Reading in 1996 it completed an amazing family double as his uncle, Gary Kelly, himself only 21, was already on the pitch. In summer 1996 Ian earned his first full cap against Croatia, yet the homesick Irish lad had been on the verge of leaving Leeds two months into his two-year apprenticeship. He stuck it out at Leeds and after playing in a variety of positions for the juniors and reserves settled in at left-back. Although not the quickest, he had great attacking flair and a left foot capable of switching play in an instant. Once established in the Leeds side he became an adept free-kick and penalty taker, something he was able to translate to international level. Ian figured for the Republic in the 1998 and

2002 World Cup Finals. As Leeds went into decline after their Champions League adventure, his form dipped and a move became inevitable. He joined newly promoted Spanish outfit Levante and later linked up with former Eire teammate Roy Keane at Sunderland.

HARVEY David

Goalkeeper

Born: Leeds, 7 February 1948.
5ft 11in, 12st 3lb (1972).
Career: Foxwood and Seacroft Grange Schools, Leeds. LEEDS UNITED February 1965. Vancouver Whitecaps (Canada) £40,000 March 1979. Drogheda 1980–81. Vancouver Whitecaps (Canada) March 1980. LEEDS UNITED March 1983. Partick Thistle loan February 1985. Bradford City February 1985. Whitby Town player-manager May 1985–86. Harrogate Town 1987. Carlisle United non-contract 1987–88.

■ One of United's most popular goalkeepers, David served a long apprenticeship in the shadow of Gary Sprake. He worked in a shoe factory then joined his home club as a professional and made about 200 Central League appearances before Don Revie finally gave him a regular first-team place in 1971–72. He kept goal as United lifted the 1972 FA Cup and later in the year won the first of his 16 Scottish caps, qualifying because his father was born north of the border. A bad car accident in February 1975 saw him temporarily lose his place to David Stewart and he missed out on a

European Cup Final appearance. After playing in Canada, David returned to Leeds in March 1983 as a 35-year-old and took over from the unsettled John Lukic. David went on to total 350 League games in his two spells with the Whites – a fine tally considering how many reserve games he played. He also packed a pretty powerful shot in training, but missed the penalty which saw United lose the 1974 Charity Shield to Liverpool in a shoot-out at Wembley. David had a variety of occupations, including running a pub, delivering fruit and vegetables to hotels, being a postman and, finally, moving to a farmhouse and smallholding on the island of Sanday in the Orkneys.

HASSELBAINK Jerrel 'Jimmy' Floyd

Forward

Born: Surinam, 27 March 1972.
6ft 2in, 13st 4lb (1997).
Career: Telstar (Holland). AZ Alkmaar (Holland) 1991. Camponmaiorense (Portugal) August 1995. Boavista (Portugal). LEEDS UNITED £2 million July 1997. Atletico Madrid (Spain) £12 million August 1999. Chelsea £15 million July 2000. Middlesbrough free July 2004. Charlton Athletic July 2006. Cardiff City August 2007.

■ George Graham pulled off a smart piece of business when he signed Jimmy Floyd from Portuguese football. The exotically-named striker packed a thunderous shot and a debut goal against Arsenal at Elland Road made him an instant terrace hero. Born in Surinam on the north-east coast of South America, he moved to Holland when he was just five but made his name in Portugal, winning a Portuguese Cup-winners' medal with Boavista. Graham's gamble paid big dividends as a blunt Leeds attack was transformed by Jimmy's sledgehammer shooting. He pounded in 22 goals in 1997–98 and earned a first call-up to the Dutch national team. He was top scorer the following season when United qualified for the UEFA Cup, but at the end of the campaign Jimmy rejected a new and improved contract. When Spanish club Atletico Madrid came in with a £12 million offer, United made a £10 million profit on their prize

asset. Jimmy's goals could not save Atletico from La Liga relegation, and within a year he was back in the Premiership with Chelsea. He spent four productive goalscoring seasons there before joining Middlesbrough, where he was often paired up front with ex-Leeds star Mark Viduka. Jimmy appeared for Holland 23 times, scoring nine goals.

HASTIE John Kenneth George

Inside-forward

Born: Cape Town, South Africa, 6 September 1928.
5ft 10in, 11st 12lb (1952).
Career: Clyde Athletic (South Africa). LEEDS UNITED August 1952.

■ United must have thought they had unearthed a South African diamond when Ken made a two-goal debut in a 2–2 draw at Birmingham on 17 September 1952. But he could not maintain that standard, played just three more times for Leeds and slipped into the background. A printer by trade, versatile Ken was spotted in South Africa playing at full-back against Newcastle in 1951. The club followed up their interest and threw him in at the deep end after just one reserve game, but overall it was a gamble that did not pay off.

HATELEY Mark Wayne

Forward

Born: Wallasey, Merseyside, 7 November 1961.
6ft 3in, 13st (1997).

Career: Coventry City apprentice, professional December 1978. Detroit Express (US) loan April 1980. Portsmouth £190,000 June 1983. AC Milan (Italy) £1 million June 1984. Monaco (France) June 1987. Rangers £500,000 June 1990. Queen's Park Rangers £1.5 million November 1995. LEEDS UNITED loan August 1996. Rangers £300,000 March 1997. Hull City free August 1997, player-manager December 1998–June 1999. Ross County 1999.

■ Howard Wilkinson swooped for former England striker Mark just after the start of the 1996–97 season because of injuries to Brian Deane and Tony Yeboah. It did not really work out, and after his month's loan deal was up, he returned to Queen's Park Rangers. The son of Tony Hateley, a powerful forward with Notts County, Aston Villa, Chelsea, Liverpool, Coventry and Birmingham among others, Mark inherited his father's aerial power. He won the first of his 10 Under-21 caps with Coventry before moving to Portsmouth with whom he made his full international debut. His career took off, scoring in a famous win over Brazil in the Maracana Stadium, which prompted a move to Italy. His golden period came at Rangers, where he won the last of his 32 caps but formed a prolific striking partnership with Ally McCoist. Both men scored at Elland Road as the Glasgow side knocked Leeds out of the European Cup in 1992. Mark won three Scottish titles, two Scottish Cups, two League Cups and was the first Englishman to become Scottish

Footballer of the Year in 1993–94. He now commentates on Scottish football for the Setanta television channel.

HAWKINS Dennis Ronald

Forward

Born: Swansea, 22 October 1947.
5ft 7in, 10st 12lb (1968).
Career: Wales Schools. LEEDS UNITED apprentice, professional October 1964. Shrewsbury Town October 1968. Chester loan September 1970. Workington March 1972. Newport County May 1972. Telford United 1973. Nuneaton Borough. Tadcaster Albion manager.

■ Dennis found it tough to break into the Leeds first team during the early years of the Revie era. The nippy little forward earned the first of his six Welsh Under-23 caps before making his United League debut. He had more opportunities in the lower divisions plus a spell as boss of Northern Counties East League side Tadcaster.

HAWKSBY John Frederick

Inside-forward

Born: York, 12 June 1942.
5ft 9in, 10st 10lb (1962).
Career: York and Yorkshire Schools. LEEDS UNITED amateur July 1957, professional June 1959. Lincoln City August 1964. York City £4,000 March 1966. King's Lynn July 1968. Cambridge City 1970. Kettering Town August 1972. Dunstable Town £4,000 July 1974. Stevenage. Rushden Town. Desborough Town.

■ John shot to prominence at Leeds when he was capped three times at England Youth level in 1959 against Wales, Scotland and East Germany. A big future seemed assured when he forced his way into the United first team at 18, scoring in each of his first two League games. His career stalled, however, and he moved on and later combined work as a painter and decorator with non-League football.

HAWLEY John East

Forward

Born: Withernsea, East Yorkshire, 8 May 1954.
6ft 1in, 13st 5lb (1978).
Career: East Riding junior football. Hull City amateur April 1972, professional August 1976. LEEDS UNITED £81,000 May 1978. Sunderland £200,000 September 1979. Arsenal £50,000 September 1981. Leyton Orient loan October 1982. Hull City loan November 1982. Happy Valley (Hong Kong) 1983. Bradford City August 1983. Scunthorpe United July 1985–86.

■ John enjoyed one popular goal-getting season at Elland Road after joining from Hull City. He was a late arrival to the paid ranks of the game, playing as an amateur with the Tigers for four years while working in the family antiques business. Signed by Jimmy Armfield, he turned pro at 22 and netted 16 goals in 1978–79, but Jimmy Adamson sold him at a handsome profit to Adamson's old club, Sunderland. John quickly repaid Sunderland's record

fee by scoring a hat-trick on his League debut for the Rokerites against Charlton and, despite suffering a hamstring injury, playcd his part in their promotion. After an unsuccessful spell at Arsenal, John moved down the divisions and won a 1984–85 Third Division Championship medal with Bradford City. He later returned to the antiques trade and launched an auctioneer's business in 2002.

HAY Daniel John

Centre-half

Born: Auckland, New Zealand, 15 May 1975.
6ft 4in, 13st 14lb (2006).
Career: Waitakere City (New Zealand). Central United (New Zealand). Perth Glory (Australia) 1998. LEEDS UNITED £200,000 August 1999. Walsall August 2002. Auckland Kingz (New Zealand) December 2004. New Zealand Knights (New Zealand) August 2005. Perth Glory (Australia) January 2006. Waitakere United (New Zealand) October 2006.

■ Giant New Zealand international defender Danny played just a handful of games during his injury-hit time with United. He was signed as cover by David O'Leary but had more opportunities at Walsall. He returned to his homeland where he skippered the New Zealand national team, reaching the 34-cap mark, before retiring from the All Whites at the age of 32 to pursue a teaching career in Auckland.

HEALY David Jonathan

Forward

Born: Downpatrick, Northern Ireland, 5 August 1979.
5ft 8in, 11st (2006).
Career: Lisburn Youth. Down Academy High School. Manchester United from trainee November 1997. Port Vale loan

February 2000. Preston North End £1.5 million December 2000. Norwich City loan January 2003 and March 2003. LEEDS UNITED October 2004. Fulham £1.5 million July 2007.

■ Unfortunately for Leeds fans, David could not replicate his sensational goalscoring record for Northern Ireland at Elland Road. It did not help the classy penalty box predator that he found himself stuck on the right flank, as his partnership with Rob Hulse looked as good as anything in the Championship when they were paired up front. He netted a relatively modest 29 times in 111 League games for Leeds, but it was a different story for Northern Ireland – his record-breaking 13 goals in the qualifying campaign for Euro 2008 took his international haul to 33 in 62 matches. His most famous strike came when he was a Leeds player, firing home superbly at Windsor Park to beat England in a World Cup qualifier. When United dropped into League One his departure was inevitable, and he linked up with his old international boss, Laurie Sanchez, at Premiership Fulham, but found goals hard to come by.

HEATH Matthew Philip

Centre-half

Born: Leicester, 1 November 1981.
6ft 4in, 13st 13lb (2006).
Career: Leicester City trainee, professional February 2001. Stockport County loan October 2003. Coventry City £200,000 July 2005. LEEDS UNITED loan November 2006, transfer January 2007.

Colchester United loan March 2008, signed May 2008.

■ With United leaking goals at an alarming rate, new United boss Dennis Wise persuaded one of his old clubs, Coventry, to loan him giant defender Matt to replace veteran Paul Butler. The deal became permanent a couple of months later. He scored United's opening goal of the 2007–08 season in a 2–1 win at Tranmere – United's first-ever game in the third tier of English football.

HEATON William Henry

Left-winger

Born: Holbeck, Leeds, 5 October 1920.
Died: Leeds, 16 January 1990.
5ft 6in, 10st (1948).
Career: Ingram Road School, Holbeck. Leeds Boys. Yorkshire Schools. Huddersfield Town trial. Whitkirk. LEEDS UNITED amateur November 1937, professional August 1938. Southampton £7,000 February 1949. Stalybridge Celtic September 1949. Rochdale November 1950.

■ Left-winger Billy whizzed through the schoolboy ranks and won amateur international and FA XI honours with Leeds after serving in India during World War Two. A real box-of-tricks speedster, he moved on to Southampton but fell out with the Saints because he refused to move home to the south. He opted to play in the Cheshire League with Stalybridge while the issue was resolved – Southampton held his registration, and he re-entered the League with Rochdale. After retiring from football he worked for a Leeds slating and roofing company.

HENDERSON John Swinton Pryde

Inside-forward

Born: Glasgow, 13 October 1923.
5ft 6in, 11st 4lb (1956).
Career: Falkirk 1940. Third Lanark September 1948. Rotherham United November 1953. LEEDS UNITED March 1955. Weymouth June 1956. Trowbridge 1959. Frome Town 1962. Devizes manager 1972. Calne Town coach.

■ Jock saw out his professional career with a brief spell at Elland Road. He had given good service to Falkirk and appeared in the side that lost the 1948 Scottish League Cup Final to East Fife. He joined Leeds just before the transfer deadline in March 1955 and added experience to United's promotion drive. Although they missed out that season, Jock was in the side at the start of the following campaign when United did go up. He later moved to the South West where he became a familiar figure in non-League circles while working for the Gas Board.

HENDERSON Thomas Wedlock

Right-winger

Born: Larkhall, Lanarkshire, 25 July 1943.
5ft 4in, 11st (1963).
Career: Larkhall Academy. Scottish Schools. LEEDS UNITED 1959. Hearts. St Mirren. LEEDS UNITED £1,500 November 1962. Bury June 1965. Swindon Town January 1966. Stockport County July 1966. Altrincham October 1967.

■ Tiny Tommy had two spells with United. The first, as a teenager, did not last long. The Scotland Schoolboy international was released because he was homesick, and he returned home to play for Hearts and St Mirren, appearing in the 1962 Scottish Cup Final for the Love Street side against Rangers. United kept tabs on his progress and he returned to Leeds in 1962, playing in the first team until Don Revie brought in Johnny Giles. Tom won a Division Four Championship medal with Stockport in 1967.

HENDRIE John Grattan

Forward

Born: Lennoxtown, Lanarkshire, 24 October 1963.
5ft 7in, 11st 4lb (1989).
Career: Lennoxtown Boys. Possil YM. Coventry City apprentice June 1980, professional May 1981. Hereford United loan January 1984. Bradford City July 1984. Newcastle United £500,000 June 1988. LEEDS UNITED £600,000 June 1989. Middlesbrough £500,000 July 1990. Barnsley £250,000 October 1996, player-manager July 1998–April 1999.

■ John picked up a Second Division Championship medal in his only season at Leeds. Injuries restricted him to just 22 starts, which was a disappointment after Howard Wilkinson fought long and hard to prise him away from Newcastle. The Scottish Youth international joined Coventry as a 16-year-old but made his name with Bradford City, earning big-money moves to Newcastle then Leeds. But he probably hit peak form at Middlesbrough, where he helped win promotion in 1991–92 and was top scorer three seasons later. John is the cousin of Aston Villa and England midfielder Lee Hendrie and nephew of Paul Hendrie – Lee's dad – the former Birmingham player. John works as a sports law consultant.

HENRY Gerald Robert

Inside-forward

Born: Hemsworth, 5 October 1920.
Died: 1979.
5ft 5in, 11st 4lb (1946).
Career: Yorkshire Schools. Outwood Stormcocks. LEEDS UNITED October 1937. Bradford Park Avenue November 1947. Sheffield Wednesday February 1950. Halifax Town player-coach December 1951, player-manager February 1952–October 1954.

■ Gerry played for Yorkshire Schools in 1934 and joined United as a 17-year-old from nursery club Outwood Stormcocks. Most of his 10 years with Leeds coincided with the war, and he made 186 wartime appearances and scored 94 goals for United – both club records. When he was manager of Halifax he brought in Allan Ure, the former Leeds trainer, to sharpen up the Shaymen's fitness.

HIBBITT Terence Arthur

Midfield

Born: Bradford, 1 December 1947.
Died: Ponteland, nr Newcastle upon Tyne, 5 August 1994.
5ft 6½in, 9st 10lb (1970).
Career: LEEDS UNITED apprentice April 1963, professional December 1964. Newcastle United £30,000 August 1971. Birmingham City £100,000 September 1975. Newcastle United player-exchange April 1968–June 1981. Gateshead July 1981, player-coach January 1983, manager April 1986. Durham City assistant manager October 1986.

■ Terry made a dramatic entry into the Football League, scoring with his first

touch after coming on as substitute in United's 4–1 victory at Nottingham Forest on 19 February 1966. The slightly-built, bow-legged Bradfordian was a clever little player with a fine left foot who never let Leeds down, winning a Fairs Cup-winners' medal in 1968 and contributing to United's first Championship success the following season. Newcastle picked up a bargain when they signed 'Bandy' for just £30,000, and he helped steer the Magpies to the 1974 FA Cup Final, which they lost to Liverpool. After three years at Birmingham he returned to Tyneside as captain but a knee injury forced him to retire. Terry stayed in the North East to help Gateshead win the Northern Premier League title and became a newsagent and milkman before managing a pub on the outskirts of Newcastle. He died of cancer, aged just 46. Terry's brother Kenny, an England Under-23 international, played for Wolves, Coventry, Bradford and Bristol Rovers.

HIDEN Martin

Defender

Born: Stainz, Austria, 11 March 1973.
6ft, 11st 9lb (2000).
Career: Sturm Graz (Austria) August 1993. Salzburg (Austria) August 1995. Sturm Graz (Austria) August 1996. Rapid Vienna (Austria) August 1997. LEEDS UNITED £1.3 million February 1998. Salzburg (Austria) £500,000 May 2000. Rapid Vienna (Austria) October 2005. Austria Karnten (Austria) loan January 2008.

■ George Graham was always a good judge of a fine defender, and Martin

fitted into that category. Graham jetted out to Dubai to see his quarry play in a friendly before signing on the dotted line. Virtually unknown in England when he joined Leeds, the Austrian international played at centre-back, sweeper and full-back for Leeds and figured in Austria's World Cup squad before a cruciate ligament injury in November 1998 put him out of action for the rest of that season. Martin did not figure much under David O'Leary and went back to Austria, where he took his total number of caps beyond the 40 mark.

HILAIRE Vince Mark

Winger

Born: Forest Hill, London, 10 October 1959.
5ft 6in, 10st (1988).
Career: Crystal Palace apprentice, professional October 1976. San Jose Earthquakes (US) 1982. Luton Town July 1984. Portsmouth £85,000 November 1984. LEEDS UNITED £190,000 July 1988. Stoke City loan November 1989. Charlton Athletic loan April 1990. Stoke City November 1990. Exeter City September 1991. Waterlooville 1993 player-coach. Bognor Regis November 1994.

■ Winger Vince was a flair player who could dribble his way through any defence, but he never hit the heights he achieved at Palace and Portsmouth in his time at Elland Road. The England Youth player won nine Under-21 caps and made an England B appearance. As a key

member of the Pompey team that won promotion to Division Two in 1986–87, Billy Bremner hoped 'Vince the Prince' could do the same for Leeds. United offered Portsmouth £70,000, the selling club wanted £270,000 and a tribunal set the fee at £190,000.

HILL George

Winger

Born: Dronfield, nr Sheffield.
5ft 9in, 11st (1920).
Career: Birmingham. Rotherham Town September 1919. LEEDS UNITED July 1920–May 1921.

■ George figured fleetingly on either flank during United's maiden Football League season. He did not get a League game with either Birmingham or Rotherham.

HILTON Joseph

Centre-forward

Born: Bromborough, Wirral, 20 July 1931.
Died: Sheffield, June 1995.
5ft 11in, 11st 10lb (1950).
Career: Doncaster junior football. LEEDS UNITED September 1948. Scarborough loan April 1949. Chester August 1950. New Brighton 1953.

■ Although Joe figured mostly at centre-forward for United's reserve, A and junior teams, his only senior appearance in a 2–1 home defeat against Swansea was at inside-left. He opted to join Leeds in preference to Sunderland and Sheffield Wednesday but did not make much progress and moved on to Chester, where he spent three seasons.

HINDLE Thomas

Inside-forward

Born: Keighley, 22 February 1921.
5ft 8in, 11st (1950).
Career: Ingrow Council School, Keighley. Keighley Boys. Keighley Town. LEEDS UNITED September 1943. York City player-exchange February 1949. Halifax Town September 1949. Rochdale March 1952. Wigan Athletic 1953. Nelson 1955.

■ After working for an engineering firm, Tom had trials with Bradford Park Avenue before joining Leeds. He played almost 100 wartime games for United and was in the first team when peacetime football resumed. An exchange deal involving Jimmy Rudd took him to York City.

HIRD Kevin

Full-back/Midfield

Born: Colne, Lancashire, 11 February 1952.
5ft 7in, 10st 6lb (1979).
Career: Lord Street School, Colne. Blackburn Rovers apprentice October 1970, professional February 1973. LEEDS UNITED £357,000 March 1979. Burnley free July 1984–May 1986. Colne Dynamos 1986. Barnoldswick Town September 1991, Kelbrook. Blackburn Rovers academy coaching staff.

■ United paid a British record fee for a full-back when they signed Kevin from Blackburn. He was one of Jimmy Adamson's better buys, but the manager never seemed able to decide where to play him. Kevin's attacking instincts saw him thrust on the right wing, where his mazy dribbling skills and long-range shooting came in to play. Dubbed 'Jasper' by the fans because of his likeness to comedian Jasper Carrott, enigmatic Kevin never gave anything less than 100 per cent. He took on the responsibility of penalty taking and scored several spectacular goals before dropping into Division Three with Burnley, where he scored 21 League and Cup goals from midfield in 1984–85 even though the Clarets were relegated. A cash crisis at Turf Moor saw Kevin's contract terminated, and he played local football

while working for a timber merchants. Since then he has run his own soccer school and coached at Blackburn's Centre of Excellence.

HODGE Stephen Brian

Midfield

Born: Nottingham, 25 October 1962.
5ft 8in, 10st 3lb (1993).
Career: Nottinghamshire County Boys. Nottingham Forest apprentice May 1978, professional October 1980. Aston Villa £450,000 August 1985. Tottenham Hotspur £650,000 December 1986. Nottingham Forest £575,000 August 1988. LEEDS UNITED £900,000 July 1991. Derby County loan August 1994. Queen's Park Rangers £300,000 October 1994. Watford free February 1995. Hong Kong football January 1996. Leyton Orient August 1977. Chesterfield coaching. Notts County Under-14 coach. Nottingham Forest and Leicester City academy coach.

■ Former England international midfielder Steve made an instant impact with Leeds, coming on as a substitute on his debut and scoring a point-saving goal against Sheffield Wednesday. He made only a dozen starts during that 1991–92 Championship season after signing from Nottingham Forest, and he did not really command a regular place during his injury-blighted time at Elland Road. Steve won eight England Under-21 caps and gained his first full cap as a Villa player against the USSR. He was a member of the 1986 World Cup team and played in the infamous 'Hand of God' game against Argentina. He swapped shirts with Diego Maradona after the game and has since loaned it to the National Football Museum in Preston. 'Harry' was captain at Villa, played in the side that lost to Coventry in the 1987 FA Cup Final, won Littlewoods Cup-winners' medals with Forest in 1989 and 1990, and regained his place in the England squad. Steve also appeared as substitute for Forest in the 1991 FA Cup Final against Tottenham, having played his last League game for the Reds against Leeds the previous week. He was unable to add to his tally of 24 international caps at Elland Road and is now a media pundit.

HODGKINSON Edwin Slack

Right-half

Born: Ilkeston, Derbyshire, 27 November 1920.
Died: Mansfield, October 2004.
5ft 8in, 11st 8lb (1948).
Career: Sorrento FC. LEEDS UNITED December 1946. Halifax Town July 1948.

■ Eddie was a keep-fit fanatic who made his Leeds debut in the final match of the 1946–47 season – a 2–1 defeat at Everton. He made just one more appearance before moving to Halifax after the Shaymen beat Mansfield, Stockport and Bournemouth to his signature.

HODGSON Gordon

Centre-forward

Born: Johannesburg, South Africa, 16 April 1904.
Died: Stoke, 14 June 1951.
6ft, 12st 7lb (1938).
Career: Benoni (South Africa). Rustenburg (South Africa) 1921. Pretorian (South Africa) 1922–23. Transvaal (South Africa) 1924–25. Liverpool November 1925. Aston Villa £3,000 January 1936. LEEDS UNITED £1,500 March 1937, youth coach 1942. Hartlepools United and York City wartime guest. Port Vale manager October 1946–June 1951.

■ South African boilermaker Gordon was a powerhouse centre-forward with a

fantastic scoring record in England. He joined Leeds just a month short of his 34th birthday and remains the only United player to score five goals in a game – against Leicester City on 1 October 1938. In 86 League and Cup matches for Leeds he netted 51 goals and continued to lead the line during the war before going on to coach the club's younger players. Gordon shot to prominence on the South African national team's 1925 tour of England. Liverpool signed him and he banged in 233 goals in 258 League games for the Reds. Such stats brought him three England caps, four England Amateur appearances and three representative games for the Football League. Gordon arrived at Leeds after a short spell at Aston Villa and moved on from Elland Road to manage Port Vale. He was still in office when he died of cancer, aged 47. An accomplished cricketer, Gordon was also a fast bowler with Lancashire CCC.

HODGSON John Percival

Goalkeeper

Born: Dawdon, Co. Durham,10 May 1922.
Died: 1973.
5ft 11½in, 11st 8lb (1945).
Career: Murton Colliery. LEEDS UNITED 1944. Middlesbrough player-exchange March 1948–55.

■ United fielded some fine goalkeepers during World War Two and Jack was among them. The miner was signed from Murton Colliery but was on the receiving end of an 8–1 hammering at York City in his first match in February 1944. However, he turned in some thrilling displays and battled it out with Harry Fearnley for a first-team place in the first season after hostilities ceased. Both eventually lost out to Jim Twomey and Jack moved to Middlesbrough in a player exchange deal involving Jim McCabe.

HOLLEY Thomas

Centre-half

Born: Sunderland, 15 November 1913.
Died: October 1992.
6ft 2in, 13st (1938).
Career: Wolverhampton Boys. Sunderland. Barnsley September 1932. LEEDS UNITED £3,750 July 1936–49. Fulham wartime guest.

■ Big Tom came from excellent footballing stock. His dad, George, was a free-scoring inside-forward with Sunderland, winning 10 England caps. Tom was destined to follow in George's stud prints, starring for Wolverhampton Boys while his father was trainer at Molineux. George's beloved Sunderland signed Tom as a youngster, but he did not make the first team. However, he established himself as a teak-tough centre-half with Barnsley and succeeded Bob Kane as United's stopper. He captained United and was an outstanding club man, making 164 League appearances and 104 more in wartime. Tom saw active service in India and, together with George Ainsley, was in an FA party that coached in Norway in summer 1946. He remained at Leeds a further three years before entering journalism and was a football writer for the *Yorkshire Evening Post* and the *Sunday People* before retiring to Majorca.

HOPKIN David

Midfield

Born: Greenock, 21 August 1970.
5ft 9in, 11st (1997).
Career: Port Glasgow Boys' Club. Greenock Morton July 1989. Chelsea £300,000 September 1992. Crystal Palace £850,000 July 1995. LEEDS UNITED £3.25 million July 1997. Bradford City £2.5 million July 2000. Crystal Palace £1.5 million March 2001. Greenock

Morton August 2002–03, joint caretaker manager. Port Glasgow coach and assistant manager.

■ David arrived at Elland Road with a reputation of being the complete midfielder and was made club captain by George Graham. The classy Scot's last act at Palace before his big-money transfer to Leeds was to curl in a brilliant 25-yard late winner against Sheffield United in the Play-off Final at Wembley to take the London club to the Premiership. Although David won five of his seven Scottish caps as a Leeds player, the Whites' fans never really saw the best of him. Injury and illness ruled him out of several games and after three seasons he moved on to Bradford City, but injuries continued to take their toll. After a second spell at Palace, he returned to his first club, Morton, where he went on to take a coaching role before running a newsagents.

HORNBY Cyril Frederick

Half-back/Inside-forward

Born: West Bromwich, 25 April 1907.
Died: West Bromwich, third quarter 1964.
5ft 11in, 11st 4lb (1930).
Career: Oakengates Town. LEEDS UNITED May 1929. Sunderland February 1936. Oakengates Town player-manager July 1937. Brierley Hill Alliance December 1937. Cradley Heath August 1938.

■ Hard-working Cyril's versatility made him a key player at Elland Road in the

1930s. Signed from Birmingham League side Oakengates, he was primarily a left-half, but slotted into a variety of positions as United established themselves as a First Division side. He had 88 League games to his credit by the time he joined Sunderland.

HORSFIELD Geoffrey Malcolm

Striker

Born: Barnsley, 1 November 1973.
6ft, 11st 7lb (2006).
Career: Scarborough apprentice, professional July 1992. Halifax Town March 1994. Witton Albion 1994. Halifax Town October 1996. Fulham

£325,000 September 1998. Birmingham City £2 million July 2000. Wigan Athletic £1 million September 2003. West Bromwich Albion £1 million December 2003. Sheffield United loan February–May 2006, £1.2 million May 2006–May 2008. LEEDS UNITED loan August 2006. Leicester City loan February–May 2007. Scunthorpe United loan January 2008.

■ Geoff arrived on a season-long loan as part of the deal that saw Rob Hulse sold to Sheffield United. He netted in his second game at Queen's Park Rangers and was sent off five days later at Crystal Palace. He found goals hard to come by in an injury-hit stay and returned to Bramall Lane after five months. Early in his career he worked on building sites while playing non-League football with Witton and Halifax, but worked hard at his game and became a million-pound player.

HOWARTH James Thomas

Centre-forward

Born: Bury, 15 April 1890.
Died: Rochdale, 20 September 1969.
5ft 8in, 12st (1922).
Career: Bury. Bristol City January 1914. LEEDS UNITED £1,750 March 1921. Bristol Rovers £500 November 1922. Lovells Athletic £750 May 1923, player-manager August 1923.

■ Tommy enjoyed a scoring debut for United, netting in a 1–1 draw against his home-town club, Bury. An all-action player with a reputation as a fiery customer, he first shot to prominence by scoring all Bristol City's goals in their run to the 1920 FA Cup semi-finals. He

joined Leeds the following year, receiving £460 of the £1,750 transfer fee, and was top scorer in 1921–22 before going to Bristol Rovers. He became player-manager at Lovells Athletic and steered them to the Western League Division Two title, making several appearances in goal. His son, Sid, played for Swansea Town, Merthyr Town, Aston Villa and Walsall.

HOWSON Jonathan

Midfield

Born: Morley, Leeds, 21 May 1988.
5ft 11in, 12st 1lb (2007).
Career: Morley Victoria Primary and Bruntcliffe High Schools. Churwell Lions. LEEDS UNITED School of Excellence, trainee July 2006.

■ One of the few shafts of light in the gloomy 2006–07 campaign was the emergence of local teenager Jonathan. He signed a three-year deal under Kevin Blackwell in September but did not make his debut until he was 18, when Dennis Wise gave him his chance in the 0–0 home draw with Hull just before Christmas. He was named United's Young Player of the Year in 2007–08, writing himself into Leeds folklore by scoring both goals at Carlisle in the League One Play-off semi-final – the winner coming in injury time – which saw the Whites overturn a 2–1 home deficit to grab a place at Wembley.

HUCKERBY Darren Carl

Forward

Born: Nottingham, 23 April 1976.
5ft 10in, 11st 12lb (1999).
Career: Lincoln City trainee 1992, professional July 1993. Newcastle United £400,000 November 1995. Millwall loan September 1996. Coventry City £1 million

November 1996. LEEDS UNITED £4 million August 1999. Manchester City £2.5 million December 2000. Nottingham Forest February 2003. Norwich City £750,000 September 2003–May 2008.

■ Lightning-quick England Under-21 international Darren destroyed United's defence with a hat-trick for Coventry in a 3–3 draw at Elland Road in April 1998. From that moment on, he became a Leeds target and the Whites got their man for £4 million the following year. Given the size of the fee, he was used surprisingly sparingly, and after 16 months spent mostly warming the bench, Darren moved on to Manchester City. Rejected as a kid by Notts County because he was too small, he scored within five minutes of his League debut for Lincoln at Shrewsbury after coming on as a 17-year-old substitute. Darren's peak form was at Coventry, where he was chosen for England B against Chile, and at Norwich, where he was in blistering form as Nigel Worthington's team stormed to the 2003–04 Championship title.

HUDSON William Albert

Right-winger

Born: Swansea, 10 March 1928.
5ft 8in, 10st 9lb (1951).
Career: Pembroke Dock. Manchester City trials. LEEDS UNITED May 1951. Sheffield United May 1952. Mansfield Town free May 1954.

■ Welsh amateur international Billy made his League debut in United's 2–1 home win over Cardiff after just one appearance in the reserves. After coming out of the Forces, he joined Pembroke Dock on the recommendation of his uncle, Albert, a former Fulham, Llanelli and Pembroke player. He was rejected by Manchester City after trials and within weeks became a Leeds player, but he did not make a lasting impression.

HUGHES Andrew John

Midfield/Full-back

Born: Manchester, 2 December 1978.
5ft 11in, 12st 1lb (2007).
Career: Oldham Athletic trainee, professional January 1996. Notts County £150,000 January 1998. Reading free July 2001. Norwich City £500,000 July 2005. LEEDS UNITED August 2007.

■ Busy midfielder Andy joined the Whites on a two-year deal after relegation from the Championship, and he impressed with his commitment. He also filled in at full-back and skippered the side on occasions during their 2007–08 League One campaign.

HUGHES Charles

Left-winger

Born: Manchester, 17 September 1927.
5ft 6½in, 9st 9lb (1950).
Career: Manchester United September 1946. Altrincham August 1950. LEEDS UNITED September 1950–52.

■ Former Manchester United junior Charlie was put straight into the Leeds first team after joining from Cheshire League side Altrincham. His debut came in a 2–2 home draw with Barnsley just a month after being released by the Old Trafford club. The left winger was also tried at left-back as cover for Grenville Hair for a few games.

HUGHES Philip Anthony

Goalkeeper

Born: Manchester, 19 November 1964.
5ft 11in, 12st 7lb (1985).
Career: Manchester United apprentice. LEEDS UNITED January 1983. Bury free June 1985. Wigan Athletic £35,000 November 1987. Scarborough free October 1991. Guiseley. Pontefract Collieries.

■ Leeds moved quickly to sign Phil when he was released by Manchester United after serving his apprenticeship. The Northern Ireland Youth international, qualifying via parentage, was unable to dislodge David Harvey and left for Bury. Two years later he won the first of his three full caps when he played at Wembley in a 3–0 European Championship qualifier.

HULSE Robert William

Forward

Born: Crewe, 25 October 1979.
6ft 1in, 11st 4lb (2005).
Career: Crewe Alexandra trainee, professional June 1998. West Bromwich Albion £750,000 August 2003. LEEDS UNITED loan February 2005, £800,000 May 2005. Sheffield United £2 million July 2006.

■ Rob was a popular striker during his short stay at Elland Road. He struck an instant rapport with the United fans thanks to a two-goal debut in a 3–1 home

win over Reading and it was not long before his loan deal with West Brom was converted into a cash move. He helped Leeds to the 2006 Championship Play-off Final against Watford at Cardiff, scoring a 12-minute hat-trick against Derby in the regulation season. That Final was his last Leeds appearance, as promoted Sheffield United moved in with a big bid to give him Premiership football. He suffered a double fracture of his left leg against Chelsea in March 2007 and was out for nine months.

HUMPHREYS Alan

Goalkeeper

Born: Chester, 18 October 1939.

5ft 11½in, 11st 5lb (1960).
Career: Overleigh School, Chester. Lache Youth Club. Shrewsbury Town October 1956. LEEDS UNITED February 1960. Gravesend & Northfleet July 1962. Mansfield Town January 1964. Chesterfield July 1968.

■ Highly promising Alan was rated as one of the best young goalkeepers in the country and was called up as reserve for the England Under-23 squad when he was at Elland Road. He had been a centre-half as a youngster but became a 'keeper before getting his big break with Shrewsbury. Alan did not fulfil his potential at Leeds but later spent five seasons at Mansfield and won a Division Four Championship medal with Chesterfield. He later worked as commercial manager for Derbyshire CCC.

HUMPHRIES William McCauley

Right-winger

Born: Belfast, 8 June 1936.
5ft 4½in, 9st 12lb (1958).
Career: Glentoran amateur. Ards. LEEDS UNITED £5,000 September 1958. Ards November 1959. Coventry City April 1962. Swansea Town £14,000 March 1965. Ards 1968. Bangor manager 1983–April 1985.

■ Leeds were the first club to recognise

Billy's talent but did not reap the full reward of his skills. He was a rugby scrum-half at school but also sparkled at football and played for Glentoran as an amateur while working as a clerical officer in the Belfast Transport Department. United beat Blackpool to his signature, but the little man did not really settle in Yorkshire and returned to Ireland to play for Ards. His second spell in English football was much happier, free-scoring from the wing with Coventry and making more than 100 appearances for Swansea. Willie won 14 Northern Ireland caps, none of them at Leeds, and also represented the Irish League eight times, winning an Irish Cup medal with Ards in 1969.

HUNTER Norman

Defender

Born: Eighton Banks, Co. Durham, 24 October 1943.
5ft 11½in, 12st 8lb (1973).
Career: Birtley Secondary Modern School. Birtley Juniors. Chester-le-Street. LEEDS UNITED apprentice November 1960, professional April 1961. Bristol City October 1976. Barnsley player-coach June 1979, manager September 1980–February 1984. West Bromwich Albion assistant manager. Rotherham United manager June 1985–December 1987. LEEDS UNITED coaching staff February 1988–October 1988. Bradford City assistant manager February 1989–February 1990.

■ Norman was one of the toughest competitors to pull on a Leeds shirt. The former electrical fitter certainly made the sparks fly with his tackling, prompting the popular phrase 'Norman Bites Yer Legs', but that reputation overshadowed the fact that he was an outstanding player. He did not look back after making his debut as a teenager in a 2–0 win at Swansea on 5 September 1962 and went on to be a bedrock of the Don Revie era. Norman was remarkably consistent, playing in five ever-present seasons during 14 years at Elland Road and featuring in all of United's League and Cup triumphs from 1965 to 1975, finishing with two League titles, FA Cup and League Cup-winners' medals, two Fairs Cup-

Norman Hunter

winners' medals and a Second Division Championship medal. The first Professional Footballers' Association Player of the Year in 1973, Norman won three England Under-23 caps and 28 at senior level and would have undoubtedly won many more but for the presence of England captain Bobby Moore. Norman was the first England player to be capped as a substitute when he came on against West Germany in September 1966. He also represented the Football League six times before his glorious reign at Leeds ended in October 1976 when he joined Bristol City. He then worked as a player-coach under Allan Clarke at Barnsley, taking over the hot seat when Clarke became Leeds boss. Norman took the Tykes into Division Two, held a variety of managerial and assistant roles, as well as a spell back at Leeds on the coaching staff. He retired in 1983 and ran a couple of sports shops, sold life insurance and became a summariser on BBC Radio Leeds in 1993.

HUNTINGTON Paul David

Central-defender

Born: Carlisle, 17 September 1987.
6ft 3in, 12st 8lb (2007).
Career: Trinity School, Cumbria. Newcastle United trainee, professional June 2005. LEEDS UNITED August 2007.

■ Former England Youth international Paul was snapped up from Premiership outfit Newcastle after Leeds were relegated to Division One. He marked his full debut for the Whites with the winner in a Johnstone's Paint Trophy tie at Darlington. He had to bide his time for a

first-team spot but took his chance while Rui Marques was on African Nations Cup Final duty with Angola.

HUTCHINSON George Henry

Forward

Born: Allerton Bywater, nr Castleford, 31 October 1929.
Died: Sheffield, August 1996.
5ft 8in, 10st 2lb (1955).
Career: Huddersfield Town amateur December 1946, professional January 1947. Sheffield United player-exchange March 1958. Tottenham Hotspur June 1955. Guildford City July 1954. LEEDS UNITED August 1955. Halifax Town July 1957.

■ George began with a flurry of goals for Leeds, including one on his debut in a 3–0 victory over Doncaster Rovers on 3 December 1955. After five goals in seven games his form tailed off, and he lost his place to George Meek and eventually moved to Halifax. Earlier he had left Huddersfield for Sheffield United in an exchange deal involving Albert Nightingale, who also became a Leeds player later in his career.

HYDES Arthur

Forward

Born: Barnsley, 24 November 1910.
Died: Barnsley, June 1990.
5ft 9in, 10st 6lb (1930).
Career: Central School, Barnsley amateur 1928. Southport trial May 1929. Ardsley Recreation. LEEDS UNITED May 1930. Newport County May 1938. York City, Exeter City, Nottingham Forest, Barnsley and Bradford City wartime guest. Exeter City February 1946.

■ Former toffee factory worker Arthur gave defences a sticky time during his eight years at Leeds. After arriving from amateurs Ardsley, the spiky-haired forward fired in a stack of goals in the reserves and scored United's goal in a 3–1 defeat at Blackburn when he made his debut as a 19-year-old. Aggressive and speedy, he was United's top scorer for three successive seasons from 1933 to 1936. His finest game came in the FA Cup third round, when his hat-trick at Newcastle gave Leeds a sparkling 3–0 win. Injuries left Arthur on the sidelines for a spell and he moved on to Newport, where he was a leading light in the County side that won the 1938–39 Division Three South title.

I

IGGLEDEN Horatio

Inside-forward

Born: Hull, 17 March 1925.
Died: Hull, 17 December 2003.
6ft, 11st 10lb (1951).
Career: Constable Street Old Boys, Hull.
Leicester City amateur July 1941,
professional March 1942. Grimsby Town
wartime guest. LEEDS UNITED player-
exchange December 1948. Exeter City July
1955. Goole Town 1956.

■ Former Royal Marine Ray arrived at
Elland Road from Leicester in an
exchange deal with Ken Chisholm.
United were certainly happy with their
part of the bargain as Ray's partnership
with winger Harold Williams was highly
effective. Ray, a former Hull dock worker,
was United's top scorer in 1951–52 and
grabbed a memorable hat-trick against
his old club, Leicester, in January 1954.
Strong in the air and the possessor of a
powerful shot, he scored exactly half a
century of goals for Leeds.

INGHAM Anthony

Half-back

Born: Harrogate, 18 February 1925.
5ft 11in, 11st 5lb (1950).

Career: Harrogate Hotspurs. LEEDS
UNITED April 1947. Queen's Park
Rangers £5,000 June 1950–May 1963, then
trainer, commercial manager and director.

■ Former electrical apprentice Tony was
captain and centre-half of amateur club
Harrogate Hotspurs before joining
United in summer 1947. He made just
three appearances before moving to
Queen's Park Rangers, where he became
one of the London club's all-time greats
after a successful conversion to left-back,
amassing a club record 548 appearances.
After retiring he had a spell as Queen's
Park Rangers' trainer, then commercial
manager and, after a spell as acting
secretary, joined the Queen's Park
Rangers board.

IRWIN Denis Joseph

Right-back

Born: Cork, Ireland, 31 October 1965.
5ft 8in, 11st (1983).
Career: Turners Cross College, Cork.
Ireland Schools. LEEDS UNITED
February 1982. Oldham Athletic £60,000
May 1986. Manchester United £625,000
June 1990. Wolverhampton Wanderers free
July 2002–May 2004.

■ Denis's premature departure from
Elland Road must rank as one of the
club's biggest mistakes. The neat and tidy
full-back looked to have a long Leeds
career ahead of him when he was
surprisingly sold to Oldham by Billy
Bremner and went on to become a
multi-medal winner at Manchester
United and a top-class Republic of
Ireland defender. Denis skippered the
juniors and reserves at Leeds before
breaking into the senior ranks and
already possessed Youth and Under-21
honours before his switch to Boundary
Park. He figured in the Oldham side
defeated in the 1990 Littlewoods Cup
Final but compensation lay in wait at
Old Trafford where he was a member of
the Red Devils' 1994 and 1996 double-
winning squad. Denis's medal haul also
included the Premiership in 1992–93,
European Cup-Winners' Cup in 1991,
FA Cup in 1995 and League Cup in 1992.
Cool, calm and collected, he featured in
Jack Charlton's 1994 World Cup side,
finishing his international career with 56
appearances. He now works as a
presenter on MUTV.

J

JACKLIN Harold

Goalkeeper

Born: Chesterfield, 8 March 1902.
Died: 1967.
5ft 11in, 11st 4lb (1925).
Career: Sheffield junior football. Blackpool 1919. LEEDS UNITED August 1920. Doncaster Rovers 1922–26.

■ Harold was the second-string goalkeeper for United's first two Football League seasons. He had won a Central League medal with Blackpool and spent the bulk of his time at Leeds in the reserves before sharing goalkeeping duties at Doncaster with another ex-Leeds man, David Russell.

JACKSON Mark Graham

Defender/Midfield

Born: Leeds, 30 September 1977.
6ft, 11st 12lb (1996).
Career: LEEDS UNITED trainee July 1995. Huddersfield Town loan October 1968. Barnsley loan January 2000. Scunthorpe United March 2000. Kidderminster Harriers February 2005. Rochdale £35,000 January 2006. Farsley Celtic June 2007.

■ England Youth international Mark was used as a defensive midfielder by George Graham, even though he was the regular junior and reserve centre-half.

He made his debut as an 18-year-old in the wake of United's disastrous Coca-Cola Cup Final defeat in 1996 and had a decent run in the side the following season. He was a useful centre-back at Scunthorpe, where he played 150 games.

JACKSON William

Left-winger

Born: Farnworth, Lancashire, 15 July 1902.
Died: Blackpool, November 1975.
5ft 8in, 11st 3lb (1925).
Career: Leyland. Altrincham 1922. Darwen 1923. Sunderland May 1924. LEEDS UNITED May 1925. West Ham United May 1927. Chelsea February 1928. Leicester City May 1931. Ashford Town loan 1932. Bristol Rovers May 1932. Cardiff City May 1934. Watford January 1935. Chorley 1935. Netherfield September 1936.

■ Two-footed winger Billy had itchy feet with a large number of clubs in a short space of time. His season at Leeds was one of his longer stops but for the most part he was a reserve at his other clubs in an 11-year career. His brother, Robert, was a Bury player.

JENNINGS Thomas Hamilton Oliver

Centre-forward

Born: Strathaven, Lanarkshire, 8 March 1925.
Died: Johnstone, 2 July 1973.
5ft 8in, 12st (1925).
Career: Strathaven Academy. Cadzow St Annes. Tottenham Hotspur trials. Raith Rovers January 1921. LEEDS UNITED March 1925. Chester June 1931. Bangor City manager. Third Lanark manager.

■ Tom held United's scoring records before John Charles burst on the scene. The Scot banged in 112 League goals for United, including a seasonal best of 35 in 1926–27 when he netted three successive hat-tricks – a feat equalled only by Liverpool's Jack Balmer in 1947 and West Brom's Gilbert Allsop in 1939. Despite Tom's deadly marksmanship, United

were relegated that season. Tom continued to score at a rapid rate and would have added to his tally but was laid low by bouts of blood poisoning. It was surprising that he did not get the nod from the Scottish selectors, although he played in a trial, scoring for the Anglo-Scots in a 1–1 draw with the Home Scots in March 1928. As a youngster he won a Scottish Juvenile Cup-winners' medal with Cadzow St Annes, but was rejected by Spurs after trials. Tom joined Raith, where his brother Charlie also played, and was a member of the Rovers team shipwrecked en route to the Canary Islands. After Leeds, Tom had a productive season with Chester before having a go at management.

JOACHIM Julian Kevin

Forward

Born: Boston, Lincolnshire, 20 September 1974.
5ft 6in, 12st 2lb (2004).
Career: Leicester City trainee July 1991, professional September 1992. Aston Villa £1.5 million February 1996. Coventry City July 2001. LEEDS UNITED free July 2004. Walsall loan March 2005. Boston United free August 2005. Darlington August 2006.

■ Julian had pace to burn as a young striker and could still turn on the speed

when he joined United after their relegation from the Premiership. He did not find goals easy to come by but found his touch when he dropped down a division when on loan at Walsall. Julian had burst on the scene as a teenager at Leicester, scoring a flurry of spectacular goals that earned him nine Under-21 caps to add to his England Youth honours. He won an European Under-18 Championship medal in 1993 and continued to shine after a big-money move to Villa.

JOBSON Richard

Defender

Born: Hull, 9 May 1963.
6ft 1in, 13st 5lb (1995).
Career: Birmingham City trials. Burton Albion. Watford £22,000 November 1982. Hull City £40,000 February 1985. Oldham Athletic £460,000 August 1990. LEEDS UNITED £1 million November 1995. Southend United loan January 1998. Manchester City free March 1998. Watford loan November 2000. Tranmere Rovers loan December 2000–February 2001

transfer March 2001. Tranmere Rovers free December 2000. Rochdale free September 2001, reserve team player-coach 2002, retiring 2003.

■ Richard, a £1 million signing from Oldham in 1990, managed just a dozen appearances before injury blocked his career at Leeds. Howard Wilkinson had tried to sign the defender the previous year, but the deal fell through because he had an ankle problem. Originally he played part-time with Burton Albion while studying for a civil engineering degree at Nottingham University. When Watford came in with a £22,000 offer for the English Universities player Richard turned pro, helping the Hornets to runners-up spot in Division One in his first full season. He gained a Second Division Championship medal with Oldham in 1991, and England manager Graham Taylor, who had sold him at Watford, called him up for the full England squad against Norway. Although Richard did not win a full cap he made a couple of starts for England B. After giving up playing he became chairman, then chief executive, of the PFA.

JOHANNESON Albert Louis

Left-winger

Born: Johannesburg, South Africa, 13 March 1942.
Died: Leeds, 29 September 1995.
5ft 7in, 10st 3lb (1969).
Career: Germiston Coloured School, Germiston Callies (South Africa). LEEDS UNITED trial January 1961, signing April 1961. York City July 1970–71.

■ Flying winger Albert was a twinkling star in the early days of the Revie era whose life ended in well-documented tragedy. Nicknamed 'Hurry, Hurry' in his native South Africa, he was recommended to Leeds by a school teacher and soon warmed to the task, despite arriving in Yorkshire at the height of winter 1961. The United staff were soon purring in admiration at his dazzling ball skills and blistering speed. Albert forced his way into the first team and was leading scorer when United swept to the 1964 Division Two title. The following year he became the first black player to feature in an FA Cup Final at Wembley when Leeds lost to Liverpool. The emergence of Eddie Gray – and Albert's increasing reliance on alcohol – gradually saw him nudged to the fringes of the action. 'The Black Flash', as Leeds fans called him, had a season at York before moving back to South Africa for a spell of coaching. He returned to Leeds where he lost his personal battle with the bottle and was found dead, aged 55, in his high-rise flat in Leeds in 1995. For United fans, the abiding memory of Albert will be of his explosive runs down the left wing. His nephew, Carl, became the British super-featherweight boxing champion in 2006.

JOHNSON Adam

Winger/Midfield

Born: Sunderland, 14 July 1987.
5ft 9in, 9st 11lb (2006).
Career: Middlesbrough trainee, professional May 2005. LEEDS UNITED loan October 2006. Watford loan September 2007.

■ England Under-19 winger Adam had a handful of games on loan from Middlesbrough, mainly during John Carver's interim spell as manager in 2006–07.

JOHNSON, Bradley Paul

Midfield/Left-Back

Born: Hackney, London, 28 April 1987.
6ft, 12st 10lb (2007).
Career: Cambridge United junior, professional November 2004. Northampton Town May 2005. Gravesend & Northfleet loan November 2006. LEEDS UNITED £250,000 January 2008.

■ In-demand youngster Bradley was snapped up by Dennis Wise from Northampton in the 2008 January transfer window. Talks took place on the eve of United's 3–0 home win over the Cobblers – a game Bradley sat out – and he made the switch to Elland Road a couple of days later.

JOHNSON Jemal Pierre

Forward

Born: Peterson, New Jersey, US, 3 May 1984.
5ft 8in, 11st 5lb (2006).
Career: Blackburn Rovers trainee, professional May 2002. Preston North End

loan October 2005. Darlington loan March 2006. Wolverhampton. Wanderers £100,000 August 2006. LEEDS UNITED loan March 2007. Milton Keynes Dons free August 2007.

■ American speedster Jemal was drafted in on loan from Wolves to add pace to United's heavy-legged attack, but his opportunities were few and far between as United spiralled towards Championship relegation.

JOHNSON Rodney

Centre-forward

Born: Leeds, 8 January 1945.
5ft 9in, 10st 12lb (1963).
Career: Cow Close School, Leeds. Leeds City Boys. Reading trials. LEEDS UNITED March 1962. Doncaster Rovers £5,000 March 1968. Rotherham United December 1970. Bradford City £9,000 December 1972. Chicago Sting (US) May 1975. Gainsborough Trinity July 1979. Garforth Town September 1982, later as coach.

■ Rod played in the successful Leeds Boys team that included Paul Madeley, Paul Reaney and Kevin Hector – who all went on to play for England. After an unsuccessful trial at Reading, Rod joined United, and England Youth honours followed, as well as an appearance for the English amateur side against Scotland in 1962. He made his Leeds debut the same year, when he scored and was carried off in a 2–0 win at Swansea. Despite his early credentials Rod could not keep a regular

first team berth and much of his career was spent in the lower divisions. At Doncaster he won a Fourth Division Championship medal and went on to skipper and coach Bradford City. He later worked as an insurance salesman after a season in America.

JOHNSON Seth Art Maurice

Midfield

Born: Birmingham, 12 March 1979.
5ft 10in, 11st (1999).
Career: Holmes Chapel Comprehensive School, Cheshire. Crewe Alexandra trainee, professional July 1996. Derby County £3 million May 1999. LEEDS UNITED £7 million October 2001. Derby County free August 2005–June 2007.

■ At the height of their lavish spending, United splashed out £7 million on aggressive Derby midfielder Seth. Unfortunately, the bulk of his four years at Leeds was spent on the treatment table and, with financial meltdown pending, Leeds allowed him to go back to the Rams on a free. His highlight at Leeds was scoring both goals in a 2–1 home win over Blackburn in October 2003. Seth had been well schooled at Dario Gradi's Crewe and Derby beat off competition from Liverpool to sign him in 1999. An England Under-21 regular, Seth won a full England cap as a substitute against Italy in November 2000, when Peter Taylor was temporarily in charge of the national team.

JOHNSON Simon Ainsley

Forward

Born: West Bromwich, 9 March 1983.
5ft 9in, 12st (2001).
Career: LEEDS UNITED trainee, professional July 2000. Hull City loan August 2002. Blackpool loan December 2003. Sunderland loan September 2004. Doncaster Rovers loan December 2004. Barnsley loan February 2005. Darlington free July 2005. Hereford United August 2007.

■ England Youth international Simon had a handful of outings for United, in which his blistering pace was an asset. He then became a bit of a loan ranger and was farmed out to five different clubs before securing a move to Darlington.

JOHNSON William

Goalkeeper

Born: Sheffield.
5ft 11in, 11st (1925).
Career: Sheffield junior football. Wombwell 1921. LEEDS UNITED May 1923. Chester June 1931. Bangor City. Crewe Alexandra September 1933.

■ Goalkeeper Bill spent eight seasons at Elland Road, mostly in the reserves, making his debut in a 1–0 win at Southampton in the 1924 Second Division Championship-winning season. His progress was checked when he ruptured a kidney against Sheffield United in November that year. He recovered to play in 29 of United's first 30 Division One games in 1925–26 before losing his place to Jimmy Potts.

JONES Alfred

Right-back

Born: Liverpool, 2 March 1937.
5ft 8in, 12st 6lb (1960).
Career: Cow Close School, Leeds. Leeds City Boys. Reading trials. Marine. LEEDS UNITED April 1960. Lincoln City £4,000 June 1962. Wigan Athletic 1967. Horwich RMI 1968.

■ Alf turned professional on the day he completed his national service with the Royal Army Medical Corps at Crookham after playing as an amateur in United's North Midlands Combination side. Most of his Leeds first-team games were at right-back, and he was first choice at Lincoln for five seasons. After giving up the full-time game he worked in a car factory.

JONES Matthew Graham

Midfield

Born: Llanelli, 1 September 1980.
5ft 11in, 11st 5lb (2000).
Career: LEEDS UNITED trainee, professional September 1997. Leicester City £3.25 million December 2000–May 2003. Llanelli September 2007.

■ Fate dealt Matthew a rough hand after his big-money move from Leeds to Leicester. Recommended by former United goalkeeper Glan Letheran, he joined Leeds' junior ranks at 12 and was an FA Youth Cup winner in 1997. The Welsh Youth international proved a

sharp-tackling, energetic midfielder and considering that he made just 11 Premiership starts, his move to the Foxes was good business for Leeds. He suffered from injuries to his knees and back, forcing him to quit at the age of just 23. His last competitive match was for Wales against US in May 2003 – it was an unlucky 13th cap, as he was sent off. Five of those caps were won as a Leeds player. Matthew also made seven Under-21 appearances and one at B level. A TV pundit, he started a comeback with his home-town club in 2007.

JONES Michael David

Centre-forward

Born: Worksop, 24 April 1945.
5ft 10in, 11st 9lb (1969).
Career: Priory Primary School, Worksop. Worksop Boys. Rotherham Boys. Dinnington Miners' Welfare. Sheffield United November 1962. LEEDS UNITED £100,000 September 1967–October 1975.

■ Three England caps were scant reward for all the effort Mick put into the game. His partnership with Allan Clarke was deadly, with Mick's strength, aggression and aerial power being the perfect foil for Clarke's rapier-like finishing skills. Mick excelled as a child, once scoring 14 goals in a school game, and he was working in a cycle factory when he joined Sheffield United. He won nine England Under-23 international caps and played twice for the full national team in May 1965 before

being discarded. Two years later he became Leeds' first £100,000 purchase and featured in the Whites' major triumphs of the period, winning two League Championships and two Fairs Cups. He was one of the heroes of the FA Cup Final victory over Arsenal when he laid on the winner for Clarke. In the dying minutes he damaged a shoulder and Norman Hunter had to lead him up to the Royal Box with his arm in a sling to receive his winners' medal. Mick's form earned him an England recall against Holland, but he was not required again after the 0–0 draw. After United's second title success he suffered a serious knee injury, which brought a premature end to his career. He then had his own shop selling sportswear before running a market stall selling sports clothing with his son.

JONES Vincent Peter

Midfield

Born: Watford, 5 January 1965.
5ft 11in, 11st 10lb (1989).
Career: Wealdstone. Wimbledon £10,000 November 1986. LEEDS UNITED £650,000 June 1989. Sheffield United £700,000 September 1990. Chelsea £575,000 August 1991. Wimbledon £700,000 September 1992. Queen's Park Rangers £500,000 March 1998, assistant manager August 1998, retiring March 1999.

■ Hard-man Vinnie became a cult figure in United's Second Division Championship winning season in 1989–90. Dubbed 'Psycho' by the national media, he arrived at Leeds with a notorious reputation for his aggressive tackling. Conference side Wealdstone first spotted the hod carrier's potential as a ball-winning midfielder in parks football and he went on to join Wimbledon, where he was an integral part of the 'Crazy Gang' culture. A member of the Dons' side that stunned Liverpool in the 1988 FA Cup Final, he joined Leeds the following year. The

sensational transfer proved to be a clever move by Howard Wilkinson as Vinnie's presence in the team galvanised the Elland Road fans. The possessor of a prodigiously long throw, Vinnie weighed in with some useful goals before the arrival of Gary McAllister saw him move on. He later played for Wales nine times, qualifying through his grandparents. He had the briefest of spells as assistant manager to Mick Harford at Queen's Park Rangers but left to pursue a career in movies after his successful film debut in *Lock, Stock and Two Smoking Barrels*.

JORDAN Joseph

Centre-forward

Born: Carluke, Lanarkshire, 15 December 1951.
6ft, 11st 3lb (1973).
Career: St Aidan's School, Wishaw. Blantyre Victoria. West Bromwich Albion trials. Greenock Morton October 1968. LEEDS UNITED £15,000 October 1970. Manchester United £350,000 January 1978. AC Milan (Italy) £325,000 July 1981. Verona (Italy) 1983. Southampton £100,000 August 1984. Bristol City February 1987, assistant player-manager November 1987, manager March 1988–June 1990. Heart of Midlothian manager September 1990–May 1993.

Celtic assistant manager June 1993. Stoke City manager November 1993–September 1994. Bristol City manager November 1994–March 1997. Huddersfield Town assistant manager and coach December 2000–May 2002. Southampton coach. Portsmouth coach, caretaker manager November 2004 and December 2005.

■ Joe was a superb successor to Mick Jones as leader of the United attack. An 18-year-old recruit from Morton, he was the recommendation of old Leeds favourite Bobby Collins, who was manager of the Greenock club. Joe gave up his job in an architect's office to be a pro footballer. Strong and brave, he was an unselfish and inspirational leader. His toothless grin earned him the nickname 'Jaws' and his development continued apace with his first Scottish cap in 1973. The following year he became a national hero when his goal against Czechoslovakia took Scotland to the World Cup Finals. Joe, who won 52 full caps and one at Under-23 level, collected a League Championship medal and played in the 1975 European Cup Final with Leeds before a record fee of £350,000 took him to Manchester United. He entered management with Bristol City, taking over from former Leeds teammate Terry Cooper, and took the Robins to the Littlewood Cup semi-finals in 1989 and promotion from the Third Division the following year.

K

KAMARA Christopher

Midfield

Born: Middlesbrough, 25 December 1957.
6ft 1in, 12st (1989).
Career: St Thomas's School, Middlesbrough. Portsmouth apprentice January 1976, professional January 1976. Swindon Town £20,000 August 1977. Portsmouth £50,000 August 1981. Brentford player-exchange October 1981. Swindon Town August 1985. Stoke City July 1998. LEEDS UNITED £150,000 January 1990. Luton Town £150,000 November 1991. Sheffield United loan December 1992. Middlesbrough loan February 1993. Sheffield United free June 1993. Bradford City player-assistant manager July 1994, manager March 1996–January 1998. Stoke City manager January–April 1998.

■ United snatched experienced Chris from under the noses of Middlesbrough to help propel them towards their 1990 Division Two title triumph. The midfielder seemed all set to join his home-town club but instead the former Teesside dockyard apprentice made the switch to Leeds. The bulk of his career was as a journeyman footballer but he had a stab at management at Bradford City. Within two months of being appointed manager, Chris led the Paraders out at Wembley in the Division Two Play-off Final against Notts County. He then had a nightmare 12-week spell in charge at Stoke before becoming a Sky TV presenter and analyst.

KANDOL Tresor Osmar

Forward

Born: Banga, DR Congo, 30 August 1981.
6ft 2in, 11st 7lb (2006).
Career: Luton Town trainee, professional September 2001. Cambridge United August 2001. Heybridge Swifts loan September 2001. Bournemouth October 2001. Thurrock August 2003. Dagenham & Redbridge May 2005. Darlington loan November 2005. Barnet £50,000 January 2006. LEEDS UNITED loan November 2006–January 2007, £200,000 January 2007.

■ After a flurry of goals for Barnet, Tresor was a surprise signing by Dennis Wise and marked his home debut with a goal in a 2–2 draw with Barnsley. When his loan spell was up, United struck a deal with the North London club. Kandol lost his way after breaking through with his first club, Luton, but he was a prolific scorer in non-League football. His form in 2007–08 earned him a call-up to the DR Congo squad.

KANE Robert

Centre-half

Born: Cambuslang, Lanarkshire, 17 July 1911.
Died: Cambuslang, January 1985.
5ft 11½in, 11st 10lb (1946).
Career: Rutherglen Rosebank. St Rochs. LEEDS UNITED August 1935–May 1947. Hibernian wartime football.

■ Bertie was one of the few players to turn out for United either side of the war. Although he was provisionally signed by Celtic in 1934–35 he remained with Scottish Central League side St Rochs, from whom he joined Leeds. Groomed as a successor to Jock McDougall, he battled it out with Tom Holley for the number-five shirt. During the war he served with the Royal Artillery in Gibraltar and Finnarts Bay, near Stranraer. He retired in 1947 and returned to Cambuslang to work in a Hoover factory.

KEANE Robert David

Forward

Born: Dublin, 8 July 1980.
5ft 9in, 11st 10lb (1946).
Career: Crumlin United. Fettercairn (trial). Wolverhampton Wanderers trainee June 1996, professional July 1997. Coventry City £6 million August 1999. Inter Milan (Italy) £13 million July 2000. LEEDS UNITED loan December 2000, £12 million May 2001. Tottenham Hotspur £7 million August 2002.

■ Many Leeds fans were disappointed when Republic of Ireland striker Robbie was sold at a £5 million loss to Spurs. With his trademark somersault goal celebration, he had been a popular, if underused, player at Elland Road. Two goals on his debut as a 17-year-old for Wolves marked him out as star material, and a year later he became his country's youngest-ever goalscorer and is now Eire's all-time best marksman. In-demand Robbie moved for huge fees and his energy helped United to the Champions League semi-finals before finances dictated that he be sold. At Spurs he captained both club and country and has proved one of Tottenham's most

highly regarded players in recent decades, scoring more than 100 goals for the White Hart Lane side.

KEETLEY Charles Frederick

Centre-forward

Born: Derby, 10 March 1906.
Died: 1979.
5ft 9in, 12st (1946).
Career: Alvaston & Boulton. LEEDS UNITED July 1927. Bradford City October 1934. Reading June 1935.

■ Former Rolls-Royce foundry worker Charlie was the youngest of a set of Derby brothers who played League football between the wars. Nine of his 10 brothers played for the same Victoria Ironworks team, but Charlie was at Alvaston & Boulton, where he hammered in 80 goals in 1926–27, triggering a move to Elland Road. He learned a lot from Tom Jennings and put it to good use in the reserves, scoring seven goals in a Central League game against Bolton. Charlie, nicknamed Wag, made a scoring debut in Division Two and finished the 1927–28 promotion

season with 18 goals from only 16 starts. He topped the club's scoring charts for three successive years and was reserve for the Football League against the Irish League in September 1932. He later returned to foundry life and also ran pubs in Derby and Chellaston. Of his brothers, Frank, Harold, Joe and Tom all played for Doncaster. Frank also aided Derby, while Albert played for Burton United, Jack assisted Hull City and Arthur was on Tottenham's books.

KELLY Dominic

Centre-half

Born: Sandbach, Cheshire, 23 June 1917.
6ft 1in, 13st (1943).
Career: Selsdon Wanderers. Sandbach Ramblers. LEEDS UNITED September 1935. Newcastle United £1,165 November 1938–March 1946.

■ Of Irish descent, Dom was one of three Kellys – including John 'Mick' – who played for Leeds in the 1930s. Tall and strong in the air, Dom was unable to dislodge Tom Holley after joining from Sandbach and moved on to Newcastle. He served in the Middle East during the war and played plenty of services football. Ligament damage ended his football career and he joined the Newcastle police force.

KELLY Gary Oliver

Right-back

Born: Drogheda, Ireland, 9 July 1974.
5ft 8in, 11st 8lb (2006).
Career: Home Farm. LEEDS UNITED July 1991–May 2007.

■ From struggling reserve-team front man to World Cup full-back – that was Gary's remarkable rise in 1993–94. The youngest of a family of 13, he was signed from Dublin club Home Farm and pitched into first-team action as a 17-year-old substitute winger in a League Cup tie against Scunthorpe with only 15 minutes of reserve-team football under his belt. Apart from brief substitute appearances, he did not re-emerge until the start of the 1993–94 season, when Howard Wilkinson fielded him at right-back on the opening day at Manchester City. Gary's blinding speed and tenacity made him a daunting opponent for any

winger and he matured so rapidly that within months Jack Charlton took him to the 1994 World Cup Finals. Gary netted in a 2–0 Ireland win in Germany before opening his Leeds account but the one-club man, a rarity in the modern game, went on to top 500 games, even though he missed all of the 1998–99 season with shin splints. The holder of 52 Irish caps, Gary gained a deserved club testimonial against Celtic at Elland Road. He donated the proceeds to build a cancer hospice in his homeland, which he later opened, after the disease claimed the life of his sister. He often played in the same Leeds team as his nephew, Ian Harte.

KELLY Jack

Centre-forward

Born: Hetton-le-Hole, nr Sunderland, 2 March 1913.
Died: Hetton-le-Hole, nr Sunderland, 1997.
5ft 8in, 11st 8lb (1934).
Career: Hetton Juniors. Burnley amateur October 1930, professional October 1931. Newcastle United April 1933. LEEDS UNITED £1,150 February 1935. Birmingham January 1938. Bury May 1939.

■ Former butcher's assistant Jack was a proven marksman in Central League football with Leeds and formed a useful partnership with the experienced George Brown before going to Birmingham. A part-time magician, his individual style meant he did not find it easy to pull first-team goals out of a hat at his other clubs.

KELLY John 'Mick'

Centre-forward

Born: Sandbach, Cheshire, c.1913.
5ft 10½in, 12st (1933).
Career: Accrington Stanley. LEEDS UNITED 1933. Barnsley October 1935. Bedford Town 1935–36.

■ 'Mick' was added to John's name to distinguish him from his United namesake Jack Kelly. He arrived from Accrington with a reputation as a free-scoring forward and netted more than 50 Central League and Yorkshire Midweek League goals for Leeds, but could not translate that form to the first team. During the war he served in the Irish Guards.

KEMP John

Left-winger

Born: Clydebank, 11 April 1934.
5ft 6in, 9st 10lb (1957).
Career: Clyde. LEEDS UNITED December 1957. Barrow March 1959. Crewe Alexandra December 1963.

■ John's stay at Leeds was not the happiest. He broke a bone in a foot and his only senior game was a disastrous 4–0 home defeat at the hands of Manchester City in February 1959. The following month he was transferred to Barrow, where he played 170 League games.

KENNEDY David

Centre-half

Born: Sunderland, 30 November 1950.
6ft ½in, 12st (1970).
Career: LEEDS UNITED apprentice, professional May 1968. Lincoln City free July 1971–September 1972.

■ Rookie centre-half David scored United's only goal in an infamous 4–1 defeat at Derby on Easter Monday 1970, when United fielded a reserve side and were fined £5,000. He also scored on his Lincoln debut at Stockport.

KENTON, Darren Edward

Central-defender/Full-back
Born: Wandsworth, London, 13 September 1978.
5ft 10in, 11st 11lb (2007).
Career: Norwich City trainee then professional July 1997. Southampton May

2003. Leicester City loan March–May 2005, transfer July 2006. LEEDS UNITED loan, signed January 2008–May 2008.

■ Experienced Darren worked with Leeds boss Dennis Wise at both Southampton and Leicester, and the pair linked up briefly at Elland Road before Wise's decision to join Newcastle. Darren initially arrived on loan as cover for Rui Marques, who was on African Nations Cup duty with Angola, but the deal was made permanent before the January transfer window closed.

KEOGH Andrew Declan

Forward

Born: Dublin, 16 May 1986.
6ft, 11st 7lb (2004).
Career: LEEDS UNITED from trainee May 2003. Scunthorpe United loan August 2004. Bury loan January 2005. Scunthorpe United £50,000 March 2005. Wolverhampton Wanderers £600,000 January 2007.

■ Academy product Andy's only taste of senior football with Leeds was as a substitute in a 2–1 Carling Cup defeat at Portsmouth in October 2004. His sale to Scunthorpe included cash sell-on clauses, and the Republic of Ireland Under-21 international's goals helped shoot the Iron to promotion to League One in 2006. He earned a move to Wolves, United receiving £100,000 from the deal. He made his first full Eire appearance against Ecuador in New York after another former Leeds junior, Caleb Folan, pulled out of the squad.

KERFOOT Eric

Wing-half

Born: Ashton-under-Lyne, Lancashire, 31 July 1924.
Died: 1980.
5ft 9in, 10st 7lb (1951).
Career: Stalybridge Celtic. LEEDS UNITED December 1949. Chesterfield July 1959.

■ Eric took to Second Division football like a duck to water after joining from non-League football. He was 25 when he turned pro, having built an excellent reputation at Stalybridge. Leeds bid £3,000 for Eric – £1,000 more than Bradford City – and he proved a snip. After just one Central League game he made his full debut and became one of United's most consistent players, featuring in four ever-present seasons including the 1955–56 promotion campaign. He had a spell as skipper before moving to Chesterfield, where he was among 23 professionals released in summer 1960 after a poor season. He later ran a pub in Duckinfield.

KERR Dylan

Left-back

Born: Valletta, Malta, 14 January 1967.
5ft 11in, 12st 5lb (1933).
Career: Doncaster Rovers. Sheffield Wednesday from YTS August 1984. Arcadia Shepherds (South Africa). LEEDS UNITED non-contract December 1988, transfer February 1989. Doncaster Rovers loan August 1991. Blackpool loan December 1991. Reading £75,000 July 1993. Carlisle United October 1996. Kilmarnock October 1996. Slough Town June 2000. Kidderminster Harriers September 2000. Clydebank November 2000. Hamilton Academicals January 2001. Exeter City August 2001. Greenock Morton October 2001. Harrogate Town September 2002. East Stirlingshire trial January 2003. Hamilton Academicals February 2003– May 2003. Kilmarnock youth coach. Kilwinning Rangers February 2005. West Valley United (US) youth coach. Argyll and Bute Council's Football Development Officer July 2005.

■ Although born in Malta, Dylan learned his soccer at Maple Road School in Mexborough, South Yorkshire. He had a great left foot and provided useful cover for Tony Dorigo. A real football traveller, his long-range goals contributed to Reading's Division Two Championship success in 1994. He won the Scottish Cup with Kilmarnock in 1997.

KERSLAKE David

Right-back

Born: Stepney, London, 19 June 1966.
5ft 8in, 11st (1993).

Career: East London, Inner London, London District and England Schools. Queen's Park Rangers amateur, schoolboy forms June 1982, professional June 1983. Swindon Town November 1989. LEEDS UNITED £500,000 March 1993. Tottenham Hotspur £450,000 September 1993. Swindon Town loan November 1996. Ipswich Town August 1997. Wycombe Wanderers loan December 1997. Swindon Town March 1998–June 1999. Tottenham Hotspur Academy coach. Northampton Town reserve-team manager 2002. Nottingham Forest assistant manager May 2006.

■ With right-back Mel Sterland facing a lengthy lay-off because of injury, Leeds turned to former England Under-21 international David to fill the vacancy. However, injury curtailed his season and he was released after only six months at Elland Road, United taking a £50,000 loss when he joined Tottenham. He started with Queen's Park Rangers and was capped at Youth, Under-19 and Under-21 level before working under Glenn Hoddle at Swindon.

KEWELL Harold

Forward/Winger

Born: Smithfield, Sydney, Australia, 22 September 1978.
6ft, 11st 10lb (1993).
Career: Smithfield Public School, Sydney. New South Wales Soccer Academy. LEEDS UNITED December 1995. Liverpool £5m July 2003–May 2008.

■ Howard Wilkinson pulled off a

masterstroke when he snapped up young Aussie Harry from the New South Wales Soccer Academy just before Christmas 1995. The youngster broke into the Leeds senior side as a left wing-back and was an integral part of the United side that won the 1997 Youth Cup. He made his international debut against Chile after just two Premiership appearances and his career took off after he switched to an attacking role. Instant control, dribbling skills at speed and fierce shooting marked him out as a star on the rise. His sensational form saw him named PFA Young Player of the Year in 2000 and he continued to sparkle in United's Champions League and UEFA Cup campaigns. But as Leeds went into decline the Wizard of Oz's form dipped – partly as a result of injuries – and he left the club in acrimonious circumstances involving a row over his agent's cut of the transfer fee to Liverpool. He continued to battle against injuries at Anfield but won 2005 Champions League and 2006 FA Cup-winners' medals despite limping off in both games. The best player to come out of Australia, Harry played in the 2006 World Cup Finals. He is married to *Emmerdale* soap star Sheree Murphy.

KILFORD John Douglas

Forward/Winger

Born: Derby, 18 November 1938.
5ft 10½in, 12st 6lb (1961).
Career: Stainsby House School, Smalley. Derby Corinthians. Notts County

amateur, professional July 1957. LEEDS UNITED February 1959. Tonbridge 1962.

■ John was ordained into the church after his playing days, which included a stint at Leeds. He worked at a Burton brewery while playing as an amateur with Notts County before joining Leeds and skippering the reserves from full-back. Unable to keep a regular first team place, he joined ex-Leeds players Gerry Francis and Alan Shackleton at non-League Tonbridge. After working as an estate agent's wages clerk he went to Oak Hill Theology College in 1973 and entered the ministry.

KILGALLON Matthew Shaun

Centre-back

Born: York, 8 January 1984.
6ft 1in, 12st 4lb (2006).
Career: Tadcaster Grammar and North Yorkshire Schools. LEEDS UNITED trainee, professional January 2001. West Ham United loan August 2003. Sheffield United £1.75 million rising to £2 million January 2007.

■ Battling centre-back Matthew was one of the few bright spots to emerge in United's 2003–04 relegation season and he continued to develop in the Championship. The Under-21 international, dubbed 'Killer', added speed to a creaking Leeds backline and enjoyed a few forays forward, playing a handful of games at left-back, including the Play-off Final against Watford at Cardiff in 2006. Linked with a move to promoted Sheffield United, he eventually joined the Blades in January 2007.

KILKENNY, Neil Martin

Midfield

Born: Enfield, London, 19 December 1985.
5ft 8in, 10st 8lb (2008).
Career: Arsenal trainee. Birmingham City January 2004. Oldham Athletic loan January 2004 and August 2007. LEEDS UNITED £150,000 January 2008.

■ Just four days after helping Oldham become the first side to end United's unbeaten League One home record on New Year's Day 2008, midfielder Neil signed a three-and-a-half year deal with Leeds. He had done well in two loan spells with the Latics but struggled to nail a first==team place at parent club Birmingham where he was sent off for handball on his full home debut against Liverpool. Although born in London, Neil was raised in Brisbane, Australia, and won a full international cap for the Aussies when he came on as a substitute in the 3–1 2006 World Cup warm-up win over Liechtenstein. He hss also played four times for the Under-21s and featured in the Australian Olyroos team in their 2008 Bejing Olympics qualifying campaign.

KING Marlon Francis

Striker

Born: Dulwich, 26 April 1980.
6ft 1in, 11st 12lb (2006).
Career: Barnet trainee, professional September 1998. Gillingham £225,000 June 2000. Nottingham Forest £950,000 November 2003. LEEDS UNITED loan March 2005. Watford £500,000 July 2005. Wigan Athletic £5m January 2008.

■ Powerful Nottingham Forest striker Marlon was utilised as a wide player during a rather unproductive loan spell towards the end of 2004–05 by Kevin Blackwell. In the summer he joined Watford, immediately hit the kind of goalscoring form he had shown early in his career at Gillingham, and helped to fire the Hornets to the Premiership. He was in the Watford side that hammered Leeds 3–0 in the 2006 Championship Play-off at Cardiff.

KIRBY Dennis

Left-half

Born: Holbeck, Leeds, 8 November 1924.
Career: LEEDS UNITED September 1942. Shrewsbury Town loan August 1948. Scarborough loan October 1948. Halifax Town August 1950. Stalybridge Celtic.

■ International Schoolboy player Dennis appeared in a few wartime games for Leeds and featured in the 1947–48 League season. His career did not develop and he later worked as a milkman and ran fish-and-chip and fruit-and-veg shops. He was a brother-in-law of David Cochrane.

KIRK Roy

Wing-half

Born: Shuttlewood, Derbyshire, 11 June 1929.
Died: 1983.
5ft 9½in, 11st 9½lb (1951).
Career: Bolsover Colliery. LEEDS UNITED October 1948. Coventry City £10,000 March 1953. Cambridge United player-coach 1960. Cambridge City manager 1967.

■ Blooded in the Yorkshire Midweek League, Roy figured at centre-half, centre-forward, right-half and outside-right in the United senior side. That versatility may have worked against him as he settled in well as Coventry's regular centre-back, playing 329 League games in eight seasons. At Highfield Road he had the unwanted distinction of scoring two own goals in a 2–2 draw with Leyton Orient on 20 September 1954.

KIRKPATRICK James Maxwell

Left-back

Born: Annan, Dumfriesshire, 7 December 1901.
5ft 7in, 11st (1924).

Career: Annan. Queen of the South. Solway Star September 1921. Workington 1922. LEEDS UNITED £150 May 1924. Watford free June 1927. Solway Star August 1928–29.

■ Jim proved a capable deputy to Bill Menzies in the 1920s First Division days after arriving from North Eastern League side Workington. His elder brother, John, played up front with Workington and Accrington Stanley.

KISHISHEV Radostin Prodanov

Midfield

Born: Burgas, Bulgaria, 30 July 1974. 5ft 10in, 12st 4lb (2006). Career: Neftokhimik Burgas (Bulgaria). Bursapor (Bulgaria) August 1997. Liteks Lovech (Bulgaria) August 1999. Charlton Athletic £300,000 August 2000. LEEDS UNITED loan March 2007. Leicester City June 2007. LEEDS UNITED loan October 2007–January 2008.

■ Radostin, winner of 63 Bulgarian caps, brought much-needed class to United's

midfield towards the end of the dreadful 2006–07 season. He arrived on loan from Charlton and although he helped improve performances United could not avoid the drop. He returned the following season for another loan spell. Radostin topped 150 games for Charlton and figured in his country's campaigns in Euro 96 and the 1998 World Cup Finals.

KNARVIK Tommy

Midfield

Born: Bergen, Norway, 1 November 1979. 5ft 7in, 11st (2000). Career: Skjergard (Norway) August 1992. LEEDS UNITED June 1997. SK Brann (Norway) May 2000. Bryne (Norway) loan 2004. Sogndal (Norway) 2005. Sandefjord (Norway) 2006. Tromso (Norway) November 2007.

■ Norwegian Youth and Under-21 international Tommy's brief taste of United action came as a substitute in a

5–1 FA Cup win at Portsmouth. He returned home in 2000 and was converted to striker by Brann in his home-town of Bergen.

KORSTEN Willem

Winger/Forward

Born: Boxtel, Holland, 21 January 1975. 6ft 3in, 12st 10lb (1999). Career: NEC Nijmegen (Holland). Vitesse Arnhem (Holland) August 1993. LEEDS UNITED loan January 1998. Tottenham Hotspur £1.5 million May 1999–October 2001. NEC Nijmegen coach 2002.

■ Tall, former Dutch Under-21 winger-cum-striker Willem did well with Leeds after being snapped up on a three-month loan. A £1.5 million deal was almost complete when the player turned down the move and opted to join Spurs. But he suffered badly from injuries at White Hart Lane and had to retire at the age of 26, becoming a Dutch TV reporter on the Premiership.

L

LAMBERT John

Centre-forward

Born: Greasborough, nr Rotherham, 25 May 1902.
Died: Enfield, London, December 1940.
5ft 9in, 12st 6lb (1928).
Career: Methley Perseverence. Sheffield Wednesday trial. LEEDS UNITED November 1922. Rotherham County. Doncaster Rovers December 1924. Arsenal £2,000 June 1926. Fulham £2,500 October 1933. Margate player-manager.

■ Jack's goalscoring talents slipped through United's fingers. He played once for Leeds, in a 2–0 defeat at Leicester on 8 September 1923. He went to Rotherham County but the League ordered him to return to Elland Road and fined County heavily for poaching Jack. But it was at Arsenal where he made his name, scoring 95 goals in 146 games, including 32 when Arsenal won the Championship in 1930–31. He also netted one of the goals as the Gunners beat Huddersfield in the 1930 FA Cup Final. Jack was on the Arsenal coaching staff when he died, aged just 36, as a result of injuries sustained in a road accident in North London.

LAMPH Thomas

Right-half

Born: Gateshead, 16 November 1892.
Died: Leeds, 24 February 1926.
5ft 9½in, 11st (1921).
Career: Pelaw United. Spennymoor United. LEEDS CITY May 1914. Manchester City £800 October 1919. Derby County March 1920. LEEDS UNITED February 1921.

■ Tommy and Ivan Sharpe are the only two players to play for both Leeds City and United. Tommy represented the North Eastern League against the Southern and Central Leagues in his early days and made a handful of City appearances before being auctioned to Manchester City. He returned to Elland Road via Derby but retired in 1922 through ill health and died, aged 32, in February 1926.

LANGLEY Ernest James

Left-back

Born: Kilburn, London, 7 February 1929.
Died: Ruislip, 9 December 2007.
5ft 9½in, 11st 5lb (1957).
Career: Evelyns Yiewsley Senior School, Kilburn. Yiewsley. Hounslow. Uxbridge. Hayes. Brentford 1946. Guildford City 1949. LEEDS UNITED June 1952. Brighton & Hove Albion July 1953. Fulham £12,000 February 1957. Queen's Park Rangers July 1965. Hillingdon Borough manager September 1967. Crystal Palace trainer-coach August 1971.

■ Jim rose from second team left-winger with Leeds to England full-back. Highly regarded as an amateur player, he joined United after his army service but did not blossom as a top-class defender until he joined Brighton, where he won an England B cap while a Third Division player. At Fulham he was World Cup winner George Cohen's full-back partner and won three England caps. Jim was 37 when he won a League Cup-winners' and Third Division Championship medals with Queen's Park Rangers and returned to Wembley as manager of Hillington in the 1971 FA Trophy Final. He was later steward at West Drayton British Legion Club in Middlesex.

LAURENT Pierre

Winger

Born: Tulle, France, 13 December 1970.
5ft 10in, 9st 12lb (1996).

Career: ESA Brive (France) 1990. Bastia (France) 1994. LEEDS UNITED £250,000 March 1997. Bastia (France) £250,000 January 1998. Strasbourg (France) July 2002, retired 2003.

■ Leeds fans hardly got a glimpse of French winger Pierre, who struggled to handle the highly charged Premiership atmosphere and returned to Corsica after eight months.

LAWSON Frederick Ian

Forward

Born: Onslow, Co. Durham, 24 March 1939.
5ft 11in, 11st 8lb (1963).
Career: Pelton and Durham Schools. Burnley March 1956. LEEDS UNITED £20,000 March 1962. Crystal Palace £9,000 June 1965. Port Vale August 1966. Barnsley August 1967.

■ England Youth international Ian's first game for Leeds at Huddersfield on 3 March 1962 was player-manager Don Revie's last. He had made a sensational impact as a teenager at Burnley, scoring four goals on his debut in a 7–0 landslide over Chesterfield in the League Cup and a hat-trick three weeks later as New Brighton were slaughtered 9–0. Ian played his part in the 1963–64 Second Division title success, scoring 11 goals, but did not feature much in the top flight.

LENNON Aaron Justin

Right-winger

Born: Leeds, 16 April 1987.
5ft 5in, 9st 12lb (2004).
Career: LEEDS UNITED trainee,
professional August 2003. Tottenham
Hotspur £1 million July 2005.

■ Leeds fans could only dream of what might have been if they had been able to hold onto local lad Aaron. A remarkable talent, he became the youngest Premiership player at the time when he featured as a substitute for United at Tottenham, aged just 16 years 129 days. The following season he netted on his first Championship start – a 3–2 win at champions Sunderland on Boxing Day 2004. With Leeds up to their necks in a cash crisis it was soon clear they would have to sell their little gem. Spurs won the scramble to sign the jet-heeled winger, who was soon tearing Premiership defences to shreds with his fabulous skills. He shot through the Under-19, Under-21 and England B ranks to full international honours and featured in the 2006 World Cup campaign.

LETHERAN Glan

Goalkeeper

Born: Llanelli, 1 May 1956.
6ft 1½in, 12st 4lb (1977).
Career: Llanelli. LEEDS UNITED May
1973. Scunthorpe United loan August
1976. Notts County September 1977.
Chesterfield £10,000 December 1977.
Swansea City £50,000 September 1979.
Oxford City. Scarborough. Bangor City.
Swansea goalkeeping coach 1998–October

2001. St Kitts & Nevis, St Vincent and Haiti coach. LEEDS UNITED scout 1992–98. Wales women's manager January 1997. Wales FA coach. Southampton scout. Swansea City goalkeeping coach May 2002. Leicester City goalkeeping coach July 2004.

■ Welsh Youth international Glan became an overnight hero after a match-winning debut in a UEFA Cup tie. With David Harvey injured, United went to Hibernian after a goalless first leg, with reserve John Shaw as first choice and teenager Glan on the bench. Shaw was injured and Letheran came on to keep a clean sheet and survived a penalty shoot-out as Leeds squeezed through 5–4. The holder of two Under-21 caps, he made just one League appearance before joining Chesterfield. Glan played at Wembley for Bangor City in the 1984 FA Trophy Final against Northwich and was later goalkeeping coach at Swansea, a scout for Leeds and had a spell coaching in the West Indies. His son, Kyle, a Welsh Under-21 international, has played for Swansea and Barnsley.

LEWIS Edward James

Left-winger

Born: Cerritos, US, 17 May 1974.

5ft 11in, 11st 2lb (2006).
Career: Cerritos High School and UCLA (US). San Jose Clash (US) 1996. Fulham £1.3 million March 2000. Preston North End September 2002. LEEDS UNITED free July 2005. Derby County August 2007.

■ Multi-capped American international Eddie was a key member of the Leeds squad which reached the 2006 Championship Play-off. He produced some stunning free-kick goals from the left-wing berth and went to his second World Cup in Germany in the summer. United rejected a bid from Wolves before the start of the 2006–07 season and when Dennis Wise was appointed United manager Eddie was temporarily switched to left-back, where he had played a few times for his country. He later moved back into the Premiership with Derby County.

LIDDELL Gary

Forward

Born: Bannockburn, Stirlingshire, 27 August 1954.
5ft 9in, 9st 12lb (1975).
Career: St Modan's High School, Stirling. LEEDS UNITED apprentice, professional September 1971. Grimsby Town March 1977. Heart of Midlothian February 1981. Doncaster Rovers March 1982–83.

■ Gary went to the same school as Billy Bremner and came through United's youth ranks to play a smattering of games in the mid-1970s. He later played under Bremner at Doncaster. Gary's son, Andy, a Scottish Under-21 international, has played with Barnsley, Wigan, Sheffield United and Oldham.

LILLEY Derek Symon

Forward

Born: Paisley, 9 February 1974.
5ft 11in, 12st 7lb (1975).
Career: Everton Boys Club August 1990. Greenock Morton August 1991. LEEDS UNITED £500,000 March 1997. Heart of Midlothian loan December 1998–February 1999. Bury loan March 1999–April 1999. Oxford United £75,000 August 1999. Dundee United £75,000 December 2000. Livingston free July 2003. Greenock Morton June 2005. St Johnstone January 2007. Stirling Albion July 2007. Forfar May 2008.

■ Scottish Youth international Derek struggled to adapt to the English game after being signed from Morton for £500,000 by George Graham. He arrived from the Greenock club as a 23-year-old with more than half a century of goals under his belt, but his only one for Leeds was a late winner at Barnsley as United came from 2–0 down to claim a 3–2 victory. Back in Scotland he went on to top 100 SL goals and win a League Cup-winners' medal with Livingston.

LINIGHAN Andrew

Centre-half

Born: Hartlepool, 18 June 1962.
6ft 4in, 13st 7lb (1985).
Career: Durham Boys. Smiths Boys Club. Smiths Dock. Hartlepool United free September 1980. LEEDS UNITED £20,000 May 1984. Oldham Athletic £65,000 January 1986. Norwich City £350,000 March 1988. Arsenal £1.25 million July 1990. Crystal Palace £150,000 January 1997. Queen's Park Rangers loan March 1999. Oxford United October 2000–May 2001. St Albans June 2001. Oxford United youth coach.

■ Former Hartlepool Council plumber Andy plugged a big gap in United's central defence during Eddie Gray's first spell as manager and was an ever present in his maiden season. But Andy, one of the tallest men to play for Leeds, was transferred by Billy Bremner to Oldham, where he was joined by United clubmates Denis Irwin, Tommy Wright and Andy Ritchie. Linighan shone at all his clubs and became an England B international but took time to win over the fans at Highbury. However,

he became the toast of the North Bank when he netted Arsenal's late FA Cup Final replay extra-time winner against Sheffield Wednesday in 1993. Andy came from a football family, making his debut for Hartlepool with brother David, who also had trials with Leeds in March 1985 before starring with Ipswich. Their dad, Brian, played for Darlington as well as their uncle, Michael, and twin brothers Brian and John joined Sheffield Wednesday. Andy started his own plumbing business in 2001 after his spell at St Albans.

LOMAS Albert

Goalkeeper

Born: Tyldesley, nr Bolton, 14 October 1924.
Career: Bolton Wanderers amateur. LEEDS UNITED September 1948. Mossley 1949. Rochdale May 1950. Chesterfield July 1951. Wigan Athletic 1952.

■ Albert was one of four goalkeepers used in 1948–49, his only appearance coming in a 3–1 defeat at home to West Brom on 2 October 1948.

LONGDEN Eric

Inside-right

Born: Goldthorpe, nr Rotherham, 18 May 1904.
Died: Blackpool, 7 September 1983.
5ft 11½in, 12st 4lb (1930).
Career: Goldthorpe United. Doncaster Rovers March 1926. LEEDS UNITED January 1929. Hull City October 1930. Blackpool January 1931. Hull City December 1932–April 1935.

■ Eric was among the most powerful tacklers of his day and weighed in with his share of goals. He moved on after the emergence of Billy Furness and won a Third Division North winners' medal in his second spell at Hull.

LORIMER Peter Patrick

Forward/Midfield

Born: Broughty Ferry, Dundee, 14 December 1946.
Career: Eastern and Stobswell Schools. Dundee Schools. Broughty YMCA. LEEDS UNITED amateur May 1962, professional December 1963. Cape Town City (South Africa) guest 1969. Toronto Blizzard

(Canada) £25,000 March 1979. York City September 1979. Vancouver Whitecaps (Canada) player-manager March 1980. LEEDS UNITED December 1983. Whitby Town December 1985. Hapoel Haifa (Israel) player-coach.

■ Peter's sledgehammer shooting terrorised defences for the best part of 20 years. He is the only player to have scored more than 200 goals for Leeds and is also the club's youngest debutant. Don Revie was in such a hurry to sign the Scottish teenager that he was stopped for speeding on his way north of the border. But Revie beat off a stack of other clubs to sign the young goal machine who had scored 176 goals in a season for his school team. Peter was just 15 years, 289 days old when he made his debut against Southampton in a Second Division game on 29 September 1962, and the Scottish Schools international won amateur caps on a tour of Kenya before turning pro on his 17th birthday. Peter was largely used on the right flank, but his ability to cut in and take a pot-shot at goal spelled trouble for opposition defences – his shot had been measured at a staggering 90 miles an hour. Goals and domestic honours flowed in equal measure while Peter's return of 21 full caps and two at Under-23 level should have been greater. He did enjoy a fine World Cup in 1974 and, after a spell in Canada and a season at York, rejoined United in December 1983. He was 37 at the time and older than his manager, Eddie Gray, but played a key

role in midfield, helping to nurture a talented crop of players. Peter overtook John Charles' goalscoring record in that second coming at Elland Road before being moved on by Gray's replacement, Billy Bremner. He went on to run the Commercial pub in Leeds and became a United board member in March 2004.

LUCAS David Anthony

Goalkeeper

Born: Preston, 23 November 1977.
6ft 2in, 13st 3lb (2007).
Career: Preston North End December 1994. Darlington loan December 1995 and October–November 1996. Scunthorpe United loan December 1996–February 1997. Sheffield Wednesday loans October–November 2003 and December 2003–February 2004, £100,000 June 2004–May 2006. Barnsley January 2007. LEEDS UNITED September 2007.

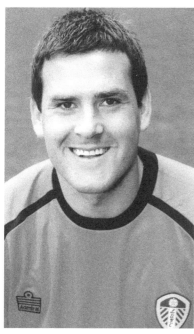

■ David, a former England Youth international, had more than 200 League games under his belt – mostly with home-town club Preston – when he arrived as cover for Casper Ankergren.

LUCIC Teddy

Defender

Born: Biskopsgaard, Sweden, 15 April 1973.
6ft 1in, 11st 10lb (2002).

Career: Vasta Froluda (Sweden). Lundby (Sweden). Gothenburg (Sweden) August 1995. Bologna (Italy) August 1998. AIK Solna (Sweden) August 1999. LEEDS UNITED loan August 2002. Bayer Leverkusen (Germany) May 2003. Hacken (Sweden) July 2005. IF Elfsborg (Sweden) January 2008.

■ Experienced Swedish international defender Teddy spent a season on loan at Elland Road after appearing in the 2002 World Cup Finals. He proved a versatile performer capable of playing right across the back four and in 2006 took his total of full caps beyond the 80 mark.

LUKIC Jovan

Goalkeeper

Born: Chesterfield, 11 December 1960.
6ft 4in, 13st 7lb (1982).
Career: Old Hall Junior and Newbold Green Secondary schools. Chesterfield and Derbyshire Schools. LEEDS UNITED December 1978. Arsenal July 1983 £125,000. LEEDS UNITED £1 million May 1990. Arsenal July 1996–2000.

■ John topped 400 appearances for Leeds in two spells with the club. He learned his trade at Elland Road under David Harvey, and after breaking into the League side at Brighton in October 1979 he went on to make a club record 146 successive League games. His run ended when he asked for a transfer and was promptly dropped.

Arsenal took him to Highbury, where he won a 1988–89 Championship medal and a 1987 League Cup-winners' medal. John won Youth and Under-21 honours but did not gain a full cap. Howard Wilkinson brought John back to Leeds and was rewarded as his goalkeeper had a magnificent season when United won the League title in 1991–92. He then went back to Arsenal and spent some time as the Gunners' goalkeeping coach.

LUMSDEN James

Inside-forward

Born: Glasgow, 7 November 1947.
5ft 5in, 12st 7lb (1970).
Career: Kinning Park. Glasgow Schools. LEEDS UNITED November 1964. Southend United September 1970. Greenock Morton 1971. St Mirren December 1972. Cork Hibernians 1973. Greenock Morton November 1973. Clydebank 1975. Celtic youth-team coach. LEEDS UNITED assistant manager July 1982–October 1985. Rochdale assistant manager December 1986–December 1987. Bristol City assistant manager, manager September 1990–February 1992. Preston North End first-team coach July 2000. Everton first-team coach May 2002.

■ Opportunities at Leeds were few and far between for Jimmy, but he forged a healthy career in the game. He was Eddie Gray's managerial assistant at Elland Road in the 1980s and the pair also teamed up at Rochdale. Jimmy also assisted Joe Jordan at Bristol City and took over as manager at Ashton Gate when Joe took the manager's job at Hearts.

LYDON George Michael

Left-winger

Born: Sunderland, 5 November 1933.
5ft 8½in, 10st 7½lb (1957).
Career: St Bennet's School, Sunderland. Sunderland and Durham County Boys. Hylton Juniors. Sunderland December 1950. LEEDS UNITED June 1954. Gateshead November 1955.

▪ Micky enjoyed an outstanding schoolboy career and won two England Youth caps in 1959. The following year he joined

Sunderland from Durham junior football but did not make the first team and joined United. First-team opportunities were slim at Leeds, but he made more than 100 League appearances for Gateshead.

LYON John

Inside-left

Born: Prescot, Lancashire, 3 November 1893.
5ft 9in, 11st 10lb (1920).
Career: Prescot. Hull City October 1913. LEEDS UNITED £300 July 1920. Prescot 1921. New Brighton August 1921. Mold August 1924. Prescot 1926.

▪ Jack was a relatively expensive signing who made a useful contribution to the 1920–21 season. He won a Welsh

Championship medal with Mold in 1924–25. Jack's elder brother, Sam, played for Prescot, Hull and Burnley.

M

McADAM David Frederick

Half-back

Born: Hereford, 3 April 1923.
5ft 9½in, 10st 4lb (1949).
Career: Abingdon School, Berkshire. Army football. Stapenhill WMC. LEEDS UNITED May 1948. Wrexham May 1950. Burton Albion 1951. Matlock Town 1959. Stapenhill WMC.

■ David was plucked from non-League football by Major Frank Buckley and enjoyed a brief spell with Leeds. He joined the army in 1941, serving with the 1st Battalion Wiltshire Regiment in India, Burma and on the North-West Frontier. David played a lot of services football, and on demob in September 1946 he worked at Branston Ordnance Depot, near Burton, playing for nearby Stapenhill. He was quickly elevated to the United first team but did not last the course and moved on to Wrexham.

McADAMS William John

Centre-forward

Born: Manchester, 20 January 1931.
Died: Barrow, 13 October 2002.
5ft 9½in, 11st 7lb (1959).
Career: Grosvenor Secondary School, Belfast. Bainbridge Town. Glenavon. Distillery. Manchester City £10,000 December 1953. Bolton Wanderers £15,000 September 1960. LEEDS UNITED December 1961. Brentford £8,000 July 1962. Queen's Park Rangers £5,000 September 1964. Barrow £5,000 July 1964. Netherfield.

■ The phrase 'luck of the Irish' hardly applied to Billy, who spent just seven months at Elland Road. The former apprentice heating engineer was the first player from Northern Ireland to move to an English club for a five-figure fee. He missed successive FA Cup Finals with Manchester City and Bolton through injury but rejoined old City teammate Don Revie, who needed someone to boost United's shot-shy attack. The move did not work out and Billy, who suffered from illness a lot during his career, soon moved on. He won his 15th and final cap at Leeds, and his international highlight

was a hat-trick against West Germany in a game the Irish lost. He died after a battle against cancer, aged 71.

McALLISTER Gary

Midfield

Born: Motherwell, 25 December 1964.
5ft 10in, 10st 1lb (1995).
Career: Fir Park Boys' Club. Motherwell 1981. Leicester City £250,000 August 1985. LEEDS UNITED £1 million July 1990. Coventry City £3 million July 1996, Liverpool free July 2000. Coventry City free player-manager April 2002–January 2004. LEEDS UNITED manager January 2008.

■ Playmaker Gary was an articulate and intelligent figure in six seasons at Elland Road. After United won the Second Division, Howard Wilkinson invested £1 million in the rising Leicester City star to add to the midfield mix with Gordon Strachan, David Batty and Gary Speed. The international quartet were at the hub of some superb football as United pipped arch rivals Manchester United to the 1991–92 Championship. Gary's wonderful range of passing and long-range shooting stamped him as one of Europe's best creative midfielders. He captained his country and won the vast majority of his 57 caps as a Leeds player. He arrived from Leicester after rejecting a £1.15 million move to Nottingham Forest, because he was unimpressed by Brian Clough's blunt

approach. Forest's loss was United's gain. He later had two spells at Coventry, the second as player-manager, and a highly successful time at Liverpool in the autumn of his career, winning the FA Cup, League Cup, UEFA Cup and European Super Cup in 2001. He returned to Elland Road as manager within days of predecessor Dennis Wise joining Newcastle (See Leeds City and United managers) and took United to the League One Play-off Final.

McCABE James Joseph

Half-back

Born: Draperstown, nr Derry, 17 September 1918.
Died: Cleveland, July 1989.
5ft 10in, 11st 10lb (1951).
Career: Billingham Synthonia Juniors. South Bank East End. Middlesbrough May 1937. LEEDS UNITED £10,000 and player-exchange March 1948. Peterborough May 1954.

■ Jim could fill a variety of positions but his best displays were at wing-half. He missed a huge slice of his career to the war, serving with the Green Howards in France and the Middle East. He arrived from Middlesbrough, with goalkeeper John Hodgson going in the opposite direction. Within months of going to Leeds, Jim won the first of six Irish caps and topped 150 appearances before moving to Peterborough.

McCALL Andrew

Inside-forward

Born: Hamilton, Lanarkshire, 15 March 1925.
5ft 6in, 9st 6lb (1954).
Career: Woodside School, Hamilton. Bent Royal Oak PSA. Blantyre Celtic. Blackpool April 1947. West Bromwich Albion January 1951. LEEDS UNITED August 1952. Lovells Athletic 1955. Halifax Town July 1956–61.

■ Andy, father of Scottish international Stuart, spent three seasons with Leeds in the mid-1950s. He served with both the Royal Navy and the army during the war before joining Blantyre Celtic and won a Scottish Junior cap against Ireland. At

Blackpool he played between the two great Stanleys – Matthews and Mortensen – and was an effective performer with United. Andy was among those who received treatment for burns as a result of the tragic Valley Parade fire in 1986.

McCLELLAND John

Centre-half

Born: Belfast, 7 December 1955.
6ft 2in, 13st 5lb (1989).
Career: Portadown. Cardiff City February 1974. Bangor City free 1975. Mansfield Town £8,000 May 1978. Glasgow Rangers £90,000 May 1981. Watford £225,000 November 1984. LEEDS UNITED £100,000 June 1989. Watford loan January 1990. Notts County loan March 1992. St Johnstone player-coach 1992, acting player-manager December 1992–November 1993. Carrick Rangers. Arbroath. Wycombe Wanderers non-contract February 1994. Yeovil Town non-contract March 1994. Doncaster Rovers coach January 1995–June 1995. Farsley Celtic August 1995. Bradford City assistant manager March 1996. Darlington October 1996.

■ Injury restricted distinguished Northern Ireland international John to just 22 League starts. The square-shouldered defender utilised his vast experience to out-manoeuvre quicker, younger players during his time at Elland Road, where he won the last of his 53 Irish caps. He played for a plethora of clubs, most notably Watford and Rangers. John played in the 1982 and 1986 World Cups and represented the Football League against the Rest of the World at Wembley in August 1987. At Bradford City he was assistant to Chris Kamara, then broke a leg on his only appearance for Darlington and now hosts tours of Elland Road.

McCLUSKEY George McKinlay Cassidy

Forward

Born: Hamilton, Lanarkshire, 19 September 1957.
5ft 11in, 12st (1985).
Career: St Catherine's Secondary School, Uddingston. Holy Cross, Hamilton. Celtic Boys Club 1968. Thorniwood loan 1973. Celtic July 1974. LEEDS UNITED July 1983–May 1986. Hibernian June 1986. Hamilton Academicals September 1989–May 1992. Kilmarnock July 1992, player-coach August 1994. Clyde October 1994.

■ Super-skilled George was a major hit with Celtic, but he could not produce the goods on a regular basis for Leeds. He won five Scottish Schools caps and four at Youth level before scoring the Hoops' winner against Rangers in the 1980 Scottish Cup Final. Capped seven times by the Under-21s, he was in the provisional squad of 40 for the 1982 World Cup but was never capped at senior level. At Elland Road he showed superb touch but found it difficult to adapt to the speed and aggression of the English game. He is now a taxi driver in Glasgow.

McCOLE John

Centre-forward

Born: Gorbals, Glasgow, 18 September 1936.
Died: Gweedore, Donegal, Ireland, 1982.
5ft 10½in, 11st 9lb (1960).
Career: Vale of Leven. Falkirk 1956. Bradford City September 1958. LEEDS UNITED £10,000 September 1959. Bradford City October 1961. New York Rangers (US) 1962. Rotherham United December 1962. Shelbourne 1963. Newport County October 1964. Cork Hibernians February 1965. Dundalk. US football.

■ John is the only United player to have scored four goals in a League Cup tie, achieving the feat against Brentford in September 1961. He maintained an excellent scoring record at Leeds but his 22 League goals in 1959–60 were not enough to save United from relegation to Division Two. His time at Elland Road was sandwiched between spells at Bradford City, and his career in England was ended by a broken leg with Rotherham in 1963.

McCONNELL Peter

Half-back/Inside-forward

Born: Reddish, nr Stockport, 3 March 1937.
5ft 9in, 11st 9lb (1961).
Career: North Reddish Primary, Stockport Grammar, Stockport and Cheshire

Schools. LEEDS UNITED March 1954. Carlisle United August 1962. Bradford City July 1969. Scarborough player-coach 1971.

■ Peter was a 15-year-old triallist running the line in a first team versus reserves match when one of the players was injured and he was given the opportunity to show what he could do. He earned a pro contract and spent over eight years at Elland Road, mainly on the fringes, before going to Carlisle where former Leeds trainer Ivor Powell was in charge. He made more than 300 appearances for the Cumbrians, skippering them to the Third Division title in 1964–65. After a spell as player-coach at Scarborough he became a licensee.

McDONALD Robert Wood

Left-back

Born: Aberdeen, 13 April 1955.
5ft 10in, 12st 1lb (1987).
Career: King Street Sports Club, Aberdeen. Aston Villa 1971, professional 1972. Coventry City £40,000 August 1976. Manchester City £270,000 October 1980. Oxford United September 1983. LEEDS UNITED loan February 1987, transfer £25,000 March 1987. Wolverhampton Wanderers February 1988–May 1988. VS Rugby 1988. Burton Albion 1989. Nuneaton Borough September 1989. Worcester City October 1990. Sutton Coldfield Town January 1991. Armitage Town 1991. Redditch United 1992.

■ Elland Road was just one port of call for the vastly experienced Bobby, who

amassed 500 appearances in his career. He possessed a cultured left foot but injury restricted his progress in a white shirt. A Scottish Schools and Youth international, he played in the 1972 Little World Cup, with Frank Gray and Kenny Burns among his teammates. He won a League Cup-winners' medal with Villa in 1975, made 161 consecutive appearances for Manchester City and helped Oxford win successive promotions to the First Division. After helping Billy Bremner's side to the Play-offs he was loaned to Wolves but injuries ended his pro career. He's since worked for the Scottish Ambulance Service and as a TV rigger.

McDOUGALL John

Centre-half

Born: Port Glasgow, Renfrewshire, 21 September 1901.
Died: Port Glasgow, Renfrewshire, 26 September 1973.
5ft 11in, 12st 4lb (1925).
Career: Kilmalcolm Amateurs. Port Glasgow Juniors. Airdrie November 1921. Sunderland £4,500 May 1929. LEEDS UNITED £6,000 November 1934–37.

■ Scottish international stopper Jock saw out his career at Elland Road. The former Clydeside marine engineer was strong, solid and reliable, choosing Leeds above Plymouth after both clubs bid for the Sunderland skipper. Vastly experienced, Jock was a Scottish Cup winner with Airdrie in 1924 and played against Northern Ireland two years

later before racking up 167 League appearances for the Rokerites. His younger brother, Jimmy, also played for Liverpool, Partick Thistle and Scotland.

McGEE John

Right-back

Born: Rothesay, Isle of Bute, Scotland, 13 July 1896.
5ft 11in, 12st 6lb (1920).
Career: Bute Comrades. LEEDS UNITED 1920. Harrogate 1921. Hull City £200 March 1922–27.

■ Jock did not play League football for United but featured in the FA Cup extra preliminary-round tie against Boothtown in 1920, which Leeds won 5–2. Ironically it was a broken leg in an FA Cup tie against Wolves seven years later, when he was a Hull player, that ended his career. During World War One he played military football for RFA Battery and moved to Yorkshire when his family found work on the estate of Lord Furness at Grantley, near Ripon.

McGHIE William Lambert

Forward

Born: Lanark, 19 January 1958.
5ft 9in, 11st 8lb (1977).
Career: Doncaster Boys. Arsenal trials. LEEDS UNITED apprentice, professional January 1976. York City £5,000 December 1979–November 1981. Boldspilkclub (Denmark).

■ Bushy-haired Scottish Youth international Billy scored within 19 minutes of his League debut for United,

an Allan Clarke penalty sealing a 2–1 victory over Ipswich on 16 April 1977. He had been preparing to travel with the reserves to Bury when Jimmy Armfield handed him a shock debut. Billy, whose family moved to Yorkshire when he was four, broke a leg in a reserve game against Bolton and moved on to York on the recommendation of Peter Lorimer.

McGINLEY William David

Midfield

Born: Dumfries, 12 November 1954.
5ft 5½in, 9st 10lb (1972).
Career: LEEDS UNITED apprentice, professional January 1972. Huddersfield Town September 1974. Bradford City June 1975. Crewe Alexandra August 1977.

■ Both of Billy's Leeds appearances were as a substitute, coming on in a 2–1 defeat at Birmingham on 30 April 1973, and a 6–1 UEFA Cup home win against Norwegian side Stroemgodset five months later.

McGOLDRICK John

Right-back

Born: Coatbridge, Lanarkshire, 23 September 1963.
5ft 11in, 10st 7lb (1983).
Career: Celtic Boys Club. Celtic. LEEDS UNITED free June 1983. Motherwell free July 1985.

■ John was unlucky enough to make his Leeds debut on one of the most humiliating nights in the club's history – the League Cup defeat to bottom-of-the-league Chester. Never a regular, he moved back to Scotland with Motherwell but a persistent knee injury, first incurred as a reserve at Celtic, forced him to retire. He then joined a car dealership.

McGOVERN John Prescott

Midfield

Born: Montrose, 28 October 1949.
5ft 10in, 10st 13lb (1983).
Career: Hartlepools United apprentice, professional May 1967. Derby County £7,500 September 1968. LEEDS UNITED August 1974. Nottingham Forest February 1975. Bolton Wanderers player-manager June 1982–January 1985. Horwich RMI February 1985. Chorley assistant manager December 1989, manager March 1990. Plymouth Argyle assistant manager March 1992. Rotherham United joint manager September 1994–September 1996. Woking manager June 1997–September 1998. Hull City assistant manager November 1998–April 2000. Ilkeston Town manager October 2000–March 2001.

■ Brian Clough signing John inherited the number-four shirt worn by Billy Bremner during the Leeds skipper's lengthy suspension following his dismissal in the 1974 Charity Shield at Wembley. John failed to show his true form during Clough's short, turbulent reign at Elland Road and was no doubt relieved to rejoin his old mentor at

Nottingham Forest, captaining them to two European Cup successes. Clough first signed John at Hartlepools and followed him to Derby. At just 19 he had appeared in all four divisions, and he played a key role in the Derby team that pipped Leeds to the 1971–72 Championship. He arrived at Leeds with John O'Hare for a joint fee of £125,000, but after Clough's departure both found themselves on the fringes. At Forest he also won the League title in 1977–78 and League Cup in 1978 and 1979. John is a pundit on BBC Radio Nottingham.

McGREGOR John Reid

Midfield/Defender

Born: Airdrie, Lanarkshire, 5 January 1963.
5ft 11in, 12st (1986).
Career: Airdrie Academy. Queen's Park. Liverpool June 1982. St Mirren loan April 1984. LEEDS UNITED loan October 1985. Glasgow Rangers £70,000 June 1987, then reserve-team coach until February 2003.

■ Despite being bought and sold by Liverpool, John's only taste of League football was during a month's loan with Leeds. He won a Scottish League Cup-winners' medal in his first season at Rangers, where he joined the coaching staff after a knee injury ended his career.

McGUGAN John Hannah

Centre-half

Born: Airdrie, Lanarkshire, 12 June 1939.
5ft 10½in, 11st 11½lb (1960).
Career: Pollok. St Mirren 1956. LEEDS UNITED £15,000 August 1960. Tranmere Rovers £12,000 February 1961. Cambridge City.

■ Injuries restricted Jackie to just one game during his six months at Elland Road. At St Mirren he won a Scottish Cup-winners' medal in 1959 and was capped at Under-23 level. He joined Leeds after going on tour with Scotland to Austria, Hungary and Turkey, but did not get a senior cap. Tranmere paid a record fee to sign Jackie from Leeds. He later ran a pub in Cambridge.

McINROY Albert

Goalkeeper

Born: Walton-le-Dale, nr Preston, 23 April 1901.

Died: Houghton-le-Spring, Co. Durham, 7 January 1985.

5ft 11in, 13st (1935).

Career: St Thomas School, Preston. Upper Walton 1919. Great Harwood. High Walton. Coppull Central. Preston North End amateur 1921–22. Great Harwood. Leyland November 1922. Sunderland May 1923. Newcastle United £2,750 October 1929. Sunderland June 1934. LEEDS UNITED May 1935. Gateshead June 1937–39.

■ Although already a veteran, Albert turned in some high-class displays between the sticks for Leeds. He was a relatively late starter, working as a packer at Preston Co-op while playing local football as a winger. It was not until he donned the goalkeeping jersey that he really caught the attention and joined Sunderland, where he was first choice for six years, winning an England cap against Northern Ireland in 1926. At Newcastle he won an FA Cup-winners' medal in 1932, before a second spell at Sunderland. He was 34 when he arrived at Elland Road but had lost none of his daring and agility. A real dressing room comic, he later ran a pub in Houghton-le-Spring.

McKENNA Frank

Centre-forward

Born: Blaydon, Newcastle upon Tyne, 8 January 1933.

5ft 9in, 11st 10lb (1956).

Career: North Shields. Bishop Auckland. LEEDS UNITED July 1956. Carlisle United February 1958. Hartlepools United July 1959. North Shields 1960. Gateshead 1962.

■ An outstanding amateur player, Frank enjoyed a two-goal debut for Leeds against his native Newcastle. Four goals in six League appearances was not enough to earn him a protracted stay at Elland Road and he moved on to Carlisle after 15 months. A joiner by trade, he starred in the Northern League and was in the Bishop Auckland side that beat Corinthian Casuals in the 1956 FA Amateur Cup Final. Frank also won three England amateur caps and played for Great Britain in an Olympic Games preliminary round match against Bulgaria.

McKENZIE Duncan

Forward

Born: Grimsby, 10 June 1950.

5ft 8in, 11st 3lb (1975).

Career: Old Clee Junior School, Grimsby. Notre Dame. Old Clee. Nottingham Forest apprentice July 1967, professional June 1968. Mansfield Town loan March 1970 and February 1973. LEEDS UNITED £240,000 August 1974. Anderlecht (Belgium) £200,000 June 1976. Everton £200,000 December 1976. Chelsea £165,000 September 1978. Blackburn Rovers £80,000 March 1969–May 1981. Tulsa Roughnecks (US) June 1981. Chicago Sting (US) May 1982. Warrington Sunday League. Bulova (Hong Kong) June 1983. Everton Football in the Community officer.

■ Brian Clough did not win too many friends during his brief managerial stay at Leeds but Duncan was one of his legacies. The showman striker was idolised by Leeds fans during his two

seasons in a white shirt. His stunning skills helped him score some brilliant solo goals and his individualistic approach provided supporters with something different after the more rigid approach of the Revie era. Highly athletic, he once arranged to jump over a Mini car at Elland Road – a stunt which further endeared him to fans. Top scorer in 1975–76, he scored 150 goals for 10 clubs worldwide and was on the England substitute's bench for the 1973–74 Home Internationals after topping the Second Division scoring charts with Forest. Duncan is an accomplished after-dinner speaker.

McMASTER Jamie

Forward/Midfield

Born: Sydney, Australia, 29 November 1982.

5ft 10in, 11st 13lb (2004).

Career: Westfield High School. Umina United (Australia). Australian National Institute of Sport. LEEDS UNITED trainee, professional November 1999. Coventry City loan November 2002. Chesterfield loan January 2004. Swindon Town loan September 2004. Peterborough United loan January 2005. Chesterfield free March 2005. Aarhus (Denmark) July 2005. Central Coast Mariners (Australia) 2005–07.

■ United picked up young Aussie talent Jamie as a 16-year-old and brought him through the Academy ranks. He won England Youth honours, but injuries held him back and he rarely figured in the Leeds first-team picture. After a series of loans he was released by Kevin Blackwell for a breach of discipline.

McMORRAN Edward James

Inside-forward

Born: Larne, 2 September 1923.
Died: Larne, 27 January 1984.
5ft 11½in, 13st (1949).
Career: Larne School. Ballyclare. Larne Olympic. Belfast Celtic. Manchester City £7,000 July 1947. LEEDS UNITED January 1949. Barnsley £10,000 July 1950. Doncaster Rovers £8,000 February 1953. Crewe Alexandra November 1957. Frickley Colliery 1958. Dodsworth Miners' Welfare coach August 1960.

■ One-time blacksmith Eddie forged a football career which included an 18-month stint at Elland Road. He shot to prominence at Belfast Celtic, scoring 60 goals in 1945–46. After the war he won an Irish Cup-winners' medal and was capped against England, triggering a move to Manchester City. He did not show his best form with Leeds and none of his 15 caps were won while a United player, although he rediscovered his touch after moving to Barnsley.

McNAB Neil

Midfield

Born: Greenock, 4 June 1957.
5ft 7in, 10st 10b (1982).
Career: Greenock and Scotland Schools. Greenock Morton. Tottenham Hotspur £40,000 amateur February 1974, professional June 1974. Bolton Wanderers £250,000 November 1978. Brighton & Hove Albion £220,000 February 1980. LEEDS UNITED loan December 1982.

Portsmouth loan March 1983. Manchester City £30,000 July 1983. Tranmere Rovers £125,000 January 1990. Huddersfield Town loan January 1992. Ayr United August 1993. Darlington September 1993. Derry City 1993. Witton Albion. Long Island Roughriders (US). Manchester City youth coach 1994–May 1997. Portsmouth youth coach. Exeter City manager October 2002–February 2003. Georgia (US) coach.

■ Cash-strapped United wanted to buy Brighton midfielder Neil after a successful loan spell but could not afford the £65,000 asking price. A boy star, he made his Scottish League debut for Morton when still only 15 and won Schools, Youth and Under-21 honours. He left Spurs after the arrival of Argentina duo Ossie Ardiles and Ricky Villa. Neil could be a fiery customer (he was once suspended for pushing a referee) but he matured and served several clubs well, notably Brighton and Manchester City, winning two promotions to Division One with the latter. He was in the preliminary Scottish squad for the 1978 World Cup Finals but was omitted from the final 22 and did not receive full honours.

McNEISH Samuel

Forward

Born: Bo'ness, West Lothian, 4 August 1930.
Died: Bo'ness, West Lothian, 1998.
5ft 10in, 10st 9lb (1951).
Career: Linlithgow Rose. LEEDS UNITED February 1951.

■ Sam played just once for Leeds, in a 4–1 defeat at Manchester City on 4 March 1951. During his national service he played for the Royal Scots against the Royal Lancers in Berlin's Olympic Stadium.

McNESTRY George

Right-winger

Born: Chopwell, Co. Durham, 7 January 1908.
Died: Gateshead, March 1998.
5ft 9in, 12st (1928).
Career: Chopwell Institute. Arsenal trial July 1926. Bradford Park Avenue August 1926. Doncaster Rovers May 1927. LEEDS UNITED November 1928. Sunderland November 1929. Luton Town August 1920. Bristol Rovers £650 May 1932. Coventry

City June 1935, retired 1937.

■ Leeds was one of seven League clubs George played for in a 10-year career. The winger only managed three outings for United but topped a century of appearances at Bristol Rovers. He won a winners' medal with the Pirates in the 1935 Division Three South Final and collected another the following year with Coventry, where his career was ended by a knee injury.

McNIVEN David Scott

Forward

Born: Stonehouse, Lanarkshire, 9 September 1955.
5ft 6in, 11st 4lb (1977).
Career: LEEDS UNITED apprentice, professional September 1972. Bradford City £25,000 February 1978. Blackpool February 1983–May 1984. Portland Timbers (US). Pittsburgh Spirit (US). Halifax Town March 1985. Morecambe 1985.

■ David enjoyed a period as United's supersub, coming off the bench to score vital goals against Manchester City, Liverpool and Leicester. The Scottish Schools international, nicknamed 'Daisy', also won three Under-21 caps before a move to Bradford City, where he played for six years. His father, Tom, the former Hibernian physiotherapist, was Scotland's physio for the 1974, 1978 and 1982 World Cups, and David's twin sons, Scott and David, played for Oldham. David senior later worked as a milkman.

McPHAIL Stephen John Paul

Midfield

Born: Westminster, London, 9 December 1979.
5ft 10in, 12st (2002).
Career: LEEDS UNITED trainee, professional December 1996. Millwall loan March 2002. Nottingham Forest loan August 2003. Barnsley free July 2004. Cardiff City August 2006.

■ A member of United's 1997 FA Youth Cup-winning side, Stephen was a cultured midfield player for Leeds with a magic wand of a left foot. The Republic of Ireland international flitted in and out of the Leeds team and was not helped by a series of injuries. He teamed up with his former Leeds youth-team boss Paul Hart in a loan spell at Nottingham Forest before joining Barnsley, helping guide them to Championship promotion via the Play-offs. He also skippered Cardiff in the 2008 FA Cup Final at Wembley when they lost to Portsmouth.

McQUEEN Gordon

Centre-half

Born: Kilbirnie, Ayrshire, 26 June 1952.
6ft 3½in, 13st (1977).
Career: Largs Thistle. Liverpool trials. Glasgow Rangers trials. St Mirren 1970. LEEDS UNITED £30,000 September 1972. Manchester United £495,000 February 1978. Seiko (Hong Kong) player-coach August 1985. Airdrie manager June 1987–May 1989. St Mirren coach June 1989. Middlesbrough reserve-team coach July 1994, first-team coach 1999–June 2001.

■ Big Gordon succeeded the incomparable Jack Charlton in the Leeds

number-five shirt. He was pretty raw when he arrived, but by the time he moved on to Manchester United for a then British record fee of £495,000 he was the finished article. Virtually unbeatable in the air, he was a massive presence in the heart of the Leeds defence, where he weighed in with a decent goal return from set pieces. A cornerstone of the 1973–74 title success, he missed the following season's European Cup Final against Bayern Munich after being sent off in the semi-final at Barcelona. A bad achilles tendon injury caused him to miss much of the following season and his exit was on the cards after a bout of fisticuffs with goalkeeper David Harvey in an FA Cup tie against Manchester City at Elland Road. He soon followed Joe Jordan to Manchester United and was on the winning side in the 1983 FA Cup Final against Brighton. Gordon's father, Tom, was a goalkeeper with Hibernian, Berwick Rangers, East Fife and Accrington Stanley and Gordon was a 'keeper at school. He is now a Sky TV football pundit.

MADDEN Simon

Right-back

Born: Dublin, 1 May 1988.
(2007).
5ft 11in, 12st (2007).
Career: Cherry Orchard. Shelbourne. LEEDS UNITED July 2007–April 2008.

■ Republic of Ireland Under-19 international Simon's senior debut came in the 2–1 Johnstone's Paint Trophy defeat against Bury in November 2007. Leeds let him go on trial with League One rivals Cheltenham in April 2008, shortly before releasing him from his contract.

MADELEY Paul Edward

Utility player

Born: Leeds, 20 September 1944.
6ft, 12st 13lb (1974).
Career: Cross Flatts Park, Parkside Secondary and Leeds Schools. Middleton Parkside Youth. Farsley Celtic. LEEDS UNITED May 1962–May 1980.

■ 'Play-anywhere' star Paul figured in every outfield position in a glittering 18-year career at Elland Road. The England Schools international worked in an insurance broker's office and played for amateur side Farsley Celtic. Originally groomed as Jack Charlton's successor, the 'Rolls-Royce' fitted smoothly into any position he was asked to fill by Don Revie. Ignored at Under-23 level, he played for the Football League and toured Canada with an FA squad. He was omitted from the original 1970 World Cup squad for Mexico, but when teammate Paul Reaney missed out with a broken leg, Paul was called up but opted not to go. The following year he won the first of his 24 caps and featured for his country at right-back, left-back, centre-half and midfield. In Leeds squads noted for their tough outlook, Paul was booked just twice in more than 700 appearances, and he figured in all the major successes of the Revie years, scoring in the Fairs Cup Final against Juventus in Italy. In later seasons he was deployed solely as a

defender, retiring in 1980 to keep an interest in the successful family home decor business. His elder brother, John, had a spell as chairman of Halifax Town.

MAGUIRE Peter Jason

Forward

Born: Holmfirth, 11 September 1969.
5ft 9in, 11st 4lb (1988).
Career: LEEDS UNITED YTS July 1986, professional July 1988. IFK Osby (Sweden) loan April–July 1989. Huddersfield Town loan September 1989, £10,000 October 1989. Stockport County loan August 1990. Emley. Elgin City 2000. Forres Mechanics. Lossiemouth January 2002.

■ Peter made his debut in the final game of the 1987–88 season, a 1–0 home win over Crystal Palace, but could not bridge the gap between reserve and first-team football. When playing for the juniors he helped save the life of a Sheffield United opponent who had swallowed his tongue by giving prompt medical attention.

MAHON John

Right-winger

Born: Gillingham, 28 December 1911.
Died: Hull, December 1993.
5ft 8in, 10st 13lb (1935).
Career: New Brompton Excelsior. Doncaster Grammar School. Doncaster Rovers 1928. LEEDS UNITED June 1929. West Bromwich Albion £4,000 September 1935. Huddersfield Town £4,250 September 1939. York City August 1945–September 1946. Aldershot, Bradford City, Chelsea, Halifax Town, LEEDS UNITED, Millwall, Queen's Park Rangers, Reading, Torquay and West Ham United wartime guest. IF Elsborg (Denmark) coach 1947–50. IFK Gothenberg (Sweden) 1950–54. Malaya coach. LEEDS UNITED coaching staff. Hull City coach 1952–54.

■ Jack was a swift, direct goalscoring winger, who operated on the right after arriving from Doncaster Rovers. United banked £4,000 when he moved on to West Brom, but Jack later had the misfortune to fracture a shin bone on his Huddersfield debut. He toured South Africa with the FA in 1939 and was in demand as a wartime guest with a stack of clubs. He was later a sports master at Hull Trinity School, where he was a noted boxing coach.

MAKINSON James

Right-half

Born: Aspull, nr Wigan, 25 January 1913.
Died: 1979.
5ft 9in, 10st 10lb (1935).
Career: Clitheroe. LEEDS UNITED November 1935–44.

■ Jim lost his best playing years to World War Two. He signed from Lancashire Combination club Clitheroe and made 68 League appearances before serving in the navy, who discharged him with an injured shoulder. He had a special support made so he could play more games and turned out over 100 times in wartime games for United until retiring in 1944.

MANGNALL David

Forward

Born: Wigan, 21 September 1905.
Died: Penzance, 10 April 1962.
5ft 10in, 11st 4lb (1933).
Career: Maltby New Church. Maltby Colliery. Huddersfield Town trials. Rotherham United trials. Doncaster Rovers amateur 1926. LEEDS UNITED November 1927. Huddersfield Town £3,000 December 1929. Birmingham February 1934. West Ham United £2,950 March 1935. Millwall May 1936. Queen's Park Rangers May 1939, manager 1944–June 1952. Millwall, Fulham and Southend United wartime guest.

■ Free-scoring forward Dave's departure from Elland Road seemed premature. The former miner scored goals for fun at junior level and smashed in 10 in the 13–0 demolition of Stockport in a Northern Midweek League game on 25 September 1929. Three days later he made his United senior debut in a 3–0 Division One victory over Burnley. Although he did not score against the Clarets, he netted six goals in nine successive appearances before being surprisingly sold to neighbours Huddersfield, where he broke the Terriers' scoring record with 42 League and Cup goals in 1931–32. In all, he scored 141 goals in 218 appearances between the wars and, after serving as a member of the Civil Defence, managed Queen's Park Rangers for eight years before being replaced by Jack Taylor, who later became boss of Leeds.

MANN James Arthur

Forward

Born: Goole, 15 December 1952.
5ft 6in, 11st 11lb (1973).
Career: Goole and Yorkshire Schools. LEEDS UNITED apprentice, professional December 1969. Bristol City free May 1974. Barnsley February 1982. Scunthorpe United non-contract December 1982. Doncaster Rovers February 1983–May 1983.

■ Jimmy had a smattering of outings for United in the early 1970s, but the busy little player did not really shine until he joined Bristol City, where, operating largely in midfield, he totalled more than 200 League appearances. As City hit dire financial straits, he was one of eight players who agreed to have their contracts cancelled to help save the club. He worked as a security officer and a milkman before becoming a jetty master for Associated British Ports in Bristol.

MARQUES Rui Manuel

Defender

Born: Luanda, Angola, 3 September 1977.
5ft 11in, 12st (2005).
Career: Baden (Germany). Benfica (Portugal). SSV Ulm 1846 (Germany) 1999. VfB Stuttgart (Germany) July 2001–May 2004. Maritimo (Portugal) July 2004. LEEDS UNITED August 2005. Hull City loan March 2006.

■ Rui played more times for Angola than he did for United in his initial spell at the club. He rejected offers from Southampton and Ipswich to join Leeds but only featured at right-back in a Carling Cup victory over Oldham in his first 16 months. However, he did feature for his country in the 2006 World Cup in Germany before being given a chance by Dennis Wise. He developed into one of United's best defenders in 2007–08 and was also in prime form with Angola as they reached the quarter-finals of the African Nations Cup.

MARSDEN John

Centre-half

Born: Leeds, 17 December 1931.
5ft 11½in, 11st 12lb (1951).
Career: Osmondthorpe YMCA. LEEDS UNITED August 1948. Barrow March 1959. Carlisle United September 1960. Doncaster Rovers July 1964.

■ Former French polisher Jack was a devoted Leeds clubman, who earned a testimonial despite playing in only 71 League matches for United. The former Leeds Red Triangle League defender acted as stand-in for John Charles and Jack Charlton for 11 years before moving to Barrow with winger John Kemp.

MARSH Clifford

Inside-forward

Born: Atherton, nr Manchester, 29 December 1920.
Died: Bournemouth, December 1990.
Career: Tyldesley United. Winsford United. LEEDS UNITED £300 September 1948. Bournemouth May 1949. Yeovil Town June 1952.

■ Cliff made a scoring debut against West Brom in a 3–1 home defeat, a few weeks after joining from Cheshire League club Winsford. He had rejected Grimsby to join Leeds, but only stayed eight months.

MARTIN Cornelius Joseph

Left-half/Centre-half

Born: Dublin, 20 March 1923.
6ft 1in, 13st (1948).
Career: Drumcondra 1941. Glentoran March 1946. LEEDS UNITED £8,000 December 1946. Aston Villa £10,000 September 1948. Waterford player-manager July 1956. Shelbourne manager. Cork Hibernians assistant manager.

■ United rebuilt their side with the £10,000 they received from Aston Villa for versatile dual Irish international Con. He was first capped at Glentoran before joining Leeds, where he starred at left-back, left-half, inside-left and centre-half. He was a major star at Villa and even played in goal several times. His confident handling came from his teenage days as a Gaelic footballer, helping Dublin win the Leinster title.

Con finished with 30 Republic of Ireland caps and six Northern Ireland appearances, but that total was surpassed by his son, Mick, who played in 51 Eire internationals while with Bohemians, Manchester United and Newcastle. Con's grandson, Owen Garvan, plays for Ipswich.

MARTIN Geoffrey

Left-winger

Born: New Tupton, Derbyshire, 9 March 1940.
5ft 9in, 11st 7lb (1960).
Career: Parkhouse Colliery. Chesterfield October 1958. LEEDS UNITED May 1960. Darlington July 1961. Carlisle United May 1962. Workington £3,000 December 1962. Grimsby Town £7,000 November 1966. Chesterfield £3,000 July 1968.

■ Geoff's only Leeds outing was in a 4–0 League Cup victory against his old club, Chesterfield. The left-winger buzzed about with good effect in the lower divisions and won a Division Four Championship medal in his second spell with the Spireites in 1970.

MARTIN John

Left-winger

Born: Bishop Auckland, 10 December 1904.
Died: Gateshead March 1984.
5ft 9½in, 11st 7lb (1924).
Career: Hebburn Colliery. Darlington 1920. LEEDS UNITED £250 July 1924. Accrington Stanley June 1926. Connah's Quay August 1928. Bury May 1929. Reading June 1930. Doncaster Rovers August 1931–May 1932.

■ Speedy winger Jack managed a couple of games for Leeds after making his name in non-League football in the North-East.

MARTYN Anthony Nigel

Goalkeeper

Born: Bethel, nr St Austell, 11 August 1966.
6ft 2in, 14st (2004).
Career: Cornwall Schools. Heavy Transport. Bugle. St Blazey. Bristol Rovers August 1987. Crystal Palace £1 million November 1989. LEEDS UNITED £2.25

million July 1996. Everton £500,000 September 2003–August 2006. Bradford City goalkeeping coach March 2007.

■ Nigel, the most expensive goalkeeper in United's history, was full value for his £2.25 million fee. Wonderfully consistent, he commanded his area with calm assurance, could produce breath-taking saves and had a superb sense of positioning. Twenty of his 23 England caps were won during his seven years at Elland Road and he also played for England B six times and the Under-21s on 11 occasions. Nigel worked in a plastics factory and for a coal merchant when he played for St Blazey in the South-Western League. He was Britain's first £1 million 'keeper when he moved to Crystal Palace from Bristol Rovers and topped 300 games for the Selhurst Park side, winning promotions and playing in the 1990 FA Cup Final. He lost his place at Leeds to Paul Robinson in 2001–02 and did not play a senior game that season but enjoyed a renaissance at Everton, where he took his career total to over 800 matches before retiring due to injury.

MASINGA Philomen Raul

Forward

Born: Kerksdorp, Johannesburg, South Africa, 28 June 1969.
6ft 2in, 12st 7lb (1995).
Career: Jomo Cosmos (South Africa) 1990. Mamelodi Sundowns (South Africa) 1991. LEEDS UNITED £250,000 August 1994. St Gallen (Switzerland) July 1996. Salernitana (Italy) October 1996. Bari (Italy) August 1997–August 2001. Al-

Wahada (United Arab Emirates) 2002. PJ Stars (South Africa) coach 2006.

■ Once South Africa's all-time international top scorer Phil arrived at Leeds with Lucas Radebe in 1994 after being spotted by scout Geoff Sleight playing against Zambia. While Radebe developed into a major player for Leeds, striker Phil was largely used as a substitute, enjoying a nine-minute extra-time hat-trick after coming on as a substitute in an FA Cup replay against Walsall. Tall and leggy, his individual style did not always fit into Howard Wilkinson's plans. Although he continued to progress on the international stage, he was unable to stay at Elland Road as he could not get his work permit renewed. After a spell in Switzerland he settled in Italy but a proposed return to England with Gordon Strachan's Coventry in summer 2001 fell through owing to work permit problems once more. He returned to South Africa, where he had won an African Cup of Nations winners' medal alongside skipper Radebe. He now runs a football academy in his homeland and is a 2010 World Cup ambassador.

MASON Clifford Ernest

Full-back

Born: York, 27 November 1929.
5ft 10in, 11st 9lb (1962).
Career: Sunderland January 1950. Darlington July 1952. Sheffield United August 1955. LEEDS UNITED £10,000 March 1962. Scunthorpe United February 1964. Chesterfield July 1964.

■ Experienced Cliff was brought in from Darlington to stabilise a shaky United defence towards the end of the 1962–63 season. Although not the quickest, he was a sharp tackler and enjoyed his best days at Sheffield United, whom he skippered in Division One before his switch to Leeds. After failing to land the job as player-manager at Doncaster, he joined Chesterfield on a part-time basis while working as a printer.

MASON George

Right-winger

Born: Church Gresley, nr Burton upon Trent, 16 September 1896.
Died: Durham, July 1987.
5ft 8in, 11st (1922).
Career: Frickley Colliery. LEEDS UNITED July 1920. Swindon Town June 1923–May 1924.

■ George was United's first-choice right-winger in their maiden Football League season. The former Frickley man was quick and direct but eventually lost his place to Alan Noble and moved on to Swindon.

MASON Robert

Centre-half

Born: Whitburn, nr Sunderland.
Died: 1981.
5ft 10in, 12st (1925).
Career: Whitburn. LEEDS UNITED March 1922. Bristol Rovers July 1927. Hartlepools United 1928. West Stanley.

■ Bobby was a stand-in for international centre-half Ernie Hart. At Hartlepools he replaced ex-Leeds player Billy Poyntz as skipper.

MATTEO Dominic

Defender/Midfield

Born: Dumfries, 28 April 1974.
6ft 1in, 11st 12lb (2003).
Career: Liverpool associate schoolboy September 1989, trainee June 1990, professional May 1992. Sunderland loan March 1995. LEEDS UNITED £4.75 million August 2000. Blackburn Rovers June 2004. Stoke City January 2007.

■ Dom proved an inspirational leader in four roller-coaster years with United. He scored one of the most famous goals in the club's history when his header at AC Milan secured a 1–1 draw that sent the Whites into the second phase of the Champions League. He went on to top a century of appearances for Leeds before moving on to Blackburn after relegation in 2004. Dom learned his trade at Liverpool, where he won England B, Under-21 and Youth honours. He was called into the senior squad by Glenn Hoddle but did not figure at full international level. However, he was also eligible for Scotland and figured in six games for the country of his birth, although he called time on his international career because of injuries and did not have too much luck with full fitness while at Blackburn.

MATTHEWS Lee Joseph

Striker

Born: Middlesbrough, 16 January 1979.
6ft 3in, 12st 6lb (1997).
Career: LEEDS UNITED trainee, professional February 1996. Notts County

loan September 1998. Gillingham loan March 2000. Bristol City £100,000 March 2001. Darlington loan December 2003. Bristol Rovers loan January 2004. Yeovil Town loan March 2004. Port Vale free July 2004. Crewe Alexandra August 2006. Livingston August 2007.

■ One of a crop of highly-rated youngsters who helped United lift the FA Youth Cup in 1997, Lee had only a sniff of first-team action. Injuries did not help the young striker's progress but he commanded a decent fee when he moved on to Bristol City. Despite showing promise at all his clubs, he was bedevilled by injury.

MAYBURY Alan Paul

Midfield/Defender

Born: Dublin, 8 August 1978.
5ft 11in, 11st 7lb (1999).
Career: St Kevin's Boys Club. LEEDS UNITED August 1995. Reading loan March 1999. Crewe Alexandra loan October 2000. Heart of Midlothian £100,000 October 2001. Leicester City £100,000 January 2005. Aberdeen loan January 2008.

■ Alan made his debut as a 17-year-old in a 3–0 defeat at Aston Villa on 3 February 1996, when Leeds were decimated by injuries. Honoured at every level by the Republic of Ireland, his first two caps at senior level came in his time at Leeds,

which was mainly spent in the reserves. He was sent off on his debut at loan club Reading but blossomed in Scotland with Hearts under manager Craig Levein, for whom he played at Leicester.

MAYERS Derek

Right-winger

Born: Liverpool, 24 January 1935.
5ft 8in, 10st 5lb (1961).
Career: Everton amateur April 1950, professional August 1952. Preston North End May 1957. LEEDS UNITED June 1961. Bury July 1962. Wrexham October 1963–April 1964. Australian football.

■ Derek spent a season at Leeds after being signed by Don Revie, but the winger, who had a fair degree of success at Preston, could not produce the goods for United on a consistent basis.

MEARS Frank

Centre-forward

Born: Openshaw, Chorlton, 11 May 1899.
5ft 10in, 12st 7lb (1928).
Career: Stalybridge Celtic. LEEDS UNITED April 1924. Barnsley May 1928.

■ Frank had a couple of games as understudy to the prolific Tom Jennings. An Arthur Fairclough signing, he was a regular marksman in the reserves and also played for Fairclough at Barnsley.

MEEK George

Winger

Born: Glasgow, 15 February 1934.
5ft 3in, 10st 7lb (1949).
Career: Thorniewood United. Hamilton Academicals 1951. LEEDS UNITED £500 August 1952. Walsall loan January 1954. Leicester City £7,000 August 1960. Walsall July 1961. Dudley Town March 1965. Rushall Olympic 1965. Stourbridge Town.

■ Nippy little winger George fell just short of 200 appearances with United. Happy on either flank, he was good value for the £500 paid in two annual instalments to Hamilton Academicals. He did his national service with the Royal Armoured Corps at Aldershot, spending time on loan at Walsall, and played for the army against a Scottish XI at Ibrox in January 1955. On his return to Elland Road he played a key role in promotion to Division One in 1956. After a short spell at Leicester, twinkle-toed George served Walsall with some distinction and had an extended career in non-League football, working as a postman in Walsall.

MELROSE James Millsopp

Forward

Born: Glasgow, 7 October 1958.
5ft 9in, 10st (1987).
Career: Whitehill School, Glasgow. Scotland Schools. Eastercraigs. Sighthill

Amateurs. Partick Thistle July 1975. Leicester City £250,000 July 1980. Coventry City player-exchange September 1982. Glasgow Celtic £100,000 August 1983. Wolverhampton Wanderers loan September 1984. Manchester City £40,000 November 1984. Charlton Athletic £45,000 March 1986. LEEDS UNITED £50,000 September 1987. Shrewsbury Town £45,000 February 1988. Macclesfield Town August 1990. St Mirren trial. Curzon Ashton October 1990. Halesowen Harriers 1991. Bollington Athletic manager. Leicester City chief scout.

■ Flame-haired Jim scored a last-minute winner against United which helped Charlton scrape through the 1987 Play-offs, but within months of condemning Leeds to more Second Division football, he was signed by Billy Bremner. It was not a fruitful stay, and after a handful of appearances, he moved on to Shrewsbury and became the first player to successfully sue a fellow professional for damages after an on-the-field incident with Swindon's Chris Kamara, the former Leeds player. Jim was a high-flier in his younger days, making his Partick debut at 16, winning eight Under-21 caps and representing the Scottish League before joining Leicester. A football nomad, he scored a hat-trick on his home debut for Coventry against Everton and helped both Charlton and Manchester City to promotion.

MENZIES William John

Left-back

Born: Bucksburn, nr Aberdeen, 10 July 1901.
Died: 3 January 1979.
5ft 8in, 11st (1925).
Career: Mugiemoss. LEEDS UNITED March 1922. Goole Town September 1933–34.

■ Bill was one of the unsung heroes of United's early history. He arrived on a month's trial from Scottish club Mugiemoss and after a fine debut went on to help United into Division One for the first time in their history. He first played for the senior side on a 2–2 Christmas Day draw at Oldham in 1923 and was virtually unchallenged for the left-back slot for the next six years. He relied on skill rather than brawn to clear his lines and after over 250 games made his final appearance for the club in the last game of the 1931–32 promotion season. He later became a coach with the West Riding FA.

MICHALIK Lubomir

Centre-back

Born: Cadca, Slovakia, 13 August 1983.
6ft 4in, 13st (2007).
Career: Senec (Slovakia) July 2005. Bolton Wanderers January 2007. LEEDS UNITED loan March–April 2007, £500,000 January 2008.

■ Giant Slovakian defender Lubomir helped plug United's leaking defence towards the end of the 2007 relegation season. He was snapped up by Bolton from Senec in the January transfer window and loaned to Leeds to gain experience a few weeks later. Lubomir scored a last-gasp winner against Plymouth to temporarily keep United's hopes of staying up alive, but he was recalled by Bolton because of a defensive crisis and netted against Chelsea on his first Premiership start. United kept tabs on the big man and signed him before the 2008 January transfer window closed.

MILBURN George William

Right-back

Born: Ashington, Northumberland, 24 June 1910.
Died: Chesterfield, 24 June 1980.
5ft 10in, 13st (1935).
Career: Ashington. LEEDS UNITED March 1928. Chesterfield May 1937, assistant manager 1947. LEEDS UNITED and Yeovil Town wartime guest.

■ George was one of three full-back brothers who served United with great distinction. He started as a centre-half with his native Ashington but was converted to right-back and quickly dropped into the consistent groove that was a family hallmark. George partnered older brother Jack regularly – they were both ever present in 1932–33 – until the emergence of Bert Sproston. George did not moan about his

demotion and went on to captain United to their only Central League Championship in 1936–37 before joining Chesterfield. When he was with the Spireites George linked up with another brother, Stan, and became one of the few players to score a hat-trick of penalties, achieving the feat in a 4–2 victory over Sheffield Wednesday on 7 June 1947. George retired the same year and became Chesterfield's assistant manager.

MILBURN John

Left-back

Born: Ashington, Northumberland, 18 March 1908.
Died: Leeds, 21 August 1979.
5ft 10in, 12st 2lb (1935).
Career: Spen Black and White. LEEDS UNITED November 1928. Norwich City £2,000 February 1939. Bolton Wanderers, LEEDS UNITED, Bradford City and Darlington wartime guest. Bradford City player-coach October 1946, player-manager January 1947–July 1948, then assistant manager until May 1949.

■ Jack was the oldest of the Milburn clan to represent Leeds and was as tough as old boots. He gave up a life in the North East coalfields to turn pro with United and started at Elland Road as a right-back but generally played on the left when he

partnered brother George. Jack was a fierce tackler, master of the shoulder charge and possessor of a thumping kick. He established himself as top-drawer penalty-taker, belting home a club record nine spot kicks in 1935–36. Jack was rarely out of the side for 10 years and enjoyed three ever-present seasons on his way to 400-plus appearances. He also played for Leeds during the war, recovering quickly from a broken leg sustained against Barnsley in August 1943. At his peak Jack was touted for international honours, and although he went with England to Czechoslovakia and Hungary in 1934 he did not get a game. He was married to United goalkeeper Jimmy Potts's sister, Isobella.

MILBURN James

Full-back

Born: Ashington, Northumberland, 21 September 1919.
Died: Wakefield, January 1985.
5ft 6in, 11st 1½lb (1949).
Career: Ashington. LEEDS UNITED November 1935. Bradford Park Avenue June 1952.

■ 'Iron Man' Jim was the youngest of the famous Leeds full-backs. Like George, he was signed from Ashington, but there was to be no easy path to the first team. Although Jim was signed in November 1935 he did not make a senior

appearance until the final match of the aborted 1939–40 season – a 1–0 home defeat against Sheffield United. Jim had to wait another seven years for his next League game. After playing 52 wartime games with the club and seeing service in India before being wounded in Belgium, Jim, who also served with the Civil Defence, picked up the threads of his football career. He made up for lost time with a series of stirring displays and even had a run out at centre-forward when United were short of goals. After 208 League appearances he left for Bradford Park Avenue, severing a 24-year link between the three Milburns and United. However, the family ties were continued by their nephew, Jack Charlton, who was recommended to the club by Jim. For good measure, the Milburns' cousin, Jackie Milburn, was a legendary forward at Newcastle.

MILLER Ernest George

Inside-right

Born: South Africa, 17 October 1927.
5ft 6½in, 10st 3½lb (1951).
Career: Arcadia (South Africa). LEEDS UNITED November 1950. Workington March 1952.

■ George was playing for Western Province side Arcadia in South Africa when he was recommended to Leeds by a friend of Major Frank Buckley. George had to acclimatise to snowbound pitches within weeks of his arrival but,

unable to make a lasting impression, he joined Workington a couple of months after a move to Preston in January 1952 fell through.

MILLER Liam William Peter

Inside-right

Born: Cork, Ireland, 13 February 1981.
5ft 8in, 10st 6lb (2006).
Career: Ballincollig. Glasgow Celtic October 1997. Aarhus (Denmark) loan August 2001. Manchester United July 2004. LEEDS UNITED loan November 2005. Sunderland September 2006.

■ The Republic of Ireland midfielder spent six months on loan from Manchester United, helping Leeds to the 2006 Play-offs at Cardiff. He scored the winner on his second Leeds outing, when the Whites stormed back from being 3–0 down with 19 minutes remaining to win 4–3 at Southampton. It proved to be his only goal for Leeds, and although Kevin Blackwell wanted to sign him at the end of the season Liam opted to return to Old Trafford before joining his old Red Devils teammate Roy Keane at Sunderland.

MILLS Daniel John

Right-back

Born: Norwich, 18 May 1977.
5ft 11in, 11st 9lb (2003).
Career: Norwich City trainee, professional November 1994. Charlton Athletic £350,000 March 1998. LEEDS UNITED £4.37 million July 1999. Middlesbrough loan August 2003. Manchester City free July 2004. Hull City loan September–November 2006. Charlton Athletic loan August–December 2007. Derby County loan January 2008.

■ Marauding full-back Danny peaked during his three seasons at Leeds. He had already won half a dozen Under-21 England caps with Charlton when a big-money move brought him to Elland Road. His development continued apace with Leeds, adding more Under-21 appearances before breaking into the full England set-up. After starring for Leeds at home and in Europe, Danny had an outstanding 2002 World Cup and won 19 full caps in all, the last few while on a season's loan at Middlesbrough as United offloaded their big-earning stars. He won a Carling Cup-winners' medal while at Boro in 2004.

MILLS Donald

Inside-forward

Born: Bramley, nr Rotherham, 17 August 1928.
Died: Torquay, February 1994.
5ft 10in, 10st 5lb (1957).
Career: Queen's Park Rangers October 1945. Torquay United loan March 1949. Cardiff City £12,500 February 1951. LEEDS UNITED £12,000 September 1951. Torquay United December 1952–62, coach and scout until 1970s.

■ Don had a lengthy career which included 15 months at Elland Road. He was 17 when he turned pro with Queen's Park Rangers, where his boss was David Mangnall, the former Leeds player. He had a loan spell at Torquay, where he was so popular that the fans tried to raise money to buy him. That did not come off but after playing for Cardiff and Leeds he returned to Plainmoor in December 1952, staying 20 years and becoming one of their all-time greats as a player, coach and scout. He later became a traffic warden at the Devon resort.

MILLS Frederick

Wing-half

Born: Hanley-on-Trent, Staffordshire, 7 August 1911.
Died: Biggleswade, Bedfordshire, March 1990.
5ft 8½in, 11st 4lb (1938).
Career: East Woodvale School, Hanley. Middleport. Port Vale April 1932. LEEDS UNITED June 1934.

■ Fred made a two-goal League debut for United at centre-forward in a 4–2 home loss against Middlesbrough. However, they were his only goals for the club as he played the bulk of his games at wing-half. Fred broke a leg playing for Leeds at Leicester in November 1934 and missed the entire 1935–36 season. He fought back to earn a first-team spot but retired during the war. Fred started his League career as an amateur with Port Vale after working at a pottery in Hanley.

MILNER James Philip

Midfield

Born: Leeds, 4 January 1986.
5ft 9in, 11st (2004).

Career: LEEDS UNITED from trainee February 2003. Swindon Town loan September 2003. Newcastle United £3.6 million July 2004. Aston Villa loan August 2005–May 2006.

■ Rising Leeds star James became the Premiership's youngest scorer at 16 years 356 days when he netted the winner at Sunderland on Boxing Day 2002. That record has since fallen to Everton's James Vaughan, but the Leeds-born winger has developed into a top-class player and a regular for the England Under-21 side. Able to play on either flank, James looked set for a long Leeds career until the club's deep financial troubles were unearthed. When Newcastle came in with a big bid, the keepers of Elland Road's purse strings had little option but to take the money to help balance the books.

MITCHELL Ronald Gilbert

Right-back

Born: Morecambe, Lancashire, 13 February 1935.
5ft 10½in, 12st 7lb (1959).
Career: Greaves School, Lancaster. Lancaster Schools. Preston North End juniors. Bolton-le-Sands. Morecambe. LEEDS UNITED £1,000 November 1958.

■ Ron was a contemporary of Blackpool and England centre-forward Ray Charnley at school and Lancashire Combination club Morecambe. United signed Ron for £1,000, plus £1,500 if he played six senior matches. They did not have to shell out the extra money though, as he only managed four games.

MITCHELL Thomas Morris

Left-winger

Born: Spennymoor, Co. Durham, 30 September 1899.
Died: York, 22 November 1984.
5ft 9in, 11st 6lb (1930).
Career: Parkside United. Tudhoe United. Spennymoor United. Blyth Spartans. Newcastle United £100 May 1920. LEEDS UNITED £785 November 1926. York City September 1931–May 1933, manager March 1937–February 1950. Norway FA coach 1945. Yorkshire Schools coach.

■ Tom was one of United's most popular players of the inter-war years. The flying

winger did not play much football at school but was persuaded by mates to play for Durham area junior club Parkside United, and at 21 he was on Newcastle's books. He won FA XI representative honours in 1924 but was mainly a reserve at St James' Park. He opted to join Leeds, and it proved a wise decision, as he was an ever present in the 1927–28 promotion season. His skill and speed delighted the crowds until he left for York in 1931, going on to manage the Minstermen. He coached in Norway for several summers and was stationed there briefly with the RAF in the war. He quit York in 1950 and set up a sports shop in the city – he had previously run one in Newcastle – and later became a director of the Bootham Crescent club and ran a pub in Leeds.

MOLENAAR Robert

Centre-half

Born: Zaandam, Holland, 27 February 1969.
6ft 2in, 14st 4lb (1998).
Career: Zilvermeuwen (Holland). Volendam (Holland) August 1992. LEEDS UNITED £1 million January 1997. Bradford City £500,000 December 2000. Roosendal BC (Holland) June 2003–07.

■ Dubbed the 'Terminator' by Leeds fans, former electrician Robert was a no frills defender – powerful in the air and tidy on the deck. He was rated as one of the best centre-backs in his native Holland when he was snapped up by George Graham and quickly established himself as a terrace hero with his no-nonsense style. Robert formed a fine defensive barrier with Lucas Radebe until he suffered a cruciate injury at Arsenal and, after getting back to fitness, moved on to Bradford City.

MOLLATT Ronald Vincent

Wing-half

Born: Edwinstowe, Nottinghamshire, 24 February 1932.
Died: York, January 2001.
5ft 11in, 11st 7lb (1959).
Career: Nottinghamshire Schools. Thoresby Colliery. LEEDS UNITED February 1950. York City July 1955. Bradford City July 1960. Frickley Colliery August 1963. Bridlington Trinity 1966, player-manager 1967. Tadcaster Albion manager March 1980. York Railway Institute manager November 1982–May 1989.

■ Ron came through the junior ranks at Elland Road, playing for the West Riding youth team and taking part in England Youth trials. He proved a good squad man without having a regular run in the first team and after completing his

national service with the 12th Lancers joined York City, where he played well over 100 times. He later became familiar on the Yorkshire non-League scene while working as a painter and decorator. He also worked at a brewer based in Tadcaster and did some scouting for Barnsley.

MOORE Ian Ronald

Forward

Born: Birkenhead, 26 August 1976.
5ft 11in, 12st 7lb (2005).
Career: Tranmere Rovers apprentice July 1992, professional July 1994. Bradford City loan September 1996. Nottingham Forest £1 million March 1997. West Ham United loan September 1997. Stockport County £800,000 July 1998. Burnley £1 million November 2000. LEEDS UNITED £50,000 March 2005. Hartlepool United July 2007. Tranmere Rovers January 2008.

■ Hard-working Ian found it a struggle to cement a regular place at Elland Road and had to wait 18 months to get off the goal mark, scoring twice in Kevin Blackwell's last game in charge – a 3–1 home win over Barnet. He won England Youth honours and the first of his seven Under-21 caps at Tranmere, where his

dad, Ronnie, had been a scoring legend. At Burnley he formed a fine partnership with Robbie Blake but at Elland Road was often asked to fill a wide role rather than play as a central striker.

MOORE James

Inside-forward

Born: Boldon, Co. Durham, 1 September 1891.
Died: December 1972.
5ft 8in, 10st 8lb (1922).
Career: Boldon Colliery. Ardsley Nelson. Barnsley August 1911. Southampton wartime guest, free May 1919. LEEDS UNITED May 1921. Brighton & Hove Albion June 1922. Halifax Town September 1923. Queen's Park Rangers November 1924. Crewe Alexandra July 1925–26. NAC Breda (Holland) coach March 1926.

■ Experienced Jim was a fairly regular fixture in United's second League season. A carpenter by trade, he built his reputation at Barnsley, winning an FA Cup-winners' medal in 1912. He put his woodworking skills to effect at an Isle of Wight aircraft factory during World War One and guested for Southampton, joining them on a permanent basis in 1919. Noted for his stern expression, he was the first Saints player to be sent off – against Grimsby on December 1920 – and returned north to join Leeds for family reasons several months later. After coaching in Holland he settled in Barnsley to run a pub, then a greengrocer's business and later became a director at Oakwell.

MOORE Stanley

Goalkeeper

Born: Worksop, Nottinghamshire, 13 December 1912.
Died: Leeds 1983.
5ft 10in, 11st 5lb (1931).
Career: Worksop Town. LEEDS UNITED August 1931. Swansea June 1935.

■ United had two goalkeepers called Moore on their books in the inter-war period – Stan and Bill – but they were not related. Of the two, Stan was the better known, sealing a transfer to Elland Road after a great display for Worksop against United in a pre-season friendly. An ever present in 1933–34, he broke a leg at Huddersfield in February 1935 and lost his place to Reg Savage. After being transfer-listed, Stan joined Swansea and was the Welsh club's regular 'keeper until he retired in World War Two.

MOORE William Riddell

Goalkeeper

Born: Sunderland, 10 March 1903.
Died: 1962.
5ft 10in, 12st 7lb (1931).
Career: Limited Yard Apprentices, Sunderland. Blackburn Rovers trial. Seaham Colliery. LEEDS UNITED March 1924. Southend United June 1925. Hartlepools United 1936.

■ Bill was one of the most colourful characters United have ever had on their books. He took up goalkeeping at school and took time off his job as a shipyard carpenter to practise his skills at a Sunderland fairground. He was offered professional terms by Blackburn after trials but turned them down in order to complete his carpentry apprenticeship. Once that was out of the way he joined Leeds and although he only made six appearances, he was a popular member of the dressing room as well as a pianist in a dance band. He gave Southend United 10 years' excellent service before returning to the North East with Hartlepools.

MORRIS Jody Steven

Midfield

Born: Hammersmith, 22 December 1978.
5ft 5in, 10st 12lb (2003).
Career: Chelsea trainee, professional

January 1996. LEEDS UNITED free July 2003. Rotherham United free March 2004. Millwall free July 2004–June 2007. Charlton Athletic trial. Yeovil Town trial January 2008. St Johnstone February 2008.

■ After doing well at Chelsea, midfield terrier Jody was expected to add bite to United's squad. But his stay at Elland Road was blighted by a series of off-field problems and he was released from his contract after just sevens months. Jody dropped down a division with Rotherham before returning to London with Millwall. At Chelsea he won seven England Under-21 caps and Youth honours, gained an FA Cup-winners' medal in 2000 and featured in the squad that won the European Cup-Winners' Cup two years earlier. The side that won the competition by beating Stuttgart 1–0 featured future Leeds players Danny Granville and Michael Duberry, as well as United management duo Dennis Wise and Gus Poyet.

MORTON Norman

Centre-forward

Born: Barnsley, 22 May 1925.
Died: 1977.
Career: Sunderland. Woolley Colliery. LEEDS UNITED December 1945.

■ Norman made just one senior appearance for United – a 6–1 defeat at Luton on 27 December 1947. He also had a wartime outing with Leeds while on Sunderland's books and that also ended in a 6–1 defeat at Chesterfield in the final game of the 1944–45 season, although he did score the United goal.

MOSS Jack

Inside-right

Born: Blackrod, nr Bolton, 1 September 1923.
5ft 6in, 10st 13lb (1950).
Career: Bury wartime. Rochdale January 1947. LEEDS UNITED January 1949. Halifax Town June 1951.

■ United struck an unusual deal when Jack moved to Halifax. A few weeks before the move, the Shaymen paid a substantial fee for his Leeds teammate Des Frost. That left little money in Halifax's coffers, so Leeds generously waived the fee for Moss. He was also an accomplished Leeds League cricketer.

MUMBY Peter

Forward

Born: Bradford, 22 February 1969.
5ft 9in, 11st 8lb (1986).
Career: Rhodesway Upper School, Bradford. Bradford and Yorkshire Schools. LEEDS UNITED schoolboy forms November 1983, professional September 1987. Shamrock Rovers loan 1989. Burnley July 1989–April 1992. Chorley. Bradford Park Avenue. Field.

■ Peter was a member of a well-known rugby League family but opted for football. He represented Bradford Boys at rugby league and looked set to follow his brother Keith, who played for Bradford Northern and Great Britain, and Colin, who played for Halifax RL. Slightly built for a forward, he did not get much of an opportunity with Leeds but did better at Burnley, where Roger Eli was a teammate.

MURRAY Thomas

Right-winger

Born: Belshill, nr Airdrie, 14 January 1933.
5ft 7in, 11st (1960).
Career: Dalry Thistle Juniors. Falkirk 1955. Queen of the South. LEEDS UNITED £3,000 August 1960. Tranmere Rovers £3,000 March 1961.

■ Tommy was a typical nippy, box-of-tricks Scottish winger but flitted in and out of the Leeds team in the 1960–61 season. After playing army football he joined Falkirk, winning a Scottish FA Cup medal in 1957. His time at Tranmere was disrupted by injuries.

MUSGROVE Robert

Right-half

Born: Ryehope, nr Sunderland, 16 August 1893.
Died: November 1934.
5ft 9in, 11st 4lb (1921).
Career: Durham City. LEEDS UNITED July 1920. Durham City July 1921, later player-manager.

■ Bob was one of the top players in the North East immediately after World War One. He captained England Schools against Wales in 1907 and was a regular in Leeds' maiden season, sandwiched between productive times at Durham City, where he also operated as player-manager.

N

NEAL Thomas Walker

Left-half

Born: New Washington, nr Gateshead, 28 November 1910.
Died: 1936.
5ft 9½in, 9st 13lb (1934).
Career: Usworth Colliery. LEEDS UNITED February 1931. Hull City May 1936.

■ Former miner Tom joined United from North East amateur side Usworth Colliery, the club that produced Billy Furness. Tom was used as cover for Wilf Copping, Cyril Hornby and Bobby Browne in his five years at Elland Road. He moved to Hull City but did not play a senior game after suffering badly from severe head pains before the start of the new season. He was admitted to Newcastle Infirmary and subsequently died.

NEWSOME Jonathan

Central-defender

Born: Sheffield, 6 September 1970.
6ft 2in, 13st 11lb (1994).
Career: Sheffield Wednesday July 1989. LEEDS UNITED £275,000 with David Wetherall June 1991. Norwich City £1 million June 1994. Sheffield Wednesday £1.2 million March 1996–May 2000. Bolton Wanderers loan November 1998. Sheffield Wednesday Academy coach. Grimsby Town Centre of Excellence coach

and scout. Gresley Rovers player-manager April 2002–June 2003. Spalding United August 2004.

■ Several eyebrows were raised when Howard Wilkinson raided his old club Sheffield Wednesday and forked out £275,000 for fringe players Jon Newsome and David Wetherall. But Wilko's faith was rewarded by both players. Strong and powerful, Jon broke into the Leeds team as the 1991–92 Championship race reached its climax and scored one of the goals in United's 3–2 triumph at Sheffield United on the day the Whites won the title. United reaped a handsome profit when he became Norwich's first £1 million player. He skippered the Canaries before returning to Wednesday, where he was forced to retire at 29 with a knee injury. He then started his own car dealership.

NICHOLLS Kevin John Richard

Midfield

Born: Newham, London, 2 January 1979.
6ft, 11st (2006).
Career: Charlton Athletic trainee, professional January 1996. Brighton & Hove Albion loan February 1999. Wigan Athletic £250,000 June 1999. Luton Town £150,000 August 2001. LEEDS UNITED £700,000 July 2006. Preston North End July 2007.

■ One of Dennis Wise's first jobs as Leeds boss was to make Kevin captain, even though the midfielder was a long-term injury victim. The driving force was signed by Kevin Blackwell and had acquired hero status at Luton, having already skippered England at Under-18, 19 and 20 level. His Leeds debut was delayed by a pre-season injury, and after only five games he was carried off with a cruciate knee ligament injury. On his return, wearing the captain's armband for the first time, he was sent off at Ipswich. Kevin did lead the side nine times before being stripped of the captaincy after telling Wise that joining Leeds was a mistake and that he wanted to rejoin fellow Championship strugglers Luton.

NIGHTINGALE Albert

Inside-forward

Born: Thryburgh, nr Rotherham, 10 November 1923.
Died: Liverpool, 26 February 2006.
5ft 8in, 10st 3lb (1954).
Career: Thurcroft. Sheffield United June 1941. Grimsby Town, Doncaster Rovers and Rotherham United wartime guest. Huddersfield Town March 1948. Blackburn Rovers £12,000 October 1951. LEEDS UNITED £10,000 October 1952.

■ Dashing inside-forward Albert put the fun into football. He had a sense of

humour on the field and a great rapport with the fans at Leeds, who finally got their man at the third time of asking. United were twice beaten to his signature by Huddersfield and Blackburn, but a £10,000 bid secured his services from Rovers in October 1952. Albert marked his Leeds debut with a goal in a 2–1 defeat at one of his old clubs, Sheffield United. With his jet-black moustache and slicked-back hair he was an instantly recognisable figure who made stamina-sapping runs, and his surges into the box won plenty of penalties. He was a great foil for John Charles and fell just short of half a century of Leeds goals – a landmark he would surely have reached but for a bad knee injury on the opening day of the 1956–57 season against Everton, which proved his final League game. He then became a greenkeeper. His nephew, Lol Morgan, played for Huddersfield, Rotherham and Darlington.

NIMMO William Brown

Goalkeeper

Born: Forth, Lanarkshire, 11 January 1934.
Died: Inveresk, East Lothian, 1991.

5ft 11in, 11st (1957).
Career: Heart of Midlothian. Edinburgh Thistle. Alloa Athletic 1955. LEEDS UNITED £1,250 February 1956. Doncaster Rovers player exchange March 1958. Mansfield Town July 1962.

■ Willie kept a clean sheet in his only senior Leeds appearance, a 2–0 win at Bolton. He was only 16 when he played for the Hearts A team in the East of Scotland League, but a serious injury triggered his release. Willie rebuilt his career at Alloa but his brief stay at Leeds ended in an exchange deal with Doncaster Rovers 'keeper Ted Burgin.

NOBLE Alan Hugh

Right-winger

Born: Southampton, 19 June 1900.
Died: Southampton, 1 April 1973.
5ft 8in, 11st (1925).
Career: Southampton 1920. Bournemouth amateur 1921. LEEDS UNITED May 1922. Brentford May 1925. Millwall May 1927.

■ Winger Alan made his Leeds debut alongside Percy Whipp in a 3–1 victory against West Ham on 4 November 1922.

The following season he played in exactly half of United's games in the Division Two Championship campaign but moved on to Brentford, who successfully converted him to right-half.

NOTEMAN Kevin Simon

Forward

Born: Preston, 15 October 1969.
5ft 9in, 11st 2lb (1988).
Career: Primrose Hill High School, Leeds. Leeds City Boys. LEEDS UNITED June 1988. Doncaster Rovers £10,000 November 1989. Mansfield Town £25,000 March 1992. Chester City September 1995–May 1997. Hibernians (Malta). Boston United August 1999. Ilkeston Town February 2000. Gainsborough Trinity 2000. Hucknall Town. Harrogate Town November 2000. Matlock Town January 2001. Buxton September 2002. South Normanton Athletic 2002. Retford United 2004.

■ Kevin was an apprentice when he scored on his Leeds debut in a 3–0 Simod Cup victory over Sheffield United. He was unable to build on that fine start and a couple of years later moved on to Doncaster Rovers, later helping Mansfield win promotion to Division Three.

O

O'BRIEN George

Inside-forward

Born: Dunfermline, 22 November 1935.
5ft 6in, 10st 11lb (1958).
Career: Blairhall Colliery. Dunfermline 1952. LEEDS UNITED March 1957. Southampton £10,000 July 1959. Leyton Orient March 1966. Aldershot December 1966–67.

■ Little George spent just over a year at Elland Road after being signed by Raich Carter. He began with Fife club Blairhall Colliery before winning promotion to the Scottish League First Division with Dunfermline from whom he joined Leeds. He was not at his best with Leeds but his thunderous shooting produced 154 goals in 243 League games in seven years with Southampton. Outside football he was a sub-postmaster and publican.

O'DOHERTY Eugene F.J.

Inside-forward

Born: Ballaghaderreen, Co. Roscommon, Ireland, c. 1896.
5ft 8in, 11st 7lb (1920).
Career: Blackpool. LEEDS UNITED £250 August 1920. Ashton National loan 1921. Halifax Town May 1922. Blackpool May 1923. Walsall May 1923. Morecambe.

■ Eugene's only action for Leeds came in the FA Cup in the club's first season. He scored a hat-trick against Boothtown in the extra preliminary round and was also on target a fortnight later in the 7–0 demolition of Leeds Steelworks. He was loaned out to Ashton National for a season, and although he scored 30 goals for the Manchester club, Leeds let him go.

O'DONNELL Christopher

Centre-half

Born: Newcastle upon Tyne, 26 May 1968.
5ft 9in, 12st (1989).
Career: Ipswich Town from apprentice June 1985. Northampton Town loan January 1988. LEEDS UNITED free July 1989. Exeter City August 1991. Gateshead.

■ Stocky red-haired central-defender Chris suffered with injuries at Leeds and his only senior action for the Whites was as a half-time substitute for Jim Beglin in the thrilling 4–3 home win over Hull City in the Division Two title-winning season of 1989–90.

O'GRADY Harold

Inside-forward

Born: Tunstall, Staffordshire, 16 March 1907.
Died: Bucknall, 12 April 1990.
5ft 11in, 11st (1932).
Career: Northwich Victoria. Nantwich

trial 1929. Witton Albion 1929. Port Vale November 1929. Southampton August 1931. LEEDS UNITED August 1932. Burnley May 1933. Bury May 1934. Millwall June 1935. Carlisle United August 1936. Accrington Stanley May 1937. Tunbridge Wells Rangers October 1938.

■ Harry spent a year at Leeds in a career that encompassed eight League clubs. He had pre-season trials with Leeds under the name of 'Cousins' before being signed by Dick Ray. He made a scoring debut in a 3–2 victory over Wolves in Division One.

O'GRADY Michael

Winger

Born: Leeds, 11 October 1942.
5ft 9½in, 11st 2lb (1968).
Career: Corpus Christi School, Leeds. Huddersfield Town October 1959. LEEDS UNITED £30,000 October 1965. Wolverhampton Wanderers £80,000 September 1969. Birmingham City loan February 1972. Rotherham United November 1972–May 1974.

■ Mike was a player who slipped through United's fingers as a kid. Although he was Leeds-born, it was at West Riding neighbours Huddersfield where he made his name, winning three England Under-23 caps. That proved the springboard for a full England cap, and

he scored twice in Belfast in October 1962 only to be promptly dropped. Don Revie forked out £30,000 to take him back to his home-town club and although he did not have the best of luck with injuries, did make another England appearance, scoring again in a 5–0 win over France. He won a Fairs Cup-winners' medal and a League Championship medal, and scored one of the quickest goals in the club's history when he netted after 35 seconds in the 10–0 European Cup rout against Lyn Oslo. Within a few days of that quickfire goal, transfer-listed Mike, who also represented the Football League three times, was on his way to Wolves.

O'HARE John

Centre-forward

Born: Renton, nr Dumbarton, 24 September 1946.
5ft 8½in, 11st 7lb (1974).
Career: St Martin's School, Renton. St Patrick's High School, Dumbarton. Drumchapel Amateurs. Sunderland juniors August 1961, professional October 1963. Derby County £22,000 August 1967. LEEDS UNITED £50,000 August 1974. Nottingham Forest February 1975–81. Dallas Tornado (US) loan April 1977 and May 1978. Belper Town August 1981. Carriage and Wagon 1982. Ockbrook manager. Stanton manager March 1988.

■ Scottish international forward John had a short period at Leeds after being brought in by his mentor, Brian Clough, who had

first spotted his talents as Sunderland's youth coach. John arrived with John McGovern from Derby, where they had enjoyed great success with Cloughie. Neither player made a lasting mark at Leeds and rejoined Clough at Forest, where both played starring roles. John, who only made seven starts for the Whites, won 15 caps and featured in three Under-23 internationals. He won Division One medals with both Derby and Forest, adding two League Cups and the European Cup, coming on as substitute in the 1980 Final against Hamburg in Madrid, in what was his last appearance for the Reds. He later worked in the licensed trade, for a combustion firm and a Derby-based car dealer.

OKON Paul Michael

Midfield

Born: Sydney, Australia, 5 April 1972.
5ft 11in, 11st 12lb (2002).
Career: Patrician Brothers College, Fairfield (Australia). Marconi Stallions (Australia) 1989. Club Brugge (Belgium) August 1991–May 1996. Lazio (Italy) August 1996–May 1999. Fiorentina (Italy) July 1999. Middlesbrough July 2000. Watford loan January 2002–April 2002. LEEDS UNITED August 2002. Vicenza (Italy) August 2003. Oostende (Belgium) 2004. Apoel Nicosia (Cyprus) 2005. Newcastle Jets (Australia) May 2006–June 2007.

■ Former Australia boss Terry Venables recruited experienced Socceroo skipper Paul Okon from Middlesbrough to shore up United's midfield. Injury delayed his debut for nearly five months and although he led the Aussies to a famous win over

England at Upton Park during his time at Elland Road, Paul's lack of mobility did not really win over the Leeds fans. There was no doubting his pedigree, with spells in Serie A and being named Belgium's Player of the Year in 1995 when at Brugge and Oceania Player of the Year in 1996.

O'LEARY David Anthony

Central-defender

Born: Stoke Newington, London, 2 May 1958.
6ft 2in, 12st 6lb (1993).
Career: St Kevin's School, Glasnevin. Ireland Schools. Shelbourne juniors. Manchester United trials. Arsenal apprentice June 1973, professional July 1975. LEEDS UNITED July 1993–95, assistant manager September 1996, manager October 1998–June 2002, Aston Villa manager May 2003–July 2006.

■ David's exploits as United's manager overshadowed the fact that he also played 10 League games for the club after a long and distinguished career with Arsenal. He was signed on a three-year contract at the age of 35 by Howard Wilkinson to assist young central-defenders David Wetherall and Jon Newsome, but his playing career was ended by achilles tendon problems. After assisting Wilkinson's successor, George Graham, David moved into the Elland Road hot seat (see Leeds City and United Managers). He acquired legendary status at Highbury, amassing a club record 558 League appearances for the Gunners, winning League, Cup and League Cup

medals twice and representing the Republic of Ireland 68 times. His brother, Pierce, also played for Ireland, Shamrock Rovers and Celtic. His nephew, Ryan, plays for Kilmarnock.

OLEMBE Salomon Rene

Midfield

Born: Yaounde, Cameroon, 8 December 1980.
5ft 7in, 10st 4lb (2003).
Career: Nantes (France) August 1997. Marseille (France) January 2002–September 2007. LEEDS UNITED loan August 2003–May 2004. Al Rayyan (Qatar) loan September 2005. Derby County trial 2007. Wigan Athletic September 2007. Kayseriespor (Turkey) April 2008.

■ Cameroon international Salomon was one of three players signed on a season-long loan from Marseille by Peter Reid. He had figured in the 1998 and 2002 World Cup squads and reputedly attracted the interest of Liverpool before Leeds moved in. He figured in midfield and left-back, but after returning from international duty in the African Cup of Nations, he found himself overlooked by Reid's replacement, Eddie Gray.

O'NEILL James

Full-back

Born: Belfast, 24 February 1952.
5ft 9½in, 12st 2lb (1973).
Career: LEEDS UNITED apprentice, professional May 1967. Chesterfield free July 1974. Staveley Works 1985. Dundee United assistant manager 1993.

■ Jimmy's three appearances in a United shirt were all as a substitute. Like many of his young contemporaries at Leeds he found it near impossible to force his way into the starting line up because of the huge array of international talent on the books. It was a different story at Chesterfield, though, where he made nearly 450 League appearances in a 12-year career. He was known throughout his playing days as Sean.

ORMEROD Brett Ryan

Forward

Born: Blackburn, 18 October 1976.
5ft 11in, 11st 4lb (2005).
Career: Accrington Stanley August 1996. Blackpool £50,000 March 1997. Southampton £1.75 million December 2001. LEEDS UNITED loan September 2004. Wigan Athletic loan March 2005. Preston North End January 2006. Nottingham Forest loan March 2008.

■ Grafting forward Brett endured a tough six-match loan spell with Leeds, missing a penalty on his debut against Sunderland and failing to score in any of his games after arriving from Southampton. Later in the campaign he flourished at Wigan, helping propel the Latics to the Premiership.

ORMSBY Brendan Thomas Christopher

Centre-half

Born: Birmingham, 1 October 1960.
5ft 11in, 11st 9½lb (1986).
Career: Ladywood Comprehensive and Birmingham Schools. Aston Villa apprentice March 1976, professional October 1978. LEEDS UNITED £65,000 February 1986. Shrewsbury Town loan January 1990. Doncaster Rovers July 1990. Scarborough August 1992. Waterford

United player-coach 1992–April 1994. Wigan Athletic August–September 1994. Farsley Celtic assistant manager November 1994. Garforth Town.

■ Inspirational skipper Brendan led United to the FA Cup semi-final and the promotion Play-offs in 1986–87. His thumping header knocked out First Division Queen's Park Rangers on that Cup run but in the Play-off he severely damaged a cartilage and was only able to make a brief comeback nearly two years later. He played under Billy Bremner at Doncaster alongside his old playing partner Jack Ashurst before a spell in Ireland and non-League football. Brendan had come through the ranks at Villa, winning England Schools and Youth honours and making over 100 League apearances for the Villains. He later worked as a postman.

OSTER John Morgan

Midfield

Born: Boston, Lincolnshire, 8 December 1978.
5ft 9in, 10st 8lb (1996).
Career: Ladywood Comprehensive and Birmingham Schools. Grimsby Town from trainee, July 1996. Everton £1.5 million July 1997. Sunderland £1 million August 1999. Barnsley loan October 2001. Grimsby Town loan November 2002 and February 2003. LEEDS UNITED loan November 2004. Burnley free January 2005. Reading free August 2005.

■ John provided some flair on the right flank during a loan spell with United

during 2004–05. However, the Welsh international was sent back to parent club Sunderland after a breach of discipline. After a spell at Burnley, he joined Reading, helping the Royals into the Premiership. The holder of 13 Welsh caps, he earned a big-money transfer from his first club, Grimsby, to Everton as a 19-year-old.

OVERFIELD John

Winger

Born: Leeds, 14 May 1932.
6ft 1in, 10st 12lb (1957).
Career: Victoria Road School, Leeds. Ashley Road Methodists. Yorkshire Amateurs. Sheffield United trial. Bolton Wanderers trial. LEEDS UNITED May 1953. Sunderland £11,500 August 1960.

Peterborough United February 1963. Bradford City July 1964–May 1965.

■ Tall, slimline winger Jack was nearly taken from under United's noses as a youngster. He trialled at both Sheffield United and Bolton before the Leeds-born player joined the Elland Road set-up from Yorkshire League football. During his national service he played in several RAF representative matches and on demob settled into United's 1955–56 promotion-winning side. He marked United's return to Division One with a goal against Everton after just two minutes of the new season in a 5–1 victory. He played in every game in that campaign but the Everton goal was his only strike. He totalled 20 goals in 159 League appearances for United.

P

PALMER Carlton Lloyd

Midfield/Central-defender

Born: Rowley Regis, nr Oldbury, 5 December 1965.
6ft 2in, 11st 10lb (1995).
Career: St Michael's Junior School, Oldbury, Rowley Regis and District Boys. Newton Albion. Netherton. Dudley Town. West Bromwich Albion YTS July 1983, professional October 1984. Sheffield Wednesday £750,000 February 1989. LEEDS UNITED £2.6 million June 1994. Southampton £1 million September 1997. Nottingham Forest £1.1 million January 1999. Coventry City £500,000 September 1999. Watford loan December 2000. Sheffield Wednesday loan February 2001 and September 2001. Stockport County player-manager November 2001–February 2003, manager until September 2003. Dublin City August 2004. Mansfield Town manager March 2005–September 2005.

■ Long-legged midfielder Carlton was also deployed as a centre-back by Howard Wilkinson at Leeds and skippered the side on several occasions. The former England man made exactly 100 Premiership starts for the Whites. His telescopic legs made many a key tackle, and his energetic long-striding style produced vital late goals as United

surged into a European place in 1994–95. However, he fell from favour under George Graham and moved on to Southampton, later having a spell as player-manager with Stockport, with whom he went through the 700-plus career appearances barrier. Carlton emerged at West Brom as a youngster to win four Under-21 caps and hit top gear in his first spell at Sheffield Wednesday, leading them to the 1993 FA Cup Final and picking up 18 England caps under Graham Taylor. He works as a pundit for BBC's *Final Score*, owns a pub in Sheffield and runs an online estate agency.

PARKER Benjamin Brian Colin

Left-back/Centre-back

Born: Pontefract, 8 November 1987.
5ft 11in, 11st 6lb (2007).
Career: LEEDS UNITED trainee, professional January 2004. Bradford City loan July 2006. Darlington loan February 2008.

■ Ben, an England Under-18 international, benefited from a season-long loan at Bradford City, before being given a chance by Dennis Wise in 2007–08.

PARKER Neil

Left-back

Born: Blackburn, 19 October 1957.
5ft 6in, 10st 3lb (1978).
Career: Billinge School, Blackburn. LEEDS UNITED apprentice, professional October 1975. Scarborough free July 1981. Harrogate Town.

■ Neil's brief contribution came as a half-time substitute for Peter Hampton in a 1–0 defeat at Liverpool on 11 March 1978. He joined Scarborough on a free after the Seasiders played United in a friendly behind closed doors before the start of the 1981–82 season.

PARKINSON Keith James

Centre-half

Born: Preston, 28 January 1956.
6ft 1in, 12st 6lb (1981).
Career: LEEDS UNITED apprentice, professional February 1973. Hull City loan November 1981. Doncaster Rovers non-contract January 1982.

■ Whole-hearted Keith never gave less than 100 per cent in United's colours when he got the chance. Most of his time was confined to junior and reserve action, and he gave up the game, aged 26, when he was released by Billy Bremner at

Doncaster. He joined the West Yorkshire Police and has nearly 25 years' service with the force.

PARLANE Derek James

Forward

Born: Helensburgh, Dunbartonshire, 5 May 1953.
6ft, 11st 10lb (1981).
Career: Queen's Park. Glasgow Rangers April 1970. LEEDS UNITED £160,000 March 1980. Bulova (Hong Kong) loan October 1981. Manchester City free April 1982. Swansea City January 1985. North Shore (Hong Kong) May 1985. Racing Jette (Belgium). Rochdale December 1986. Airdrie January 1988. Macclesfield Town June 1988. Curzon Ashton.

■ Scottish international striker Derek struggled for goals in a poor Leeds team after arriving from Rangers, where he

won a pile of honours. He started as a midfielder at Queen's Park, but burst on to the scene at Ibrox by scoring on his debut against Bayern Munich in the semi-final of the European Cup-Winners' Cup in 1972. Adept in the air, he won 12 full caps, five at Under-23 level and one as an Under-21, and he represented the Scottish League twice. Derek won plenty of domestic medals for the Gers before his move to Leeds. Although it did not work out at Elland Road, he thrived at Manchester City. He later played at Rochdale under Eddie Gray before becoming a sportswear salesman.

PARRY William

Left-half

Born: Denaby, nr Doncaster, 20 October 1914.
5ft 9in, 12st (1939).
Career: Mexborough. Denaby United. 1936. Frickley 1937. LEEDS UNITED October 1937. Chelmsford City June 1939.

■ United were Bill's only League club, and he played six games in the final season before World War Two. He had shone in the Midland League as a 16-year-old but was unable to live up to his early promise at Elland Road and moved to Southern League Chelmsford.

PEACOCK Alan

Centre-forward

Born: Middlesbrough, 29 October 1937.
6ft 1in, 11st 9lb (1963).
Career: Lawson Secondary School. Middlesbrough apprentice, professional November 1954. LEEDS UNITED £53,000 February 1964. Plymouth Argyle October 1967–March 1968.

■ Alan's goals helped power United to the Second Division title in 1965. He arrived in February and rattled in eight goals in 14 games, including two in the 3–0 win at Swansea, which clinched promotion. He missed the first half of the following season through injury but continued his impressive strike rate and played in the FA Cup Final against Liverpool. His heading ability was of the top order and he added two England caps while at Leeds to the four he had won at Middlesbrough, where he formed a prolific partnership with

Brian Clough. Alan scored 126 goals in 218 games for Boro before opting to join Leeds in preference to Spurs or Everton. His last couple of years with United were injury-ridden, and he tried to make a fresh start with Plymouth but was forced to retire because of a knee problem in 1968. He later ran a newsagents in Middlesbrough.

PEARSON John Stuart

Centre-forward

Born: Sheffield, 1 September 1963.
6ft 2in, 13st 1lb (1987).
Career: Wisewood School, Sheffield. Sheffield Wednesday apprentice June 1979, professional May 1981. Charlton Athletic £100,000 May 1985. LEEDS UNITED £72,000 January 1987. Rotherham United loan March 1991. Barnsley £135,000 July 1991. Hull City loan January 1992. Carlisle United August 1993. Mansfield Town non-contract November 1994. Cardiff City January 1995. Merthyr Town. Chorley September 1996. Sheffield manager 1997–2000.

■ Nearly half of big John's 127 games for Leeds were as a substitute. 'Big Bird's' height helped him to open up defences but he was hardly a prolific scorer. However, the former Wednesdayite did have the satisfaction of scoring his only Leeds hat-trick in the 5–0 rout of Sheffield United on 8 March 1988. Born just 100 yards from Hillsborough, the

England Youth international made a fantastic start with the Owls, scoring in his opening four matches and recording a rare treble of debut goals on his League, FA Cup and League Cup debuts. John suffered badly with injuries in the latter part of his career and gave up the game with a neck injury, although he did spend three seasons as manager of Sheffield FC, the world's oldest football team.

PEMBERTON John Matthew

Defender

Born: Oldham, 18 November 1964.
5ft 11in, 11st 9lb (1993).
Career: Chadderton and Oldham Boys. Rochdale September 1984. Crewe Alexandra March 1985. Crystal Palace £80,000 March 1988. Sheffield United £300,000 July 1990. LEEDS UNITED £250,000 November 1993. Crewe Alexandra free August 1997–August 1998. Nottingham Forest assistant academy manager, then reserve-team coach.

■ Quick and aggressive, John was a versatile defender brought in midway through the 1992–93 season to bolster the Leeds squad. Vastly experienced, he had featured in the Crystal Palace squad promoted to the top flight in 1989 and figured in their FA Cup Final side the following year against Manchester United. 'Pembo' was fully committed at Leeds and there was even a hint he could be used as a striker to pep up a shot-shy attack after his hat-trick as an emergency

centre-forward against Middlesbrough in a reserve game. But a knee injury virtually ended his career at Leeds, and he packed in after a one-game comeback with one of his former clubs, Crewe.

PENNANT Jermaine Lloyd

Winger

Born: Nottingham, 15 January 1983.
5ft 6in, 10st (2004).
Career: Notts County associated schoolboy. Arsenal £1.5 million January 1999. Watford loan January 2002 and

November 2002. LEEDS UNITED loan August 2003. Birmingham City £500,000 January 2005. Liverpool £6.7 million July 2006.

■ Jermaine's speed and quick feet could not prevent United from sliding out of the Premiership. The England Under-21 international arrived on loan from Arsenal and proved an entertaining acquisition, later earning big-money moves to Birmingham and Liverpool. After just a smattering of appearances for Notts County as a 16-year-old he joined Arsenal for £1.5 million and was inducted into their academy.

PETERSON Paul Wayne

Left-back

Born: Luton, 22 December 1949.
5ft 6in, 10st 6½lb (1970).
Career: LEEDS UNITED apprentice, professional December 1969. Swindon Town June 1971. Stevenage Borough coach and assistant manager.

■ Reserve left-back Paul served his apprenticeship with United and made his debut on Easter Monday 1970 in a United reserve side that lost 4–1 at Derby. At Stevenage he worked with Derek Montgomery after playing with him in United's junior sides in the late 1960s.

PEYTON Noel

Inside-forward

Born: Dublin, 4 December 1935.
5ft 5in, 10st (1958).
Career: East Wall. Shamrock Rovers 1953. LEEDS UNITED £5,000 January 1958. York City £4,000 July 1963. Barnstaple Town player-manager May 1965. St Patrick's Athletic.

■ Republic of Ireland schemer Noel clocked up a century of appearances for United. Speedy and skilful, he won five of his six full caps at Elland Road and a string of domestic honours with Shamrock, including a Championship medal in 1957 and an FAI Cup-winners' medal the previous year. By the time he joined Leeds he had already turned out five times for the League of Ireland representative side and made his full international debut in a famous victory over West Germany.

PHELAN Terence Michael

Full-back

Born: Manchester, 16 March 1967.
5ft 8in, 10st (1986).
Career: Cathedral High School, Manchester. Salford and Greater Manchester Schools. Manchester City associate schoolboy. LEEDS UNITED trainee August 1984. Swansea City May 1986. Wimbledon £100,000 July 1987. Manchester City £2.5 million September 1992. Chelsea £700,00 November 1995. Everton £850,000 January 1997–May 1999. Crystal Palace loan October–December 1999. Fulham free February 2000. Sheffield United free August 2001. Charleston Battery (US) November 2001. Otago United (New Zealand) player-coach October 2005.

■ Jet-heeled Terry was converted from a winger to a full-back by Eddie Gray. It was a move that ultimately paid off for Terry, but he was released by Gray's successor, Billy Bremner. He rebuilt his career at Swansea and when he joined Manchester City – the club that had released him as a schoolboy – the £2.5 million fee was a world record for a defender. Although a Mancunian, he qualified to play for the Republic of Ireland as his mother hailed from County Sligo. He won the first of his 41 caps against Hungary in 1991 and played in the 1994 World Cup Finals. Terry, who won an FA Cup-winners' medal with Wimbledon in 1988, took up a coaching job in South Carolina in the United States before stepping into management in New Zealand.

POTTS James Forster

Goalkeeper

Born: Morpeth, Northumberland, 22 January 1904.
Died: Northumberland, October 1986.
6ft 1in, 12st 9lb (1930).
Career: Blyth Spartans. Ashington Colliery. LEEDS UNITED February 1926. Port Vale May 1934–36.

■ The North East has always been a rich seam of footballing talent for United, and goalkeeper Jimmy was no exception. A brother-in-law of the famous Milburn clan, Jimmy worked as a coal hewer at Ashington before turning professional with Leeds, making his debut in a 3–1 defeat at Huddersfield just two days after joining the Elland Road club. Athletic and powerful, he dominated his area for the best part of eight seasons, making him the best of United's 'keepers of the inter-war years. He was 35 when he moved to Port Vale, where he missed just two games in two seasons before retiring.

POTTS Joseph

Right-back

Born: Newcastle upon Tyne, 25 February 1889.
5ft 11in, 12st 4lb (1922).
Career: Ashington. Hull City March 1912. Portsmouth 1914. LEEDS UNITED June 1921. Chesterfield June 1923. Bradford Park Avenue 1925–27.

■ Although he had skippered Portsmouth, strong-tackling Joe struggled to dislodge Jimmy Frew at Leeds after he arrived from Fratton Park. He moved on to Chesterfield, where he was an ever present in his first season.

POWELL Aubrey

Inside-forward

Born: Cynlais, nr Pontardawe, Glamorgan, 19 April 1918.
5ft 5in, 10st 2lb (1938).
Career: Cwm Wanderers. Swansea Town amateur 1933. LEEDS UNITED November 1935. Everton £10,000 July 1948. Birmingham City £7,000 August 1950. Wellington Town August 1951–52.

■ Aubrey defied the doctors' diagnosis to make a stirring comeback from a broken leg. After the fracture in United's game at Preston on 20 March 1937 he was told he would never play again but battled back to form a highly effective partnership with David Cochrane until the outbreak of the war. Aubrey played 126 times for Leeds in wartime games and won his first official Welsh cap in October 1946. During the war he served in Belgium. A compact player and mazy dribbler, Aubrey packed a punch with his shooting, but hard-up United sold him to Everton. After finishing his football days he worked as a confectionary rep in Leeds.

POWELL Samuel

Centre-forward

Born: Holmes, nr Rotherham, 25 May 1899.
Died: Sheffield, 21 June 1961.
5ft 9in, 11st (1922).
Career: Thornhill. LEEDS UNITED January 1921. Sheffield Wednesday March 1925. Stafford Rangers 1930. Sheffield Wednesday reserve-team trainer, first-team trainer 1937.

■ Sam spent most of his time at Elland Road in the reserves, but his sale to Sheffield Wednesday proved a smart piece of business, as it enabled Leeds to raise funds to purchase Russell Wainscoat from Middlesbrough. Sam did not pull up many trees as a player at Hillsborough but served the Owls faithfully for 30 years as one of the backroom staff.

POYNTZ William Ivor

Inside-forward

Born: Tylerstown, Glamorgan, 18 March 1894.
Died: Leeds, 5 April 1966.
5ft 11in, 11st 10lb (1921).
Career: Gorseind United. Llanelli. LEEDS UNITED 1921. Doncaster Rovers November 1923. Northampton Town May 1924. Bradford Park Avenue 1925. Crewe Alexandra December 1926. Hartlepools United 1927. Bury coach. LEEDS UNITED training staff. Newport County trainer October 1937.

■ Billy holds the unwanted record of being the first United player to be sent off, on 11 February 1922 against Bury. He was back in the headlines the following week when he got married on the morning of the match against Leicester City and scored a hat-trick in the afternoon. Billy shuffled around several clubs before finishing his career at Hartlepools, where he was made centre-half and skipper by manager Bill Norman, one-time assistant to Arthur Fairclough at Leeds. He later returned to Elland Road for nine years on the staff after qualifying as a physiotherapist at Leeds General Infirmary.

PRICE Arthur

Half-back

Born: Rowlands Gill, Co. Durham, 12 January 1921.
Died: Gateshead, June 1995.
5ft 6in, 10st 8lb (1946).
Career: Consett. LEEDS UNITED amateur September 1945.

■ United beat Newcastle in the race to sign Arthur from North Durham League side Consett. He was working as a maintainence engineer at Hebburn and chose to play for Leeds as an amateur. He played in six of the opening eight games of the 1946–47 season before losing his place to Gerry Henry.

PRUTTON David Thomas Michael

Midfield

Born: Hull, 12 September 1981.
6ft 1in, 11st 10lb (2007).
Career: Nottingham Forest trainee, professional October 1998. Southampton £2.5 million January 2003. Nottingham Forest loan January 2007. LEEDS UNITED August 2007.

■ Midfielder David played 25 times for the England Under-21 side but did not make the breakthrough at full international level despite good form with Southampton. A broken metatarsal checked his progress and he returned to his first club Nottingham Forest on loan before joining Leeds, after featuring heavily in their 2007 pre-season games while the future of the club was being secured. He proved to be one of United's most consistent performers as they defied the odds to reach the League One Play-offs despite the club being deducted 15 points at the start of the season. At Saints he incurred a 10-match ban and £6,000 fine after pushing referee Alan Wiley following a red card against Arsenal.

PUGH Daniel Adam

Left-winger/Left-back

Born: Bacup, Lancashire, 2 April 1987.
5ft 11in, 11st 5lb (2005).
Career: Manchester United trainee July 2000. LEEDS UNITED July 2004. Preston North End £250,000 June 2006. Stoke City loan November 2007, £500,000 January 2008.

■ When cult hero Alan Smith went to Manchester United, Danny made the journey in the opposite direction. The Red Devils reserve proved he was more than a makeweight in the deal with a flurry of early goals, including many fine strikes from a distance. Surprisingly, he did not make a Championship start in 2005–06 and moved on to Preston in the summer. Together with ex-Leeds men Richard Cresswell and Dominic Matteo, he helped Stoke to the Premiership in 2008.

R

RADEBE Lucas Valeriu

Defender

Born: Soweto, Johannesburg, South Africa, 12 April 1969.
6ft 1in, 11st 9lb (2005).
Career: Bophuthatswana (South Africa). ICL Birds (South Africa). Kaiser Chiefs (South Africa) April 1990. LEEDS UNITED £250,000 August 1994–July 2005.

■ Versatile South African star Lucas is one of the most popular Leeds players of the post-Revie era. He was a marvellous ambassador for the club during his 11 years at Elland Road. He arrived with countryman Phil Masinga for £250,000 in summer 1994 – a gamble by Howard Wilkinson that paid big dividends. Early injuries meant Lucas took time to find his best position, but by 1996 he had settled as a defender and won an African Cup of Nations medal. A superb tackler and reader of the game, he grew in stature both at Leeds and at home, making 70 appearances for his country, many of them as skipper. 'The Chief', one of 14 children, played in the 1998 and 2002 World Cup Finals and maintained a high level of performance in his 200 League games, despite suffering from a succession of injuries in his last few seasons with Leeds. Originally a

goalkeeper at junior club level in South Africa, he also pulled on the goalkeeping jersey in a couple of matches for United after an injury to John Lukic and a red card for Mark Beeney. His testimonial attracted 38,000 to Elland Road and it was typical of the smiling Lucas that he shared the money raised between charities in Great Britain and Africa.

REANEY Paul

Right-back

Born: Fulham, 22 October 1944.
5ft 10in, 11st 3lb (1971).
Career: Cross Green School, Leeds. Middleton Parkside Juniors. LEEDS UNITED groundstaff October 1961, Bradford City June 1978. Newcastle United (Australia) 1980.

■ Only Jack Charlton and Billy Bremner have played more games for Leeds than Paul. He was only a few weeks old when his family left London for Leeds, where he attended Cross Green School and was an apprentice motor mechanic when he joined the United groundstaff in 1961. Originally a winger, 'Speedy' Reaney made the number-two shirt his own, winning heaps of medals during his 17 years with the club. He was one of the best man-markers in the game and could also supplement the attack, providing pin-point crosses for the likes of Allan Clarke and Mick Jones. Three England caps and five at Under-23 level seem a poor reward for such a consistent performer. A broken leg at West Ham

towards the end of the 1969–70 season forced Paul out of England's World Cup squad, but he made a full recovery to give United further sterling service before moving on to Bradford City. He had a spell in Australia with New South Wales club Newcastle United and was named Australia's Player of the Year before returning to Yorkshire to run coaching courses at schools and holiday camps.

REED George

Left-half

Born: Altofts, nr Wakefield, 7 February 1904.
5ft 8in, 11st 2lb (1930).
Career: Altofts. LEEDS UNITED October 1924. Plymouth Argyle May 1931. Crystal Palace June 1934. Clapton Orient April 1936. Crystal Palace trainer. Plymouth Argyle trainer 1950s.

■ Sharp-tackling George only cost United a signing-on fee when he arrived from Altofts. He broke into the first team midway through the 1926–27 season and missed only eight League games in the next three-and-a-half years. His consistency earned him a joint benefit game with Harry Roberts against Manchester United in April 1930, and he joined Roberts at Plymouth the following year. He was later reserve-team trainer at Crystal Palace and trainer at Plymouth.

RENNIE David

Defender/Midfield

Born: Edinburgh, 29 August 1964.
5ft 11in, 11st 12lb (1986).
Career: Leicester City apprentice July 1980, professional May 1982. LEEDS UNITED £45,000 January 1986. Bristol City £175,000 July 1989. Birmingham City £120,000 February 1993. Coventry City £100,000 March 1993. Birmingham City loan February 1996. Northampton Town August 1996. Peterborough United December 1997. Boston United 1999–2000. Burton Albion 2000–2002.

■ David was used as a central-defender and ball-winning midfielder by manager Billy Bremner. He was full value for his

modest fee, making over 100 appearances for the Whites, and netted the opening goal in the 1987 FA Cup semi-final against Coventry – a club he was to skipper later in his career. David started at Leicester, where he won 20 Scottish Youth caps and played in his country's European Youth Championship-winning side in 1982.

REVIE Donald George

Inside-right

Born: Middlesbrough, 10 July 1927.
Died: Edinburgh, 26 May 1989.
5ft 11in, 12st 9lb (1959).
Career: Archibald Road School, Middlesbrough. Newport Boys Club. Middlesbrough Swifts. Leicester City August 1944. Hull City £20,000 November 1949. Manchester City £25,000 October 1951. Sunderland £22,000 November 1956. LEEDS UNITED £12,000 December 1958, player-manager March 1961, retiring as a player 1963. England manager April 1974. United Arab Emirates coach July 1977–May 1980. Egypt coaching.

■ Don's achievements as United manager have tended to overshadow his illustrious playing career. Developed as a youngster by Leicester, he scored twice against Portsmouth in their 1949 FA Cup semi-final victory but missed the Final against Wolves with broken blood vessels in his nose. His football education continued at Hull alongside player-manager Raich

Carter, who later took charge at Leeds. The peak of his playing days was at Manchester City, where he created 'The Revie Plan', playing as a deep-lying centre-forward in both the 1955 and 1956 FA Cup Finals and winning the 1955 Footballer of the Year award. His exploits earned him six appearances and four goals for England, plus two representative games for the Football League. A clever and intelligent player, he suffered relegation at Sunderland in 1957–58 and arrived at Elland Road for his first stab at management. Initially he found the going tough as he juggled playing with managing and eventually hung up his boots at the end of the 1962–63 season, aged 35, to concentrate on off-field matters, taking Leeds to previously unknown heights (see Leeds City and United Managers).

RIBEIRO Bruno Miguel Fernandes

Midfield

Born: Setubal, Portugal, 22 October 1975.
5ft 8in, 12st 2lb (1997).
Career: Vitoria Setubal (Portugal). LEEDS UNITED £500,000 July 1997. Sheffield United £500,000 October 1999. Uniao Leiria (Portugal) July 2001. Beira-Mar (Portugal) 2001. Santa Clara 2002 (Portugal). Vitoria Setubal (Portugal) 2003.

■ Compact little Portuguese midfielder Bruno was virtually unknown when he

arrived at Elland Road in summer 1997 with Jimmy Floyd Hasselbaink. Bruno was earmarked as one for the future but made rapid progress to quickly earn a first-team place. His neat skills and powerful shooting reminded fans of a mini-Johnny Giles and he was soon tipped for international honours. Injury saw him lose his place, and after dropping down the pecking order he had a brief spell at Sheffield United before returning to Portugal.

RICHARDSON Frazer

Right-back/Midfield

Born: Rotherham, 29 October 1982.
5ft 11in, 12st 1lb (2006).
Career: LEEDS UNITED from trainee November 1999. Stoke City loan January 2003 and November 2003.

■ England Youth international Frazer was regarded as the natural successor to long-serving right-back Gary Kelly. The Irishman's consistency limited Frazer's

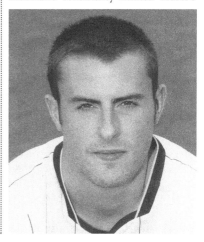

defensive chances, but he was often called on to fill in on the right side of midfield and netted the second goal in the 2006 Play-off semi-final victory at Preston.

RICHMOND Joseph

Centre-forward

Born: Leasingthorne, Co. Durham, 1 April 1897.
Died: Norwich, 6 March 1955.
5ft 11in, 11st 10lb (1925).
Career: Leeholme School. Durham Schools. Sittingbourne. Shildon March 1922. LEEDS UNITED December 1922. Barnsley February 1926. Norwich City July 1926–30. Letchworth Town coach.

■ Joe led United's front line with great enthusiasm as they surged to the 1924 Division Two League title, scoring 15 goals – three of them in a 5–2 home win against Hull. Goals were much harder to come by at the top level, and he moved on to Barnsley and later operated at full-back for Norwich, making 130 appearances. He then ran a couple of pubs in the East Anglian city. Before becoming a professional footballer, Joe served with the Royal Flying Corps as a flight-sergeant, winning the French *Medaille Militaire* in World War One.

RICKETTS Michael Barrington

Forward

Born: Birmingham, 4 December 1978.
6ft 2in, 11st 12lb (2005).
Career: Walsall from trainee September 1996. Bolton Wanderers £500,000 July 2000. Middlesbrough £2.2 million January 2003. LEEDS UNITED free July 2004. Stoke City loan February 2005. Cardiff City loan August 2005. Burnley loan January 2006. Southend United June 2006. Preston North End free January 2007. Oldham Athletic July 2007–January 2008. Walsall loan November 2007. Southampton trial March 2008. Columbus Crew (US) trial April 2008. San Jose Earthquakes (US) trial April 2008.

■ Michael suffered a miserable time at Elland Road, struggling for match fitness and failing to score a League goal. He had arrived at Leeds as part of the deal that saw Mark Viduka move to Middlesbrough, but the former England

man never really let his strong physique dominate defences. It had been a different story as a youngster at Walsall, where a flurry of goals earned him a big move to Bolton. Here, he won his only England cap against Holland, but he failed to live up to his £2.2 million fee at Middlesbrough.

RILEY Valentine

Inside-forward

Born: Hebburn, nr South Shields, 1 January 1904.
Died: 1966.
5ft 8in, 11st (1928).
Career: Washington County. Middlesbrough October 1923. Wood Skinners. LEEDS UNITED November 1924. Annfield Plain. Newport County August 1928. West Stanley August 1931. West Stanley. Southampton August 1932. Jarrow.

■ Fringe player Valentine's only senior appearance for United came in the FA Cup fourth-round 3–0 replay defeat at Bolton in 1927, when Bobby Turnbull and Albert Sissons were unable to play.

RIPLEY Stanley Keith

Wing-half

Born: Normanton, nr Wakefield, 29 March 1935.
6ft 1in, 11st 2lb (1957).
Career: Normanton Secondary School. Altofts YMCA. LEEDS UNITED April 1952. Norwich City August 1958. Mansfield Town £4,000 November 1958.

Peterborough United July 1960. Doncaster Rovers August 1962–June 1966.

■ Keith opted to join Leeds ahead of Blackpool and West Brom in 1952. The tall youngster had been a centre-half at school but caught United's eye as a wing-half with local club Altofts. Raich Carter gave him a run in the forward line in 1955 and Keith responded with a clutch of goals, including a hat-trick in a 4–1 win against Rotherham. Keith did his national service with the Royal Signals and played for the army against a Scotland XI at Ibrox Park. On demob he returned to Elland Road, where his versatility proved a great asset before moving on to Norwich. He won a Fourth Division Championship medal with Peterborough.

RITCHIE Andrew Timothy

Forward

Born: Manchester, 28 November 1960.
5ft 10in, 11st 11lb (1984).
Career: Moseley Grammar School and Stockport Schools. Whitside. Manchester United associate schoolboy October 1975, apprentice September 1977, professional December 1977. Brighton & Hove Albion £500,000 October 1980. LEEDS UNITED player-exchange March 1983. Oldham Athletic £50,000 August 1987. Scarborough player-coach August 1995. Oldham Athletic February 1997, player-manager May 1998, retired as a player July 2001. LEEDS UNITED Academy director October 2001–2003. Barnsley Academy

manager April 2003, first-team coach March 2004, manager March 2005–November 2006. Huddersfield Town manager April 2007–April 2008.

■ Leeds suffered against Andy when he scored a hat-trick for Manchester United in March 1979. He won eight England Schools caps under skipper Brendan Ormsby and looked set for a lengthy career at Old Trafford after 13 goals in just 26 League starts. However, he was surprisingly sold to Brighton, where he won an England Under-21 cap against Poland. A swap deal with Terry Connor saw Andy arrive at Elland Road, where he ran his socks off for the Whites' cause. He once scored six goals in a reserve game against Grimsby and netted 40 times in the League before his time at Leeds ended in a dispute over his contract. He was on a week-to-week deal before transferring to Oldham, where he helped the Latics reach the League Cup Final and win the old Second Division title in 1991. Andy later returned to Boundary Park as player-manager, making his last appearance as a 40-year-old, and also guided Barnsley to promotion to the Championship via the Play-offs in 2006.

ROBERTS Harold

Right-back

Born: Crofton, nr Wakefield, 27 June 1904.
Died: Plymouth, 18 May 1968.

5ft 7in, 11st 9lb (1930).
Career: Castleford Town. LEEDS UNITED February 1925. Plymouth Argyle November 1930. Bristol Rovers £820 September 1937. Frickley Colliery August 1939. Plymouth Argyle wartime guest.

■ Like Bert Duffield, his predecessor at right-back, Harry was recruited from Midland League side Castleford. He was 20 when he arrived at Elland Road and broke into the first team on a regular basis in 1926–27. His move to Plymouth was a roaring success, with 248 appearances, putting in numerous crunching tackles and blasting in goals from the penalty spot. He was nicknamed 'The Rock of Gibraltar' at Home Park, and he ran a stall in Plymouth market after giving up the game.

ROBERTSON David

Left-back

Born: Aberdeen, 17 October 1968.
5ft 11in, 11st (1998).
Career: Deeside Boys Club. Aberdeen July 1985. Glasgow Rangers £970,000 July 1991. LEEDS UNITED £500,000 May 1997–May 2001. Montrose coach, then joint player-manager May 2002. Elgin City manager March 2003–December 2005. Montrose manager September 2006–January 2007.

■ Scottish international left-back David was snapped up by George Graham as his contract with Rangers was due to expire. But he was bedevilled by injuries, and cartilage trouble ended his career prematurely, although he did have a few games for Montrose at the end of 2001–02. He won plenty of honours at Ibrox and played for his country three times, against Nigeria, Sweden and Holland.

ROBINSON David

Left-back

Born: Langholm, Dumfriesshire, 4 June 1899.
Died: 1986.
5ft 7in, 11st 6lb (1928).
Career: Workington. Aston Villa trials. Carlisle United. Solway Star. LEEDS UNITED May 1926. Southend United May 1928–40, then assistant trainer and later groundsman.

■ The son of a pattern weaver, Scottish defender David started life as a winger with Workington and had trials with Aston Villa. Carlisle converted him to a defensive role but he did not get many opportunities at Leeds. It was a different story at Southend, where he played 317 games for the Shrimpers and was assistant trainer for 13 years, working under Wilf Copping. He was also groundsman at Roots Hall until retirement in 1970.

ROBINSON Paul William

Goalkeeper

Born: Beverley, East Yorkshire, 15 October 1979.
6ft 2in, 13st 4lb (2001).
Career: LEEDS UNITED from trainee May 1997. Tottenham Hotspur May 2004 £1.5 million.

■ The promise shown by FA Youth Cup winner Paul bore rich fruit at Elland Road. He patiently bided his time, warming the bench as understudy to the excellent Nigel Martyn, whose rib injury against Roma allowed agile Paul a run in the team. He showed that the number-one spot would be in safe hands, with his superb reflexes saving the team many times. He also played his part in United's thrilling run to the Champions League semi-finals and won 11 Under-21 caps. After eventually taking over from Martyn on a regular basis, Paul won the first four of his full caps as a substitute and became England's first choice after joining Tottenham following United's relegation from the Premiership. A member of the Euro 2004 squad, he played in all England's games in the 2006 World Cup. He won a 2008 League Cup-winners' medal with Spurs.

ROBINSON Ronald

Left-back

Born: Sunderland, 22 October 1966.
5ft 9in, 11st (1986).
Career: Sunderland and Wearside Schools. Vaux Breweries August 1983. Ipswich Town October 1984. LEEDS UNITED November 1985. Doncaster Rovers £5,000 February 1987. West Bromwich Albion £80,000 March 1989. Rotherham United £40,000 August 1989. Peterborough United free December 1991. Exeter City £25,000 July 1993. Huddersfield Town loan January 1994. Scarborough August 1995.

■ Ronnie, an Ipswich reserve recruited on a free transfer, was handed his League debut in a 2–1 United victory at Carlisle

United in November 1985. Thirteen months later he made his last senior Leeds appearance in a 7–2 thumping at Stoke. He later rejoined Bremner at Doncaster, where he was successfully remodelled as a centre-half and moved to West Brom in a £200,000 package with Rovers teammate Paul Raven.

ROBSON Cuthbert

Outside-right

Born: High Wheatley, Co. Durham, 19 October 1900.
Died: Durham, October 1972.
5ft 7in, 11st (1925).
Career: Thornley Albion. Cockfield Albion. LEEDS UNITED July 1924. Southend United May 1926. Hartlepools United 1927. Connah's Quay. Bristol City 1930. Chester October 1931.

■ Cuthbert, nicknamed 'Cud', was among the most popular players in North East amateur football before turning pro with Leeds. He made a scoring debut in a 3–1 defeat at West Brom in October 1924 and made all his appearances for United in Division One before suffering a knee injury.

ROBSON William

Right-winger

Born: Shildon, Co. Durham, c. 1900.
5ft 7in, 11st 7lb (1924).
Career: Shildon Athletic. Cockfield. LEEDS UNITED December 1921. Mansfield Town 1924. Frickley Colliery January 1925. Gainsborough Trinity December 1925. Ashington 1926.

■ Bill was one of many Robsons who came out of amateur football in the

North East to play League football. He and Walter Coates, another player from the North East, represented the Yorkshire Midweek League in March 1923.

ROCASTLE David Carlyle

Midfield

Born: Lewisham, London, 2 May 1967.
Died: Slough, 31 March 2001.
5ft 9in, 12st 10lb (1993).
Career: Roger Manwood's School, London. Arsenal apprentice August 1983, professional December 1984. LEEDS UNITED £2 million August 1992. Manchester City £1.25 million December 1993. Chelsea £1.25 million August 1994–March 1998. Hertha Berlin (Germany) trials 1996. Norwich City loan January 1997. Hull City loan October 1997. Sabah Rhinos (Malaysia) April 1998.

■ Elegant England midfielder David became United's most expensive signing when he left his boyhood club Arsenal for £2 million. Howard Wilkinson saw 'Rocky' as the natural successor to Gordon Strachan for the champions, but the powers of the Scot showed no signs of diminishing while David struggled with form and fitness. He made just 19 starts in all competitions for Leeds and his miserable 16-month stay ended with a switch to Manchester City, with the more direct David White moving in the opposite direction. At Highbury, David had won two Championship medals, a League Cup-winners' medal and 14 England caps, but his career drifted after

his time at Elland Road and he was never able to rediscover the dazzling form which saw him light up the Gunners in over 200 games. David died of cancer aged just 33. Just six weeks after his death, his son, Ryan, was Arsenal's mascot in the FA Cup Final against Liverpool. Arsenal named their youth team's indoor training facility after David.

RODGERSON Ralph

Left-back

Born: Sunderland, 30 December 1892.
5ft 9in, 12st (1921).
Career: Pallion Institute. Burnley. Huddersfield Town February 1913. LEEDS UNITED March 1921. Wearside League football. Dundee January 1923.

■ Ralph played regular wartime football at Huddersfield Town for Arthur Fairclough, who signed the defender a season after taking over at Leeds. Ralph's experience served United at both first-team and reserve level. United kept his registration as he spent most of the 1922–23 season in the Wearside League before joining Dundee.

ROPER Harold

Inside-forward

Born: Romiley, nr Stockport, 13 April 1910.
Died: 16 April 1983.
5ft 10in, 10st 7lb (1930).
Career: New Mills. LEEDS UNITED August 1929. Cardiff City May 1935. Stockport County October 1937.

■ Former warehouse clerk Harry waited three years for his debut after signing from non-League New Mills. He marked his first start with United's goal in a 2–1 defeat at Blackpool in the second game of the 1932–33 season. Cartilage problems meant Harry was unable to build on that promising start and he was transferred to Cardiff.

ROQUE JUNIOR Jose Vitor

Centre-back

Born: Santa Rita do Spaucai, Brazil, 31 August 1976.
6ft 1in, 12st 11lb (2003).
Career: Sao Jose (Brazil) 1994. Palmeiras (Brazil) 1995. AC Milan (Italy) June

2000–July 2004. LEEDS UNITED loan September 2003–January 2004. Siena (Italy) loan January 2004. Bayer Leverkusen (Germany) July 2004. Duisburg (Germany) October 2007–February 2008. Al Rayyan (Qatar) April 2008.

■ World Cup winner Roque Junior was a high-profile loan signing who struggled to adapt to the demands of the Premiership. In the five League starts made by the Brazilian defender, United let in 20 goals as the club tumbled towards relegation. He was sent off in his second appearance and netted twice in a 3–2 League Cup defeat against Manchester United. During this colourful spell he also continued to represent Brazil, with whom he won the World Cup in 2002, lifting his haul of caps to nearly 50.

ROSS Robert Alexander

Full-back

Born: Wishaw, Lanarkshire, 25 May 1927.
Died: Leeds, March 1992.
5ft 8in, 10st 9½lb (1951).
Career: Workington. LEEDS UNITED £500 July 1950. Stockport County June 1954.

■ Bobby made all his five United appearances in the 1951–52 season. He had little chance to develop, with Jimmy Dunn and Jim Milburn holding down the full-back spots and Grenville Hair emerging in the reserves.

RUDD John James

Outside-left

Born: Hull, 25 October 1919.
Died: Manchester, 13 December 1985.
5ft 6in, 10st (1949).
Career: Fearons. Tenure Athletic. Manchester City January 1938. York City March 1947. LEEDS UNITED player-exchange February 1949. Rotherham United October 1949. Scunthorpe United October 1951. Workington September 1952. Northwich Victoria 1953. Stafford Rangers.

■ Skilful Jimmy was tipped for a big future after joining Manchester City from Dublin club football. After just one game for the Maine Road club, he was picked to face England as an 18-year-old, but his club refused to release him, saying he was not ready for international football. He was stationed in North Yorkshire with the Durham Light Infantry, guesting for York City. He joined Leeds from the Minstermen in an exchange deal with Tom Hindle but only stayed eight months and his career did not really ignite until he joined Rotherham. He scored two goals direct from corners in a game against Wrexham in August 1950, going on to help Rotherham to the Division Three North title. He later settled in Manchester, where he worked for Kelloggs as a cooker operator and served a union secretary for 21 years. He later worked as a kitchen porter and a match-day steward at Manchester City. His nephew, Billy, played for Birmingham, York, Grimsby, Rochdale and Bury.

RUSH Ian James

Forward/Midfield

Born: St Asaph, Denbighshire, 20 October 1961.
6ft, 12st 6lb (1993).
Career: St Richard Gwyn Catholic High School. Chester City apprentice, professional September 1979. Liverpool £300,000 May 1980. Juventus (Italy) £3.2 million July 1987. Liverpool loan July 1986, £2.8 million August 1988. LEEDS UNITED May 1996. Newcastle United August 1997. Sheffield United loan February 1998. Wrexham player-coach August 1998–July 1999. Sydney Olympic

(Australia) 1999. Chester City manager August 2004–April 2005. Welsh Football Trust elite performance director September 2007.

■ Liverpool goalscoring legend Ian was well past his best when he arrived at Leeds from Anfield. It took him 15 games to get off the mark, although George Graham, who had replaced Howard Wilkinson shortly after the start of the season, deployed him on the right of midfield to add some creativity. He managed just three goals in his one season at Elland Road, which was in stark contrast to his Liverpool stats. He was the Reds' greatest scorer with a remarkable 346 goals in two spells at Anfield. The Player of the Year in 1984, he is Wales' leading scorer with 28 strikes in 73 games. A model pro, Ian won five League titles with Liverpool, three FA Cup and five League Cup winners' medals and was in the Reds' side that won the 1984 European Cup on penalties against Roma.

RUSSELL David Page

Goalkeeper

Born: Crossgates, nr Dunfermline, 13 November 1895.
Died: Kirkcaldy, Fife, 15 August 1972.
5ft 10in, 11st 5lb (1925).
Career: Hearts of Beath. Kilsyth Rangers. Doncaster Rovers August 1923. LEEDS UNITED player-exchange January 1925. Watford August 1926. Lincoln City July 1927–28.

■ Although he had little experience, David was thrown in at the deep end to make his Leeds debut against West Riding neighbours Huddersfield Town, a match which United lost 2–0. A Scottish junior international, he was understudy to ex-Leeds 'keeper Harold Jacklin at Doncaster, joining Leeds in exchange for forward Jack Lambert.

S

SÁ Armando de Miguel Correira

Defender

Born: Maputo, Mozambique, 16 September 1975.
5ft 9in, 11st 2lb (2007).
Career: Belenenses (Portugal) 1992. Vilafranquense (Portugal) 1994. Braganca (Portugal) 1996. Villa Real de Santo Antonio (Portugal) 1997. Rio Ave (Portugal) 1998. Benfica (Portugal) 2001. Villareal (Spain) 2004. Espanyol (Spain). LEEDS UNITED loan January 2007. Foolad (Iran).

■ With United struggling near the foot of the Championship, manager Dennis Wise snapped up Mozambique international defender Armando on loan from Spanish club Espanyol, where he won the Spanish Cup in 2006. He also won a Portuguese Cup with Benfica and had 21 caps when he arrived at Elland Road.

SABELLA Alejandro

Midfield

Born: Buenos Aires, Argentina, 5 November 1954.
5ft 8in, 10st 13lb (1981).
Career: River Plate (Argentina). Sheffield United £160,000 July 1978. LEEDS UNITED £400,000 May 1980. Estudiantes (Argentina) £120,000 January 1982. Gremio (Brazil) 1985. Estudiantes 1987. Ferro Carril Oeste (Argentina) 1987. River

Plate (Argentina) assistant coach. Argentina assistant coach 1994–99. Uruguay assistant coach 1999–2001. Monterrey (Mexico) assistant coach 2002–2004. Corinthians (Brazil) assistant coach 2005. River Plate (Argentina) assistant coach 2006.

■ Alex became the first South American to represent United when he moved up the M1 from Sheffield United. The Blades had originally been in the market for a young Diego Maradona, but their £180,000 bid was laughed off and they took Alex instead. His wonderful ball skills made him popular at Bramall Lane, and when Leeds came in with a bid, he rejected a £600,000 move to Sunderland, then in Division Two, to play in the top flight. He found it difficult to impose himself in a struggling Leeds outfit and returned to Argentina, where he reignited his career with Estudiantes, winning four full caps. Alex then worked as assistant to Daniel Passarella, including a spell running the national team.

SAKHO Lamine

Forward

Born: Louga, Senegal, 28 September 1977.
5ft 10in, 11st 2lb (2003).
Career: Nimes (France) 1998. Lens (France) July 1999. Marseille (France) January 2002. LEEDS UNITED loan August 2003. St Etienne (France) January 2005. Montpellier (France) January 2007.

■ Lamine was one of several players to join United in long-term loan deals in the ill-fated 2003–04 season. However, he dropped out of the picture when Eddie Gray took over from Peter Reid. He did, however, represent Senegal in the African Cup of Nations Finals while at Elland Road.

SAVAGE Reginald

Goalkeeper

Born: Eccles, Lancashire, 5 July 1912.
Died: Salford, October 1997.
5ft 11½in, 11st (1931).
Career: Taylor Brothers. Stalybridge Celtic. LEEDS UNITED February 1931. Queen of the South July 1939. Nottingham Forest

and Blackpool wartime guest. Nottingham Forest December 1946. Accrington Stanley August 1947–April 1948.

■ Reg replaced ex-England international Albert McInroy at Leeds but was ousted by another international – Ireland's Jim Twomey. He was a solid, if unspectacular, performer and won a League Cup North winners' medal and a Cup-winners' medal while guesting for Blackpool in 1943.

SCAIFE George

Full-back

Born: Bradford, 23 December 1914.
Died: Bradford, June 1990.
Career: LEEDS UNITED amateur August 1936, professional May 1937. Millwall wartime guest.

■ George played all his senior games for United in the last full season before the war. He played mostly as an amateur in the reserves, as a left-back.

SCOTT John Alfred

Goalkeeper

Born: Crosby, nr Whitehaven, 18 July 1928.
5ft 11in, 11st 2½lb (1951).
Career: Crosby. Workington. LEEDS UNITED May 1950. Workington 1956.

■ Goalkeeper John was an ever present in the 1952–53 season. A former blacksmith at Birkby Colliery in Cumberland, he was a fairly late starter in football. He did not play much at school but was bitten by the soccer bug when some pals asked him to go in goal for a kickabout. He was playing in the North Eastern League with Workington when he was invited to Hull for trials by Major Frank Buckley. John was not taken on but when the Major became Leeds boss, John joined the Elland Road roster. A noted golfer, he returned to Cumberland in summer 1956.

SEARSON Harold Vincent

Goalkeeper

Born: Mansfield, 3 June 1924.
6ft 1in, 12st 7lb (1949).

Career: High Oakham, Mansfield and Nottinghamshire Schools. Bilsthorpe Colliery 1941. Sheffield Wednesday amateur 1942, professional August 1946. Mansfield Town June 1947. LEEDS UNITED £2,000 January 1949. York City November 1952. Corby Town 1954.

■ Harry contested the goalkeeping slot with John Scott before moving on to neighbours York. 'Polly' served with the Fleet Air Arm in India before becoming a footballer. He had a safe pair of hands and would pluck crosses out of the air with the greatest of ease before thumping the ball deep downfield. One of the few post-war players to play on his wedding day, Harry, a noted club cricketer, was football coach to Hunslet Boys' Club during his time at Elland Road.

SELLARS Scott

Midfield

Born: Sheffield, 27 November 1965.
5ft 6in, 10st (1986).
Career: Hindle House School, Sheffield. LEEDS UNITED apprentice, professional July 1983. Blackburn Rovers £20,000 July 1986. LEEDS UNITED £800,000 July 1992. Newcastle United £700,000 March 1993. Bolton Wanderers £720,000 December 1995. Huddersfield Town July 1999. Aarhus (Denmark) April 2001. Port Vale January 2002. Mansfield Town March 2002, later player-coach March 2005. Sheffield United Academy Under-18 coach. Chesterfield assistant manager February 2008.

■ Scott made his debut as a 17-year-old in a goalless draw at Shrewsbury in the final game of the 1982–83 season. That was the opening chapter in a fine career for the midfielder with a magical left foot. After asking for a transfer he was sold to Blackburn and helped Rovers to promotion, but before he could establish them as a force in the Premiership he returned to Leeds for a big fee. His second spell at Elland Road was wrecked by injuries and he only managed half-a-dozen Premiership starts before another sizeable transfer saw him join Newcastle. He proved to be a free-kick expert, helping the Magpies to the First Division title.

SHACKLETON Alan

Centre-forward

Born: Padiham, nr Burnley, 3 February 1934.
5ft 11in, 11st 5lb (1959).
Career: Burnley amateur. Bolton Wanderers amateur. Burnley May 1954. LEEDS UNITED £8,000 October 1958. Everton September 1959. Nelson July 1960. Oldham Athletic £1,200 August 1961–May 1962. Tonbridge.

■ Alan's best season was with Leeds, finishing top scorer with 16 League goals in 1958–59. That total included a hat-trick against Blackburn in his fourth game, but after pulling on a Leeds shirt just twice in the following campaign he moved to First Division Everton. Despite having a great scoring ratio wherever he played, Alan could not always command a regular first-team place away from Leeds.

SHARP Kevin Philip

Full-back

Born: Ontario, Canada, 19 September 1974.
5ft 9in, 11st 11lb (1995).
Career: Poulton-le-Fylde. Blackpool Town. FA National School of Excellence. Auxerre (France) 1991. LEEDS UNITED £120,000 September 1992. Wigan Athletic £50,000 December 1995. Wrexham November 2001. Huddersfield Town August 2002. Scunthorpe United July 2003. Shrewsbury Town July 2005–April 2006. Guiseley October 2006. Hamilton Academicals November 2006. Northwich Victoria player-coach June–December 2007.

■ A member of the 1993 FA Youth Cup-winning squad, Kevin provided effective cover for left-back Tony Dorigo. Although born in Canada, he moved to England aged 18 months and his dad, Frank, had trials with Tranmere. As a youngster Kevin was pigeon-toed and had to wear special shoes to correct the problem, but it did not prevent his development as a footballer and he attended the FA National School of Excellence. He was a teenager with Auxerre in France before joining Leeds for £120,000 with Jamie Forrester. Kevin was capped at every level from Under-15 to Under-18 but did not break through at the highest tier and fashioned a good career in the lower divisions, playing in Wigan's Division Three Championship side of 1997.

SHARPE Ivan Gordon

Winger

Born: St Albans, Hertfordshire, 15 June 1889.
Died: Southport, 9 February 1968.
5ft 6in, 10st 2lb (1913).
Career: St Albans Abbey. Watford October 1907. Glossop August 1908–September 1911. Brighton & Hove Albion guest February 1911. Derby County October 1911. LEEDS CITY June 1913. Nottingham Forest guest. Luton Town guest. Glossop 1915. LEEDS UNITED November 1920–23. Yorkshire Amateur.

■ English amateur international winger Ivan Sharpe and Tommy Lamph are the only two Leeds players to have played for United and City. Ivan's only United game was in a 4–0 home win against Coventry on 1 December 1920.

SHARPE Lee Stuart

Winger

Born: Halesowen, nr Birmingham, 27 May 1971.
6ft, 12st 2lb (1998).
Career: Hagley High School, Halesowen and Stourbridge Schools. Birmingham City associate schoolboy July 1986. Torquay United trainee August 1987, professional May 1988. Manchester United £185,000 June 1988. LEEDS UNITED £4.5 million August 1996. Bradford City £200,000 March 1999. Portsmouth loan February 2001. Exeter City August 2002. Grindalvik (Iceland) 2003. Garforth Town September 2004.

■ United had to take a massive loss when they sold former England winger Lee to Bradford City for just £200,000, having arrived at Elland Road for £4.5 million three years earlier. That made him Leeds' record signing at the time and proved to be Howard Wilkinson's last purchase for the club. Leeds fans saw only glimpses of Lee's best in his injury-hit spell with the club, which included missing the whole of 1997–98 with knee ligament damage. In his younger days at Old Trafford he was a destructive winger with an eye for goal. Lee, a former Young Player of the Year, won eight England caps and a further eight at Under-21 level after being snapped up from Torquay, where he had made his debut as a 16-year-old.

SHAW John

Goalkeeper

Born: Stirling, 4 February 1954.
6ft 1in, 13st 7lb (1971).
Career: LEEDS UNITED apprentice, professional February 1971. Bristol City May 1974. Exeter City July 1985. Gloucester City 1988.

■ John's only two United games were in Europe and he came off at half-time in both. Holding a 2–0 first leg lead against Belgian outfit Lierse, 17-year-old John started the second leg in goal but was replaced by Gary Sprake after letting in three goals, United eventually losing 4–0. Two years later he gave a great display in a dramatic match against Hibernian. He went in as third choice with David Harvey injured and David Stewart ineligible but broke a couple of fingers and was replaced at the interval by Glan Letheran. John later played 295 times for Bristol City and had more than 100 outings for Exeter.

SHEEHAN Alan Michael Anthony

Left-back

Born: Athlone, 14 September 1986.
5ft 10in, 11st 2lb (2008).
Career: Belvedere August 2002. Leicester City July 2003. Mansfield Town loan September 2006. LEEDS UNITED loan January 2008.

■ A Republic of Ireland international, Alan joined United on loan just before the January transfer window closed in 2008 and was one of three players handed his Leeds debut by new boss Gary McAllister in the 2–0 home defeat at the hands of Tranmere a couple of days later.

SHEPHERD Paul David

Midfield

Born: Leeds, 17 November 1977.
5ft 8in, 10st 3lb (2001).
Career: LEEDS UNITED apprentice, professional September 1995. Ayr United loan March 1997. Tranmere Rovers loan February 1999. Ayr United 1999. Keflavik (Iceland) summer 2000. Scunthorpe United September 2000. Cambridge United. Crewe Alexandra trial. Wimbledon trial. Luton Town March 2001. Oldham Athletic October 2001. Scarborough loan December 2001–March 2002, transfer July 2002. Leigh RMI August 2003. Harrogate Town August 2004. Stalybridge Celtic February–May 2005.

■ Leeds-born England Under-18 international Paul was thrown in at the deep end when a lengthy injury list led George Graham to give him his only start in a 3–0 defeat at Arsenal in October 1996.

SHERIDAN John Joseph

Midfield

Born: Stretford, Manchester, 1 October 1964.

5ft 9in, 10st 8lb (1986).

Career: St Mary's School, Manchester. Manchester City schoolboy. LEEDS UNITED March 1982. Nottingham Forest £650,000 August 1989. Sheffield Wednesday £500,000 November 1989. Birmingham City loan February 1996. Bolton Wanderers £180,000 November 1996. Doncaster Rovers August 1998. Oldham Athletic October 1998, caretaker manager December 2003, assistant manager March 2004, manager June 2006.

■ Discarded Manchester City teenager John became a star performer with United. Within six months of arriving from Maine Road he stamped his authority on the Leeds midfield with a wonderful array of passing. He recovered from a broken leg at Barnsley in October 1983 to figure in over 250 games for the Whites. He played for the Republic of Ireland through parental qualification at all levels, making his senior debut in March 1988 against Romania, featuring in Jack Charlton's 1990 and 1994 World Cup squads and finishing with 34 caps. He spent three awkward months under Brian Clough at Nottingham Forest, where he did not get a League game, before going to Sheffield Wednesday. John scored the only goal in the 1991 League Cup Final to beat Manchester United and

won a First Division Championship with Bolton in 1997. He finished his playing career with Oldham at the age of 39 and later became boss of the Latics. His brother, Darren, started on Leeds's books before playing for Barnsley.

SHERWIN Harry

Right-half

Born: Walsall, 11 October 1893.

Died: Leeds, 8 January 1953.

5ft 8in, 11st 4lb (1925).

Career: Walsall Schools. Darlaston. Sunderland December 1913. Sunderland Rovers (1915–16) and LEEDS CITY wartime guest (1916–18). LEEDS UNITED May 1921. Barnsley March 1925. LEEDS UNITED assistant trainer June 1926. Bradford City trainer 1936.

■ Hard-nut Harry was a key component of the half-back line which provided the base for United's 1923–24 Division Two Championship success. The son of a master chimney sweep, fierce-tackling Harry was certainly not afraid to clean up opposition forwards. He played alongside Ernie Hart and Jim Baker for United and made 91 wartime appearances for Leeds City, including an ever-present 1917–18, before returning to parent club Sunderland. After over a century of United games he had just over a year at Barnsley before returning to Elland Road as assistant trainer. Harry also played against Wales in 1907 in England's first Schoolboy international.

SHORT John David

Inside-left

Born: Gateshead, 25 January 1921.

Died: Nottingham, June 1986.

5ft 10in, 12st (1953).

Career: St Hilda's. LEEDS UNITED February 1937. Newcastle United and Hartlepool United wartime guest. Millwall £4,000 November 1948, trainer-coach November 1955. Huddersfield Town coach June 1960. Sheffield United coach 1961, assistant manager August 1969, later chief scout and youth-team manager. Gillingham physiotherapist January 1978. Chesterfield physiotherapist October 1981. Notts County 1983 trainer, retiring 1984.

■ John emerged during wartime football after joining United from Gateshead junior club St Hilda's. He scored 36 goals in 58 wartime games before making his League debut on the opening day of the 1946–47 season. The probing inside-forward then made 243 League appearances for Millwall, where he also worked as player-coach.

SHUTT Carl Steven

Forward

Born: Sheffield, 10 October 1961.

5ft 10in, 11st 10lb (1989).

Career: Spalding. Sheffield Wednesday May 1985. Bristol City £55,000 October 1987. LEEDS UNITED £50,000 and player exchange March 1989. Malmo (Sweden) loan August 1990. Birmingham City £50,000 August 1993. Manchester

City loan December 1993. Bradford City £75,000 August 1994. Darlington March 1997–June 1999. Kettering Town September 1999, then player-manager. Bradford Park Avenue 2004–May 2005.

■ Carl arrived at Leeds from Bristol City in a player-exchange for Bob Taylor, Leeds receiving £200,000 for Taylor and paying £50,000 for Carl, who marked his debut with a hat-trick against Bournemouth. He provided excellent back-up to the strike force for four-and-a-half years, with his most famous goal coming in Barcelona's Nou Camp Stadium when he came off the bench to score the winner against Stuttgart in United's replayed European Cup tie. Carl, who had served Howard Wilkinson well at Sheffield Wednesday, was a relatively late starter in League football at the age of 23. The Owls had snapped him up from Spalding, where his manager was Mick Hennigan, later to become Wilko's number-two at Leeds.

SIBBALD Robert Louis

Full-back

Born: Hebburn, Co. Durham, 25 January 1948.
5ft 7in, 10st 3lb (1966).
Career: Jarrow, Felling and Hebburn Boys. Airdrie trials. LEEDS UNITED amateur 1963, professional January 1965. York City February 1969. Southport August 1971–February 1977. Witton Albion December 1977. Los Angeles Aztecs (US) 1975–80, then assistant coach.

■ Bobby could not cut the mustard at Leeds, making just one start, but went on to play alongside some of the world's greatest players. After playing 240 League games for Southport he teamed up with Los Angeles Aztecs in the North American Soccer League, playing alongside George Best and Johan Cruyff. While living in America it was reported he had had a big win in a US lottery.

SIMMONDS Robert Lyndon

Forward

Born: Pontypool, Gwent, 11 November 1966.
5ft 4in, 9st 10lb (1986).
Career: Blackwood Comprehensive, Ebbw Vale, Gwent and South Wales Schools. Arsenal trials. Cardiff City schoolboy. LEEDS UNITED apprentice, professional July 1983. Swansea City loan October 1986. Rochdale loan February 1987, £4,000 May 1987, retiring 1988.

■ Diminutive Lyndon scored piles of goals in the juniors and reserves, winning five Welsh Youth caps and 11 at Schoolboy level. He scored both goals in a 2–1 win over Portsmouth on his full debut but could not maintain his blazing start. His goals saved Rochdale from relegation from the Football League during a loan spell in 1987, and not surprisingly he joined the Dale on a full-time basis, linking up with Derek Parlane. However, he had to quit at the age of 21 because of a pelvic injury.

SINCLAIR Ronald McDonald

Goalkeeper

Born: Stirling, 19 November 1964.
5ft 11in, 11st 9lb (1983).
Career: Nottingham Forest apprentice, professional October 1982. Wrexham loan March 1984. Derby County loan November 1984. Sheffield United loan August 1985. LEEDS UNITED loan March 1986, £10,000 June 1986. Halifax Town loans March 1987 and December 1988. Bristol City September 1989. Walsall loan September 1991. Stoke City £25,000 November 1991. Bradford City loan August 1994. Chester City August 1996–October 1998. Stoke City coaching staff. Leek Town 1999. Witton Albion December 1999.

■ Scottish Youth and schools international Ronnie was an able deputy for Mervyn Day in the 1980s. Although not the tallest, he was an excellent shot-stopper and was taken on from Nottingham Forest after a period on loan. Much of his time was spent on loan at a variety of clubs, his best period being at Stoke, where he won a Second Division Championship in 1992–93.

SISSONS Albert Edward

Outside-right

Born: Kiveton Park, Sheffield, 5 July 1903. Died: Erdlington, Birmingham, 4 October 1975.
5ft 11in, 11st 12lb (1926).
Career: Kiveton Park Colliery. Arsenal trial. Doncaster Rovers July 1923. LEEDS UNITED £1,000 October 1925. Southport

July 1928. Northampton Town July 1928. Worksop Town October 1931.

■ Albert made a useful contribution as understudy to England international Bobby Turnbull at Leeds with his direct, forceful running. He left school at 14 to become a pit-pony driver at his local mine at Kiveton Park and had trials with Arsenal, but it was displays at Doncaster under Dick Ray's management that caught United's attention. Albert died, aged 72, from an overdose of asprin while suffering from pneumonia, and the inquest recorded a verdict of misadventure. His son, Graham, played for Birmingham and Peterborough, while a cousin, Bill Sissons, played in goal for Lincoln.

SMELT Alfred

Left-back

Born: Rotherham
5ft 8in, 12st 3lb (1920).
Career: Mexborough Town. LEEDS UNITED July 1920.

■ Alf played in one League game against Stockport as a replacement for Jimmy Frew after turning out in United's team that thrashed Leeds Steelworks 11–0 in the FA Cup preliminary round in 1920. Three of Alf's brothers played League football – Len (Gainsborough, Burnley and Barrow), Tom (Accrington, Exeter, Chesterfield, Manchester City, Oldham, Crewe and Rotherham) and John (Portsmouth and Sheffield Wednesday). John also played for Leeds City in World War One.

SMITH Alan

Forward

Born: Rothwell, nr Leeds, 28 October 1980.
5ft 9in, 11st 10lb (2000).
Career: LEEDS UNITED trainee, professional March 1998. Manchester United £6 million May 2004. Newcastle United £6 million August 2007.

■ Leeds fans were genuinely shocked when cult hero Alan joined arch-enemy Manchester United. His love affair with the Whites ended in tears after relegation in 2004, and many supporters could not stomach his choice of new club. But there was never any doubting his commitment to Leeds' cause from the moment he burst

on to the scene in November 1998. After an England Under-18 tour to the Middle East was called off, Alan found himself on the bench at Anfield, coming on to score with his first touch to cement a famous 3–1 win over Liverpool. The following week he again came on to score on his home debut in a 4–1 win over Charlton and his career was up and running. His aggressive style did not give defenders a moment's peace but also earned him plenty of red cards. Fiery Alan won 10 Under-21 caps and won the first of 17 full caps as a sub in a 4–0 win over Mexico at Derby in May 2001. Alan also had a spell on the right side of midfield, and although his goal output dipped he still netted 56 Leeds goals, including all four in a UEFA Cup victory over Hapoel Tel Aviv. After his £7 million transfer he soon won over sceptics at Old Trafford, but his career took a turn for the worse when he badly fractured an ankle against Liverpool in an FA Cup tie. After battling back to fitness he found himself down the Red Devils' pecking order, and in summer 2007 he joined Mark Viduka and James Milner at Newcastle.

SMITH John Eric

Right-half

Born: Glasgow, 29 July 1934.
Died: Dubai, 12 June 1991.
5ft 5in, 11st 5½lb (1963).
Career: St Andrew's Juveniles. Pollok 1951. Glasgow Benburb. Glasgow Celtic 1953. LEEDS UNITED £10,000 June 1960. Greenock Morton June 1964–66 then coaching staff, then manager 1972. Pezoporikos (Cyprus) coach. Hamilton Academicals manager 1972. Sharjah (United Arab Emirates) manager April 1978. Al Nasr (United Arab Emirates) assistant manager June 1982–May 1983. Al Shaab (United Arab Emirates) 1984. Pezoporikos (Cyprus) coach 1980s.

■ Experienced Eric suffered a broken leg in his first season at Leeds after a high-profile move from Celtic. Jack Taylor believed the Scottish international wing-half's experience and spirit would add more backbone to the United defence after relegation to Division Two in 1960. A regular under Don Revie the following campaign, Eric was among the players who helped the club stabilise before joining Morton – the first port of call in a successful coaching career that included a spell in the Middle East under Revie. Eric, whose two Scottish caps came against Holland and Portugal, topped 100 appearances for Celtic, where he won a winners' medal in the 1956 Scottish Cup. He died from a heart attack while on holiday in Dubai.

SMITH Joseph Barry

Centre-forward

Born: South Kirkby, Yorkshire, 15 March 1934.
Died: New Zealand, February 2007.
5ft 10in, 12st 3lb (1951).
Career: St Walburga's School, Shipley. Bradford Boys. Bradford United. Bradford Park Avenue groundstaff. Farsley Celtic. LEEDS UNITED October 1951. Bradford Park Avenue May 1955. Wrexham June 1957. Stockport County July 1958. Headington United October 1959. Oldham Athletic August 1960. Bangor City December 1960. Southport August 1961. Accrington Stanley October 1961.

■ Barry had a fairytale debut for United, scoring as an 18-year-old in a 2–0 home win over Fulham on 13 September 1952. The former apprentice plumber, who had played in the West Riding County youth team, made just one more appearance and was stationed at Oswestry while doing his national service with the Royal Artillery. He joined Bradford, where he had previously been a member of the Park Avenue groundstaff. After football he ran an industrial equipment business in Bradford and died on a sailing holiday in New Zealand.

SMITH Leonard

Left-half

Born: Birmingham or Worcester 1903.
5ft 10in, 12st 6lb (1925).
Career: Redditch Town. LEEDS UNITED

May 1921. Bristol Rovers June 1926–March 1928. Merthyr Town June 1929. Wolverhampton Wanderers May 1930. Evesham Town 1931. Witley Wanderers September 1932.

■ Reserve left-half Len made a crucial contribution to United's 1923–24 Division Two Championship-winning side, playing in the final nine games as cover for skipper Jim Baker and the experienced Harry Sherwin. He also had a decent run in the middle of the following season, but when his senior appearances became more sporadic he moved to Bristol Rovers. He later featured in Merthyr Town's final match before leaving the League in 1930.

SNODIN Glynn

Full-back/Midfield

Born: Rotherham, 14 February 1960.
5ft 6in, 9st 6lb (1987).
Career: Doncaster Rovers apprentice, professional October 1977. Sheffield Wednesday £135,000 June 1985. LEEDS UNITED £150,000 July 1987. Oldham Athletic loan August 1991. Rotherham United loan February 1992. Hearts March 1992–May 1993. Barnsley July 1993. Carlisle United June 1995, retiring to become chief scout. Gainsborough Trinity 1995–96. Scarborough youth team manager June 1997. Doncaster Rovers coach 1998–2000. Charlton Athletic reserve team manager 2001. Southampton coach March 2006, then assistant manager. Northern Ireland assistant manager June 2007. West Ham United coach June 2007.

■ Glynn followed his younger brother Ian to Leeds, but the siblings did not play in the same United side. The pair were developed by Doncaster, where Glynn started as a 16-year-old. He played 300 times for Rovers, many of them alongside Ian, before the partnership ended. Ian headed to Leeds in May 1985, and Glynn joined Sheffield Wednesday the following month. Two years later Glynn arrived at Elland Road, where he played at full-back and in midfield. He knocked in some spectacular goals for Leeds but glandular fever, a viral illness and injury meant he endured a stop-start time at Elland Road. He later became a respected coach, steering Charlton's reserves to regular title success before becoming a highly regarded coach with Southampton and West Ham. He also assisted ex-Leeds man Nigel Worthington on a part-time basis with Northern Ireland.

SNODIN Ian

Midfield

Born: Rotherham, 15 August 1963.
5ft 10in, 11st (1985).
Career: Doncaster Rovers apprentice April 1979, professional August 1980. LEEDS UNITED £200,000 May 1985. Everton £840,000 January 1987. Sunderland loan October 1994. Oldham Athletic January 1995. Scarborough August 1997. Doncaster Rovers player-manager August 1998, manager to April 2000. Armthorpe Welfare August 2000.

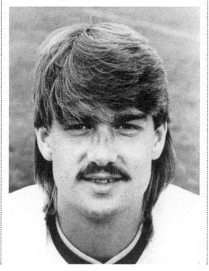

■ Ian was the more high-profile player of the Snodin brothers, coming within a whisker of a full England cap. He followed Billy Bremner from Doncaster to Second Division Leeds, already with a good pedigree, having earned England Youth and Under-23 recognition while still playing in the Third Division. He showed his undoubted midfield class with Leeds, succeeding Peter Lorimer as skipper. Ian was a real driving force and despite his fiery temperament was consistently linked to top-flight clubs such as Liverpool. United banked a club record fee of £840,000 when he went to Everton, winning a League Championship medal in 1986–87. The Toffees converted him into a fine full-back and he was called up for England to face Greece in February 1989, but withdrew through injury and was never called up again. He missed nearly two complete seasons at Goodison through injury but managed a couple of England B outings. He now does radio and TV work.

SPEAK George

Left-back

Born: Blackburn, 7 November 1890.
Died: Blackburn 10 March 1953.
5ft 8½in, 11st 7lb (1922).
Career: Clitheroe Central. Darwen. Liverpool trials. Grimsby Town May 1911. Gainsborough Trinity July 1913. West Ham United May 1914. Preston North End March 1919. LEEDS UNITED £250 August 1923–25.

■ George rounded off his career by winning a Division Two Championship medal with United in 1923–24 but did not feature too regularly in the latter part

of that great campaign. He was energetic, tough and fearless but lost many of his best years to the war, when he guested for Preston.

SPEED Gary Andrew

Midfield

Born: Mancot, Flintshire, 8 September 1969.
6ft, 12st (1989).
Career: Hawarden Grammar School. Blue Star. LEEDS UNITED trainee April 1986, professional June 1988. Everton £3.5 million July 1996. Newcastle United £5.5 million February 1998. Bolton Wanderers £750,000 July 2004, first-team coach May–October 2007. Sheffield United £250,000 January 2008.

■ Gary made a massive contribution to United's success under the guidance of Howard Wilkinson and has become one of the most respected players in the Premiership. He played for Manchester City nursery side Blue Star before being snapped up by Leeds. His first-team chance came after scoring in 12 consecutive Northern Intermediate League games, and he did not look back, making his mark in the 1990 promotion campaign. He provided the balance on the left-hand side of midfield, was ever present in United's first season back in the top flight and missed just one game as United lifted the 1992 title. A complete all-rounder, whose ability in the air was an added bonus to his skill on the ground, he totalled 85 caps for Wales – just seven short of Neville Southall's

record. United rejected a big bid from Everton in March 1996 but the Blues came back three months later with a deal that saw Gary join the club he supported as a boy. He left Goodison under a cloud but went on to give sterling service to Newcastle and Bolton, becoming the first player to break through the 400 and 500 appearance barriers in the Premiership.

SPRAKE Gareth

Goalkeeper

Born: Winch Wen, nr Swansea, 3 April 1945.
6ft, 13st 3lb (1971).
Career: Llansamlet School and Swansea Schools. Cwn Youth. LEEDS UNITED apprentice June 1960, professional May 1962. Birmingham City £100,000 October 1973–December 1975.

■ Gary made a flying start to his Leeds career – literally. He made his debut as a 16-year-old apprentice in dramatic circumstances, when number-one Tommy Younger fell ill on the eve of United's game at Southampton on 17 March 1962. Gary did not know he was needed until five hours before kick-off and was still in his digs in Leeds. He was whisked to Hampshire via taxi and plane from Manchester and arrived for the

kick-off, which was delayed by 15 minutes. United lost 4–1 but had unearthed a star in Gary, who became first choice the following season. He became Wales' youngest-ever goalkeeper at 18 years, 7 months and 17 days when he faced Scotland in November 1963. Gary won 37 Welsh caps, 32 of them as a Leeds player, plus five at Under-23 level. He was acrobatic and athletic, turning in one of his best performances in the 0–0 draw in Budapest that enabled United to beat Ferencvaros 1–0 on aggregate and lift the Fairs Cup. An ever present in United's 1968–69 Championship-winning side, well-built Gary made more appearances than any other Leeds 'keeper with over 500 appearances. Much has been made in some quarters about his lack of concentration and mistakes – particularly the day he threw the ball into his own net at Liverpool in November 1966 – but they can't disguise the fact that he was an outstanding goalkeeper capable of pulling off impossible saves. After losing his place to David Harvey he moved on to Birmingham but had to retire through illness. He has since suffered from heart problems, leading to a couple of by-pass operations. In 1988 he retired from his job as training officer for Solihull Council.

SPRING Matthew John

Midfield

Born: Harlow, 17 November 1979.
5ft 11in, 11st 5lb (2004).
Career: Luton Town apprentice, professional July 1997. LEEDS UNITED July 2004. Watford £150,000 August 2005. Luton Town £300,000 January 2007.

■ Creative midfielder Matthew suffered during his one season at Elland Road. After more than 200 games at Luton he underwent groin surgery while at Leeds and made only four League starts before being sold to Watford, where he instantly found his best form. He was in the Hornets side that thumped Leeds 3–0 at Cardiff in the 2006 Championship Play-off Final.

SPROSTON Bert

Right-back

Born: Elworth, nr Sandbach, 22 June 1914.
Died: Bolton, 27 January 2000.
5ft 7½in, 11st 10lb (1938).
Career: Sandbach Ramblers. Huddersfield Town trials. LEEDS UNITED May 1933. Tottenham Hotspur £9,500 June 1938. Manchester City £9,500 December 1938. Aldershot, Wrexham, Port Vale and Millwall wartime guest. Ashton United August 1950. Bolton Wanderers trainer and scout July 1951.

■ Bert was a class act at full-back and undoubtedly one of United's stars of the 1930s. After being rejected by Huddersfield as a kid, he played for non-League Sandbach, joining Leeds as a 17-year-old. He did not take long to get in the first team and won his first England cap in 1936

against Wales. By the time he was sold to Spurs for a near-record £9,500 he had represented his country eight times. He did not settle in London and returned north to play for Manchester City six months later. He made an unusual debut for City, travelling up with the Tottenham party on Friday, completing his transfer that night, and turning out against his old team the following day. He won a Second Division Championship medal in 1946–47 to add to his 11 England caps, two wartime international appearances and Football League representative honours.

STACEY Alexander

Right-half

Born: London, 3 June 1904.
Died: Leeds, September 1993.
5ft 8in, 10st 12lb (1930).
Career: Grove House Lads Club, Manchester. Northwich Victoria. New Mills. LEEDS UNITED October 1927. Sheffield United November 1933–May 1937. Kidderminster Harriers.

■ Solidly built Alex was a replacement for classy half-back Willis Edwards, who was laid low by cartilage trouble. Alex was a regular in the reserves for six years and had opportunities to move away but stuck by United and was granted a benefit for his loyalty. He moved on to Sheffield United but within six months fractured a leg which effectively ended his career.

STACK Graham Christopher

Goalkeeper

Born: Hampstead, London, 26 September 1981.
6ft 2in, 12st 6lb (2006).

Career: Arsenal trainee, professional July 2000. Beveren (Belgium) loan July 2002–June 2003. Millwall loan July 2004–May 2005. Reading loan July 2005–May 2006, free August 2006. LEEDS UNITED loans October 2006 and January 2007–May 2007. Wolverhampton Wanderers loan August 2007.

■ Goalkeeper Graham was one of Dennis Wise's first recruits. The former Arsenal Youth Cup-winning shot-stopper had played with Wise at Millwall.

STEPHENSON Joseph Eric

Inside-left

Born: Bexleyheath, Kent, September 1914.
Died: Burma, 8 September 1944.
5ft 6½in, 10st 2lb (1938).
Career: Tom Hood School, Leytonstone. Leeds Schools. Outwood Stormcocks. Harrogate 1931. LEEDS UNITED amateur January 1933, professional September 1934–September 1944.

■ England international Eric was tragically cut down in his prime while serving as a major with the Gurkha Rifles and is buried in Taukkyan War Cemetery in Burma. His parents moved to Leeds when he was a youngster and United picked him up from Harrogate, where

his talent emerged in the Northern League. A creator rather than taker of goals, he quickly rose through the ranks after turning pro and had a sparkling 1937–38 season, topped by a hat-trick in a 4–3 home win against Sunderland. Towards the end of the campaign Eric was rewarded with his England debut against Scotland and also played in a 7–0 win against Ireland in November 1938. He turned out for United during a couple of wartime seasons, and the club played Celtic in a benefit game for his widow in 1946–47. Eric's younger brother also died in the war.

STERLAND Melvyn

Right-back

Born: Sheffield, 1 October 1961.
5ft 10in, 12st 10lb (1989).
Career: Waltheof School, Sheffield. Sheffield Wednesday apprentice June 1978, professional October 1979. Glasgow Rangers £800,000 March 1989. LEEDS UNITED £600,000 July 1989. Boston United player-manager 1994–May 1996. Stalybridge Celtic manager.

■ Buccaneering right-back Mel was a huge hit when he linked up with his old mentor Howard Wilkinson at Leeds. He had worked with Wilko at Sheffield Wednesday, joining them from school, and was immensely popular at Hillsborough. Owls fans dubbed him 'Zico' – a nickname which was transferred to Elland Road. Mel had played a key role

in Wednesday's promotion to Division One in 1984 before a brief spell at Rangers, where he won a Scottish League Championship medal. He opted to work for Wilkinson again and provided United with tremendous thrust down the right flank, delivering pin-point crosses and long throw-ins for Lee Chapman to pile in the goals and booming in several efforts himself – many of them thunderous free-kicks. Mel was a key component as Leeds stormed to the First and Second Division titles before injuries forced him to quit. He was capped once against Saudi Arabia and seven times by the Under-21s, all as a Wednesday player.

STEVENSON Ernest

Inside-left

Born: Rotherham, 28 December 1923.
Died: St Helens, 15 October 1970.
5ft 6in, 10st 6lb (1951).
Career: Wath Wanderers. Wolverhampton Wanderers 1943. Cardiff City October 1948. Southampton February 1950. LEEDS UNITED player-exchange February 1951. Wisbech Town £1,000 July 1952.

■ Like so many of his contemporaries, Ernie's career was severely disrupted by the war. He played for Wolves' nursery side, Wath Wanderers, and featured in the Finals of the League North Cup and War Cup for Wolverhampton. He was signed for Leeds by his old Wolves boss, Major Frank Buckley, but he rarely featured in 1951–52 and left for non-League side Wisbech.

STEVENSON William Byron

Midfield/Defender

Born: Llanelli, 7 September 1956.
Died: 6 September 2007.
6ft 1in, 11st (1977).
Career: LEEDS UNITED apprentice April 1972, professional September 1973. Birmingham City player-exchange March 1982. Bristol Rovers July 1985. Garforth Town player-manager 1986–August 1989.

■ Slimline Byron capably filled a variety of positions for United without any of his managers really finding him a regular place in nearly a decade at the club. He was being groomed as a successor to

Norman Hunter but found himself filling in right across the back four before moving in to midfield. With Leeds in desperate need of a striker, Byron was traded by Allan Clarke for Birmingham's Frank Worthington. He was a regular for Wales until he was sent off in Turkey for violent conduct, receiving a four-year ban – a sentence that was later reduced. After giving up the full-time game he played in the Northern Counties East League with Garforth before having to retire with knee problems. Byron ran pubs in the Leeds area for several years and died, aged 50, of throat cancer.

STEWART David Steel

Goalkeeper

Born: Glasgow, 11 March 1947.
6ft 1½in, 12st (1977).
Career: Wellshot. Shettleston Violet. Kilsyth Rangers. Ayr United 1967. LEEDS UNITED £30,000 October 1973. West Bromwich Albion £70,000 November 1978. Swansea City £60,000 February 1980. Ryoden (Hong Kong) July 1982.

■ David was United's goalkeeper in the 1975 European Cup Final. Blessed with lightning reflexes, he sparkled in the semi-final in Barcelona, having patiently waited as understudy to David Harvey. His form was so good that he won a full Scottish cap in September 1977, saving a penalty in a 1–0 defeat in East Germany. The Glaswegian worked as an upholsterer and carpet fitter when he won a Scottish Junior Cup medal with

Kilsyth Rangers. He continued as a part-timer with Ayr, winning Under-23 honours, before moving to Leeds. He did not get a game at West Brom and after finishing at Swansea worked as a goldsmith in the Welsh city.

STEWART James Gordon

Inside-forward

Born: Durban, South Africa, 7 August 1927.
Died: Northern Natal, South Africa, December 1980.
5ft 7in, 10st (1952).
Career: Parkhill (South Africa). LEEDS UNITED October 1951–53.

■ United scouts Willis Edwards and Frank Taylor saw Gordon playing in his native South Africa against a touring Wolves side. They liked what they saw and he sailed aboard the liner Caernarfon with another inside-forward called Skene, who was not taken on. Within three months of his arrival Gordon made his senior debut in a 3–1 home win against West Ham on 26 January 1952, but he was largely confined to the reserves and returned home in 1953. He worked as an engineering rep and died, aged 73, as a result of injuries sustained in a car crash.

STILES John Charles

Midfield

Born: Manchester, 6 May 1964.
5ft 9½in, 10st 12lb (1986).
Career: Shamrock Rovers 1981. Vancouver Whitecaps (Canada). LEEDS UNITED

April 1984. Doncaster Rovers £40,000 August 1989. Rochdale loan March 1992. Irish football. Gainsborough Trinity. Armthorpe Welfare August 2000.

■ John had a fantastic pedigree – son of World Cup winner Nobby and nephew of United legend Johnny Giles. It was uncle Johnny who gave John his first break in football at Shamrock Rovers before he joined Leeds via Vancouver Whitecaps. John was neat on the ball but struggled with the rugged aspects of the game and his Leeds highlight was a long-range strike at Wigan that set up United's 2–0 FA Cup sixth-round win in 1987. He was one of Billy Bremner's first signings for Doncaster and after retiring from football worked for an insurance company, spent some time as a players' agent and now works as a stand-up comedian.

STONE Stephen Brian

Midfield

Born: Gateshead, 20 August 1971.
5ft 8in, 12st 7lb (2006).
Career: Nottingham Forest apprentice June 1987, professional May 1989. Aston Villa £5.5 million March 1999. Portsmouth loan October 2002, transfer December 2002. LEEDS UNITED July 2005–December 2006.

■ Experienced ex-England ace Steve was seen by Kevin Blackwell as the man to play on the right of midfield to supply balance to United's line-up. But an achilles tendon injury virtually ruled him out for the entire 2005–06

campaign, although he did manage to start in United's final match of the regular season – a 2–0 defeat at Preston. Steve did begin the following season but sustained another injury. After Blackwell was replaced by Dennis Wise, Steve's contract was cancelled by mutual consent and he retired. Steve, a busy, forceful midfielder, won nine England caps, a First Division Championship medal with Forest – where he made over 200 appearances – and promotion to the Premiership with Portsmouth.

STORRIE James

Centre-forward

Born: Kirkintilloch, Lanarkshire, 31 March 1940.
5ft 8½in, 11st 4lb (1963).
Career: Kilsyth Rangers. Airdrie December 1957. LEEDS UNITED £15,650 June 1962. Aberdeen February 1967. Rotherham United December 1967. Portsmouth December 1969. Aldershot loan February 1972. St Mirren player-coach October 1972. Waterlooville player-manager. Airdrie coach. St Johnstone manager.

■ Jim's goals helped United establish themselves as a force to be reckoned with on their return to Division One in 1965. He had been a prolific marksman north of the border with Airdrie and commanded a decent fee when Don Revie signed him in summer 1962. He marked his debut with the winning goal at Stoke on the opening day of the new campaign and finished it with 25 goals.

He was top scorer as they finished runners-up on their return to the top flight, but after losing his place went to Aberdeen and featured in the 1967 Scottish Cup Final, missing a penalty as the Dons lost 2–0 to Celtic.

STRACHAN Gordon David

Midfield

Born: Edinburgh, 9 February 1957.
5ft 6in, 10st 3lb (1989).
Career: Craigroyston and Edinburgh Schools. Dundee October 1971. Aberdeen £50,000 November 1977. Manchester

United £500,000 August 1984. LEEDS UNITED £300,000 March 1989. Coventry City March 1995, player-manager November 1996–June 1997, manager to September 2001. Southampton manager October 2001–February 2004. Glasgow Celtic manager May 2005.

■ Gordon proved the catalyst that helped revive the Leeds glory days in the early 1990s, and Howard Wilkinson pulled off a masterstroke when he signed the 32-year-old Scottish international from Manchester United. A revitalised Gordon was named skipper and was at the hub of the Leeds revival, lifting both the Second and First Division Championships and earning a recall to the national team despite being in the autumn of his career. Voted Footballer of the Year in 1991, he was supremely fit, physically and mentally, helped by a much-publicised diet of seaweed pills and bananas. Blessed with supreme skill and stamina, his midfield combination with Gary McAllister, David Batty and Gary Speed will rank as one of the best seen at Elland Road. Gordon could dribble, shoot with power, deliver free-kicks and corners to the inch and always seemed to play with a touch of cheek and fun. Copper-haired Gordon was made an OBE in New Year 1993 and was strongly tipped to replace Wilkinson as boss, but he actually went on to extend his illustrious playing career at Coventry, who also gave him his first taste of management. Gordon hung up his boots in June 1997 with 50 caps to his credit and a string of medals and honours with Aberdeen and Manchester United to add to his successes at Elland Road. A key figure in Scotland's 1982 and 1986 World Cup campaigns, he was Scottish Player of the Year in 1980. His son, Gavin, a former Leeds YTS player, played for Gordon at Highfield Road.

STRANDLI Frank

Forward

Born: Kristiansand, Norway, 16 May 1972.
6ft 1in, 13st 13lb (1994).
Career: IK Start (Norway) 1989. LEEDS UNITED £250,000 January 1993. SK Brann (Norway) loan June 1994, transfer November 1994. Lillestroem (Norway) 1995. Panathinaikos (Greece) August 1998. Aalborg (Denmark) January 1999–February 2002.

■ Frank, a card-carrying member of the Leeds United Supporters' Club, earned a dream move to Elland Road. The fairytale continued within days of his arrival, coming on as substitute for Rod Wallace and scoring within minutes of a 3–0 home win over Middlesbrough. But the dream died as Frank could not adapt to the pace of English football, and after a lengthy spell in the reserves he returned to his native Norway, for whom he won the first of his 24 caps against Bermuda as a 17-year-old. United wanted him to come to England in October 1992, but the deal was delayed a few months because of difficulties in getting a work permit while he completed his national service with the Norwegian army. His career was ended, aged 28, by a recurring groin strain while with Danish side Aalborg.

STUART George Ernest

Wing-half

Born: East Wemyss, Fife, 4 July 1895.
Died: Dundee, 1989.
5ft 7in, 11st 7lb (1920).
Career: Dundee. LEEDS UNITED (July 1920).

■ Recruited for United's maiden season in the Football League, George played in just a couple of FA Cup preliminary ties and one League game, when he and Ernie Hart made their debuts in a 2–0 home defeat against Stockport.

SULLIVAN Neil

Goalkeeper

Born: Sutton, London, 24 February 1970.
6ft, 12st 1lb (2005).
Career: Wimbledon from trainee July 1988. Crystal Palace loan May 1992. Tottenham Hotspur June 2000. Chelsea August 2003. LEEDS UNITED August 2003. Doncaster Rovers loans November 2006 and February–April 2007, transfer June 2007.

■ Neil, Chelsea's third-choice 'keeper, was one of the best of the free transfers picked up by Kevin Blackwell and proved a fine last line of defence for the two seasons after relegation from the Premiership. An excellent shot-stopper, he saved four penalties in an ever-present 2004–05 campaign and even earned a recall to the Scotland national squad, but he did not add to his 27 caps. Prior to his arrival in Yorkshire he had spent all his time with London clubs, doing particularly well at Wimbledon, where he played more than 200 times. Shortly after leaving Leeds he appeared in Doncaster's Johnstone's Paint Trophy Final-winning team at the Millennium Stadium, Cardiff, where he had suffered Play-off heartbreak the previous year with United. Neil was in the Doncaster side that beat Leeds in the 2008 League One Play-off Final.

SUTHERLAND Harry Ross

Centre-forward

Born: Salford, 30 July 1915.
Career: Sedgeley Park. LEEDS UNITED July 1938. Southport, Rochdale, Accrington Stanley, Doncaster Rovers and Chesterfield wartime guest. Exeter City May 1947. Bournemouth July 1948–May 1949.

■ Harry joined Leeds from Sedgeley Park with a big goalscoring reputation, and a two-goal debut in the reserves clinched him a professional contract. He also scored United's goal in a 4–1 defeat at Wolves on his League debut in 1939. Like many, his career was badly disrupted by the war, and he only played a couple more times before moving on after the war.

SWAN Jack

Forward

Born: Easington, Co. Durham, 10 July 1893.
Died: Hendon, January 1990.
5ft 10in, 11st 7lb (1922).
Career: Seaham Harbour. Huddersfield Town October 1919. LEEDS UNITED November 1921. Watford £1,000 September 1925. Queen's Park Rangers £300 February 1927. Thames July 1928. Lovells Athletic October 1929.

■ Jack was United's top scorer in the 1923–24 Second Division Championship-winning campaign, averaging a goal every other game from 36 starts. Many of them were missile-like shots from his trusty left foot, which brought him exactly 50 goals in Leeds colours. He first shot to prominence at neighbouring Huddersfield, playing in the 1920 FA Cup Final defeat to Aston Villa. After losing his place in the Terriers' team to England international Clem Stephenson, who had guested for United in World War One, Jack was transferred to Leeds. He went AWOL while at Elland Road and received a club suspension, suffering a similar fate at his next club,

Watford. For a decade before his death he was the longest-living FA Cup finalist.

SWAN Peter Harold

Defender/Forward

Born: Leeds, 28 September 1966.
6ft, 11st 12lb (1987).
Career: Middleton Park and Leeds Schools. Yorkshire Schools. Yorkshire Amateur. LEEDS UNITED apprentice, professional August 1984. Hull City £200,000 March 1989. Port Vale £300,000 August 1991. Plymouth Argyle £300,000 July 1994. Burnley £200,000 August 1995. Bury £50,000 August 1997. Burnley August 1998. York City March 2000. Ossett Town player-manager November 2000–02. Northampton Town youth coach 2004.

■ Peter was not a graceful player, but he was powerful and highly effective. A strong, muscular Leeds lad, 'Swanny' made his breakthrough shortly after Billy Bremner took over from Eddie Gray, scoring twice on his second home League appearance, a 4–0 win against Stoke. Mainly a defender but also a useful attacking target man, Peter was excellent in the air and it needed a Hull record fee to prise him away from Elland Road. He forged a fine career, particularly at Port Vale, playing twice at Wembley in 1993. He was in the side that won the Autoglass Trophy but eight days later joined the select band of players to be dismissed at the Twin Towers when Vale lost to West Brom in the Second Division Play-off Final.

SWEENEY, Peter Henry

Midfield

Born: Glasgow, 25 September 1984.
6ft, 12st 1lb (2007).
Career: Welling Secondary, England and Scotland Schools. Elms FC. Millwall junior, then professional December 2000. Stoke City July 2005. Yeovil Town loan January 2007. LEEDS UNITED January 2008.

■ Peter was drafted in midway through the 2007–08 season to provide more width to United's midfield. He had worked with manager Dennis Wise at Millwall, where he played against Manchester United in the 2004 FA Cup Final. Peter has the unusual distinction of playing for both England and Scotland Schools. Born in Glasgow, he was brought up in London and played a couple of times for England as a schoolboy until the FA realised he was a Scot. He qualified for England because he attended an English school, but the FA had an agreement with the other home nations that a non-England schoolboy could not play for England, so he was snapped up by the Scottish selectors. He has since played eight times for the Scottish Under-21 side.

SWINBURNE Trevor

Goalkeeper

Born: East Rainton, Co. Durham, 20 June 1953.
6ft, 14st 7lb (1985).
Career: Lambton and Hetton Boys. East Rainton Youths. Sunderland apprentice July 1968, professional June 1970. Sheffield United loan December 1976. Carlisle United May 1977. Brentford August 1983. LEEDS UNITED June 1985. Doncaster Rovers loan September 1985. Lincoln City February 1986–May 1987.

■ Trevor provided solid back-up to regular number-one Mervyn Day at Leeds, playing just a couple of games. He had been deputy to Jim Montgomery at

Sunderland for seven years but topped 350 appearances for Carlisle before arriving at Elland Road as a 32-year-old. His dad, Tom, played in goal for Newcastle and won a wartime England cap, while brother Alan also played for Oldham. After retiring in May 1987 Trevor became a prison officer in Leicestershire.

TAYLOR Francis Gerald

Outside-left

Born: Magherafelt, Co. Londonderry, 2 January 1923.
5ft 6in, 11st (1950).
Career: Bangor. LEEDS UNITED July 1949.

■ Irish junior international Frank had a Christmas to remember in 1949, making his Leeds debut in a 3–1 home win over Preston on 24 December, and he kept his place for the 1–1 draw on Boxing Day. Frank, who worked as a draughtsman in Ireland, made just one more appearance for United.

TAYLOR John Brian

Goalkeeper

Born: Rossington, nr Doncaster, 7 October 1931.
5ft 10in, 11st 3lb (1951).
Career: Sheffield Wednesday amateur. Doncaster Rovers March 1949. Worksop Town. LEEDS UNITED March 1951. King's Lynn 1953. Bradford Park Avenue June 1954.

■ United called Brian back from his national service in York to make his League debut at Birmingham City on 22 August 1951. That was the start of a run of 11 successive games – his only United appearances.

TAYLOR John Robert

Forward

Born: Horden, Co. Durham, 3 February 1967.
5ft 10in, 11st 2lb (1986).
Career: Dene House School, Peterlee. Hartlepool United trial. Newcastle United trial. Horden Colliery August 1985. LEEDS UNITED March 1986. Bristol City £175,000 March 1989. West Bromwich Albion £300,000 January 1992. Bolton Wanderers loan January 1998, transfer May 1998. West Bromwich Albion £90,000 March 2000. Cheltenham Town August 2003. Tamworth June 2004–June 2006. Kidderminster Harriers September 2006– January 2007.

■ Teen striker Bob was recommended to

United by Horden Colliery manager Dick Malone, a member of the 1973 Sunderland side that beat Leeds in the FA Cup Final. Local council worker Bob went to Elland Road for trials and scored a hat-trick in his first game for the juniors. The following season he was top scorer for the reserves and was gradually introduced to the senior side by Billy Bremner. He left United in an exchange deal for Carl Shutt and rattled in 50 goals for Bristol City, helping them win promotion when he finished the Third Division's top scorer. That triggered a move to West Brom, where he scored 113 goals in two spells, earning Baggies legend status.

THOM John

Centre-forward

Born: Hurlford, Ayrshire, 18 May 1899.
Died: 1966.
5ft 8in, 12st (1924).
Career: Hurlford Thistle. Birmingham trials. Nottingham Forest August 1922. Workington 1923. LEEDS UNITED £430 May 1924. Bristol Rovers £175 June 1927. Workington August 1928. Aldershot June 1930. Guildford 1933. Aldershot reserve team trainer.

■ Jock usually scored goals wherever he played, including three for Leeds in seven starts. Having failed to make the League breakthrough with Nottingham

Forest, he joined Workington, where his 30 goals in 1923–24 attracted United's attention. He scored over a century of goals for Aldershot, including a staggering 68 in 1930–31.

THOMAS David Gwyn

Midfield

Born: Swansea, 26 September 1957.
5ft 8in, 11st (1982).
Career: LEEDS UNITED apprentice, professional July 1975. Barnsley £40,000 March 1984. Hull City £25,000 March 1990. Carlisle United August 1991–92.

■ Welsh Schools international Gwyn was a prolific scorer at junior and reserve level and scored on his first League start in the first team, a 2–0 home win over Bristol City on 30 April 1977. However, the vast majority of his games for the senior side were in midfield. A familiar figure with his socks rolled down to his ankles, he had limitless energy and won three Under-21 caps but missed out on a full international because of injury. He broke a leg at Hull and damaged cruciate ligaments in both knees at Barnsley.

THOMAS Michael Reginald

Midfield

Born: Mochdre, nr Colwyn Bay, 7 July 1954.
5ft 6in, 10st 7lb (1990).
Career: Pendorlan Secondary School, Colwyn Bay. Clwyd, Conwy and North Wales Schools. Quinton Hazell. Wrexham amateur 1969, apprentice 1971, professional April 1972. Manchester United £300,000 November 1978. Everton £450,000 August

1981. Brighton £400,000 November 1981. Stoke City £200,000 August 1982. Chelsea £75,000 January 1984. West Bromwich Albion September 1985. Derby County loan March 1986. Wichita Wings (US) August 1986. Shrewsbury Town August 1988. LEEDS UNITED £10,000 June 1989. Stoke City loan March 1990, transfer August 1990. Wrexham August 1991. Conwy United July 1993–August 1993. Inter Cardiff 1995. Portmadog manager. Amlwch Town 1998–99.

■ While the 1989–90 Division Two campaign was one of celebration for United, it brought frustration for experienced Welsh international Mickey. He started the first three games of that promotion season but suffered a knee injury at Blackburn. By the time he was fit there was no room in the side for the feisty midfielder and he went on loan to Stoke, eventually joining on a permanent basis. One of the most colourful characters ever to play football, Mickey won the first of his 51 Welsh caps at Wrexham and earned a string of big-money moves between some of English football's biggest clubs. An outspoken dynamic firebrand, he was shipped out of Everton after just three months for refusing to play in a reserve game and was jailed in his second stint at Wrexham for handling counterfeit money. Despite such scrapes he enjoyed a career that brought him 101 goals in 729 appearances and plenty of medals.

THOMPSON Alan

Midfield

Born: Newcastle upon Tyne, 22 December 1973.
6ft, 12st 8lb (2007).
Career: Newcastle United schoolboy forms 1989, professional March 1991. Bolton Wanderers £350,000 July 1993. Aston Villa £4.5 million June 1998. Glasgow Celtic £2.75 million September 2000. LEEDS UNITED loan January–May 2007, free August 2007–May 2008. Hartlepool United loan January 2008.

■ With Leeds close to the foot of the Championship table, they grabbed experienced left-sided midfielder Alan on loan from Scottish giants Celtic in the 2007 January transfer window. After relegation he was signed permanently and made skipper, and he had a brief spell as acting assistant manager when Gus Poyet joined Spurs. Alan's career almost ended in tragic circumstances before it began. In 1990 the England Youth international suffered a broken neck and back in a car crash which hospitalised several of Newcastle United's junior players, but he fought back from those career-threatening injuries to win a place in the Magpies' first XI. Frustrated by limited opportunities he joined Bolton, where his sparkling displays, embroidered by a cultured left foot and a booming shot, earned him two England Under-21 caps and a big-money move to Villa

before enjoying even greater success with Celtic. While in the SPL he won an England cap against Sweden as Sven Goran Eriksson strove to solve the national side's left-side midfield problem. He retired in May 2008.

THOMPSON Nigel David

Defender/Midfield

Born: Leeds, 1 March 1967.
5ft 7in, 10st 12lb (1986).
Career: Lawnswood, Leeds and West Yorkshire Schools. LEEDS UNITED December 1984. Rochdale loan August 1986. Chesterfield £10,000 March 1988–90. Goole Town. Colne Dynamos. Gainsborough Trinity. Alfreton Town.

■ Nigel, a member of the England Under-18 squad, had a handful of United first team outings at left-back and midfield as a teenager. He struggled to match up to Second Division standards and his League career came to a premature end at Chesterfield because of a knee injury. He started work as a postman in Leeds.

THOMPSON Robert

Centre-forward

Born: Coundon Grange, nr Bishop Auckland, 1890.
6ft, 12st (1920).
Career: Wingate Albion. Preston North End. Durham City August 1919. LEEDS UNITED July 1920. Ashington May 1921. Luton Town June 1922. Pontypridd 1923. Accrington Stanley 1924. Bury May 1925.

Hartlepools United December 1926. Goole Town January 1927. York City January 1927.

■ Bob netted United's first-ever League hat-trick, his treble coming against Notts County at Elland Road on 11 December 1920. A former winner of the famous Powderhall Sprint in Edinburgh, he topped the Leeds scoring charts in that maiden season but found himself on the sidelines when United signed Tommy Howarth, and he moved on to Ashington. Bob regularly switched clubs and had a successful 1923–24 season with Pontypridd, scoring 51 goals and earning a place in the Welsh League side that played the Irish Free State in February 1924.

THOMSON John

Inside-forward

Born: Loanhead, nr Edinburgh, 14 April 1916.
Died: Haymarket, Edinburgh, 1976.
Career: Loanhead Steelworks. LEEDS UNITED September 1934. Grimsby Town February 1939. Hereford United. York City November 1948.

■ United signed John as an 18-year-old and he made a scoring debut in a 3–0 win against Everton on 17 October 1936. He looked set for a long run in the team but was put in the shadows by the purchase of George Ainsley and moved on to Grimsby.

THORNTON Richard George

Goalkeeper

Born: Boldon, Co. Durham, 16 May 1894.
5ft 10in, 11st 4lb (1925).
Career: Esh Winning. Bearpark. LEEDS UNITED amateur May 1925, professional September 1925. Accrington Stanley November 1928. York City June 1931–May 1932. Bridlington Town. Leyland Motors. Selby Town August 1937.

■ Poor Dick's sole appearance in goal for Leeds was a disaster – a 6–3 Boxing Day defeat at Burnley, with all the Clarets' goals coming in the first half. He had been a noted amateur in North East football and had a decent stint at Accrington.

TILLOTSON Arthur

Left-back

Born: Hunslet, Leeds, 7 February 1894.
5ft 10in, 11st 10lb (1920).
Career: Sheffield United. Castleford Town. LEEDS UNITED July 1920. Castleford Town September 1920.

■ Arthur arrived at Elland Road with his Castleford full-back partner Bert Duffield. While Bert became a big hit, Arthur only turned out in the club's opening two games before returning to Castleford, where his brother Joe was also on the books.

TINKLER Mark Roland

Midfield

Born: Bishop Auckland, Co. Durham, 24 October 1974.
5ft 10in, 13st 3lb (1995).
Career: Bishop Auckland, Durham and England Schools. LEEDS UNITED November 1991. York City £85,000 March 1997. Southend United £40,000 August 1999. Hartlepool United November 2000. Livingston July 2007.

■ Another of the 1993 FA Youth Cup-winning side, Mark excelled in central defence in the Final games against Manchester United. However, it was in midfield that he played virtually all his senior football, making his debut at Sheffield United as David Batty's replacement towards the end of the 1992–93 season. Mark was a member of

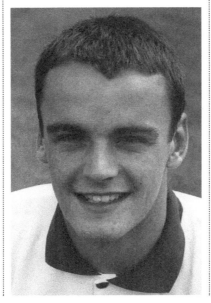

the Under-18 squad that won the European Championship but a broken ankle in a reserve team match saw him slip down the Elland Road pecking order and he was transferred to York. Since then he has amassed over 200 games for Hartlepool.

TONER James

Right-winger

Born: Shettleston, Glasgow, 23 August 1924.
5ft 6in, 11st 12lb (1954).
Career: St Mungo's Academy, Glasgow. Fauldhouse United. Dundee. LEEDS UNITED June 1954.

■ Persistent Leeds finally signed Jim after a lengthy pursuit of the speedy Scottish winger. His performances at Dundee caught the eye of Major Buckley, but it was Buckley's successor, Raich Carter, who eventually persuaded Jim to join Leeds. He made his debut on the opening day of the 1954–55 season in a 2–0 win over Hull City, the club whom Leeds had pipped for his signature. However, Jim was never able to hit the heights he had achieved north of the border, where he won Scottish League Cup-winners' medals in 1952 and 1953 and a Scottish Junior Cup-winners' medal with Fauldhouse. He was seriously injured and his wife, Christine, was one of two passengers killed in January 2007 when the Scotland-bound coach they were on overturned in London.

TOWNSLEY Thomas

Centre-half

Born: Polmont, Stirlingshire, 28 April 1898.
Died: Peterhead, 10 April 1976.
5ft 11in, 11st 2lb (1930).
Career: Laurieston Villa. Cowie Wanderers. Falkirk 1919. LEEDS UNITED £5,000 December 1925. Falkirk October 1931–33. Peterhead manager 1938.

■ Tom was a magnificent servant for Leeds, missing only four games in his three-and-a-half seasons at Elland Road after making his debut in a 2–2 home draw with Burnley on Christmas Day 1925. He was successfully converted from centre-half to right-back, a move

that had a dual purpose – allowing the emerging Ernie Hart to take the central defensive role while Tom plugged the problematic right-back slot. Tom was a highly mobile defender and while at Falkirk played once for Scotland against Wales in October 1925 and turned out for the Scottish League XI four times. He had a second spell with Falkirk before managing Peterhead for many years.

TRAINOR John

Centre-forward

Born: Byker, Newcastle upon Tyne, 29 August 1911.
5ft 10in, 13st (1935).
Career: Northumberland Schools. Berwick Rangers. Duns. Ashington 1934. LEEDS UNITED December 1935. Southend United May 1938.

■ Powerfully-built centre-forward Jack was a sporting all-rounder. He was a star athlete at school and played rugby union for Berwick in 1933, but eventually opted for football. Jack played at Ashington for Billy Hampson, who brought him down to Leeds when he was appointed manager at Elland Road but Jack made only three League starts before moving to Southend. Jack was a cousin of Charlie Napier, the Celtic, Derby, Sheffield Wednesday and Scottish international forward.

TURNBULL Robert

Right-winger

Born: South Bank, Middlesbrough, 17 December 1895.
Died: Middlesbrough, 19 March 1952.
5ft 10in, 11st 7lb (1925).

Career: South Bank East End. Bradford Park Avenue January 1918. LEEDS UNITED May 1925. Rhyl September 1932–33.

■ United's fans were enraptured by Bobby's dazzling skills for six seasons. The right-winger gave many a full-back a sleepless night with his rapid footwork, which brought him 45 goals in 204 League appearances in United colours. Bobby began with amateur side South Bank East End and looked destined to join Middlesbrough. However, Boro missed out on his signature in unusual circumstances. Bradford Park Avenue arrived in Middlesbrough to play a benefit game for the relatives of Boro full-back Donald McLeod, who died in World War One. Avenue were a man short, and Turnbull was persuaded to turn out for them. He gave a brilliant display and was signed by Bradford straight after the match, scoring five times on his wartime debut for Avenue against Barnsley on New Year's Day 1918. He was capped against Ireland the following year and toured South Africa with an FA squad in 1920. After retiring from football he returned to Teesside to work for Dorman Long & Company.

TURNER Charles J.

Centre-half

Born: Manchester, c. 1911.
5ft 10½in, 11st (1933).
Career: Eccles Schools. Atherton. Stalybridge Celtic. LEEDS UNITED May 1933. Southend United June 1935.

■ Charlie spent a couple of seasons at Leeds as deputy to England international Ernie Hart. He had represented Eccles Schools, playing in the same side as United goalkeeper Reg Savage.

TURNER Christopher Robert

Goalkeeper

Born: Sheffield, 15 September 1958.
6ft, 12st 4lb (1984).
Career: Sheffield Schools. Sheffield Wednesday apprentice March 1975, professional August 1976. Lincoln City loan October 1978. Sunderland July 1979. Manchester United August 1985. Sheffield Wednesday September 1988. LEEDS UNITED loan November 1989. Leyton Orient October 1991, assistant manager 1993, joint manager April 1994–April 1995. Leicester City coach 1995. Wolverhampton Wanderers youth-team coach. Hartlepool United manager February 1999–November 2002. Sheffield Wednesday November 2002–September 2004. Stockport County December 2004–December 2005. Hartlepool United director of sport February 2006.

■ Former England Youth international Chris helped United out on loan for a couple of games when Mervyn Day was injured. A good, solid goalkeeper, he won a League Cup-winners' medal with Sheffield Wednesday in 1991 and helped the Owls back into the top flight, later returning to Hillsborough as manager.

TURNER John Kipling

Right-winger

Born: Worksop, Nottinghamshire, c. 1914.
5ft 6in, 10st 7lb (1935).
Career: Worksop Town. Northern Rubber
Works, Retford. LEEDS UNITED October
1935. Mansfield Town £150 December
1937. Bristol City £250 May 1939.
Mansfield Town wartime guest.

■ Jack was signed by United after a trial in a Yorkshire Midweek League game when he scored against Mansfield under the pseudonym 'A. Newman'. Ironically, he had been recommended to Mansfield when he was a youngster on Worksop's books before turning out for North Notts League club Northern Rubber Works. Mainly confined to the reserves at Elland Road, he eventually joined the Stags in December 1937.

TWOMEY James Francis

Goalkeeper

Born: Newry, Northern Ireland, 13 April
1914.
Died: Leeds, 9 November 1984.
5ft 11in, 12st 2lb (1937).
Career: Newry Town. LEEDS UNITED
December 1937. Halifax Town August
1949, later trainer-coach.

■ Jim had the curious honour of winning his first Irish cap while still a reserve at Leeds. As a youngster he was a skilful boxer and Gaelic footballer, but opted to pursue a soccer career and

James Twomey

made his debut for Newry Town when he was only 15. He played twice for the Irish League and it was a brilliant display against the Football League at Blackpool in October 1937 that triggered the rush to sign him. Leeds boss Billy Hampson won the race and Jim gave up his job as a woodworking machinist to join United's payroll. Jim started life in Leeds reserves before making the breakthrough in March 1938. He played at Blackpool in a Central League game on the 12th, kept a clean sheet against Wales on his international debut on the 16th and made his Leeds senior debut three days later, also at Blackpool. Although he returned to his home town of Newry during the war, he returned to Leeds when peacetime football resumed and settled in the city. After finishing at

Halifax Town he did some scouting for United and did a great deal of charity work for the Leeds United ex-Players' Association.

TYRER Arthur Spencer

Left-winger

Born: Manchester, 25 February 1931.
6ft, 11st 10½lb (1951).
Career: Mossley. LEEDS UNITED
September 1950. Peterborough United July
1954. Shrewsbury June 1955. Aldershot
June 1955. Fleet 1964.

■ Arthur quit his job as a plumber to join United as a professional from Cheshire League club Mossley. An excellent crosser and possessor of a fierce shot, Arthur lacked consistency at Leeds but found his feet at Aldershot, where he made 235 League appearances.

U–V

UNDERWOOD Benjamin Riley

Left-half

Born: Alfreton, Derbyshire, 30 September 1901.
Died: 9 March 1958.
5ft 10½in, 11st 8lb (1928).
Career: Derby County. New Hucknall Colliery 1920. Sutton Town 1924. Doncaster Rovers June 1926. LEEDS UNITED May 1928. Coventry City 1931–34.

■ Rejected as a teenager by Derby, Ben had half a dozen games in three seasons with United, usually acting as cover for George Reed or Willis Edwards. He was unlucky with injuries at Leeds and it was a similar story at Coventry.

VARADI Imre

Striker

Born: Paddington, London, 8 July 1959.
5ft 8in, 11st 11lb (1989).
Career: Paddington and Central London Schools. Letchworth Garden City. Letchworth Town FC 1975. Hitchin. Sheffield United apprentice July 1975, professional April 1978. Everton £80,000 March 1979. Newcastle United £125,000 August 1981. Sheffield Wednesday £150,000 plus David Mills August 1983. West Bromwich Albion £285,000 June

1985. Manchester City player exchange with Robert Hopkins October 1986. Sheffield Wednesday player exchange with Carl Bradshaw September 1988. LEEDS UNITED £50,000 February 1990. Luton Town loan March 1992. Oxford United loan January 1993. Rotherham United March 1993. Mansfield Town August 1995. Boston United player-coach September 1995. Scunthorpe United September 1995. Matlock Town player-manager November 1995–May 1996. Guiseley player-coach 1996. Denaby United player-coach January 1997–May 1998. Stalybridge Celtic assistant manager and coach 1998–99.

■ Injuries to Bobby Davison and Carl Shutt prompted Howard Wilkinson to dip into his Sheffield Wednesday contacts book to sign Imre and keep United's Division Two Championship bandwagon rolling. It was the third time that Imre had played for Wilko, and he joined up with ex-Owls players Shutt, Lee Chapman, Mel Sterland, Glynn Snodin and John Pearson at Elland Road. Quick and direct, he played enough games to win a medal – one of the highlights of a career encompassing 13 League clubs and 151 goals in 419 League games. He later worked briefly with Mel Sterland at Boston and Stalybridge. Imre's brother, Fernando, played for Fulham.

VICKERS Peter

Forward

Born: Kilnhurst, nr Doncaster, 6 March 1934.
5ft 9in, 10st (1951).
Career: Rotherham and Yorkshire Schools. LEEDS UNITED groundstaff 1948, professional March 1951. March Town. King's Lynn July 1956. Lincoln City August 1959. Wisbech Town. Northampton Town February 1960. Scarborough 1960.

■ It was possibly a case of too much, too soon for Peter. He captained Rotherham Boys and played for Yorkshire and England Schools, joining United's groundstaff as a 14-year-old. Eight days after turning pro he made his League

debut, aged 17, in a 2–2 home draw with Queen's Park Rangers in March 1951. He played in the next game at Hull but did not re-emerge in first-team colours until August 1954, having completed his national service in Germany with the Royal Armoured Corps. He was selected for the Central League XI against champions Wolves Reserves in September 1952, but after demob his career drifted.

VIDUKA Mark Anthony

Striker

Born: Melbourne, Australia, 9 October 1975.
6ft 2in, 13st 9lb (2002).
Career: Melbourne Knights (Australia) 1993. NK Croatia Zagreb (Croatia) 1995. Glasgow Celtic December 1998. LEEDS UNITED £6 million July 2000. Middlesbrough £4.5 million July 2004. Newcastle United free June 2007.

■ Multi-talented Mark had all the weapons to be a top-class striker – sublime skill, heading prowess, power and no lack of pace for a big man. It brought him 72 goals in four years at Elland Road. The 'Duke' was unstoppable on his day, as Liverpool found out on 4 November 2000 when he scored all United's goals as Leeds fought back from 3–1 down to win 4–3 at Elland Road. However, there were times when he looked uninterested and tended to score his goals in batches – his late flurry of 13

Mark Viduka

goals in the final 10 games of the 2002–03 staving off Premiership relegation for a year. Of Croatian and Ukranian descent, Mark was so good with Melbourne Knights that they named a stand after him. After three years with Zagreb he showcased his talents at Celtic before David O'Leary signed him for Leeds. After United's relegation from the top flight Mark was inevitably sold, teaming up with Jimmy Floyd Hasslebaink in Middlesbrough's attack to help Boro lift the League Cup and reach the 2006 UEFA Cup Final. He also skippered Australia in the 2006 World Cup Finals, 12 years after winning his first cap.

W

WAINSCOAT William Russell

Inside-left

Born: East Retford, Nottinghamshire, 28 July 1898.
Died: Worthing, July 1967.
5ft 10½in, 12st (1922).
Career: Maltby Main. Barnsley March 1920. Middlesbrough £4,000 December 1923. LEEDS UNITED £2,000 March 1925. Hull City October 1931–34.

■ Russell reached his peak in his six years at Elland Road, winning an England cap against Scotland in April 1929. A classic inside-forward, he allied speed to slick passing and sharp-shooting to net 87 goals in 215 League games in United colours. He made a dream debut with his first League club, Barnsley, scoring a debut hat-trick against Fulham on 6 March 1920. He also scored on his Middlesbrough debut but after the Ayresome Park side were relegated he joined Leeds to stay in the First Division. The national selectors quickly sat up and took notice, taking Russell on the 1926 FA tour of Canada, where he scored five in a game against Thunder Bay. Despite sustaining a broken nose and a triple fracture of an arm at Leeds, Russell's performances were rarely short of excellent. He joined Hull, aged 33, helping the Tigers to the 1933 Division Three North title before retiring the following year. He then held a variety of jobs, including railway clerk, licensee, shoe shop boss, confectioner and drapery store manager. Russell was also a splendid cricketer, turning out for Barnsley in the Yorkshire Council.

WAKEFIELD Albert Joseph

Centre-forward

Born: Pontefract, 19 November 1921.
Died: December 2006.
5ft 9in, 11st (1947).
Career: Stanningley Works. LEEDS UNITED October 1942. Southend United player-exchange August 1949. Clacton July 1953.

■ Had Albert not returned to Leeds after World War Two he might well have made a name for himself in Italian football. He joined the Elland Road payroll during the war but did not manage too much wartime football at home as he was serving in Italy. He turned down offers from Italian clubs to go back to United when hostilities ended, marking his belated League debut at the age of 25 with United's goal in a 2–1 defeat at Southampton on 30 August. He knocked in a couple more on his home debut four days later in a 4–1 win against Barnsley, finishing the campaign as leading scorer with 21 goals. A swap with Frank Dudley took him to Southend, where he netted over half a century of League goals.

WALLACE Raymond George

Midfield/Full-back

Born: Lewisham, London, 2 October 1969.
5ft 6in, 11st 4lb (1991).
Career: Southampton trainee July 1986, professional April 1988. LEEDS UNITED £100,000 July 1991. Swansea City loan March 1992. Reading loan March 1994. Stoke City August 1994. Hull City loan December 1994–99. Airdrie September 1999. Altrincham September 1999. Witton Albion March 2001. Tyldesley United.

■ Marginally the youngest of the three footballing Wallace brothers from Southampton, Ray accompanied twin Rod to Elland Road. Ray was rated at £100,000, a fraction of the £1.6 million

paid for Rod. Although he had been out of the frame at Saints for 20 months, Ray had four Under-21 caps to his name. All three Wallaces – the twins and elder brother Danny, who was later to play for Manchester United and England – made history in October 1989 when they played together against Sheffield Wednesday. Ray's opportunities at Leeds were few and far between, but he shone at Stoke and topped 200 appearances.

WALLACE Rodney Seymour

Forward

Born: Lewisham, London, 2 October 1969.
5ft 7in, 11st (1992).
Career: Southampton apprentice July 1986, professional April 1988. LEEDS UNITED £1.6 million June 1991. Glasgow Rangers July 1998. Bolton Wanderers September 2001. Gillingham August 2002–May 2004. Kingstonian Under-18 assistant manager January 2008.

■ Hot Rod, twin of Ray and brother of Danny, had pace to burn. The little forward's darting runs were the perfect complement to the raw power of Lee Chapman as the striking duo enjoyed a magnificent 1991–92 League Championship season. In September 1992 he was called up for an England trip to Spain, but injury prevented him from going. Rod won 11 Under-21 caps at Southampton and played a couple of times for England B but missed out on

---

that elusive senior appearance. A thrilling individual player, his BBC Goal of the Season against Tottenham in April 1994 ranks as one of the best solo goals ever seen at Elland Road, dribbling past a swathe of defenders in a long mazy run before curling home a wonderful shot from just inside the penalty area. After 66 first-team goals Rod had great success in Scotland with Rangers.

WALTON James

Left-half

Born: Sacriston, Co. Durham, 3 December 1904.
Died: 20 November 1982.
5ft 9in, 11st 7lb (1920).
Career: Cleator Moor. West Stanley August 1919. LEEDS UNITED July 1920. Bristol Rovers August 1923. Brentford £125 November 1924–26. Hartlepools United November 1926.

■ Jimmy missed only one game in United's maiden Football League season. He was plucked from non-League football in the North East and was a fine asset but lost his first-team place when skipper Jim Baker switched to left-half. Jimmy had a spell at inside-forward before being transferred to Bristol Rovers.

WALTON Simon William

Utility player

Born: Sherburn-in-Elmet, nr Leeds, 13 September 1987.
6ft 1in, 13st 5lb (2006).
Career: Sherburn High School. Sherburn White Rose juniors. LEEDS UNITED trainee, professional September 2004. Charlton Athletic £1 million July 2006. Ipswich Town loan August 2006–January 2007. Cardiff City loan January–May 2007. Queen's Park Rangers £200,000 July 2007. Hull City loan January 2008.

■ Simon burst on to the scene as a 16-year-old, scoring a penalty on his debut in a high-profile friendly against Spanish giants Valencia, only to be sent off for a second bookable offence minutes later. His energy in midfield proved useful as United tried to stabilise after relegation from the Premiership and he also played in central defence and at full-back. He rarely featured in his second season and United accepted a £1 million bid from Charlton, who immediately sent him on loan to Ipswich and later to Cardiff, where he was sent off in the Bluebirds' 1–0 home win over Leeds on 17 February 2007.

WARNER Anthony Randolph

Goalkeeper

Born: Liverpool, 11 May 1974.
6ft 4in, 13st 9lb (2006).
Career: Liverpool junior, professional January 1994. Swindon Town loan November 1997. Glasgow Celtic November 1998. Aberdeen loan March 1999. Millwall July 1999. Cardiff City July 2004. Fulham £100,000 August 2005. LEEDS UNITED loan August 2006–January 2007. Norwich City loan February–May 2007. Barnsley loan February 2008.

■ With Neil Sullivan injured, manager Kevin Blackwell took Fulham goalkeeper Tony on loan at the start of 2006–07. However, after Dennis Wise replaced Blackwell, Tony found himself on the bench. New loan man Graham Stack took his place between the sticks, and Tony returned to his parent club.

WATERHOUSE Fred

Winger

Born: Horsforth, nr Leeds, 28 September 1897.
5ft 8in, 12st (1920).
Career: Huddersfield Town amateur. LEEDS UNITED August 1920.

■ Fred was signed at the start of United's first Football League season from neighbours Huddersfield but his only appearances came in the preliminary round of the FA Cup, when United fielded reserve sides because of clashes with Second Division fixtures.

WATSON Andrew

Midfield

Born: Aberdeen, 3 September 1959.
5ft 10in, 11st 10lb (1983).
Career: Sunnyside. Aberdeen June 1976. LEEDS UNITED £60,000 June 1983. Hearts December 1984. Hibernian 1987–May 1989. Motherwell assistant manager 1994. Hibernian assistant manager February 1998. Glasgow Rangers assistant manager December 2001. Scotland assistant manager January 2007. Birmingham City assistant manager November 2007.

■ Hard-working midfielder Andy was highly regarded north of the border and was recruited by Eddie Gray. He had pushed himself to the brink of international honours after winning four Under-23 caps while at Aberdeen, where he played alongside Gordon Strachan and won Scottish Cup and European Cup-Winners' Cup medals. At Leeds he was not at his best as he found it hard to come to terms with the pace of the English game. A knee injury ended his career at 28 with Hibs. Andy was a top-notch coach in Scotland, working as assistant to Alex McLeish at Motherwell, Hibs and Rangers before the duo were handed the reins of the national side. After coming close to taking Scotland to the 2008 European Cup Finals, they quit for Premiership side Birmingham City, only to suffer relegation at the end of the campaign.

WEBB Robert

Forward

Born: Altofts, nr Castleford, 29 November 1933.
5ft 5½in, 8st 11lb (1951).
Career: Normanton Boys. West Riding Boys. Silkstone Rovers. Whitwood Technical. LEEDS UNITED April 1951. Walsall March 1955. Bradford City July 1955. Torquay United July 1962–64.

■ Bobby was spotted in junior football by County FA coach Jimmy Frew, the former United defender, who advised the youngster to switch from full-back to inside-forward. Bobby, who was working down the mines, took the advice and was soon snapped up by United. He did his national service in Germany with the King's Own Light Infantry but only managed three Leeds appearances. He later found his feet at Bradford City, clocking up over 200 matches.

WESTLAKE Ian John

Midfield

Born: Clacton, Essex, 10 July 1983.
5ft 9in, 12st (2006).
Career: Ipswich Town trainee, professional August 2002. LEEDS UNITED August 2006. Brighton & Hove Albion loan March 2008.

■ Former England Under-18 water polo international Ian arrived at Leeds from Ipswich as Dan Harding went in the opposite direction. He had played over 100 games for the Tractor Boys but was in and out of the United side in a difficult 2006–07 season. It was a similar story the following year, but he had a productive loan spell at Brighton.

WESTON Curtis James

Midfield

Born: Greenwich, London, 24 January 1987.
5ft 11in, 11st 9lb (2007).
Career: Millwall trainee, professional July 2003. Swindon Town August 2006. LEEDS UNITED August 2007. Scunthorpe United loan March 2008.

■ Curtis made a name for himself by becoming the youngest player to appear in an FA Cup Final when he replaced Dennis Wise towards the end of Millwall's 2004 defeat against Manchester United, aged 17 years 119 days. The midfielder followed Wise to Swindon and Leeds, playing in United's first-ever game in the third tier of English football. That match proved to be his only League start for United.

WESTON Donald Philip

Centre-forward

Born: New Houghton, Derbyshire, 6 March 1936.
Died: Mansfield, 19 January 2007.
5ft 7in, 11st 6lb (1963).
Career: East Derbyshire Boys. Wrexham June 1959. Birmingham City £15,000 January 1960. Rotherham United £10,000 December 1960. LEEDS UNITED December 1962. Huddersfield Town October 1965. Rotherham United December 1966. Chester August 1968. Altrincham. Bethesda Athletic.

■ Don made the best possible start to his career with United, scoring a debut hat-

trick as Stoke were despatched 3–1 at Elland Road on 15 December 1962. He finished the following season as joint top scorer with Albert Johanneson as Leeds swept to the Second Division title. However, Don was an infrequent starter in the top division and moved on to neighbours Huddersfield. Don, who did his national service with the 31st Training Regiment Royal Artillery, had two spells with Rotherham, featuring in the 1961 League Cup Final side beaten by Aston Villa. He later ran a car dealership in Mansfield.

WETHERALL David

Central-defender

Born: Sheffield, 14 March 1971.
6ft 3in, 13st 12lb (1996).
Career: Sheffield Boys. Middlewood Rovers. Sheffield Wednesday July 1989. LEEDS UNITED £125,000 July 1991. Bradford City £1.4m July 1999–May 2008, player-caretaker manager February 2007.

■ Chemistry student David had all the elements of a top-class defender as a youngster – skills recognised by Howard Wilkinson when he was manager at Sheffield Wednesday. The England Schools captain joined the Owls, played three times for England Under-19s and played for the British Universities side which won a bronze medal in the World student Games at Sheffield. After Wilko

took over at Leeds he raided his old club for David and Jon Newsome. David improved in leaps and bounds, peaking in the mid-1990s with a series of committed, powerful displays. Bradford paid a record fee to take him to Valley Parade, where he was appointed as skipper. He has played about 300 games for the Bantams and also had a brief spell as player-caretaker manager.

WHALLEY Frederick Harold

Goalkeeper

Born: Bolton, 9 October 1898.
Died: 25 April 1976.
6ft, 12st (1922).
Career: Preston Schools. Army football. Preston North End June 1919. Grimsby Town 1920. LEEDS UNITED May 1921. Fulham March 1924–26.

■ Solid goalkeeper Fred was an ever present in 1922–23 when United finished seventh in Division Two. He was a popular chap who thought nothing of chatting to the fans behind his goal when the action was at the other end of the pitch. He moved on to Fulham after losing his place to Billy Down. A product of Preston Schools and army football, Fred enlisted in the North Lancashire Regiment at 15 and saw active service in France before becoming a professional footballer. After retiring he became a policeman in Preston.

WHARTON Clarence Norman

Goalkeeper

Born: Askham-in-Furness, 28 July 1903.
Died: Askham-in-Furness, 13 July 1961.
6ft 1in, 12st 4lb (1928).
Career: Askham. Barrow May 1922. Preston North End August 1925. Barrow September 1927. Sheffield United £250 1928. Norwich City July 1931. Doncaster Rovers May 1935. York City May 1936. LEEDS UNITED August 1939.

■ Piano-playing Norman ended a distinguished career with a couple of Leeds appearances in the truncated 1939–40 season. The talented musician was 36 when he arrived at Elland Road, having earned a reputation as a brave goalkeeper at all his clubs, peaking in 1933–34 as an ever present in Norwich's Division Three South Championship campaign. He retired during the war and returned to his native Cumbria to take up his pre-football job as an electrician.

WHEATLEY Thomas

Goalkeeper

Born: Hebburn, Co. Durham, 1 June 1929.
5ft 11½in, 10st 10lb (1953).
Career: Amble 1950. Lincoln City trials. LEEDS UNITED April 1953.

■ Goalkeeper Tom made six United appearances as deputy to John Scott. He was signed from Northern Alliance club Amble, where he won rave reviews after trials.

WHELAN Noel David

Forward

Born: Leeds, 30 December 1974.
6ft 2in, 11st 3lb (1995).
Career: LEEDS UNITED apprentice, professional March 1993. Coventry City £2 million December 1995. Middlesbrough £2.2 million August 2000. Crystal Palace loan March 2003. Millwall August 2003. Derby County January 2004. Aberdeen August 2004. Boston United July 2005. Livingston March 2006. Dunfermline August 2006–January 2007.

■ One-time United ballboy Noel went on to join the playing ranks at Elland Road after leaving school. He possessed great skill on the ball for a big lad and quickly made a name for himself, scoring one of the goals in the first leg of the 1993 FA Youth Cup Final at Manchester United and helping the England side win the European Youth Championships in the summer after making his senior United debut at Sheffield United towards the end of the season. Leeds had a hot property on their hands and his stock rose further when he scored the only goal of the game on his debut for the England Under-21 side against the Republic of Ireland at Newcastle. However, a throat virus and

the arrival of Tony Yeboah saw him lose his starting place in the Leeds line up and when Coventry tabled a £2 million bid for the young striker, United took the cash. He started well with the Sky Blues, but his progress stalled because of injury and, later in his career, drink-related problems. Noel tried to revive his career in Scotland but suffered an achilles problem after only three months at Dunfermline and was released in January 2007.

WHIPP Percy Leonard

Inside-forward

Born: Gorbals, Glasgow, 28 June 1893.
5ft 9½in, 11st 12lb (1922).
Career: West London Old Boys. Ton Pentre 1920. Clapton Orient May 1921. Sunderland £500 May 1922. LEEDS UNITED £750 November 1922. Clapton Orient June 1927. Brentford May 1929. Swindon Town May 1930. Bath City August 1931.

■ Percy quickly repaid a chunk of the large transfer fee paid to Sunderland when he scored a debut hat-trick for United against West Ham on 4 November 1922 and finished the season as top scorer. It was to be the start of five years at Leeds in which his clever play and decent goal return from inside-forward earned him the nickname 'The Arch General'. A member of the 1923–24 promotion side, he moved to Orient for a second spell after the arrival at Elland Road of Scottish international John White. Percy was a big financial gamble that paid off – he made just one appearance at Sunderland, where he was

understudy to the great Charles Buchan. Percy, the son of a master mariner, was born in Glasgow but raised in London and first attracted the interest of clubs in the capital with a Man-of-the-Match display for a Hammersmith League XI against Fulham reserves. However, before the London clubs made their move, Percy went to Wales to turn pro with Ton Pentre, returning to London the following year for his first spell with Orient. He served in the Royal Field Artillery in World War One.

WHITE David

Midfield/Winger

Born: Manchester, 30 September 1967.
6ft 1in, 12st 9lb (1993).
Career: Salford Boys. Manchester City apprentice, professional November 1985. LEEDS UNITED player exchange rated at £2 million December 1993. Sheffield United £500,000 November 1995–July 1998.

■ David White and David Rocastle were both valued at £2 million when they traded right-side midfield places, the unhappy Rocastle leaving Leeds to take White's place at Maine Road. Like Rocastle before him, David found the burden of replacing the inspirational Gordon Strachan too heavy a load to carry. Ankle injury troubles certainly did not help and United fans only saw

glimpses of the strong, powerful, direct running that earned David an England cap and over 100 goals in his dynamic Manchester City days. He was most effective coming on as a substitute and driving at tiring defences, but Leeds were happy to accept a cut-price bid from Sheffield United after two frustrating years at Elland Road. He retired as a Blades player after further ankle problems. At Maine Road, David also won two England B caps, six at Under-21 level and an outing for the England Youth team.

WHITE John

Inside-forward

Born: Coatbridge, Lanarkshire, 27 August 1897.
Died: February 1986.
5ft 8½in, 11st 7lb (1927).
Career: Bedley Juniors. Clyde 1914–15. Albion Rovers 1920. Hearts £2,700 May 1922. LEEDS UNITED £5,600 February 1927. Hearts £2,350 August 1930. Margate 1934. Leith Athletic.

■ John became one of the most expensive footballers of his day when he joined Leeds from Hearts for £5,600. It was also a pretty profound statement by the United directors, who were determined to stay in Division One. John arrived too late to save Arthur Fairclough's team from relegation, but he prospered in Dick Ray's promotion side the following season when he missed just one game and top scored with 21 goals after the Leeds board rejected a £6,000 bid from Sheffield United midway

through the campaign. John repaid their faith with some outstanding performances before rejoining Hearts at the age of 33. He had been a legend at Tynecastle, having been top scorer for five years running, netting 102 goals, including four in a game in three successive matches in 1925–26. He was Scotland's top scorer in 1922–23 and surprisingly played only three times for his country – once while at Albion Rovers and twice at Hearts. He was one of four brothers to play professionally, one of the siblings being another Hearts hero, Willie White. John was brother-in-law of Andy Anderson, who also played for Hearts and Scotland.

WHITLOW Michael William

Midfield/Full-back

Born: Davenham, nr Northwich, 13 January 1968.
5ft 11in, 12st 1lb (1989).
Career: Rudland Youth Club. Bolton Wanderers juniors 1985. Witton Albion August 1987. LEEDS UNITED November 1988. Leicester City £250,000 March 1992. Bolton Wanderers £500,000 September 1997. Sheffield United July 2003. Notts County July 2004–March 2005, coach August 2005–May 2007.

■ Mike arrived at Elland Road with teammate Neil Parsley from Northern Premier League side Witton Albion. Right-back Parsley did not make the

Leeds senior side but Whitlow grabbed his second opportunity. He had been rejected by Bolton as a youngster and joined Witton as a part-timer while working as a labourer. Howard Wilkinson expressed an interest in the Albion pair when he was boss at Sheffield Wednesday, but the Owls did not follow up their interest and when Wilkinson took over at Leeds he signed the duo. Mike could play at left-back or in midfield and proved a fine squad man for the 1990 and 1992 title-winning teams. He moved on to Leicester shortly after Leeds teammate Simon Grayson joined the Foxes, where the pair won League Cup-winners' medals.

WHYTE Christopher Anderson

Central-defender

Born: Islington, London, 2 September 1961.
6ft 1in, 11st 10lb (1993).
Career: Highbury Grove, Islington and Inner London Schools. Arsenal trainee August 1977, professional September 1978. Crystal Palace loan August 1984. Los Angeles Lazers (US) 1986. West Bromwich Albion August 1988. LEEDS UNITED £400,000 June 1990. Birmingham City £250,000 August 1993. Coventry City loan December 1995. Charlton Athletic March 1996. Detroit Neon (US) 1996. Leyton Orient January 1997. Oxford United February 1997.

■ Dependable Chris played a key role in establishing Leeds back in the big time after the Second Division Championship was lifted in 1990. Chris's spell at Elland Road was the best of his career, and he showed great skills for a defender. He was schooled at Arsenal, and although he

won four England Under-21 caps at Highbury, he found it hard to get in the Gunners' first team, where future Leeds boss David O'Leary was the lynchpin in central defence. Chris was a rock-solid investment by Leeds but as he approached his mid–30s he found his place under threat from the likes of David Wetherall and Jon Newsome. He moved on to Birmingham, where he won another Second Division title medal in 1995 and the following season played against Leeds in the Coca-Cola Cup semi-final, scoring an own goal winner for United in the first leg.

WHYTE David

Midfield

Born: Dunfermline, 2 March 1959.
5ft 9in, 11st 5lb (1978).
Career: Dunfermline Schools. LEEDS UNITED apprentice, professional March 1977. Hibernian July 1979. Bradford City non-contract. Barnsley November 1980. Northwich Victoria. Harrogate Railway Athletic.

■ Scottish midfielder David was on the fringes of the United team in the late 1970s, managing just one start and another appearance as sub. After a brief spell at Hibernian he failed to make the Bradford City and Barnsley first teams. He joined the Fire Service, stationed first at Castleford, then Moortown.

WIJNHARD Clyde

Forward

Born: Paramaribo, Surinam, 9 November 1973.
5ft 11in, 12st 4lb (1998).
Career: Ajax Amsterdam (Holland). Gronigen (Holland). RKC Waalwik (Holland) August 1995. Willem II (Holland) August 1997. LEEDS UNITED £1.5 million July 1998. Huddersfield Town £500,000 July 1999. Preston North End March 2002. Oldham Athletic August 2002. Vitoria Guimaraes (Portugal) June 2003. Beira Mar (Portugal). Darlington October 2004. Macclesfield Town October 2005. Brentford September–December 2006.

■ Clyde was pencilled in as a replacement for Rod Wallace but found the top level of English football a step too

far. With Alan Smith and Harry Kewell coming through the ranks, the Dutch recruit found himself mainly on the bench or in the reserves, where he was a consistent marksman. United took a £1 million loss when he moved to Huddersfield after a year. In September 2000 he suffered a near-fatal car crash but after a spell in Portugal returned to England to play in the lower divisions with Darlington and Macclesfield.

WILCOCKSON Ernest Stanley

Inside-forward/Left-half

Born: Poplar, London, 11 May 1905.
Died: Dartford, 3 March 1965.
5ft 11in, 11st 5lb (1935).
Career: Crittall Athletic. Crystal Palace June 1930. Dartford June 1932. York City June 1933. LEEDS UNITED June 1934. Swindon Town August 1935. Tunbridge Wells Rangers May 1939. West Ham United youth coach.

■ When Stan joined Leeds he could claim, tongue-in-cheek, that he was a movie star. After shining for York City in 1933–34, United officials opened talks with the Bootham Crescent club about Stan's transfer at the Football League annual meeting in London. The deal was struck and all that was required was the player's consent. It was known that Londoner Stan was in the capital and he was tracked down to a picture house in East Ham. The cinema manager agreed to flash a message across the screen, asking Stan to contact the York party at the meeting. The move went through the following day but Stan did not really get his name in lights at Elland Road – he only played four games.

WILCOX Jason Malcolm

Winger

Born: Farnworth, Lancashire, 15 July 1971.
5ft 11in, 11st 10lb (2000).
Career: Blackburn Rovers associate schoolboy June 1986, trainee July 1987, professional June 1989. LEEDS UNITED £3 million December 1999. Leicester City August 2004. Blackpool January 2006–May 2006 after three-month loan.

■ When United were splashing the cash as the Millennium approached, they forked out £3 million on Blackburn winger Jason. He had performed consistently well against Leeds for Rovers, having come through the Academy and played for England twice. He added a third cap against Argentina just a couple of months after moving to Elland Road, but his stay in Yorkshire was generally one of injury woe, despite his obvious class. At his best he was a quick, direct winger, able to unleash excellent crosses into the box, but also filled in for Leeds at left-back.

WILKINS Ernest George

Inside-forward

Born: Hackney, London, 27 October 1917.
Career: Hayes. Brentford February 1938. Portsmouth and West Ham United wartime guest. Bradford Park Avenue February 1947. Nottingham Forest £7,500 December 1947. LEEDS UNITED September 1949–May 1950.

■ George, father of England international Ray, ended his career with Leeds. He was something of a boy star, winning honours galore as a teenager with amateur side Hayes. He joined Brentford just before the war and played in the Bees' win against Portsmouth in the 1942 London Cup Final. The bulk of his best playing days were lost to the war, and injury limited him to just three starts for the Peacocks before he was forced him to quit the game. Two of George's other sons also played League football – Graham (Chelsea and Brentford) and Dean (Brighton and Queen's Park Rangers).

WILKINSON Charles Edward

Left-back

Born: Memdomsley, Co. Durham, 7 April 1907.
Died: Memdomsley, Co. Durham, third quarter of 1975.
5ft 10in, 11st 4lb (1930).
Career: Wallsend. Consett. LEEDS UNITED September 1928. Sheffield United October 1933. Southampton June 1938. Bournemouth player-coach August 1939.

■ Durham miner Charlie was taken on by Leeds after trials but only managed three starts in five years at Elland Road. A move to Sheffield United proved beneficial as he played in the Blades' 1936 FA Cup Final side that lost to Arsenal.

WILLIAMS Andrew

Midfield

Born: Birmingham, 29 July 1962.
6ft 1in, 11st 9lb (1988).
Career: Dudley Town. Solihull Borough.

Coventry City £20,000 July 1985. Rotherham United October 1986. LEEDS UNITED £175,000 November 1988. Port Vale loan December 1991. Notts County £115,000 February 1992. Huddersfield Town loan September 1993. Rotherham United October 1993. Hull City July 1995. Scarborough August 1996. Gainsborough Trinity. Matlock Town. Guiseley.

■ Andy was one of Howard Wilkinson's first captures and played his part in United's revival in the early 1990s. He was a relatively late starter in professional football, making his debut for Coventry at 23 after giving up his job as an accountant. His energy down Rotherham's left side prompted Wilkinson to take him on and Andy contested the number-11 shirt with John Hendrie at the start of the 1989–90 promotion season. Both lost out to Gary Speed, although Andy's case was not helped after an abcess in his groin became infected. He now works for Rotherham Council.

WILLIAMS Gary

Full back/Midfield

Born: Wolverhampton, 17 June 1960.
5ft 9in, 11st 1lb (1987).
Career: Aston Villa associate schoolboy December 1975, apprentice July 1976, professional June 1978. Walsall loan March 1980. LEEDS UNITED £230,000 July 1987. Watford January 1990. Bradford City December 1991–94. Golden (Hong Kong) 1994–95.

■ European Cup winner Gary broke his long scoring duck as a Leeds player. He

joined Aston Villa as a schoolboy and was in their title-winning side in 1981 and played in the team which beat Bayern Munich 1–0 in the Final of the continent's premier competition the following year. He was Villa's regular right-back but joined Leeds when the Birmingham club were relegated in 1987. He made 240 appearances for Villa without a League goal and played a further 19 for Leeds before belatedly opening his account against Bradford City. He then scored twice more, at West Brom and Leicester, in his next six outings. Curiously, for a player whose goals were a rarity, he scored a hat-trick for his final club, Bradford City, against Stockport in the Autoglass Trophy in January 1993.

WILLIAMS Harold

Winger

Born: Briton Ferry, Neath, 17 June 1924.
5ft 4in, 8st 11lb (1953).
Career: Bryn Hyfrd. Briton Ferry Athletic 1935–38. Swansea Town trials. Belfast Celtic and Cliftonville wartime guest. Briton Ferry Athletic 1946. Newport County November 1946. LEEDS UNITED £12,000 June 1949. Newport County March 1957. Bradford Park Avenue £750 July 1957, retiring December 1957.

■ Little Harold stood 5ft 4in in his size-five boots but played like a Colossus on the wing for United. The flying milkman had been Leeds' tormentor-in-chief as minnows Newport County pulled off a stunning 3–1 FA Cup win at Elland Road in 1949. Harold had been up in the early hours of the morning on his milk round before skimming the cream of United's defence in the afternoon. Major Frank Buckley was determined to sign Harold, who had served on Royal Navy destroyer escorts in the Atlantic during the war, and finally got his man that summer. Leeds paid out a sizable fee, plus defender Roly Depear, to get the twice-capped Welsh international. Harold, who could play on either wing, was a fantastic dribbler with a quick turn of foot and a thumping shot. He won a couple more Welsh caps as a Leeds player, against Northern Ireland and Scotland, before breaking a leg against Everton in 1952. He bounced back to full fitness and contributed to United's 1956 promotion season before returning to Newport with

211 Leeds League games to his name. After football he kept a pub near Elland Road and later at Gildersome before retiring in 1986.

WILLIAMS John

Right-back

Born: Doncaster, 14 April 1920.
Died: 1979.
Career: Denaby United. LEEDS UNITED December 1948. Denaby United August 1950.

■ Part-timer John divided his time between football and his job as an insurance salesman. Shortly after joining Leeds from Midland League side Denaby he made his sole United appearance, at right-back, in a 3–1 Boxing Day home defeat at the hands of West Ham.

WILLIAMSON Brian William

Goalkeeper

Born: Blyth, Northumberland, 6 October 1939.
6ft 1in, 12st 1lb (1963).
Career: Seaton Delaval. Gateshead October 1958. Crewe Alexandra July 1960. LEEDS UNITED December 1962. Nottingham Forest February 1966. Leicester City loan August 1967. Fulham £10,000 December 1968–May 1970.

■ Brian spent just over five years at Leeds, deputising just a handful of times for Gary Sprake. Confusingly, Leeds had two goalkeepers called B. Williamson on their books between June 1965 and February 1966. The lesser-known was Bobby, who did not get into the first team but also played with Rochdale and St Mirren. Injury forced Brian to retire when at Fulham and he became a security guard.

WILLINGHAM Charles Kenneth

Right-half

Born: Sheffield, 1 December 1912.
Died: Dewsbury, May 1975.
5ft 8in, 10st 7lb (1947).
Career: Owler Lane School, Sheffield and Yorkshire Schools. Ecclesfield. Worksop Town amateur 1928. Huddersfield Town amateur 1930, professional November

1931. Sunderland £5,000 December 1945. LEEDS UNITED March 1947–May 1948, then coach to 1950. Halifax Town coach 1952.

■ Experienced England international Ken ended his playing days with United before joining the club's coaching set-up. He was 35 when he arrived at Elland Road, having been one of Huddersfield Town's all-time greats in the 1930s. He won a dozen England caps, represented the Football League six times and played in the Terriers side that lost to Preston in the 1938 FA Cup Final. Ken was an outstanding athlete as a youngster, representing England schools after becoming Sheffield half-mile schools champion. He also played for England at shinty. After leaving football he was involved in the pub trade.

WILLIS John George

Left-winger

Born: Shotton, Co. Durham, 5 July 1937.
5ft 8in, 10st 5lb (1953).
Career: Evenwood Town. LEEDS UNITED March 1953. Hartlepools United November 1954. Blyth Spartans 1959. Horden Colliery Welfare 1961. Eppleton Colliery Welfare 1963.

■ All three of winger George's games for Leeds came in the 1953–54 season. After completing his national service with the 7th Battalion Royal Signals he returned to his native North-East as a Hartlepools player.

WILSON George McIntyre

Inside-left

Born: Kilmarnock, 23 May 1905.
Died: Huddersfield, 22 May 1984.
5ft 10½in, 11st 7lb (1930).
Career: Portobello. Clydebank August 1927. Alloa Athletic November 1927. Huddersfield Town March 1928. LEEDS UNITED March 1929. Chesterfield June 1930.

■ Former Scottish miner George appeared in United's final three games of the 1928–29 season. After giving up playing he worked for an engineering firm in Huddersfield but retired because of severe tinnitus – a continual buzzing in the ears.

WILSON James

Goalkeeper

Born: Garforth, nr Leeds, 1 January 1909.
6ft 1in, 12st (1930).
Career: Rothwell Amateurs. LEEDS UNITED March 1928. Halifax Town trial March 1930. Shrewsbury Town trial August 1930. Shirebrook August 1930. Mansfield Town £50 1931. Sutton Town loan January 1933. Bradford Park Avenue £100 June 1933. Bristol City 1934. Bristol Rovers 1938.

■ A fine performance for Rothwell against Doncaster Rovers in a reserve game heralded a move to Leeds for goalkeeper James. However, his brief opportunities at Elland Road were effectively ended when he was on the receiving end of an 8–2 thrashing at West Ham in February 1929.

WINDLE William Henry

Left-winger

Born: Maltby, 9 July 1920.
5ft 4in, 10st (1948).
Career: Hull City juniors. Goole Town. Denaby United. LEEDS UNITED October 1947. Lincoln City February 1948. Chester October 1951. New Brighton November 1955. Rhyl.

■ Little Billy was an experienced Midland League player with Denaby when he joined United for a small fee. Billy Heaton and Tom Hindle usually kept him out of the Leeds side but he gave good service to Lincoln and Chester.

WOOD Basil

Left-winger

Born: Wortley, nr Sheffield, 9 November 1900.
Died: Harrogate, 8 June 1979.
5ft 7in, 11st 6lb (1921).
Career: Crook Town. LEEDS UNITED November 1920. Sheffield Wednesday June 1922.

■ Left-winger Basil broke into United's first team in the club's very first season shortly after joining from Crook. He made his debut on Christmas Day, in a 0–0 home draw with Fulham, and held down a regular place until summer 1922. He scored just twice in 52 League games, in successive games – a 3–1 win at Blackpool on 17 September 1921 and a 2–0 home victory against Clapton Orient the following Saturday.

WOOD Royden

Goalkeeper

Born: Wallasey, Merseyside, 16 October 1930.
6ft 2in, 12st 8lb (1953).
Career: St George's School, Wallasey. Harrowby. New Brighton amateur. Clitheroe. LEEDS UNITED May 1952–59.

■ In the mid-1950s, Roy was a permanent fixture in goal for Leeds. He arrived from Lancashire Combination club Clitheroe and proved a worthy successor to John Scott. Roy was ever present for two successive seasons (1955–56 and 1956–57) and missed only one game in 1957–58. All his 196 League games were as a United player and after being transfer-listed in 1959 he decided

to retire and become a betting shop manager. He was also a member of the PFA management committee, which negotiated the abolition of the maximum wage for players. Roy was a good all-round athlete who excelled at football and hockey and was regarded as one of the best wicketkeepers in the Leeds and District Cricket League during his time at Elland Road.

WOODGATE Jonathan Simon

Central-defender

Born: Middlesbrough, 22 January 1980.
6ft 2in, 13st (2002).
Career: LEEDS UNITED trainee, professional May 1997. Newcastle United £9 million January 2003. Real Madrid (Spain) £13.4 million August 2004. Middlesbrough loan August 2006, transfer £7 million April 2007. Tottenham Hotspur £8m January 2008.

■ High-quality defender Jonathan emerged from United's FA Youth Cup-winning ranks to become a full England international. David O'Leary, himself a great centre-half, recognised Jonathan's talent and immediately promoted him to the first team after taking over the managerial reins from George Graham. A series of superb displays, marked by perfectly timed tackles, power in the air and all-round speed, saw him win his first England cap at the age of 19 after his first season. A great career beckoned, but his football world came crashing down when he and Lee Bowyer were charged with causing grievous bodily harm to a student following an incident in Leeds city centre – a charge they denied. Jonathan did not play for Leeds during the protracted high-profile court case, and he was suspended by England. He was aquitted of GBH but found guilty of affray. He was also injured during this spell but forced his way back into the Leeds team and completed 100 League starts before the cash-strapped Whites sold him to Newcastle. He suffered badly from a succession of injuries with the Magpies, who netted a huge profit when he went to Real Madrid. More injury troubles saw him miss an entire La Liga season and his long-waited Real debut against Bilbao was a disaster – Jonathan scored an own-

goal and was sent off. He did manage to establish himself in Spain and a loan move to his home-town club, Middlesbrough, saw him hit peak form and an England recall before a big-money move to Spurs. Middlesbrough banked a £1 million profit when he moved to Tottenham, where he scored the winner against Chelsea in the 2008 League Cup Final in a Spurs side that also contained ex-Leeds players Paul Robinson, Robbie Keane and Aaron Lennon.

WOODS Martin Paul

Winger

Born: Airdrie, Lanarkshire, 1 January 1986.
5ft 11in, 11st 11lb (2003).
Career: LEEDS UNITED from trainee January 2003. Hartlepool United loan September 2004. Sunderland July 2005. Rotherham United August 2006. Doncaster Rovers June 2007. Yeovil Town loan February 2008.

■ Winger Martin earned a call-up for United's 2003 pre-season tour of Ireland, and he tasted a few minutes of senior football as a substitute in United's 3–2 Boxing Day win at Sunderland. Ironically, he was to join the Black Cats 17 months later, and although he did not play too often he won a couple of Scottish Under-21 caps.

WORSLEY Herbert

Right-winger

Born: Stockport, 20 September 1911.
Died: Denton, Manchester, 25 June 1971.

5ft 7in, 10st 7lb (1934).

Career: Altrincham. Bolton Wanderers amateur. Manchester North End. LEEDS UNITED amateur August 1933, professional January 1934. Fulham June 1935.

■ Bert had the misfortune to make his debut in the worst defeat in United's history, a crushing 8–1 loss at Stoke on 27 August 1934. He played twice more for the first team before transferring to Fulham, where he played 112 times in four seasons.

WORTHINGTON Frank Stewart

Forward

Born: Halifax, 23 November 1948.
5ft 11in, 11st 8lb (1982).
Career: Sowerby Bridge Grammar School. Halifax Schools. Huddersfield Town apprentice April 1964, professional November 1966. Leicester City £80,000 August 1972. Bolton Wanderers £87,000 September 1977. Philadelphia Fury (US) loan May 1979–August 1979. Birmingham City £150,000 November 1979. Tampa Bay Rowdies (US) loan April 1981–August 1981. LEEDS UNITED player exchange March 1982. Sunderland £50,000 December 1982. Southampton June 1983. Brighton & Hove Albion May 1984. Tranmere Rovers player-manager July 1985–86. Preston North End March 1987. Stockport County November 1987. Cape Town Spurs (South Africa) April 1988. Chorley October 1988. Stalybridge Celtic December 1988. Galway United

February 1989. Weymouth September 1989. Radcliffe Borough October 1989. Guiseley player-coach November 1989. Preston North End coaching staff 1990. Hinckley Town player-coach September 1990. Cemaes Bay 1991. Halifax Town player-coach August 1991. Swindon Town coaching staff December 1993.

■ Had United been able to get their hands on flamboyant Frank a few months earlier they could have avoided the drop in 1982. The showman goalscorer boosted Leeds' under-strength attack when he arrived from Birmingham in March 1982 with Byron Stevenson going in the opposite direction. Gifted Frank weighed in with nine goals in 17 games but could not prevent Allan Clarke's team dropping into Division Two. Elland Road was just one stop in a long and colourful career that took in over 20 clubs at various levels. He was at his peak at Leicester, where he scored 78 goals in five years and won eight England caps. He was Division One's leading goalscorer with Bolton in 1978–79 and enjoyed a life that was as colourful off the field as on it.

WORTHINGTON Nigel

Defender

Born: Ballymena, Northern Ireland, 4 November 1961.
5ft 11in, 12st 8lb (1995).
Career: Ballymena. Notts County £100,000 July 1981. Sheffield Wednesday £125,000 February 1984. LEEDS UNITED £325,000 July 1994. Stoke City July 1996. Blackpool player-manager July 1997–December 1999, retiring as a player July 1999. Norwich City joint assistant manager June 2000, manager December 2000–May 2007. Leicester City manager May 2007. Northern Ireland manager June 2007.

■ Howard Wilkinson was a huge admirer of model pro Nigel, signing the Irishman three times in his managerial career. Nigel was first spotted at Ballymena, where he had won an Irish Cup medal and Northern Ireland Youth caps and joined Wilko at Notts County. When Wilkinson moved to Wednesday Nigel followed him in a £125,000 deal and 10 years on played under Wilkinson for a third time when he joined Leeds at

the age of 33. He was used as cover on the left of midfield and defence, but the high-tempo style of the game no longer suited Nigel's game. He did, however, take his Northern Ireland cap tally beyond 60 while at Elland Road. It was no surprise that Nigel moved into management, first at Blackpool and later at Norwich, after a spell assisting his former international teammate Bryan Hamilton, taking the Canaries to the First Division title in 2004. He was appointed Northern Ireland boss in June 2007, signing a two-year deal in January 2008.

WRIGHT Alan Geoffrey

Left-back

Born: Ashton-under-Lyne, 28 September 1971.
5ft 4in, 9st 9lb (2006).
Career: Blackpool apprentice August 1988, professional April 1989. Blackburn Rovers £400,000 October 1991. Aston Villa £1 million March 1995. Middlesbrough August 2003. Sheffield United October 2003. Derby County loan February 2006. LEEDS UNITED loan October 2006. Cardiff City loan November 2006. Doncaster Rovers loan February 2007. Nottingham Forest loan March 2007. Cheltenham Town October 2007.

■ Diminutive Alan had just one Leeds outing while on loan from Sheffield United – a disastrous 4–0 home defeat against Stoke. He was vastly experienced and was particularly effective at Aston Villa, where he played in the side that thumped Leeds

3–0 at Wembley in the 1996 League Cup Final. He won two Under-21 caps at Blackburn and gained international Youth honours with Blackpool.

WRIGHT Barrie

Left-back

Born: Bradford, 6 November 1945.
5ft 8½in, 11st 2lb (1962).
Career: LEEDS UNITED groundstaff, professional November 1962. New York Generals (US) loan 1964 and April 1967. Brighton & Hove Albion January 1969. Hartlepool loan September 1970. Bradford Park Avenue September 1971. Gainsborough Trinity. Thackley.

■ Barrie captained England Schools seven times, won two Youth caps and was skipper of United's Central League side. He looked a certainty to make the big time but could not keep pace with the Revie revolution in the early years and spent a couple of summers playing in America for New York Generals, then coached by former Leeds defender Freddie Goodwin. He also played for Goodwin at Brighton but quit the full-time game, aged only 25, to begin work as a warehouseman.

WRIGHT Jermaine Malaki

Midfield

Born: Greenwich, 21 October 1975.
5ft 9in, 11st 9lb (2005).
Career: Millwall apprentice, professional November 1992. Wolverhampton Wanderers £60,000 December 1994. Doncaster Rovers loan March 1996. Crewe Alexandra £25,000 February 1998.

Ipswich Town £500,000 July 1999. LEEDS UNITED July 2004. Millwall loan September 2005. Southampton loan February–May 2006, transfer July 2006

■ Midfielder Jermaine was one of eight players to join United during Kevin Blackwell's rebuilding of the cash-strapped Whites. He opted to join Leeds instead of Everton and was rewarded with a regular starting place in the Championship line up until the arrival of Shaun Derry. Jermaine is credited with scoring one of the fastest goals in United's history – 12 seconds – in the 2–1 home loss against Burnley on 4 November 2004. The former England Youth international's best form was at Ipswich, where he played over 200 games.

WRIGHT Ronald William

Inside-left

Born: Falkirk, 16 December 1940.
5ft 7in, 10st 5lb (1961).
Career: Shettleston Rovers. LEEDS UNITED June 1959. St Johnstone November 1960–63.

■ Ronnie made his United debut in the club's first-ever League Cup tie – a goalless draw against Blackpool on 28 September 1960.

WRIGHT Thomas Elliott

Forward

Born: Dunfermline, Fife, 10 January 1966.

5ft 9in, 11st (1984).
Career: St Columba's School, Dunfermline. Hutchinson Vale. LEEDS UNITED apprentice April 1992, professional January 1982. Oldham Athletic £80,000 October 1986. Leicester City £300,000 August 1989. Middlesbrough £650,000 July 1994. Bradford City July 1995. Oldham Athletic August 1997. Kilmarnock November 1997. St Johnstone December 1997. Livingston March 1998. Doncaster Rovers 1998. King's Lynn May 2000. Oldham Athletic youth coach, assistant manager June 2006.

■ Teenager Tommy was an overnight success, scoring a debut goal as a 17-year-old in a 3–3 draw at home to Fulham towards the end of 1982–83 season. Under Eddie Gray's guidance, Tommy's pace and trickery provided some rare joy after United's relegation. He was the club's top scorer in 1984–85, including a hat-trick against Notts County. After injury he lost his place and joined a growing ex-Leeds contingent at Oldham, winning a Scottish Under-21 cap in 1987. Big money moves to Leicester and Middlesbrough followed as Tommy continued his development. He is a member of a well-known sporting family: Tommy's dad, Thomas, was a Scottish international forward who played for Sunderland, Partick Thistle, East Fife and Oldham; Tommy's uncle, Jackie Sinclair, played for Dunfermline, Leicester, Newcastle, Sheffield Wednesday, Chesterfield and Stenhousemuir; while brother Barry was a National Hunt jockey.

Y

YEBOAH Anthony

Striker

Born: Kumasi, Ghana, 6 June 1966.
5ft 11in, 13st 13lb (1995).
Career: Kotoko Babies (Ghana). Omnibus Services Authority (Ghana). Neoplan Stars (Ghana). Kumasi Corner Stones (Ghana). Okwawu United (Ghana). Saarbrucken (Germany) 1988. Eintracht Frankfurt (Germany) 1990. LEEDS UNITED £3.4 million January 1995. Hamburg SV (Germany) £1 million September 1997. Al Hittad (Qatar) 2001–02.

■ Few strikers have made as much impact at Elland Road as African star Tony. He was a relatively unknown quantity outside the Bundesliga, where he had twice topped the scoring charts, piling in 68 goals in 123 games. United broke their club transfer record to pay Eintracht Frankfurt £3.4 million for the Ghanaian star. He soon picked up the pace with Leeds, scoring 13 goals in 16 starts, including a hat-trick against Ipswich that helped Leeds to a UEFA Cup place in 1996. Tony did not disappoint in Europe either, his spectacular hat-trick in Monte Carlo destroying Monaco, while the Premiership treble he notched at Wimbledon included a blistering volley.

But topping the lot was the match-winning volley that sank Liverpool at Elland Road, voted by Leeds fans as United's greatest-ever goal. Leeds had found a player of genuine star quality but injuries, many sustained on international duty, saw the goals dry up. Tony's relationship with new manager George Graham deteriorated and the player burned his bridges when he threw his shirt at the bench and went straight down the tunnel when Graham took him off in a 1–0 defeat at Tottenham in March 1997. He did not pull on a Leeds first-team jersey again, and despite 32 goals in just 61 starts he returned to Germany, seeing out his playing days in Qatar. He later opened a hotel in Ghana, where he is a sporting icon, having scored 26 goals in 59 games for his country.

YORATH Terence Charles

Midfield

Born: Cardiff, 27 March 1950.
5ft 10in, 10st 12lb (1975).
Career: Cardiff and Wales Schools. LEEDS UNITED apprentice, professional April 1967. Coventry City £125,000 August 1976. Tottenham Hotspur £265,000 August 1979. Vancouver Whitecaps (Canada) February 1981. Bradford City December 1982. Swansea City player-manager July 1986–February 1989, retiring as a player 1987. Wales manager July 1988–December 1993. Bradford City manager February 1989. Swansea City manager March 1990. Cardiff City manager August 1994–March 1995. Lebanon manager 1995–97. Sheffield Wednesday coach 2000, manager October 2001–October 2002. Huddersfield Town assistant manager 2003–December 2006.

■ But for the longevity of Billy Bremner and Johnny Giles, tenacious midfielder Terry would have notched up more than his near-200 appearance for Leeds. He was more noted at school as a rugby union scrum-half and had trials for Cardiff Schools but settled down at the round ball game. He played for Cardiff and Wales Boys before joining the Elland Road groundstaff, turning down the two Bristol clubs and his native Cardiff. He had to wait patiently in the reserves and had only one senior game under his belt when he won his first full international cap in 1969, against Italy. A real ball-winning midfielder, he was a key component of the 1974 title-winning squad, especially when Giles was out injured. Terry figured in the 1975 European Cup Final but his rugged skills were not always appreciated by United fans. He had a spell as captain under Jimmy Armfield and his leadership qualities blossomed at Coventry before he joined the likes of Ossie Ardiles, Ricardo Villa and Glenn Hoddle in the Tottenham engine room. Of Terry's 59 full caps – 42 of them as skipper – the first 28 were won as a Leeds player. He then entered coaching and management, improving the fortunes of both Wales – whom he took to the brink of the 1994 World Cup Finals – and Lebanon, who rose 60 places in FIFA's world rankings under his stewardship. Terry's son, Daniel, tragically collapsed and died, aged 15, shortly before he was due to join United as an apprentice. One of his daughters, television sports presenter Gabby Logan, represented Wales at rhythmic gymnastics at the 1990 Commonwealth Games.

YOUNGER Thomas

Goalkeeper

Born: Edinburgh, 10 April 1930.
Died: Edinburgh, 13 January 1984.
6ft 1in, 14st 11lb (1957).
Career: Hutchinson Vale. Hibernian 1948. Liverpool £9,000 June 1956. Falkirk player-manager June 1959– February 1960. Stoke City March 1960. LEEDS UNITED September 1961– October 1962. Toronto City (Canada) coach. Hibernian public relations officer October 1969.

■ Veteran Scottish international goalkeeper Tommy played out the final days of his illustrious career at Elland Road. He was 31 when Don Revie signed him and played in goal before Gary Sprake became firmly established as United's number-one. Tommy was a dedicated player, flying home to Edinburgh each weekend from his national service with BAOR in Germany to play for Hibernian. He won the first of 24 full Scottish caps while at Easter Road, won Scottish League Championship medals in 1951 and 1952 and represented the Scottish League three times before joining Liverpool. Tommy was also captain of Scotland's 1958 World Cup squad and after retiring as a player did a bit of scouting for Leeds and had a spell in Canada, but returned to Hibs where he later became a director. He was president of the Scottish FA at the time of his death

LEEDS CITY AND UNITED MANAGERS

Leeds City

Gilbert Gillies 1905–08

Frank Scott-Walford 1908–12

Herbert Chapman 1912–19

Leeds United

Arthur Fairclough 1920–27

Dick Ray 1927–35

Billy Hampson 1935–47

Willis Edwards 1947–48

Frank Buckley 1948–53

Raich Carter 1953–58

Bill Lambton 1958–59

Jack Taylor 1959–61

Don Revie 1961–74

Brian Clough 1974

Jimmy Armfield 1974–78

Jock Stein 1978

Jimmy Adamson 1978–80

Allan Clarke 1980–82

Eddie Gray 1982–85

Billy Bremner 1985–88

Howard Wilkinson 1988–96

George Graham 1996–98

David O'Leary 1998–2002

Terry Venables 2002–03

Peter Reid 2003

Eddie Gray (caretaker) 2003–04

Kevin Blackwell 2004–06

Dennis Wise 2006–08

Gary McAllister 2008–

Leeds City pictured in 1905 with Gilbert Gillies (first left on middle row).

Gilbert Gillies

1905–08

There were more than 100 applicants for the post of manager of Leeds City when it was advertised. The man selected for the job was Gilbert Gillies, a journalist, who became the club's first-ever manager on 16 March 1905. He was given a three-year contract worth £156 a year. As secretary-manager of Chesterfield, he played a key role in getting the Spirerites elected to the Football League in 1899.

City came top of the voting when they were elected to the League, and in his three years he consolidated the club as a solid Second Division outfit. Together with trainer George Swift, a former Loughborough left-back and Football League representative, Gillies attracted forwards of the calibre of Billy McLeod and Fred Croot.

Gillies, born in the parish of Glassary, Argyllshire, on 15 September 1869, was a superb organiser but felt he had under-achieved at Leeds. When his contract expired it was not immediately renewed and he took the manager's job at Bradford, where he remained until February 1911. A former Football League referee, he was out of football by 1914 and running a hotel in Matlock.

Frank Scott-Walford

1908–12

Exactly three years after Gillies's appointment, City offered the job to Frank Scott-Walford, manager of Southern League side Brighton. Born in Perry Barr, Birmingham, in 1869, he was an amateur goalkeeper on Tottenham's books before joining Isthmian League club London Caledonians. A forward thinker, he formed the Enfield and District League and became a Southern League referee.

Scott-Walford became Brighton's manager in March 1905 but soon found himself in hot water for approaching players of other clubs before their contracts had expired. He was suspended from management from 16 April until 1 August. That ban did not deter City's directors, who opened talks with Brighton to negotiate his release as he still had two years of his contract with the Sussex club to run. Brighton announced on 26 March 1908 that Frank would be leaving as soon as a replacement could be found.

Scott-Walford brought a posse of Brighton players with him – Jimmy Burnett, Davie Dougal, Dickie Joynes, Tom Rodger and Willie McDonald – but none made a lasting impression. He then switched his attention to Ireland, bringing the likes of Joe Enright and Joe Moran across the water. Many of the Irish acquisitions failed to make the grade, and with little money to buy new players City began to struggle and were forced to apply for re-election at the end of the 1911–12 season, prompting Scott-Walford to quit.

He was manager at Coventry from 1913 to 1915.

Herbert Chapman

1912–19

Had Herbert Chapman remained with Leeds after the illegal payments scandal that led to City's expulsion from the Football League, the club could have gone on to great things. This theory is based on the staggering success he had later at Arsenal and Huddersfield, setting both clubs on the road to a hat-trick of League Championships.

The son of a coal-miner from Kiveton Park, Sheffield, Chapman was born on 19 January 1878. He was a nomadic inside-forward who played for Kiveton Park, Ashton North End, Stalybridge, Rochdale, Grimsby, Swindon, Sheppey United and Worksop between 1897 and 1901 as he followed his career as a mining engineer.

Chapman did turn professional with Northampton, Notts County and Tottenham and it was in his second spell at Northampton that their directors recognised his tactical appreciation of the game and made him manager in 1907. He steered Northampton to the 1909 Southern League title and was unveiled as manager-secretary of Leeds City in May 1912. He successfully

canvassed for City's re-election to the League and came within two points of clinching promotion in his first season in charge. Receipts and profits were up and the directors were impressed with Chapman's ability to instill team spirit by getting players to speak their minds in team talks.

During the war Chapman worked at a munitions factory, and although he returned to the club in 1916 he was suspended pending investigations into illegal payments to wartime players. Chapman quit on 16 December 1919, claiming he had been harshly dealt with by the FA Commission because he was not in office when the payments were allegedly made. He became manager of an oil and coke firm in Selby and only after his appeal was upheld did he move back into management. He joined Huddersfield in September 1921 and won the 1922 FA Cup and the Division One title in 1924 and 1925.

Arsenal lured him to London in June 1925 and he repeated his success, guiding the Gunners to the League Championship in 1931 and 1933 and the FA Cup in 1930.

Chapman is also credited with introducing the 'stopper' centre-half to the game. At the height of his managerial powers, while on a scouting mission, he caught pneumonia and died on 6 January 1934, 12 days short of his 65th birthday.

Arthur Fairclough

1920–27

Division Two promotion 1923–24

The directors of the newly-formed Leeds United appointed former Huddersfield boss Arthur Fairclough as manager on 26 February 1920. He was seen as the ideal man to rebuild the club after the dismissal of Leeds City from the Football League. Fairclough named former City player Dick Ray as his assistant, and the pair scoured the country looking for football talent as the new Leeds club had, in effect, to start from scratch following the auction of the Leeds City players.

Fairclough was born in Redbrook, Barnsley, on 1 March 1873, and had an outstanding football pedigree. He had to give up as a player with a Barnsley junior side through ill-health in 1892, but four years later was elected to Barnsley's committee, becoming club secretary at Oakwell as Barnsley entered the Football League in 1898. He quit the post three years later to concentrate on other business matters but returned to football in July 1902 when he was elected to the Sheffield FA, returning to Barnsley in 1904 as manager-secretary. Fairclough took the unfancied Tykes to the 1910 FA Cup Final, which they lost to Newcastle after a replay, but two years later the south Yorkshire side were back in the Final, this time beating West Brom 1–0 in a replay.

Fairclough, who was also a Football League referee, loved the game – his weekly wage of £2 being less than that of

his club trainer and most of his players. In April 1912, he moved to Huddersfield and laid down the base for Herbert Chapman to take the Terriers to outstanding success. When Huddersfield chairman J. Hilton Crowther switched his allegiance to Leeds, Fairclough followed him to Elland Road, resigning as secretary-manager at Huddersfield just before Christmas 1919. It was a big gamble, but Fairclough and Ray got United up and running, and after Ray left to manage Doncaster, Fairclough brought in Dick Norman, the Blackpool boss, as his assistant.

Fairclough and Norman had worked in tandem at Barnsley and quickly made their mark at Leeds, steering the Peacocks into Division One for the first time in 1923–24. Top names like Willis Edwards, Russell Wainscoat, Tom Jennings and Bobby Turnbull were brought in, but United found it tough going in the top flight and Fairclough quit after relegation in 1926–27. He returned to Barnsley as manager-secretary on 12 May 1929 but resigned a year later. He became a Barnsley director in 1935, while Norman, his assistant at Leeds, went on to manage Hartlepools.

Fairclough, an important figure in United's history, died in Sheffield on 18 March 1948.

Dick Ray

1927–35

Division Two promotion 1927–28, 1931–32.

Dick Ray served Leeds as a player, captain, committee man, secretary and manager. Born in Newcastle-under-Lyme on 4 February 1876, Dick began his career in Macclesfield in 1893, joining Burslem Port Vale the following year. He also played for Manchester City, Stockport County and Chesterfield before signing for Leeds City in time for the club's inaugural season in the Football League.

A solid left-back, he captained City in 1908, retiring in 1912. After City were expelled from the League he was on the original committee formed to help get United started, running the Midland League side on a slimline budget before

Arthur Fairclough was brought in. He worked under Fairclough before becoming manager at Doncaster Rovers on their election to the Northern Section of the Third Division.

On Fairclough's resignation, Ray was appointed manager-secretary at Elland Road, responsible for both team selection and playing policy. Ray developed the likes of Bert Sproston, Billy Furness, Eric Stephenson, Wilf Copping, Arthur Hydes, Tom Cochrane and the Milburn brothers – George and Jimmy – in his eight years at the helm. Ray took United back into Division One in 1928 and two years later achieved fifth place – their highest position since being formed. They were relegated the following season, but the directors stood by Ray and were rewarded with immediate promotion.

Ray was appointed the first-ever team manager of a Football League XI as they drew 2–2 at Ibrox against the Scottish League in February 1934, receiving a gold medal for the honour.

On 5 March 1935 he decided he had taken Leeds as far as he could and quit his £1,000 a year job. The following month he was installed as Bradford City's boss, staying at Valley Parade until the axe fell in February 1938. After a spell scouting for Millwall, Ray ran a garage business in Leeds and also had an interest in billiards salons in the city.

Ray, who was also a fine cricketer with Bradford League club Laisterdyke, served

in the Royal Army Service Corps in World War One. An outstanding servant at Elland Road, Ray died in St James' Hospital, Leeds, on 28 December 1952.

Billy Hampson

1935–47

Central League Champions 1936–37.

United's directors kept their early managerial appointments 'in house'. Replacing Dick Ray was another Leeds City old boy, Billy Hampson, who was a regular guest for the club during World War One.

Born in Radcliffe on 26 August 1882, Hampson was a late developer as a player, figuring for Rochdale, Bury and Norwich before securing a £1,250 move to Newcastle in January 1914. When St James's Park closed during the war, Hampson had a lengthy guest spell at Leeds before rejoining the Magpies and belatedly winning a first-team place. At 41 years and eight months he became the oldest FA Cup finalist when Newcastle beat Aston Villa in 1924. He then played for South Shields from September 1927 to March 1930 before entering management at Carlisle, where he is credited with discovering Bill Shankly. After a spell in charge at Ashington he took the job at Elland Road, consolidating United's status as a solid First Division side.

Trips to Ireland to sign Jim Twomey, David Cochrane and Bobby Browne all paid dividends, and he continued to strengthen his pool of players with a blend of experience and youth. This helped the reserves win the 1936–37 Central League title for the first and only time in the club's history, but World War Two prevented many of those younger players reaching full football maturity.

Perhaps reflecting on his own longevity as a player, Hampson stood by his loyal squad when peacetime football returned, but age had caught up with several key players and United suffered their worst-ever season in 1946–47, finishing bottom of Division One with only six wins. Hampson stepped down and was made chief scout but only held the post for eight months. He later worked as a coach for the Northumberland Schools FA.

Hampson, who died on 23 February 1966, at Congleton, Cheshire, had two footballing brothers – Tom (Darlington) and Walter (Charlton).

Willis Edwards

1947–48

Leeds legend Willis Edwards took over from Hampson in April 1947 as their nightmare campaign was drawing to a close. The former England hero had been assistant to trainer Bob Roxburgh with prime responsibility for the Central League side immediately after the war.

Edwards faced a massive task as he overhauled an ageing squad. Although he improved fitness and lowered the age of the team, the 1947–48 season was mainly one of struggle. United dabbled with relegation for a while before finishing 18th and the decision was taken to move him back to assistant trainer in April 1948 after 12 months in charge.

Edwards remained on the backroom staff for well over a decade, expanding his association with the club to 35 years. He died, aged 85, in Leeds on 27 September 1988, having spent the last years of his working life employed in a jam factory.

Frank Buckley

1948–53

United were at a low ebb when new go-ahead chairman Sam Bolton named one of the best-known names in football, Major Frank Buckley, as the new manager. Bolton, a motor haulage contractor, had trials with Leeds City as a youngster and rose from United fan to become director in 1945. Three years on, he chose the 64-year-old Buckley to revive the club's fortunes.

The charismatic Buckley had a forceful style of management and was regarded as an innovator. Born in Urmston, Manchester, on 9 November 1883, he played at centre-half for Aston Villa, Brighton, Manchester United, Manchester City, Birmingham, Derby County and Bradford City, winning an England cap against Ireland in 1914.

He fought in the Boer War and in World War One joined the 17th Middlesex Regiment, reaching the rank of Major in 1916 and commanding the Footballers' Battalion, which was made up of soccer professionals.

His first managerial job was with Norwich City before they joined the Football League. After a stint as a commercial traveller he was appointed boss at Blackpool in October 1923 and in summer 1927 stepped up to run Wolves.

At Molineux he developed a fine youth policy and took Wanderers from the lower reaches of Division Two to Division One runners-up and an FA Cup Final. In February 1944 he broke a contract for life to join Notts County for £4,000, and within hours of his resignation at Meadow Lane in January 1946 he took charge at Hull, later joining Leeds.

Life at Elland Road was never dull with the Major around. In an attempt to improve his squad's balance and mobility, he introduced dance sessions on the pitch, with players pairing up to strut their stuff to the music coming over the public address system. A mechanical kicking machine was installed to improve heading, trapping, volleying and goal-kicking. To prove his own fitness he did press-ups and high-kicking tricks in the dressing room, much to the embarrassment of some of the less nimble senior players.

At Wolves he had created a sensation by treating his players with monkey-gland extract to sharpen their thinking and reintroduced a more advanced form of the tonic at Leeds, although no one could say if it worked.

Despite all these high-profile innovations, United continued to struggle and an embarrassing FA Cup third-round home defeat against Newport put Buckley under pressure. He did not flinch and despite criticism for selling internationals Con Martin and Aubrey Powell, pinned his faith in youth.

Gradually United's fortunes turned. In 1950 Buckley took them to the FA Cup sixth round for the first time in their history and unearthed a world star in Welsh teenager John Charles. Buckley switched Charles between defence and attack, but despite the giant Welshman's massive influence United continually missed out on promotion. At least Buckley managed to hold on to Charles – clubs were constantly knocking at United's door.

In April 1953 the Major felt as though he had taken Leeds as far as he could and, at the age of 70, became Walsall's manager, bowing out of the game two years later. He died, aged 84, on 22 December 1964 in Walsall.

Raich Carter

1953–58

Division Two promotion 1955–56.

Just as he had done at Hull five years earlier, former England inside-forward Raich Carter took over the manager's post at Leeds from Frank Buckley. The former apprentice engineer won 13 full England caps and was dubbed the 'silver-

haired maestro' as his supreme passing ability allowed him to dictate matches.

Horatio Stratton Carter was born in Sunderland on 21 December 1913 and played international schoolboy football before joining his home-town club as an amateur in 1930. He sparkled for the Rokerites and Derby County, skippering Sunderland to the First division title and becoming the only player to win FA Cup-winners' medals either side of World War Two. The master tactician transferred his on-field knowledge to management at Hull, where he was appointed player-manager in 1948 on Buckley's move to Leeds.

Carter ended his playing career with 218 goals in 451 games and soon made an impact at Boothferry Park, buying and selling fellow England star Don Revie and taking the Tigers to the Division Three North title in 1949. He resigned in September 1951 to run a sweet shop in Hull but was lured out of retirement by the Tigers as they faced relegation. He later moved to Ireland, where he took Cork Athletic to the 1953 FA of Ireland Cup Final.

At Leeds he built the team around the brilliance of John Charles and finally ended United's run of nine stagnant seasons by taking the club into the First Division in 1956, clinching promotion with victory at Boothferry Park. Pressure continued to mount on the Leeds board to sell Charles and they finally gave in when Italians giants Juventus made a £65,000 offer that was too good to turn down.

Charles was irreplaceable and predictably United had to fight to stay up, slipping to 17th in 1957–58. Less predictable was the decision to dispense with Carter's services after his five-year contract came up for renewal at the end of the campaign.

Carter, who claimed he was given only half the cash from Charles's sale to buy players, was appointed manager of Mansfield Town in February 1960 and got them promoted from Division Four. He also went to Middlesbrough, staying at Ayresome Park for just over three years. He left football in February 1966 and later became manager of the sports section at a department store in Hull.

Carter, who also played cricket for Derbyshire and Durham, died in Hull on 9 October 1994.

Bill Lambton

1958–59

After having some relatively big names at the helm, United opted for a lower-profile man to be their fifth post-war manager – Bill Lambton. Although he was only in office for three months, he is credited with bringing Don Revie to Elland Road.

Born in Nottingham on 2 December 1914, Lambton was a goalkeeper with Nottingham Forest, Exeter and Doncaster before concentrating on coaching. A fitness fanatic, Lambton

helped keep British amateur boxers in trim while he was coaching in Denmark. On his return to England he coached Scunthorpe United, and his unorthodox training methods included trampoline sessions aimed at keeping players fit and supple.

Lambton was 42 when Carter appointed him trainer-coach at Leeds in November 1957, taking over from the venerable Bob Roxburgh, who had been trainer since the mid-1930s. When Carter departed, Lambton was installed as caretaker manager before being officially handed control on 9 December 1958. Lambton's training methods did not always win the directors' approval and he quit after only three months. However, by that time he had signed Revie from Sunderland and appointed him skipper after Irish international Wilbur Cush gave up the role.

Lambton's next managerial appointment was even shorter than his tenure at Leeds. In April 1959 he spent just three days in charge at Scunthorpe, although his appointment had only been verbal. He was later in office at Chester from November 1961–July 1963.

Lambton died at his home in Sherwood, Nottingham, on 16 September 1976, aged 61.

Jack Taylor

1959–61

United were in a state of flux after Lambton's departure and the managerial picture became no clearer as the Peacocks sought his successor. Arthur Turner, the Headington United manager and former Birmingham boss, was red-hot favourite and the United programme even announced his imminent arrival. However, he was persuaded to stay at Headington where, as Oxford United, he helped them gain admission to the Football League.

Out of the confusion, Barnsley-born Jack Taylor, the QPR chief, was appointed Leeds manager in May 1959. Taylor had played for Frank Buckley at Wolves in the 1930s and later turned out for Norwich. His first stab at management came with Southern League club Weymouth and in June 1952 he replaced the Leeds forward Dave Mangnall as manager at QPR. For nine years he did a steady job with

Rangers and the Leeds board thought he would be just the man to steady the ship at Elland Road after what had been a fairly unstable period.

Within a year United were relegated and, unable to shore up a shaky defence or make headway in regaining their top-flight status, Taylor resigned on 13 March 1961. He still had a year of his £2,000-per-annum contract to run and drifted out of football. Taylor died in Barnsley on 22 February 1978, one week after his 64th birthday.

Don Revie

1961–74

Division Two champions 1963–64. FA Cup winners 1972. FA Cup finalists 1965, 1970 and 1973. FA Cup semi-finalists 1967 and 1968. Football League Cup winners 1968. Fairs Cup semi-finalists 1966. Fairs Cup finalists 1967. Fairs Cup winners 1968 and 1971. Division One champions 1968–69 and 1973–74. Charity Shield winners 1969. European Cup semi-finalists 1970. European Cup-Winners' Cup finalists 1973.

'The Don' was the man who made Leeds United. Before he took over, the club had little to shout about in terms of success but he elevated them to being one of the best in the world.

Four days after Jack Taylor's resignation Revie was appointed player-manager. Both Chester and Bournemouth had inquired about Revie's availability and director Harry Reynolds, soon to be chairman, had already drafted a letter to the Cherries singing Revie's praises. When he re-read the letter, Reynolds realised Revie was just the man to take charge at Elland

Road, tore up the letter, and persuaded the other directors to agree to the former England man's appointment. It was a turning point in United's history.

Born in Middlesbrough on 10 July 1927, Revie began his career with Leicester in 1944 and featured in four major transfer deals totalling nearly £80,000, a record at the time.

Hull paid Leicester £20,000 for Revie in November 1949, Manchester City £25,000 in October 1951, Sunderland £22,000 in November 1956 and Leeds £12,000 in November 1958.

A clever inside-right, Revie won six England caps, was Footballer of the Year in 1955 and won an FA Cup-winners' medal with Manchester City the following year. He based his innovative 'Revie Plan' of the deep-lying centre-forward on tactics formulated by the outstanding Hungarian national team in the mid-1950s and observers tipped him for a managerial future. He was still just a player, though, when he made his Leeds debut in a 3–2 win over Newcastle on 29 November 1958. He was appointed skipper but after a string of poor results Freddie Goodwin took over the job.

Revie's first job was to avoid relegation, which he achieved thanks to a 3–0 win at Newcastle on the final day of the 1961–62 season. He patiently nurtured the youth policy introduced by Lambton and Taylor, giving debuts to teenagers such as Gary Sprake, Paul Reaney and Norman Hunter. His signing of veteran Scottish international Bobby Collins was inspired and the crop of kids learned quickly from the midfield master.

Leeds stormed to the 1964 Division Two title and soon made their mark in Division One, winning two League titles, the FA Cup, Football League Cup and Fairs Cup twice under Revie's guidance. On top of that were a string of heart-breaking near misses. Some critics felt Revie, who wore a lucky blue suit on matchdays and had a string of other superstitions, was over-cautious, but the football his men produced in the final few seasons at Leeds was fantastic.

Revie assembled an outstanding backroom staff: trainer Les Cocker, the former Accrington and Stockport player; coach Syd Owen, the ex-Luton and England centre-half; and assistant

manager Maurice Lindley, who spent 17 years as an Everton player.

United's style of play in Revie's early days was tough and uncompromising, but the criticism they received bonded his squad together. He was the club's father-figure and his 'family' had an unquenchable thirst for victory. He was able to keep his squad happy even though most of the reserves would have walked into virtually any other first team in the country.

Not all Revie's glory boys were home-grown. He was also astute in the transfer market, with the bargain Johnny Giles later joined by big-money signings Allan Clarke and Mick Jones. Revie was Manager of the Year in 1969, 1970 and 1972 and was awarded the OBE in January 1970.

After United lost the 1973 FA Cup Final to Sunderland, Revie looked set to join Everton but opted to stay at Elland Road. With two more Scottish snips in the squad, Joe Jordan and Gordon McQueen, Leeds rewarded Revie with a second title in 1974, playing some magnificent football. At the end of that superb season he severed his 13-year link with Leeds to become England's manager and plot a path to the 1978 World Cup Finals. Revie, though, could not recapture the club atmosphere at national level, and his constant chopping and changing produced mixed results and dull performances.

In July 1977, he quit to take a lucrative job as coach to the United Arab Emirates on a tax-free contract reputed to be worth £60,000 a year. Revie took a huge amount of flak from the Football Association, who suspected he was negotiating his escape route to the Middle East while still in charge of the England team, and they suspended the ex-Leeds boss from working in England until he was willing to face a charge of bringing the game into disrepute. Revie later won a High Court case against the FA and was granted an injunction quashing the ban. However, it was a victory with a hollow ring, as Justice Cantley criticised aspects of Revie's character. There were also allegations in newspapers concerning Leeds matches when he was in charge at Elland Road.

While his stock at home was low, Revie was hailed a success by the UAE in his three years as coach. He took over club side Al Nasr in May 1980 and in August 1984 was appointed manager of Cairo club Al Al, but returned to Britain before Christmas. Revie did not work in full-time football again, but his court victory enabled him to take up a brief consultancy at Elland Road. Whatever his standing nationally, his place in United's folklore is guaranteed. A road near the Leeds ground was named after him and the new all-seater Geldard End Kop was renamed the Revie Stand in 1994. Indeed, many of the ground improvements at Leeds were down to Revie's great success with the Whites. His influence in the game continued after his retirement with Terry Cooper, Jack Charlton, Norman Hunter, Johnny Giles, Trevor Cherry, Terry Yorath, Joe Jordan, Billy Bremner, Eddie Gray, Allan Clarke, Bobby Collins, Gordon McQueen and Jimmy Greenhoff all making their mark in management – Clarke, Bremner and Gray each filling Revie's old seat at Leeds.

In 1988 Revie revealed he was suffering from the incurable motor-neurone disease and was confined to a wheelchair. He did manage to revisit Elland Road for a joint testimonial game for John Charles and Bobby Collins in April 1988 but died on 26 May 1989 at Murrayfield Hospital, Edinburgh.

Brian Clough

1974

On his departure from Elland Road, Don Revie advised the Leeds board that Johnny Giles would make an excellent manager. It was advice that went unheeded, though, as the directors surprised the football world by appointing Brian Clough, a fierce critic of Revie and United's style of play. While Maurice Lindley remained in temporary charge, the Leeds directors were talking to Clough, who was then in charge at Brighton.

The Leeds squad was ageing and Clough, who had been a major managerial success at Derby, was seen as the man tough enough to do the job. Like Revie, he hailed from Middlesbrough where he was born on 21 March 1935. Cloughie piled in the goals for Boro and neighbours Sunderland, winning two England caps in 1960 before injury ended his playing days with 251 League goals in 274 games. As a young manager he impressed at Hartlepools and revived the fortunes of Derby, steering them to the Championship in 1971–72 with his assistant Peter Taylor.

Clough's outspoken comments on

television and in newspapers prickled the Derby board and after a row at the Baseball Ground he joined Brighton on a five-year deal with Taylor. Leeds had to fork out huge compensation to the Seagulls for Clough, although Taylor remained at the Goldstone Ground. Clough arrived at Elland Road with trainer Jimmy Gordon, but without Taylor he seemed isolated from the players, many of whom he had blasted in the past.

Derby players John O'Hare, John McGovern and the mercurial Duncan McKenzie came in as Clough set about his changes. Early results were poor, not helped by the suspension of skipper Billy Bremner after a red card in Clough's first game in charge, the Charity Shield at Wembley. Rumours soon emerged that the dressing room was unhappy and in a remarkable U-turn Clough was sacked after just 44 days in office. Chairman Manny Cussins said the decision was made for the good of the club while Clough commented 'I think it is a very sad day for Leeds and for football.'

Newspapers were rife with talk of player power, forcing the Leeds squad to issue a statement denying they had forced Clough out. The suspended Bremner, assistant manager Lindley and chief coach Owen picked the side for the next game at Burnley, two days after Clough's exit. None of Clough's signings were in the squad.

Clough received £200,000 in compensation and emerged in January 1975, re-united with Taylor, as manager of Nottingham Forest. Forest were transformed from a mundane outfit into double European champions as Clough and Taylor worked their magic. O'Hare and McGovern shared in their triumphs, leaving Leeds fans to contemplate what might have been.

Old Big 'Ead was consistently the people's choice to manage England, but the call never came, with many suspecting the FA would not be able to handle him. Bombastic and charming in equal measure, Brian Clough OBE, retired in May 1993 after Forest's relegation from the Premiership. After battling with a drink problem he died of stomach cancer on 20 September 2004, having had a liver transplant the previous year. His son, Nigel, played at Forest, Liverpool and Nottingham Forest, and entered management with Burton Albion.

Jimmy Armfield

1974–78

European Cup finalists 1975. FA Cup semi-finalist 1977. Football League Cup semi-finalists 1978.

After the Clough debacle, Leeds needed the proverbial 'safe pair of hands' and found them in former England right-back Jimmy Armfield. 'Gentleman Jim'

end of the 1977–78 season. He has not worked in football management since. As well as being a newspaper reporter and radio summariser, he has worked as a consultant for the FA and was instrumental in the appointments of Terry Venables as national coach in 1994 and Glenn Hoddle two years later.

Jimmy was awarded the OBE in 2000 and revealed in 2007 that he was suffering from throat cancer. In February 2008 he received the Contribution to League Football award for his 54 years' service to the game.

Jock Stein

1978

Just one game into the 1978–79 season, United installed former Celtic supremo Jock Stein as manager. A big friend and old adversary of Don Revie, the Scot was a legend at Celtic Park, becoming the first boss in Britain to win the European Cup. He jumped at the chance to move to Elland Road on 21 August 1978 on a three-year contract reputed to be worth £85,000. However, he did not sign the contract and within weeks had replaced under-fire Scotland boss Ally McLeod as national team boss.

Stein spent 44 days in charge at Elland Road, the same time as Clough, and left United in mid-table. Big Jock took Scotland to the 1982 World Cup Finals in Spain and guided them to the brink of the Mexico Finals four years later. In the pandemonium which followed a tense draw in Cardiff on 10

played a record 568 League games for his home-town club Blackpool, where he was born on 21 September 1935. He was capped 43 times by England and captained his country.

A calm, quiet, pipe-smoking, unassuming man, Armfield was 38 and relatively inexperienced on the managerial front. In his first post he steered Bolton to the Third Division title in 1973. The Leeds board took their time appointing Armfield, allowing Lindley to temporarily fill the void once more. When he did take charge, Leeds were already out of the title race so Armfield opted to make few changes and gave priority to the European Cup. For the old stars in the squad it would be their last crack at the continent's top prize and they rose to the occasion, rolling

back the years with some outstanding displays.

Within a few months Armfield had achieved what Revie couldn't, taking Leeds to the European Cup Final. When they lost to Bayern Munich in Paris, United's hooligan faction rioted, triggering a European ban of four years. Armfield's reasoned arguments at the club's appeal saw the suspension cut to two years.

Armfield went about the task of replacing Revie's aging aces, bringing in talent like Tony Currie, Brian Flynn, Ray Hankin and Arthur Graham. His patient team-building saw Leeds reach the 1977 FA Cup semi-final and the League Cup semi-final the following year, but he was not given time to finish the job and the impatient board dismissed him at the

September 1985 – essential to Scotland's World Cup progress – Stein collapsed and died, aged 62. Scotland, and football in general, mourned the passing of one of Britain's greatest managers.

Born in Lanarkshire on 5 October 1922, Stein was a part-timer with Albion Rovers before turning pro at 27. He returned to his old job as a miner, this time in the South Wales coalfield, and played centre-half for Llanelli before joining Celtic in 1951. As a player he led Celtic to their first Scottish League and Cup double in 40 years in 1954 before quitting the following year. He remained at Celtic as a coach until 1960, when he moved to Dunfermline, taking them to victory in the 1961 Scottish Cup Final. Jock rejoined Celtic in 1965 and enjoyed an unprecedented run of success, winning 10 League titles – nine in a row – eight Scottish Cups, six League Cups and that European Cup.

Awarded the CBE in 1970, Stein was out of the game for ten months after a serious car accident in July 1975, followed by a heart attack and series of major operations. When he was 55 he was given the less taxing job of general manager of the Hoops, who were paving the way for Billy McNeill to take over. It was not a role he relished and he took the chance to join Leeds.

Jimmy Adamson

1978–80

Football League Cup semi-finalists 1979.

Maurice Lindley once more filled the caretaker role, picking the side for three weeks before Jimmy Adamson was appointed to the Elland Road hot seat. Adamson, who was once offered the England manager's job, took over at Leeds in October 1978 for what proved a stormy couple of years.

Born in Ashington on 4 April 1929, Adamson turned professional with Burnley on New Year's Day 1947 and went on to become one of the Clarets' all-time greats. Although never capped at full level, he skippered the Turf Moor outfit to the 1960 League Championship and two years later was named Footballer of the Year. He was included in the World Cup Finals squad for Chile in 1962, doubling up as assistant to Walter Winterbottom.

When Winterbottom later resigned,

Adamson rejected an offer to take charge because he felt he lacked the necessary managerial experience and the position was filled by Alf Ramsey. Adamson took a coaching role at Burnley and six years later was appointed manager, steering the Lancashire club back to the top division in 1973. Continually forced to sell his young star names, he quit in January 1976. In May he spent a fortnight with Sparta Rotterdam but failed to settle in Holland. Within a few months he took command at struggling Sunderland but could not prevent them dropping into Division Two.

Leeds were at a crossroads when Adamson joined them and it seemed as though he had them on the right path when United finished fifth – their best position since Don Revie's departure – a place in Europe and a League Cup semi-final place. That early promise did not materialise. Top scorer John Hawley and talented stars Tony Currie and Frank Gray were sold and their replacements were unsuccessful.

The likes of Alan Curtis, Wayne Entwistle and Brian Greenhoff all failed to make a lasting impact, leaving United fans impatient and angry. A fan base that demanded the sort of success they had enjoyed under Revie demonstrated after a dire performance against Coventry in March 1980, in front of the lowest crowd at Elland Road for 17 years. Mounted police broke up the demo but Adamson survived until the end of the season.

The start of the next campaign was poor and pressure continued to build on Adamson, who appealed for fans to stay calm as fans' protests were sapping the squad's confidence. In September 1980 Adamson bowed to the inevitable and quit, slipping out of full-time football.

Allan Clarke

1980–82

As player-manager of Barnsley, former Leeds striker Allan Clarke had made a big impression in South Yorkshire. The Elland Road directors turned to Clarke to revive Leeds' fortunes, appointing him on 16 September 1980. Confident and ambitious, Clarke declared he was a winner as a player and wanted to be a winner as a manager. He had a big job on his hands with United one place from the bottom of Division One. Circumstances demanded he concentrate on defensive work and his tactics worked, as Leeds finished the season in ninth place despite scoring only 39 League goals.

To boost the attack he spent £930,000 on West Brom winger Peter Barnes in summer 1981, but it did not have the desired effect. Leeds only managed 39 goals again, but the defence was not as tight and United lost their Division One status for the first time since 1964. Clarke and assistant Martin Wilkinson paid the price for relegation with their jobs. The pair re-emerged at Third Division Scunthorpe, who knocked Leeds out of the FA Cup the following season.

In July 1985 Clarke took over for a second time at Barnsley, succeeding another Leeds old boy, Bobby Collins. He stayed at Oakwell until midway through the 1989–90 season and then had a five-month spell as Lincoln boss before leaving full-time football.

Eddie Gray

1982–85

Relegated Leeds were strapped for cash and the board opted to name popular winger Eddie Gray as player-manager in July 1982. He had served United for nearly two decades, and although he had no managerial experience he had impressed with the way he coached the juniors during one of his lengthy spells of injury.

With virtually no money available, Gray relied heavily on blooding a batch of talented youngsters, including John Sheridan, Denis Irwin, Scott Sellars and Tommy Wright. He brought back old favourite Peter Lorimer as skipper and the tactics worked, as United played some attractive football. But his skilful, enthusiastic squad were outmuscled by more experienced opponents, and although they were promotion candidates

for three successive seasons, they never quite made the breakthrough. United made a bad start to 1985–86 but just when a run of one defeat in eight games seemed to have turned the corner, 38-year-old Gray and his assistant Jimmy Lumsden were sacked. A 6–2 vote by the board ended Gray's 22 years with the club.

Although Leeds were 14th, the decision did not go down too well with supporters, and one director, Brian Woodward, a former United reserve, resigned in protest. Lorimer handed a statement to the board condemning the timing and handling of Gray's dismissal on the eve of a home game against Middlesbrough but the board did not budge.

Coach Peter Gunby was put in temporary charge and a Lorimer penalty won the game against Boro, but Leeds fans chanted in support of Gray during the game and called for chairman Leslie Silver to go. Gray, typically, showed no bitterness and later joined former team-mate David Harvey as a player for non-League Whitby Town, where Lorimer also moved.

After a spell as Middlesbrough's reserve and youth-team coach, Gray was appointed manager at Rochdale in December 1986 then had a year as boss at Hull before returning as Whitby as manager in September 1989.

Billy Bremner

1985–88

FA Cup semi-finalists 1987

Billy Bremner, the heartbeat of Don Revie's superb squad, became the third successive former United player to take the helm at Elland Road. After finishing his magnificent playing career with Hull City, Bremner took over as manager at Doncaster Rovers, a club where cash was in short supply.

Rovers had been limping along in Division Four for several years but that changed with Bremner's appointment in November 1978. Within two years he got them promoted, only to be relegated immediately after a run of crippling injuries. Undeterred, Bremner took Doncaster back up the following season. The Leeds board saw the old warrior as the man to lead United back to the top flight but after he took over from Gray United struggled to 14th place.

The following season Bremner almost cracked it, as Leeds came close to double glory. They came within 10 minutes of gaining promotion to Division One, only to fall at the final hurdle in a Play-off replay with Charlton at Birmingham, going down 2–1 late in extra-time to a couple of goals. That shattering experience came after a thrilling FA Cup semi-final defeat to Coventry, also in extra-time.

United were installed as favourites to go up the following year and Bremner was rewarded with an extension to his contract. However, after looking well placed at the turn of the year, United had to be content with seventh place in 1987–88. Poor results at the beginning of the next campaign saw Bremner axed in September. Although he was the man who blooded future England star David Batty, too many of Bremner's signings from the lower divisions failed to pay off at Elland Road.

Coach Peter Gunby took temporary command while United searched for a replacement for Bremner, who returned to Doncaster as manager in July 1989, staying until he resigned in November 1991. It proved his last job in football. Although out of the full-time game, Bremner kept tabs on affairs at his beloved Elland Road and Leeds fans were stunned when news filtered through of his death on 7 December 1997. He succumbed to pneumonia at Doncaster Royal Infirmary, just two days short of his 55th birthday.

Howard Wilkinson

1988–96

Division Two champions 1989–90. Football League Cup semi-finalists 1991. Division One champions 1991–92. FA Charity Shield winners 1992. FA Youth Cup winners 1993. Football League Cup finalists 1996.

Leeds may have been struggling on the pitch in the early 1980s, but their pulling power remained undiminished. Although he was with First Division Sheffield Wednesday, Howard Wilkinson had no qualms about dropping a division to join Leeds.

Lack of spending power at Hillsborough had frustrated Wilkinson, who felt he could not take the Owls any further without a cash injection for players. Up the M1 at Elland Road, Leeds were a sleeping giant and Wilkinson told the United board that they could take 'route one' back to the top flight if they were prepared to back him with big transfer funds. The Leeds directors took the gamble and on 10 October 1988 Wilkinson became United's eighth manager in 14 years. His credentials were unchallenged. Born in Sheffield on 13 November 1943, Wilkinson had an unspectacular career as a winger with Wednesday, Brighton and Boston United, entering management with the latter when they were a non-League outfit.

Wilkinson gained a degree in physical education at Sheffield United, taught for a couple of years in Sheffield and managed the England semi-professional side before his burgeoning managerial career gained greater exposure in 1982. An FA regional coach, he was working at Notts County when he succeeded Jimmy Sirrell as manager in 1982, replacing Jack Charlton at Wednesday the following summer. In his first season Wilkinson got the Owls back into Division One and kept them in the top half of the table for several seasons, with a fifth-place finish in 1986–87 the high point.

His first job at Leeds was to improve the squad's fitness with the help of assistant Mick Hennigan, and staff were quickly impressed by the new manager's attention to detail and organisational skills. Leeds finished in mid-table before the board sanctioned the promised spending spree in summer 1989. Mel Sterland, John Hendrie and Vinnie Jones joined defender Chris Fairclough and inspirational veteran midfielder Gordon Strachan, who were recruited in March. His expensively assembled squad, laced with home-grown talent like David Batty and Gary Speed, was given an extra edge with the arrival of goal-grabber Lee Chapman in January 1990. It was Chapman's header at Bournemouth that gave Leeds 85 points and the title, beating Sheffield United on goal difference.

Crowds poured back to Elland Road and the Whites finished fourth on their return to the First Division, with Gary McAllister replacing Jones in midfield. Leeds won huge praise for their brand of football but it got even better the following season – the last before the advent of the Premiership. 'Sergeant Wilko's' warriors were involved in a terrific scrap before pipping Manchester United to the title, Leeds' third Championship crown. But Leeds suffered a reaction in the following campaign, failing to win an away game in

the League in 1992–93 and suffering early exits from Europe and the domestic cups. Fans' favourite Eric Cantona was sold to Manchester United and popular local ace David Batty moved on to Blackburn.

Wilkinson reshaped his side and Leeds finished fifth in 1993–94. Wilkinson, chairman of the Managers' Association, signed a new deal to keep him at Elland Road until the end of the century. However, fans were unhappy at the lack of progress, and when United were outplayed 3–0 in the League Cup Final, Wilkinson was booed off the Wembley pitch by a section of supporters.

The strong youth policy he put in place nurtured the likes of Harry Kewell and was just starting to bear fruition as the club won the Youth Cup for the first time in 1993. After two successive fifth-place finishes, United looked back on track but after the resignation of Leslie Silver as chairman, Wilkinson's position was less secure. A poor start to 1996–97, capped by a 4–0 home reverse against old rivals Manchester United, saw Wilkinson ousted.

In addition to introducing young players like Kewell, Gary Kelly and Ian Harte, Wilkinson also recruited some excellent players in Nigel Martyn, Tony Dorigo, Lee Bowyer, Tony Yeboah and Rod Wallace, leaving the new manager material to work with. Given his excellent record, Wilkinson did not have to wait long for employment. He was hired as the FA's technical director and was caretaker manager for an England friendly against France after the sacking of Glenn Hoddle in 1999.

Wilko had a relatively unsuccessful spell as Under-21 manager until June 2001, but did oversee the full national team again – drawing 0–0 with Finland in a World Cup qualifier – after Hoddle's successor, Kevin Keegan, resigned.

In 2002 he returned to club management at Sunderland, with Steve Cotterill as his assistant, but it did not work out and the Black Cats, anchored at the foot of the Premiership, sacked the pair in March 2003. After two months as coach with Chinese club Shanghai Shenua, Wilkinson had a short stint as Leicester City's coach before returning to

Notts County as a non-executive director. He also helped out with coaching at Meadow Lane until leaving the club in September 2007.

George Graham

1996–98

FA Youth Cup winners 1997.

The Leeds directors, seemingly always able to spring a surprise, whoever was on the board, brought George Graham out of exile in an effort to restore United's fortunes. The Scot, who had fantastic success at Arsenal, had been dismissed by the Gunners in February 1995 after a bung scandal. It was alleged that he had taken £425,000 in illegal payments from Norwegian agent Rune Hauge to sign John Jensen and Pal Lydersen while manager at Highbury. On top of his sacking he was banned from football for a year by the FA.

Despite that dark cloud hanging over him, Graham had an impressive CV. Born in Bargeddie, Lanarkshire, on 30 November 1944, he won 12 caps for Scotland but his club career was all in England. Nicknamed 'Stroller', he was a cultured midfielder who served Aston Villa, Chelsea, Arsenal, Manchester United, Portsmouth and Crystal Palace before entering coaching with the latter. A stint as QPR coach followed before being appointed manager of Millwall, with whom he won promotion to the old Second Division.

In May 1986 Graham became Arsenal boss and the silverware soon started to roll in, with two League Championships,

an FA Cup, two League Cups and the European Cup-Winners' Cup over an eight-year period. Leeds' directors hoped this record could be transferred to Elland Road.

Graham got right back to basics and that meant concentrating on defence to start with. United scraped together just 28 goals in 1996–97 but still finished comfortably in mid-table. Graham removed the shackles the following season and Leeds finished fifth, gaining UEFA Cup qualification. Things were looking up, but his two-year spell came to an end when it became clear that Leeds could not resist the overtures of managerless Tottenham with Graham hankering after a return to London. Although Graham had signed a three-and-a-half year contract with United the previous December, he could not resist going back to the capital.

Ironically, Graham's last Premiership game in charge of Leeds was a 3–3 draw at Spurs. Just months later Tottenham lifted the League Cup, but Graham was never popular with the White Hart Lane faithful because of his links with north London rivals Arsenal. His Tottenham tenure was ended in March 2001 and he has not worked in management since.

David O'Leary

1998–2002

UEFA Cup semi-finalists 2000, Champions League semi-finalists 2001.

Initially, Leeds wanted Leicester City's Martin O'Neill as Graham's replacement but he eventually opted to stay in the East Midlands. Once O'Neill was out of the equation the obvious choice was David O'Leary.

A legendary centre-half at Arsenal, he had been signed by Wilkinson but only made a dozen starts for Leeds before taking up coaching at Elland Road. He worked as Graham's assistant but when it became clear he was not following Graham to Tottenham, he was given the Leeds job.

Despite his wealth of playing knowledge at domestic and international level, 41-year-old O'Leary had no managerial experience. He was officially installed as manager on 25 October 1998 on a two-and-a-half year contract with

Eddie Gray, who had returned to the club as a coach, as his assistant. The pair were like a breath of fresh air, giving youngsters like Alan Smith and Jonathan Woodgate their chance to shine. With Jimmy Floyd Hasselbaink pumping in the goals, Leeds were playing an exciting brand of football and finished fourth to qualify for the UEFA Cup.

With Harry Kewell the star of the team, United shook off the £13 million exit of Hasselbaink to Atletico Madrid by signing Sunderland striker Michael Bridges, who netted 19 Premiership goals in 1999–2000. Ten successive wins in all competitions were rounded off with a 2–1 victory at Watford on 3 October, sending Leeds to the top of the table. O'Leary's young guns won unanimous praise for their exciting brand of attacking football, but the thrilling campaign hit the buffers in spring as United's form dipped. The club was plunged into mourning when fans Christopher Loftus and Kevin Speight were stabbed to death just before the UEFA Cup semi-final against Galatasary in Istanbul.

United lost 2–0 in Turkey and were held 2–2 on an emotional night at Elland Road, but the team remained undefeated in their last five Premiership games to finish third and claim a Champions League spot the following season.

Chairman Peter Ridsdale and his board splashed the cash in preparation for 2000–01, bringing in Celtic striker Mark Viduka (£6 million), Lens midfielder Olivier Dacourt (£7.2 million) and Liverpool's versatile Dominic Matteo (£4.2 million). They were joined a few months later by West Ham international Rio Ferdinand (£18m, a world record for a defender) and Inter Milan striker Robbie Keane (£12 million).

United had to go through the qualification stages for the Champions League and few gave them much hope of getting beyond the first stage, but they enjoyed a fantastic campaign, despite the ongoing Lee Bowyer and Jonathan Woodgate court case, reaching the semi-finals before being knocked out by Valencia. However, they did not do as well in the Premiership and had to settle for UEFA Cup qualification. The spending continued as Liverpool goal ace Robbie Fowler (£11 million) and Derby midfielder Seth Johnson (£7 million) were added to O'Leary's growing squad.

On New Year's Day 2002, United were top of the Premiership but nose-dived in the second half of the season, finishing sixth. By this time relations between O'Leary and Ridsdale were reported to have been strained by the publication of the manager's book, *Leeds United On Trial,* a title that did not go down too well in the dressing room given the Bowyer–Woodgate court case. O'Leary's failure to get United back into the Champions League also started to bite financially. Players had to be sold before new ones could be bought.

It emerged that Ridsdale and the board had borrowed £60 million, budgeting for a decent run in the Champions League. O'Leary had spent nearly £100 million on players in less than five years – generating good income from transfers and gate receipts too – and kept Leeds in the top six of the Premiership.

While Leeds fans braced themselves for the exit of several star players, some were surprised that O'Leary was the first departure in June 2002. After being linked with several posts, O'Leary returned to management with Aston Villa in June 2003 but could not work the magic of his early years at Leeds and left by mutual consent in July 2006.

Terry Venables

2002–2003

Celtic's Martin O'Neill was once again linked with the Leeds post, but it was

former England chief Terry Venables who accepted the challenge of leading United. Within a month Leeds, with their multi-million pound debt rising, sold Rio Ferdinand to Manchester United for £30 million. Meanwhile, Venables was restricted to modest buys as the depth of United's financial troubles, thought to amount to £80 million, became clear.

More sales followed as the relationship between Venables and chairman Peter Ridsdale became increasingly strained. The sale of Jonathan Woodgate to Newcastle United without Venables's knowledge proved the final straw and, with the club sliding towards relegation, Venables was sacked in March 2003 after eight months in charge. He later assisted Steve McClaren in the England set-up, but the pair were axed two days after England failed to qualify for the 2008 European Championships.

Venables, the 59-year-old former Chelsea, Tottenham and England player, learned his managerial trade with Crystal Palace and QPR, taking both clubs to Division Two titles.

In May 1984, 'El Tel' went to Barcelona and took the Catalan club to the League title in his first season, followed by a European Cup Final appearance. He returned to London to manage Tottenham and guided them to the FA Cup in 1991 – 24 years after playing in a Spurs Cup Final-winning

side. In January 1994 Venables, highly regarded as a coach, landed the England post despite his business dealings coming under scrutiny.

Venables led England to the semi-finals of Euro '96, which England hosted, then took Australia to the brink of their first appearance of the World Cup Finals, only to lose to Iran in a Play-off. The next stop was a short one as chairman of Portsmouth, returning to management with Crystal Palace in March 1998 and leaving the following January when the club went into administration. Two years later he was appointed Middlesbrough coach and assistant to Bryan Robson, but the pair left in June 2001, Venables re-emerging at Leeds 12 months later.

Peter Reid

2003

Leeds were in danger of relegation when Peter Reid was appointed to replace Terry Venables on 21 March 2003 until the end of the season.

Reid, the former Manchester City and Sunderland boss, stuck to his brief and United secured their Premiership status with a 3–2 win at Arsenal in the penultimate game of the season. By this time Peter Ridsdale had stood down as chairman and Professor John McKenzie,

an academic who studied at the London School of Economics, was at the helm in the boardroom. He had a sharp financial brain and told Reid to get free transfers or loan signings in the summer as he re-shaped a squad that was losing more of its star names, including Harry Kewell to Liverpool.

Many of the long-term loans were from abroad and simply not up to life in the Premiership, and after a 6–1 thrashing at Portsmouth in November the board showed him the door, having survived less time than Venables. Before the end of the season Reid was installed as manager at Coventry but left the club by mutual consent in January 2005.

Reid, who was in charge when Sunderland were promoted to the Premiership as champions in 1996, had more success as a player than a manager. After leaving Bolton he won two League Championship medals and an FA Cup-winners' medal with Everton. He was Footballer of the Year in 1985 and played for England 13 times.

Eddie Gray

2003–2004

Throughout all the chaos of the previous three years one man was a constant at the club – Eddie Gray. He had been assistant to O'Leary, Venables and Reid and

became the first man to manage Leeds twice, following his efforts in the 1980s. It was a near-impossible task, with Leeds rooted to the bottom of the table and morale even lower, and players never quite certain if they were going to be paid from one month to another.

Most of the loan players were jettisoned, but Gray could not prevent the inevitable and relegation was effectively confirmed by a 4–1 defeat at Bolton in early May. By this time United had more new faces in the boardroom including insolvency expert Gerald Krasner, who headed a takeover by local businessmen, in the chair. Gray left at the end of the season as Leeds sold off all their top players – Mark Viduka, Alan Smith and goalkeeper Paul Robinson among them – to stave off the very real threat of liquidation.

Kevin Blackwell

2004–2006

Championship Play-off finalists 2006.

It would take a brave man to step into the wreckage of free-falling Leeds United, but Kevin Blackwell took on 'Mission Impossible'.

Against a backdrop of no funds and few players, Blackwell, a former assistant to Neil Warnock at Sheffield United, took up the challenge.

He had been drafted in as coach by Peter Reid and was a relatively low-profile figure compared with many of the club's post-Revie managers.

A goalkeeper with Barnet and Boston United, he played under Warnock at Scarborough and followed the manager to Notts County, Torquay, Huddersfield and Plymouth, doubling up as a coach at the latter two clubs.

He was goalkeeping coach at Bury under Warnock and became assistant manager at Bramall Lane when his mentor took over as manager in December 1999.

At Leeds he pieced together a team of free transfers and trialists, old experienced pros with a sprinkling of younger players.

Although fans feared the club could be relegated a second successive season, Blackwell halted the slide on the field, and given the circumstances 14th place was as good as could be expected.

Midway through the season 73-year-old Ken Bates, the former Chelsea

supremo, completed his takeover of the club, Gerald Krasner having reduced the original £103m debt considerably.

Having stabilised the club on the pitch, Blackwell was given financial support by Bates, bringing in strikers Rob Hulse, David Healy, Richard Cresswell and Robbie Blake. United's strong home record and solid performances on opposition soil lifted them to third place by the end of February.

Blackwell was rewarded with a new contract but performances tailed off, and although United reached the Play-off Final at Cardiff they were thumped 3–0 by Watford, managed by a former Leeds coach, Adie Boothroyd. Blackwell's assistant, Sam Ellis, didn't have his contract renewed in the summer, and John Carver, who had replaced Boothroyd as coach, moved up to assistant.

A poor start to the next campaign saw Leeds gain just seven points from seven games, and Blackwell was shown the door.

Carver filled in for a handful of games but a dire 5–1 defeat at Luton ended his prospects of landing the job on a permanent basis.

In November 2006 Blackwell announced he was suing Leeds for wrongful dismissal after it was confirmed he was sacked for gross misconduct for press comments about the club's finances.

He returned to management with Carver as his number two, in March 2007 with Luton, where he had been born on 21 December 1958.

But it was a case of out of the frying pan into the fire. Blackwell did not have enough time to prevent Luton going down, and the following season the Hatters found themselves in dire financial straits. In December 2007 Luton went into administration, incurring a deduction of 10 points. The following month Blackwell announced he would be leaving the club in February, only to be sacked in January.

He was not out of work long. On 14 February he succeeded Bryan Robson as manager of struggling Sheffield United, where he had previously worked under Neil Warnock. With Ellis as his assistant, he agreed to take the job until the end of the season and transformed a Blades squad in danger of being embroiled in a relegation battle to one that reached the brink of the Play-offs. Blackwell's reward was a three-year deal in May 2008.

Dennis Wise

2006–2008

It was little surprise that Dennis Wise became United's next manager. He has been close to chairman Ken Bates since their days at Chelsea, where Wise spent 11 years. He and assistant Gus Poyet both arrived from Swindon, where, in the four months they worked in tandem, they had taken the Robins to second spot in League One.

They watched Leeds crash 3–1 at home to Southend in the League Cup – the Whites side being selected by reserve team coach David Geddis before taking charge the following day. Wise was quick to make changes, rooting out older players but with finances remaining a problem results were hard to gain. Relegation was confirmed in the final home game of the season against Ipswich – a 1–1 draw – and Leeds slumped to the third tier of English football for the first time in their history. United announced they were going into administration before the Derby game and were given a 10-point deduction, ensuring they finished bottom.

Worse was to follow as Leeds were deducted a further 15 points from the start of the League One campaign. Throughout the summer there had been a long-running battle to sort out United's future before Bates regained full control of the club. However, the League

Although born in Kensington on 16 December 1966, Wise was on Southampton's books as a teenager, but made his breakthrough at Wimbledon where he was part of the 'Crazy Gang' that beat Liverpool in the 1988 FA Cup Final. He won plenty of honours while at Chelsea, including 21 England caps, and was a combative midfield player.

Sacked by his next club, Leicester, after a pre-season incident in Finland, Wise returned to London with Millwall, becoming player-manager in 2003. The following year he guided the Lions to the FA Cup Final but after falling out with the chairman he left Millwall and reverted to playing, with short spells at Southampton and Coventry. He was then appointed as Swindon boss in May 2006.

Gary McAllister

2008

League One Play-off finalists 2008.

Leeds acted quickly to fill the gap created by Dennis Wise's sudden departure. Chairman Ken Bates soon thrashed out a deal at his Monaco base with former United star Gary McAllister to return to the club as manager. United, despite going through a sticky patch, were still in the Play-off hunt, and McAllister's brief was simple – win promotion. That mission was not quite achieved by McAllister and his battling squad.

The former Scotland captain initially agreed to take on the job until the end of the season and brought in Steve Staunton, the former Liverpool defender and Republic of Ireland manager and player, as his assistant. Neil McDonald, the ex-Carlisle manager, was recruited as coach. The new backroom staff replaced Dave Bassett and coach John Gannon, who had left shortly after Wise quit for Newcastle.

It took five games before the new boss recorded his first victory as his squad got to grips with passing their way up the pitch. It made for more attractive football and the victories soon began to mount up, earning McAllister a 12-month

imposed the 15-point deduction as they believed United had not followed rules on clubs entering administration – a sanction Leeds contested vigorously.

The club's future was secured just before the start of the new season, and Wise was unable to sign any new players until the issue was resolved, even paying some of the squad out of his own pocket.

Rather than crumble, the points loss bonded the team, management, fans and directors together, and Wise's side made a blazing start to the season with United winning their opening seven League games, earning Wise successive Manager of the Month awards.

Just when Leeds looked set fair, Poyet moved back to his old club, Tottenham, as assistant manager and his role at Leeds was taken by Dave Bassett, Wise's former boss at Wimbledon.

By Christmas United's fantastic charge up the table was beginning to splutter, but few predicted the next managerial move when Wise quit Leeds in January 2008 to become Newcastle United's highly paid executive director of football. Behind him he had left a solid base on which his successor could build, with United occupying a Play-off slot and a squad with a penchant for scoring vital late goals.

rolling contract. Leeds, despite their points handicap, reached the Play-offs in dramatic fashion. They trailed Carlisle 2–0 until an injury-time goal gave them hope at Brunton Park, where they duly completed the job, winning 2–0 – with another injury-time goal – to reach the League One Play-off Final. However, the Wembley game proved a match too far as United lost 1–0 to near-neighbours Doncaster.

Leeds had fought the points deduction tooth and nail, but the battle to get the points back ended just before the end of the season when an independent tribunal ruled in the League's favour. Had the points not been taken away from United, they would have been runners-up to Swansea City and regained their place in the Championship at the first attempt, but instead they had to settle for fifth place.

McAllister had left Elland Road in 1996 and played for Coventry and Liverpool, being awarded an MBE in 2001. He became manager at Coventry in April 2002, leaving in December 2003 as his wife, Denise, was suffering from cancer. After her death in March 2006, he did TV work before his Leeds managerial appointment was confirmed on 29 January 2008.

INTERNATIONALS

A total of 105 Leeds United players have been capped by 22 countries at full international level. A further four Leeds City players also won international honours while at the club. This list includes all those players, including those who were on loan at the club and those United players who were on loan at other clubs when they turned out for their countries. For example, Roque Junior's four outings for Brazil came when he was on loan from Italian club AC Milan. On the other hand, Danny Mills's final England appearance was while he was on a season-long loan at Middlesbrough. The appearances are listed in calendar years – in some cases games were played against the same opponents in successive matches and are marked (2) with the total number of caps listed at the end of each players' appearances.

Lucas Radebe is United's most capped player, making 58 appearances for South Africa. Billy Bremner is the most capped British player with 54 outings for Scotland, while Jack Charlton leads the way for England with 37. The Republic of Ireland first played as a separate nation in 1924, but Eire-born players appeared for Northern Ireland until after World War Two. Harry Duggan played for both Northern Ireland and the Republic of Ireland.

Leeds City

Ireland
J. **Enright** 1912 v Scotland (1).
J. **Moran** 1912 v Scotland (1).
B. **Scott** 1913 v Wales, England, Scotland (3).

Wales
R. **Morris** 1903 v Scotland (1).

Leeds United

Angola
R. **Marques** 2006 v Mexico, Iran; 2008 v Egypt, Morocco, South Africa, Senegal, Tunisia, Egypt (8).

Australia
J. **Burns** 2000 v Scotland; 2001 v Colombia (2).
H. **Kewell** 1996 v Chile, Saudi Arabia; 1997 v Tunisia, Iran (2), Saudi Arabia, Uruguay, Brazil; 2000 v Hungary; 2001 v France, Uruguay (2); 2003 v England (13).
P. **Okon** 2003 v England, Republic of Ireland, Jamaica (3).
M. **Viduka** 2001 v France, Uruguay (2); 2003 v England, Republic of Ireland, Jamaica; 2004 v South Africa (7).

Austria
M. **Hiden** 1998 v Hungary, US, Tunisia, France, Israel, Cyprus, San Marino (7).

Brazil
Roque Junior 2003 v Jamaica, Peru, Uruguay; 2004 v Republic of Ireland (4).

Bulgaria
R. **Kishishev** 2007 v Albania (2) (2).

Cameroon
S. **Olembe** 1998 v Egypt (1).

England
P. **Barnes** 1981 v Norway, 1982 v Holland (2).
D. **Batty** 1991 v USSR, Argentina, Australia, New Zealand, Malaysia, Germany, Turkey; 1992 v Hungary, France, Sweden, Norway; 1993 v San Marino, US, Brazil; 1999 v Hungary, Sweden, Bulgaria, Luxembourg, Poland (19).
L. **Bowyer** 2002 v Portugal (1).
J. **Charlton** 1965 v Scotland, Hungary, Yugoslavia, West Germany, Sweden, Wales, Austria, Northern Ireland, Spain; 1966 v Poland, West Germany, Scotland, Yugoslavia, Finland, Denmark, Poland, Uruguay, Mexico, France, Argentina, Portugal, West Germany, Northern Ireland, Czechoslovakia, Wales; 1967 v Scotland, Wales, Spain, 1969 v Romania, France, Wales, Holland, Portugal; 1970 v Holland, Czechoslovakia (35).
T. **Cherry** 1976 v Wales, Scotland, Brazil, Finland, Republic of Ireland, Italy; 1977 v Luxembourg, Northern Ireland, Scotland, Brazil, Argentina, Uruguay, Switzerland, Luxembourg, Italy; 1978 v Brazil, Wales, Czechoslovakia, Wales, Sweden; 1980 v Republic of Ireland, Argentina, Wales, Northern Ireland, Scotland, Australia, Spain (27).
A. **Clarke** 1970 v Czechoslovakia, East Germany; 1971 v Malta, Northern Ireland, Wales, Scotland; 1973 v Scotland, Wales, Scotland, Czechoslovakia, Poland, USSR, Italy, Austria, Poland, Italy; 1974 v Portugal; 1975 v Czechoslovakia, Portugal (19).
T. **Cooper** 1969 v France, Wales, Scotland, Mexico; 1970 v Holland, Belgium, Colombia, Ecuador, Romania, Brazil, Czechoslovakia, West Germany, East Germany; 1971 v Malta, Northern Ireland, Wales, Scotland, Switzerland (2); 1974 v Portugal (20).
W. **Copping** 1933 v Italy, Switzerland, Ireland, Wales, France; 1934 v Scotland; 1939 v Romania (7).
T. **Currie** 1978 v Brazil, Wales, Northern Ireland, Scotland, Hungary, Czechoslovakia; 1979 v Northern Ireland (2), Wales, Sweden (10).
T. **Dorigo** 1991 v Germany; 1992 v Czechoslovakia, Hungary, Brazil; 1993 v San Marino, Poland, US, Brazil, Holland (9).
W. **Edwards** 1926 v Wales, Scotland, Ireland; 1927 v Wales, Scotland, Belgium, Luxembourg, France; 1928 v Scotland, France, Belgium, Ireland, Wales; 1929 v Scotland, Ireland, Wales (16).

R. Ferdinand 2001 v Spain, Finland, Albania, Mexico, Greece, Germany, Albania, Greece, Sweden; 2002 v Holland, South Korea, Cameroon, Sweden, Argentina, Nigeria, Denmark, Brazil (17).

R. Fowler 2002 v Italy, Paraguay, Cameroon, Denmark (4).

B. Furness 1933 v Italy (1).

B. Greenhoff 1980 v Australia (1).

N. Hunter 1965 v Spain; 1966 v West Germany, Yugoslavia, Finland; 1967 v Austria; 1968 v Spain, Sweden, West Germany, Yugoslavia, USSR; 1969 v Romania, Wales; 1970 v Holland, West Germany; 1971 v Malta; 1972 v West Germany (2), Wales, Northern Ireland, Scotland, Wales; 1973 v Wales, USSR, Austria, Poland; 1974 v Northern Ireland, Scotland, Czechoslovakia (28).

M.D. Jones 1970 v Holland (1).

P. Madeley 1971 v Northern Ireland, Switzerland (2), Greece; 1972 v West Germany (2), Wales, Scotland; 1973 v Scotland, Czechoslovakia, Poland, USSR, Italy, Austria, Poland, Italy; 1974 v Czechoslovakia, Portugal; 1975 v Cyprus, Czechoslovakia, Portugal; 1976 v Finland, Republic of Ireland; 1977 v Holland (24)..

N. Martyn 1997 v South Africa, Cameroon; 1998 v Chile, Belgium, Czech Republic; 1999 v France, Luxembourg, Poland, Belgium; 2000 v Ukraine, Romania; 2001 v Spain, Mexico, Holland, Greece, Sweden; 2002 v Holland, Italy, South Korea, Cameroon (20).

D. Mills 2001 v Mexico, Holland, Sweden; 2002 v Italy, Paraguay, South Korea, Cameroon, Sweden, Argentina, Nigeria, Denmark, Brazil, Portugal; 2003 v Australia, South Africa, Serbia Montenegro, Slovakia, Croatia, Portugal (19).

M. O'Grady 1969 v France (1).

A. Peacock 1965 v Wales, Northern Ireland (2).

P. Reaney 1968 v Bulgaria, 1969 v Portugal, 1971 v Malta (3).

P. Robinson 2003 v Australia, South Africa, Croatia, Denmark (4).

A. Smith 2001 v Mexico, Greece, Holland; 2002 v Portugal, Slovakia, Macedonia; 2003 v Portugal, Sweden (8).

B. Sproston 1936 v Wales; 1937 v Ireland, Wales, Czechoslovakia; 1938 v Scotland, Germany, Switzerland, France (8).

E. Stephenson 1938 v Scotland, Ireland (2).

R. Wainscoat 1929 v Scotland (1).

J. Wilcox 2000 v Argentina (1).

J. Woodgate 1999 v Bulgaria; 2002 v Portugal, Slovakia, Macedonia (4).

France

E. Cantona 1992 v England, Belgium, Switzerland, Holland, Sweden, England, Denmark, Austria, Finland (9).

O. Dacourt 2001 v South Korea, Australia, Mexico; 2002 v Malta; 2003 v Egypt, Colombia, Japan, Turkey, Cameroon (9).

Ghana

T. Yeboah 1995 v Niger*, Norway, Congo, Sierra Leone, Egypt; 1996 v Saudi Arabia, Zimbabwe, Ivory Coast, Tunisia, Mozambique, Zaire, South Africa, Brazil; 1997 v Morocco, Zimbabwe, Sierra Leone (16).

* This match was later annulled as Niger withdrew from the African Cup of Nations.

Holland

J-F. Hasselbaink 1998 v Cameroon, Paraguay, Nigeria, Belgium, Mexico (5).

Iceland

G. Einarsson 2005 v Croatia, Italy, Hungary, South Africa, Croatia, Sweden (6).

Northern Ireland

R. Browne 1935 v England; 1936 v Wales; 1937 v England; 1938 v Wales, Scotland, England (6).

D. Cochrane 1938 v England; 1939 v Wales; 1946 v England, Scotland; 1947 v Wales, Scotland, England; 1948 v Wales, Scotland; 1949 v Wales, Scotland, England (12).

W. Cush 1957 v Italy; 1958 v Italy, Wales, Czechoslovakia, Argentina, West Germany, Czechoslovakia, France, England, Spain, Scotland; 1959 v Wales, Scotland, England; 1960 v Wales (15).

H. Duggan 1929 v England; 1930 v England, 1931 v Wales; 1932 v England, 1933 v England; 1934 v Scotland; 1935 v Wales, Scotland (8).

D. Healy 2005 v Canada, England, Poland, Germany, Malta, Azerbaijan, England, Wales, Austria, 2006 v Estonia, Finland, Iceland, Spain, Denmark, Latvia, 2007 v Liechtenstein, Sweden (17).

W. McAdams 1962 v Holland (1).

J. McCabe 1948 v Scotland; 1949 v Wales, England; 1951 v Wales; 1953 v Wales, Scotland (6).

J. McClelland 1990 v Norway (1).

C. Martin 1947 v Scotland, England; 1948 v Wales (3).

N. Worthington 1994 v Portugal, Austria, Republic of Ireland; 1995 v Republic of Ireland, Latvia, Canada, Chile, Latvia, Portugal, Leichtenstein, Austria; 1996 v Norway, Swede, Germany (14).

Norway

E. Bakke 1999 v Turkey; 2000 v Slovenia, Italy, Spain, Yugoslavia, Slovenia, Wales, Ukraine; 2001 v Northern Ireland, Bulgaria, Ukraine, Belarus, Armenia; 2002 v Sweden, Japan, Holland, Denmark, Romania, Bosnia-Herzegovina; 2003 v Luxembourg, Finland, Denmark, Romania (23).

A. Haaland 1997 v Finland, France, Switzerland; 1998 v Belgium, Saudi Arabia, Slovenia, Albania, Egypt; 1999 v Georgia, Albania (10).

G. Halle 1997 v Finland, Brazil, Iceland, Finland, Azerbaijan, Switzerland; 1998 v Belgium, Mexico, Saudi Arabia, Scotland (10).

F. Strandli 1994 v US (1).

Republic of Ireland

J. Chandler 1979 v Czechoslovakia, US (2).

J. Douglas 2006 v Holland, Cyprus, Czech Republic, San Marino; 2007 v Wales, Slovakia (6).

H. Duggan 1927 v Italy; 1930 v Belgium, 1936 v Hungary, Luxembourg (4).

P. Fitzgerald 1960 v Wales, Norway; 1961 v Scotland (3).

J. Giles 1963 v Austria (2); 1964 v Spain (2), Poland, Norway, England; 1965 v Spain (3); 1966 v Austria, Belgium, Spain, Turkey; 1967 v Turkey, Austria; 1968 v Denmark; 1969 v Czechoslovakia, Scotland; 1970 v Poland, West Germany; 1971 v Italy; 1972 v France; 1973 v USSR; 1974 v Brazil, Uruguay, Chile, USSR, Turkey; 1975 v Switzerland, USSR, Switzerland (32).

I. Harte 1997 v Croatia, Holland, Mexico, Bolivia, Liechtenstein, Macedonia, Iceland; 1997 v Wales, Macedonia, Romania, Liechtenstein, Lithuania, Iceland, Lithuania, Belgium (2); 1998 v Argentina, Mexico; 1999 v Paraguay, Croatia, Malta; 2000 v Czech Republic, Holland, Portugal, Estonia, Finland; 2001 v Cyprus, Andorra (2), Portugal, Estonia, Croatia, Holland, Cyprus, Iran (2); 2002 v Russia, Denmark, US, Nigeria, Cameroon, Germany, Saudi Arabia, Spain, Finland, Russia, Switzerland; 2003 v Scotland, Norway, Australia, Russia, Turkey, Switzerland, Canada; 2004 v Czech Republic, Poland (56).

R. Keane 2001 v Croatia, Holland, Iran (2); 2002 v Russia, Denmark, US, Nigeria, Cameroon, Germany, Saudi Arabia, Spain, Finland (13).

G. Kelly 1994 v Russia, Holand, Bolivia, Germany, Czech Republic, Norway, Holland, Latvia, Liechtenstein, Northern Ireland; 1995 v Northern Ireland, Portugal, Liechtenstein, Austria (2), Latvia, Portugal, Holland; 1997 v Wales, Romania, Liechtenstein, Iceland, Lithuania, Belgium (2); 1998 v Czech Republic, Argentina, Mexico; 1999 v Croatia, Macedonia; 2000 v Czech Republic, Holland, Finland; 2001 v Cyprus, Andorra (2), Portugal, Estonia, Croatia, Holland, Iran (2); 2002 v Russia, Denmark, US, Nigeria, Cameroon, Germany, Saudi Arabia, Spain, Finland, Switzerland (52).

S. McPhail 2000 v Scotland, US, South Africa; 2001 v Croatia, Cyprus; 2002 v Finland, Greece, 2003 v Turkey, Canada, 2004 v Nigeria (10).

C. Martin 1947 v Spain, 1948 v Portugal, Spain (3).

A. Maybury 1998 v Czech Republic, 1999 v Northern Ireland (2).

L. Miller 2006 v Sweden (1).

N. Peyton 1960 v West Germany, Sweden, Wales; 1962 v Iceland, Scotland (5).

J. Sheridan 1988 v Romania, Yugoslavia, Poland, Norway, Spain (5).

Scotland

W. Bell 1966 v Portugal, Brazil (2).

B. Bremner 1965 v Spain, Poland, Italy (2); 1966 v England, Portugal, Brazil, Wales, Northern Ireland; 1967 v England, Wales; 1968 v England, Denmark, Austria, Cyprus; 1969 v West Germany, Wales, Northern Ireland, England, Cyprus, Republic of Ireland, West Germany; 1970 v Austria; 1971 v Wales, England, Portugal, Belgium, Holland; 1972 v Northern Ireland, Wales, England, Yugoslavia, Portugal, Brazil, Denmark (2); 1973 v England, Northern Ireland, England, Switzerland, Brazil, Czechoslovakia, West Germany; 1974 v Northern Ireland, Norway, Zaire, Brazil, Yugoslavia, Spain; 1975 v Spain, Denmark (51) .

S. Caldwell 2004 v Wales, Trinidad & Tobago (2).

B. Collins 1965 v England, Spain, Poland (3).

A. Graham 1977 v East Germany, 1978 v Austria, Norway; 1979 v Wales, Northern Ireland, England, Argentina, Norway, Austria; 1980 v Wales (10).

E. Gray 1969 v England, Cyprus, West Germany, Austria; 1971 v Wales, Northern Ireland, Belgium, Holland; 1976 v Wales, England, Finland, Wales (12).

F. Gray 1976 v Switzerland; 1978 v Norway, Portugal; 1979 v Wales, Northern Ireland, England, Argentina; 1981 v Northern Ireland, England, Sweden, Portugal; 1982 v Spain, Holland, Wales, New Zealand, Brazil, USSR, East Germany, Switzerland, Belgium; 1983 v Switzerland, Wales, England, Canada (24).

D. Harvey 1972 v Denmark, Czechoslovakia; 1973 v West Germany; 1974 v Northern Ireland, Wales, England, Belgium, Zaire, Brazil, Yugoslavia, East Germany; 1975 v Spain, Denmark (2); 1976 v Finland (15).

D. Hopkin 1997 v Belarus, France; 1999 v Czech Republic, Bosnia (2) (5).

J. Jordan 1973 v England, Switzerland, Brazil, Czechoslovakia (2), West Germany; 1974 v Northern Ireland, Wales, England, Belgium, Norway, Zaire, Brazil, Yugoslavia, East Germany; 1975 v Wales, England, Belgium, Spain; 1976 v Spain, Wales, Northern Ireland, England, Czechoslovakia, Wales; 1977 v Northern Ireland, England, East Germany, Czechoslovakia, Wales (30).

P. Lorimer 1969 v Austria; 1971 v Wales, Northern Ireland; 1972 v Northern Ireland, Wales, England, Denmark (2); 1973 v England (2), West Germany; 1974 v England, Belgium, Norway, Zaire, Brazil, Yugoslavia, Spain; 1975 v Denmark (2), Romania (21).

G. McAllister 1990 v Romania, Switzerland, Bulgaria; 1991 v USSR, San Marino, Switzerland, San Marino; 1992 v Northern Ireland, Finland, US, Canada, Norway, Holland, Germany, CIS, Switzerland, Portugal, Italy; 1993 v Malta, Switzerland, Italy, Malta; 1994 v Holland, Austria, Holland, Finland, Russia, Greece; 1995 v Russia, San Marino, Greece, Finland, Sweden, San Marino; 1996 v Australia, Denmark, US, Colombia, Holland, England, Switzerland (41).

G. McQueen 1974 v Belgium, Spain; 1975 v Spain, Portugal, Wales, Northern Ireland, England, Romania, Denmark; 1976 v Czechoslovakia, Wales; 1977 v Wales, Northern Ireland, England, East Germany, Czechoslovakia, Wales (17).

D. Matteo 2000 v Australia; 2001 v Belgium, San Marino, Croatia, Belgium; 2002 v France (6).

D. Stewart 1977 v East Germany (1).

G Strachan 1989 v France; 1991 v USSR, Bulgaria, San Marino, Switzerland, Romania; 1992 v Northern Ireland, Finland (8).

Senegal

L. Sakho 2004 v Mali, Tunisia (2).

Slovakia

L. Michalik 2007 v Republic of Ireland (1).

South Africa

P. Masinga 1994 v Madagascar, Mauritius, Zambia; 1995 v Argentina, Germany; 1996 v Cameroon, Angola, Egypt, Algeria, Tunisia, Brazil, Malawi (12).

L. **Radebe** 1994 v Madagascar, Mauritius, Zambia; 1996 v Angola, Egypt, Algeria, Ghana, Tunisia, Brazil, Malawi (2), Zaire; 1997 v Zambia, Congo, Zaire, England, Holland, Zambia, Congo, France, Germany, Brazil, Uruguay; 1998 v Angola, Ivory Coast, Namibia, Morocco, DR Congo, Egypt, Zambia, Argentina, Iceland, France, Denmark, Saudi Arabia, Angola; 1999 v Mauritius, Gabon (2), Denmark, Mauritius, Zimbabwe, Sweden; 2000 v Gabon, DR Congo, Algeria, Ghana, Nigeria, Tunisia, Liberia 2001 v Burkino Faso; 2002 v Madagascar, Scotland, Turkey, Paraguay, Slovenia, Spain; 2003 v England (58).

Spain
R. **Bravo** 2003 v Armenia (1).

Sweden
T. **Lucic** 2002 v Czech Republic; 2003 v Hungary, Croatia, San Marino, Poland (5).

United States of America
E. **Lewis** 2005 Trinidad & Tobago, Mexico, Costa Rica; 2006 v Venezuela, Latvia, Czech Republic, Ghana (7).

Wales
M. **Aizlewood** 1987 v USSR, Finland, Denmark; 1988 v Sweden, Malta, Italy, Holland; 1989 v West Germany (8).

J. **Charles** 1950 v Northern Ireland; 1951 v Switzerland; 1953 v Northern Ireland, France, Yugoslavia, England, Scotland; 1954 v Northern Ireland, Austria, Yugoslavia, Scotland, England; 1955 v Northern Ireland, England, Scotland, Austria; 1956 v Northern Ireland, Scotland, England; 1957 v Northern Ireland; 1962 v Scotland (21).

A. **Curtis** 1979 v England, Wales, Malta, Republic of Ireland, West Germany, Turkey (6).

B. **Flynn** 1977 v Czechoslovakia, West Germany; 1978 v Iran, England, Scotland, Northern Ireland, Malta, Turkey; 1979 v Scotland, England, Northern Ireland, Malta, Republic of Ireland, West Germany; 1980 v England, Scotland, Northern Ireland, Iceland, Turkey, Czechoslovakia; 1981 v Republic of Ireland, Turkey, Scotland, England, USSR, Czechoslovakia, USSR; 1982 v England, Scotland, Northern Ireland, France, Norway (32).

C. **Harris** 1976 v England, Scotland; 1977 v West Germany; 1978 v Iran, England, Scotland, Northern Ireland, Malta, Turkey; 1979 v West Germany, England, Malta; 1980 v Northern Ireland, Iceland, Turkey, Czechoslovakia; 1981 v Republic of Ireland, Turkey, Scotland, England, USSR, Czechoslovakia, Iceland; 1982 v England (24).

M.G. **Jones** 1999 v Switzerland; 2000 v Qatar, Brazil, Portugal, Poland (5).

A. **Powell** 1946 v Scotland, England; 1947 v England, Scotland; 1948 v Northern Ireland (5).

G. **Speed** 1990 v Costa Rica, Denmark, Luxembourg; 1991 v Republic of Ireland, Iceland, Germany, Brazil, Germany, Luxembourg; 1992 v Republic of Ireland, Romania, Holland, Argentina, Japan, Faroe Islands, Cyprus, Belgium; 1993 v Republic of Ireland, Belgium, Faroe Islands, Republic of Czechs and Slovaks, Cyprus, Romania; 1994 v Norway, Sweden, Albania, Moldova, Georgia, Bulgaria; 1995 v Bulgaria, Germany, Moldova, Germany, Albania; 1996 v Italy, Switzerland (36).

G. **Sprake** 1963 v Scotland; 1964 v Northern Ireland, Scotland, Denmark, Greece; 1965 v England, USSR; 1966 v Northern Ireland, Scotland; 1967 v England, Scotland; 1969 v West Germany, Scotland, England, Northern Ireland, Rest of the UK, East Germany, Italy, Romania; 1971 v Scotland, England, Northern Ireland, Finland; 1972 v England, Scotland, Northern Ireland, England; 1973 v England, Poland, Scotland, Northern Ireland, Poland (32).

B. **Stevenson** 1978 v Northern Ireland, Malta, Turkey; 1979 v Scotland, England, Northern Ireland, Malta, West Germany, Turkey; 1980 v Iceland; 1981 v Czechoslovakia (11).

H. **Williams** 1950 v Northern Ireland, Scotland (2).

T. **Yorath** 1969 v Italy; 1971 v Scotland, England, Northern Ireland, Czechoslovakia; 1972 v England, Scotland, Northern Ireland; 1973 v England, Poland, Scotland, Poland; 1974 v England, Scotland, Northern Ireland, Austria, Hungary, Luxembourg; 1975 v Hungary, Luxembourg, Scotland, Austria; 1976 v England, Yugoslavia, Scotland, England, Northern Ireland, Yugoslavia (28).

APPEARANCES AND GOALS

100 consecutive appearances

League

146	John Lukic	October 1979 to March 1983
144	Jim Baker	August 1920 to December 1923
143	Eric Kerfoot	January 1955 to April 1958
133	Tom Townsley	January 1926 to March 1929
104	Grenville Hair	March 1953 to September 1955

All Matches

162	John Lukic	October 1979 to March 1983
148	Eric Kerfoot	January 1955 to April 1958
140	Jim Baker	October 1920 to December 1923
140	Tom Townsley	January 1926 to March 1929
114	Gary Kelly	August 1993 to December 1995
108	Grenville Hair	March 1953 to September 1955
105	John Lukic	October 1990 to October 1992
100	Norman Hunter	August 1970 to May 1972

Ever present in a Football League season

Leeds City

	Games	
1907–08	38	F. Croot
1910–11	38	A. Creighton
1911–12	38	H. Roberts
1912–13	38	E. Lintott, B. McLeod
1913–14	38	G. Affleck, M. Foley

Leeds United

	Games	
1920–21	42	J. Baker, W. Down, B. Duffield
1921–22	42	J. Baker
1922–23	42	J. Baker, F. Whalley
1924–25	42	J. Harris
1925–26	42	T. Jennings
1926–27	42	J.F. Potts, T. Townsley
1927–28	42	T. Mitchell, G. Reed, T. Townsley
1930–31	42	W. Copping
1931–32	42	Jack Milburn
1932–33	42	B. Furness, G. Milburn, Jack Milburn
1933–34	42	B. Moore
1937–38	42	Jack Milburn
1948–49	42	Jim Milburn
1949–50	42	T. Burden, J. Charles, H. Searson
1950–51	42	Jim Milburn
1952–53	42	T. Burden, J. Dunn, J. Scott
1953–54	42	G. Hair, E. Kerfoot
1954–55	42	G. Hair
1955–56	42	J. Dunn, E. Kerfoot, R. Wood
1956–57	42	J. Dunn, G. Hair, E. Kerfoot, J. Overfield, R. Wood
1957–58	42	E. Kerfoot
1963–64	42	N. Hunter
1968–69	42	B. Bremner, N. Hunter, P. Reaney, G. Sprake
1970–71	42	N. Hunter
1971–72	42	N. Hunter, P. Lorimer, P. Madeley
1973–74	42	B. Bremner, N. Hunter
1975–76	42	F. Gray
1976–77	42	T. Cherry
1980–81	42	J. Lukic
1981–82	42	J. Lukic
1982–83	42	F. Gray
1984–85	42	A. Linighan, J. Sheridan
1987–88	44	M. Day
1989–90	46	G. Strachan
1990–91	38	L. Chapman, J. Lukic, G. McAllister, M. Sterland, C. Whyte
1991–92	42	J. Lukic
1993–94	42	G. Kelly, G. McAllister
1994–95	42	G. Kelly, J. Lukic
1999–2000	38	N. Martyn
2000–01	38	L. Bowyer
2001–02	38	N. Martyn
2002–03	38	P. Robinson
2004–05	46	N. Sullivan

Most ever-present seasons

5	N. Hunter, J. Lukic
4	E. Kerfoot
3	J. Baker, J. Dunn, G. Hair, Jack Milburn
2	B. Bremner, T. Burden, F. Gray, G. Kelly, N. Martyn, Jim Milburn, G. McAllister, T. Townsley

(Note: Reaney made 41 appearances for four consecutive seasons prior to being an ever present in 1968–69)

Individual scoring feats

Five goals in a game (United)

G. Hodgson v Leicester City (h) Division One	1 Oct 1938

Five goals in a game (City)

B. McLeod v Hull City (a) Division Two	16 Jan 1915

Four goals in a game (United)

T. Jennings v Liverpool (a) Division One	2 Oct 1926
T. Jennings v Blackburn Rovers (h) Division One	9 Oct 1926
R. Wainscoat v West Ham Utd (h) Division One	30 Apr 1927
T. Jennings v Chelsea (h) Division Two	10 Dec 1927
A. Hydes v Middlesborough (h) Division One	28 Oct 1933
G. Hodgson v Everton (h) Division One	26 Feb 1938
J. Charles v Notts County (h) Division Two	19 Aug 1953
J. McCole v Brentford (h) League Cup	13 Sep 1961
P. Lorimer v Spora Luxembourg (a) UEFA Cup	3 Oct 1967
A. Clarke v Sutton United (a) FA Cup	24 Jan 1970
A. Clarke v Burnley (h) Division One	3 Apr 1971
M. Viduka v Liverpool (h) Premier League	4 Nov 2000

A. Smith v Hapoel Tel Aviv (a) UEFA Cup   14 Nov 2002
B. Deane v QPR (h) Championship   20 Nov 2004

Four goals in a game (City)

F. Hargraves v Morley (h) FA Cup   7 Oct 1905
D. Morris v Morley (h) FA Cup   7 Oct 1905
D. Wilson v Clapton Orient (h) Division Two 3 Mar 1906
B. McLeod v Nottingham Forest (h) Division Two 29 Nov 1913

Three goals in a game (United)

10 times	J. Charles, C. Keetley
6	P. Lorimer
4	T. Jennings
3	L. Chapman, A. Graham, A. Hydes, M. Jones, T. Yeboah
2	H. Brook, E. Cantona, A. Johanneson, A. Nightingale, A. Ritchie, A. Shackleton, J. Storrie, G. Strachan, P. Whipp
1	G. Ainsley, I. Baird, R. Belfitt, M. Bridges, L. Browning, W. Butler, A. Clarke, B. Deane, F. Dudley, H. Duggan, B. Forrest, R. Fowler, E. Gray, J. Greenhoff, G. Hodgson, R. Hulse, R. Iggleden, R. Keane, P. Masinga, G. McAllister, E. O'Doherty, J. Pearson, A. Powell, B. Poyntz, J. Richmond, K. Ripley, C. Shutt, E. Stephenson, P. Swan, B. Thompson, B. Turnbull, M. Viduka, R. Wainscoat, R.S. Wallace, D. Weston, J. White, T. Wright

Three goals in a game (City)

5 times	B. McLeod
2	A.Price
1	J. Gemmell, J. Lavery

Progressive scoring records

Bob Thompson set the first target in Leeds United's opening season, scoring 11 League goals and adding another in the FA Cup. 'Soldier' Wilson did likewise for Leeds City but Fred Hargraves was overall top scorer due to his FA Cup goals. This chart shows how individual scoring records have been equalled and beaten since then.

Leeds City

	League		All Matches	
1905–06	David Wilson	13	Fred Hargraves	19
1906–07	Billy McLeod	15		
1907–08	Billy McLeod	17		
1912–13	Billy McLeod	27	Billy McLeod	28
1913–14	Billy McLeod	27	Billy McLeod	28

Leeds United

	League		All Matches	
1920–21	Bob Thompson	11	Bob Thompson	12
1921–22	Tommy Howarth	13	Tommy Howarth	14
1922–23	Percy Whipp	15	Percy Whipp	16
1923–24	Jack Swan	18	Jack Swan	18
1925–26	Tom Jennings	26	Tom Jennings	26
1926–27	Tom Jennings	35	Tom Jennings	37
1953–54	John Charles	42	John Charles	43

Leading Scorers 1905–06 to 2007–08

Leeds City

	League		All Matches	
1905–06	D. Wilson	13	F. Hargraves	19
1906–07	B. McLeod	15	B. McLeod	16
1907–08	B. McLeod	17	B. McLeod	17
1908–09	B. McLeod	15	B. McLeod	17
1909–10	B. McLeod	15	B. McLeod	15
1910–11	B. McLeod	14	B. McLeod	14
1911–12	B. McLeod	14	B. McLeod	14
1912–13	B. McLeod	27	B. McLeod	28
1913–14	B. McLeod	27	B. McLeod	28
1914–15	B. McLeod	18	B. McLeod	19
1919–20	B. McLeod	9	B. McLeod	9

Note: The 1919–20 season ended for City after eight games and Port Vale took over and completed their remaining fixtures. The 1939–40 season was abandoned due to World War One after three games. United had not scored in any of these fixtures.

Leeds United

	League		All Matches	
1920–21	B. Thompson	11	B. Thompson	12
1921–22	T. Howarth	13	T. Howarth	14
1922–23	P. Whipp	15	P. Whipp	16
1923–24	J. Swan	18	J. Swan	18
1924–25	J. Swan	11	J. Swan	11
1925–26	T. Jennings	26	T. Jennings	26
1926–27	T. Jennings	35	T. Jennings	37
1927–28	T. Jennings	21	T. Jennings	22
	J. White	22	J. White	22
1928–29	C. Keetley	20	C. Keetley	22
1929–30	R. Wainscoat	15	R. Wainscoat	18
1930–31	C. Keetley	16	C. Keetley	16
1931–32	C. Keetley	23	C. Keetley	23
1932–33	A. Hydes	16	A. Hydes	20
1933–34	A. Hydes	16	A. Hydes	16
1934–35	A. Hydes	22	A. Hydes	25
1935–36	G. Brown	18	G. Brown	20
1936–37	A. Hydes	11	A. Hydes	11
1937–38	G. Hodgson	25	G. Hodgson	26
1938–39	G. Hodgson	20	G. Hodgson	21
1946–47	G. Ainsley	11	G. Ainsley	12
1947–48	A. Wakefield	21	A. Wakefield	21
1948–49	L. Browning	13	L. Browning	14
1949–50	F. Dudley	12	F. Dudley	16
1950–51	L. Browning	19	L. Browning	20
1951–52	R. Iggleden	19	R. Iggleden	20
1952–53	J. Charles	26	J. Charles	27
1953–54	J. Charles	42	J. Charles	43
1954–55	H. Brook	16	H. Brook	16
1955–56	J. Charles	29	J. Charles	29
1956–57	J. Charles	38	J. Charles	39
1957–58	H. Baird	20	H. Baird	20
1958–59	A. Shackleton	16	A. Shackleton	17
1959–60	J. McCole	22	J. McCole	23
1960–61	J. McCole	20	J. McCole	23

Season	League		All Matches	
1961–62	B. Bremner	11	B. Bremner	12
			J. Charlton	12
1962–63	J. Storrie	25	J. Storrie	27
1963–64	A. Johanneson	13	A. Johanneson	15
	D. Weston	13	I. Lawson	15
1964–65	J. Storrie	16	J. Storrie	19
1965–66	P. Lorimer	13	P. Lorimer	19
	J. Storrie	13		
1966–67	J. Giles	12	J. Giles	18
1967–68	P. Lorimer	16	P. Lorimer	30
1968–69	M. Jones	14	M. Jones	17
1969–70	A. Clarke	17	A. Clarke	26
			M. Jones	26
1970–71	A. Clarke	19	A. Clarke	23
1971–72	P. Lorimer	23	P. Lorimer	29
1972–73	A. Clarke	18	A. Clarke	26
1973–74	M. Jones	14	A. Clarke	16
1974–75	A. Clarke	14	A. Clarke	22
1975–76	D. McKenzie	16	D. McKenzie	17
1976–77	J. Jordan	10	J. Jordan	12
1977–78	R. Hankin	20	R. Hankin	21
1978–79	J. Hawley	16	J. Hawley	17
1979–80	K. Hird	8	K. Hird	8
1980–81	C. Harris	10	C. Harris	10
1981–82	A. Graham	9	A. Graham	9
	F. Worthington	9	F. Worthington	9
1982–83	A. Butterworth	11	A. Butterworth	13
1983–84	G. McCluskey	8	T. Wright	11
	T. Wright	8		
1984–85	T. Wright	14	T. Wright	15
1985–86	I. Baird	12	I. Baird	12
1986–87	I. Baird	15	I. Baird	19
	J. Sheridan	15		
1987–88	J. Sheridan	12	J. Sheridan	14
1988–89	B. Davison	14	B. Davison	17
1989–90	G. Strachan	16	G. Strachan	18
1990–91	L. Chapman	21	L. Chapman	31
1991–92	L. Chapman	16	L. Chapman	20
1992–93	L. Chapman	13	L. Chapman	17
1993–94	R.S. Wallace	17	R.S. Wallace	17
1994–95	T. Yeboah	12	T. Yeboah	13
1995–96	T. Yeboah	12	T. Yeboah	19
1996–97	B. Deane	5	R.S. Wallace	8
	L. Sharpe	5		
1997–98	J. Hasselbaink	16	J. Hasselbaink	22
1998–99	J. Hasselbaink	18	J. Hasselbaink	20
1999–2000	M. Bridges	19	M. Bridges	21
2000–01	M. Viduka	17	M. Viduka	22
2001–02	R. Fowler	12	M. Viduka	16
2002–03	M. Viduka	20	M. Viduka	22
2003–04	M. Viduka	11	M. Viduka	12
2004–05	D. Healy	7	D. Healy	7
			B. Deane	7
2005–06	D. Healy	12	D. Healy	14
	R. Hulse	12	R. Hulse	14
2006–07	D. Healy	10	D. Healy	10
2007–08	J. Beckford	20	J. Beckford	20

Top 20 Scorers

	All Matches			League	
1	P. Lorimer	238	1	P. Lorimer	168
2	J. Charles	157	2	J. Charles	153
3	A. Clarke	151	3	T. Jennings	112
4	T. Jennings	117	4	A. Clarke	110
5=	B. Bremner	115	5	C. Keetley	108
	J. Giles	115	6	B. Bremner	90
7	M.D. Jones	111	7	J. Giles	88
8	C. Keetley	110	8	R. Wainscoat	87
9	J. Charlton	96	9	M.D. Jones	77
10	R. Wainscoat	93	10	A. Hydes	74
11	A. Hydes	82	11	M. Viduka	72
12	L. Chapman	80	12	J. Charlton	70
13	E. Gray	69	13=	L. Chapman	62
14=	A. Johanneson	67		B. Furness	62
	J. Storrie	67	15	J. Storrie	58
16=	B. Furness	66	16	R.S. Wallace	53
	R.S. Wallace	66	17	E. Gray	52
18	H. Kewell	63	18	G. Hodgson	51
19	M. Viduka	59	19=	A. Johanneson	48
20	A. Smith	56		A. Nightingale	48
				J. Sheridan	48
			20=	H. Iggleden	47
				J. Swan	47

Totals include League, FA Cup, League Cup, League Play-offs, FA Charity Shield, European Cup, European Cup-Winners' Cup, UEFA Cup (including Inter-Cities Fairs Cup), Inter-Cities Fairs Cup Play-off, Full Members' Cup and the Football League Trophy. The only City player who would merit entry to the above columns is Billy McLeod, who scored 177 goals, including 171 in the League.

Top 20 Appearances

	All Matches			League	
1	J. Charlton	773	1	J. Charlton	629
2	B. Bremner	772/1	2	B. Bremner	586/1
3	P. Reaney	736/12	3	P. Reaney	549/8
4	N. Hunter	724/2	4	N. Hunter	540
5	P. Madeley	712/13	5	P. Madeley	528/8
6	P. Lorimer	677/28	6	P. Lorimer	503/22
7	E. Gray	561/8	7	E. Gray	441/13
8	G. Kelly	516/15	8	E. Hart	447
9	J. Giles	523/4	9	G. Hair	443
10	G. Sprake	505/2	10	J. Dunn	442
11	T. Cherry	477/8	11	G. Kelly	419/11
12	G. Hair	474	12	T. Cherry	393/33
13	E. Hart	472	13	W. Edwards	417
14	D. Harvey	445/2	14	Jack Milburn	386
15	W. Edwards	444	15	J. Giles	380/3
16	J. Dunn	443	16	G. Sprake	380
17	J. Lukic	433	17	J. Lukic	355
18	Jack Milburn	408	18	D. Harvey	350
19	F. Gray	396/9	19	E. Kerfoot	336
20	A. Clarke	361/5	20	F. Gray	327/5

Totals include League, FA Cup, League Cup, League Play-offs, FA Charity Shield, European Cup, European Cup-Winners' Cup, UEFA Cup (including Inter-Cities Fairs Cup), Inter-Cities Fairs Cup Play-off, Full Members' Cup and the Football League Trophy. The nearest City player to merit entry to the above columns is Billy McLeod, who played in 301 games, including 289 in the League.

Players of the Season

1970–71	Norman Hunter
1971–72	Peter Lorimer
1972–73	Allan Clarke
1973–74	Mick Jones
1974–75	Gordon McQueen
1975–76	Paul Madeley
1976–77	Gordon McQueen
1977–78	Tony Currie
1978–79	Brian Flynn
1979–80	John Lukic
1980–81	Trevor Cherry
1981–82	Eddie Gray
1982–83	Kenny Burns
1983–84	Tommy Wright
1984–85	Neil Aspin
1985–86	Ian Snodin
1986–87	John Sheridan
1987–88	Peter Haddock
1988–89	Ian Baird
1989–90	Chris Fairclough
1990–91	David Batty
1991–92	Tony Dorigo
1992–93	Gordon Strachan
1993–94	Gary McAllister
1994–95	Brian Deane
1995–96	Tony Yeboah
1996–97	Nigel Martyn
1997–98	Lucas Radebe
1998–99	Lee Bowyer
1999–2000	Harry Kewell
2000–01	Lee Bowyer
2001–02	Rio Ferdinand
2002–03	Paul Robinson
2003–04	Alan Smith
2004–05	Neil Sullivan
2005–06	Shaun Derry
2006–07	Eddie Lewis
2007–08	Jermaine Beckford

Leeds United Captains

1920–26	J. Baker
1926–33	J.F. Potts
1933–34	W. Copping
1934–37	J. McDougall
1937–49	T. Holley
1949–54	T. Burden
1954–55	E. Kerfoot
1955–57	J. Charles
1957–59	W. Cush
1959–60	W. Cush, D. Revie
1960–62	F. Goodwin
1962–65	B. Collins
1965–66	B. Collins, J. Charlton
1966–76	B. Bremner
1976–82	T. Cherry
1982–83	T. Cherry, D. Harvey
1983–84	D. Harvey
1984–85	P. Lorimer
1985–86	I. Snodin
1986–87	I. Snodin, B. Ormsby
1987–88	M. Aizlewood, J. Ashurst
1988–89	M. Aizlewood
1989–94	G. Strachan
1994–96	G. McAllister
1996–2000	L. Radebe
2000–01	L. Radebe, G. Kelly
2001–02	R. Ferdinand
2002–04	D. Matteo
2004–06	P. Butler
2006–07	K. Nicholls, J. Douglas
2007–08	A. Thompson, J. Douglas

OTHER APPEARANCES BY COMPETITION

European Cup and Champions League
(1969–70, 1974–75, 1992–93, 2000–01)

I. Harte 17, P. Madeley 17, A. Smith 16, M. Viduka 16, D. Mills 15/1, L. Bowyer 15, P. Lorimer 15, D. Matteo 15, B. Bremner 14, O. Dacourt 14, N. Hunter 14, P. Reaney 14, A. Clarke 13, J. Giles 13, D. Martyn 12, D. Batty 11/1, G. Kelly 11/1, E. Bakke 10/2, T. Cooper 10, L. Radebe 10, T. Yorath 8/1, M.D. Jones 8, J. Jordan 8, G. Sprake 8, E. Gray 7/1, J. Charlton 7, R. Ferdinand 7, G. McQueen 7, H. Kewell 6/3, F. Gray 6, P. Robinson 6, E. Cantona 5, L. Chapman 5, T. Dorigo 5, C. Fairclough 5, J. Lukic 5, G. McAllister 5, G. Speed 5, D. Stewart 5, G. Strachan 5, C. Whyte 5, J. Woodgate 5, D. Harvey 4/1, M. Bridges 4, M. Duberry 4, M. Bates 3/3, J. Burns 3/1, J. Newsome 3, J. Wilcox 2/3, T. Cherry 2/1, D. Rocastle 2/1, S. McPhail 1/2, R. Belfitt 1, T. Hibbitt 1, M. Jones 1, D. McKenzie 1, A. Maybury 1, M. O'Grady 1, S. Sellars 1, T. Hackworth 0/2, S. Hodge 0/2, D. Huckerby 0/2, C. Shutt 0/2, R.S. Wallace 0/2, G. Evans 0/1, C. Galvin 0/1, P. Hampton 0/1, C. Harris 0/1, D. Hay 0/1.

Goalscorers: M.D. Jones 8, Lorimer 7, Smith 7, Bowyer 6, Bremner 6, Clarke 6, Giles 4, Harte 4, Viduka 4, McQueen 3, Belfitt 2, Cantona 2, Hibbitt 2, Jordan 2, McAllister 2, Matteo 2, Bakke 1, Chapman 1, Ferdinand 1, Huckerby 1, O'Grady 1, Shutt 1, Speed 1, Strachan 1, Yorath 1, Wilcox 1.

European Cup-Winners' Cup
(1972–73)

D. Harvey 9, N. Hunter 9, P. Lorimer 9, T. Cherry 8, P. Reaney 8, B. Bremner 7, J. Giles 6/1, J. Jordan 6/1, M. Bates 6, M.D. Jones 6, P. Madeley 6, A. Clarke 5, T. Yorath 4/3, G. McQueen 2/1, J. Charlton 2, R. Ellam 2, E. Gray 2, F. Gray 1/1, C. Galvin 1.

Goalscorers: M.D. Jones 3, Jordan 3, Clarke 2, Lorimer 2, Bates 1, Cherry 1, Giles 1.

UEFA Cup and Inter-Cities Fairs Cup
(1965–66, 1966–67, 1967–68, 1968–69, 1970–71, 1971–72, 1973–74, 1979–80, 1995–96, 1998–99, 1999–2000, 2001–02, 2002–03)

B. Bremner 55, N. Hunter 54/1, P. Reaney 51/3, P. Lorimer 49/1, G. Sprake 48/2, P. Madeley 47/1, J. Charlton 46, J. Giles 41, T. Cooper 38, E. Gray 30/1, I. Harte 28, M.D. Jones 28, H. Kewell 28, G. Kelly 24, N. Martyn 24, L. Bowyer 23, R. Belfitt 22/3, E. Bakke 21/1, M. O'Grady 19, J. Greenhoff 18/1, M. Bates 17/6, W. Bell 17, L. Radebe 17, A. Clarke 15, J. Woodgate 15, S. McPhail 14/2, M. Bridges 13/2, A. Smith 12/7, D. Harvey 12/2, D. Mills 12/1, T. Cherry 10, J. Storrie 10, D. Batty 9/1, M. Viduka 9, T. Yorath 8/3, O. Dacourt 8, D. Matteo 8, J. Wilcox 7/3, A. Haaland 7/2, T. Hibbitt 7/2, R. Ferdinand 7, J. Lukic 7, D. Hopkin 6/1, R. Keane 6, P. Robinson 6, M. Duberry 5/1, F. Gray 5/1, A. Johanneson 5/1, A. Curtis 4, R. Ellam 4, B. Flynn 4, R. Hankin 4, P. Hart 4, J. Hasselbaink 4, M. Hiden 4, G. McAllister 4, R. Molenaar 4, C. Palmer 4, J. Pemberton 4, G. Speed 4, D. Wetherall 4, T. Yeboah 4, J. Jordan 3/3, N. Davey 3/2, M. Jones 3/2, N. Barmby 3, B. Collins 3, B. Deane 3, A. Graham 3, P. Hampton 3, K. Hird 3, G. McQueen 3, A. Peacock 3, N. Whelan 3, P. Beesley 2/2, C. Galvin 2/1, T. Dorigo 2, J. Faulkner 2, G. Halle 2, J. Mann 2, K. Parkinson 2, J. Shaw 2, B. Stevenson 2, D. Huckerby 1/8, C. Wijnhard 1/3, C. Harris 1/2, L. Sharpe 1/2, G. Hamson 1/1, G. Liddell 1/1, B. Ribeiro 1/1, D. White 1/1, R. Bowman 1, D. Kennedy 1, P. Okon 1, A. Couzens 0/2, J. O'Neill 0/2, M. Ford 0/1, R. Fowler 0/1, D. Granville 0/1, G. Letheran 0/1, D. Lilley 0/1, M. Kilgallon 0/1, B. McGinley 0/1, F. Richardson 0/1, K. Sharp 0/1, M. Tinkler 0/1, R.S. Wallace 0/1.

Goalscorers: Lorimer 21, Bremner 10, Charlton 10, Johanneson 8, Kewell 8, Bowyer 7, Smith 7, Belfitt 6, Clarke 6, Giles 6, J.Greenhoff 6, M.D.Jones 6, E.Gray 5, Bakke 4, Madeley 4, Graham 3, Keane 3, Viduka 3, Yeboah 3, Bates 2, Bridges 2, Cooper 2, Hart 2, Harte 2, O'Grady 2, Radebe 2, Barmby 1, Bell 1, Cherry 1, Curtis 1, Galvin 1, F.Gray 1, Hankin 1, Hasselbaink 1, Huckerby 1, Hunter 1, Liddell 1, McAllister 1, Palmer 1, Peacock 1, Speed 1, Storrie 1, Wilcox 1, Own-goal 1.

Full Members' (Simod/Zenith Data Systems) Cup
(1985–86 to 1991–92)

D. Batty 12, M. Day 11, P. Haddock 9/1, M. Sterland 9, G. Strachan 9, M. Whitlow 9, I. Baird 8, C. Fairclough 8, B. Davison 7/2, N. Aspin 6, J. Sheridan 6, A. Williams 5/2, J. Lukic 5, G. Snodin 5, C. Whyte 5, C. Shutt 4/3, G. Speed 4/3, N. Blake 4, L. Chapman 4, V. Jones 4, G. McAllister 4, D. Rennie 4, B. Taylor 3/1, J. Ashurst 3, J. Pearson 2/3, M. Aizlewood 2, J. Beglin 2, K. De Mange 2, J. Hendrie 2, V. Hilaire 2, D. Irwin 2, A. Linighan 2, P. Lorimer 2, T. Phelan 2, S. Sellars 2, J. Stiles 1/2, P. Swan 1/2, S. Grayson 1/1, L. Simmonds 1/1, N. Thompson 1/1, I. Varadi 1/1, M. Adams 1, J. Buckley 1, T. Dorigo 1, K. Edwards 1, N. Edwards 1, G. Hamson 1, C. Kamara 1, G. McCluskey 1, J. Newsome 1, K. Noteman 1, B. Ormsby 1, D. Kerr 0/4, R.S. Wallace 0/1, T. Wright 0/1.

Goalscorers: Chapman 3, Davison 3, Shutt 3, Sterland 2, Strachan 2, Williams 2, Aizlewood 1, Lorimer 1, McAllister 1, Noteman 1, Rennie 1, Sellars 1, Taylor 1, Varadi 1, Wallace 1.

Inter-Cities Fairs Cup Play-off

(1971–72)

R. Belfitt 1, B. Bremner 1, J. Charlton 1, N. Davey 1, C. Galvin 1, J. Giles 1, N. Hunter 1, J. Jordan 1, P. Lorimer 1, P. Reaney 1, G. Sprake 1.

Goalscorer: Jordan 1.

FA Charity Shield

(1969–70, 1974–75, 1992–93)

B. Bremner 2, A. Clarke 2, J. Giles 2, E. Gray 2, N. Hunter 2, P. Reaney 2, P. Lorimer 1/1, D. Batty 1, E. Cantona 1, L. Chapman 1, J. Charlton 1, T. Cherry 1, T. Cooper 1, T. Dorigo 1, C. Fairclough 1, D. Harvey 1, M.D. Jones 1, J. Jordan 1, J. Lukic 1, P. Madeley 1, G. McAllister 1, G. McQueen 1, J. Newsome 1, G. Speed 1, G. Sprake 1, R.S. Wallace 1, C. Whyte 1, S. Hodge 0/1, D. McKenzie 0/1, G. Strachan 0/1.

Goalscorers: Cantona 3, Charlton 1, Cherry 1, Dorigo 1, Gray 1.

Football League (Johnstones' Paint) Trophy

(2007–08)

M. De Vries 2, J. Howson 2, P. Huntington 2, D. Lucas 2, B. Parker 2, P. Da Costa 1/1, M. Heath 1/1, W. Andrews 1, S. Carole 1, L. Constantine 1, S. Madden 1, R. Marques 1, D. Prutton 1, F. Richardson 1, A. Thompson 1, I. Westlake 1, C. Weston 1, T. Ameobi 0/1, J. Clapham 0/1, J. Douglas 0/1, T. Kandol 0/1.

Goalscorers: Constantine 1, Huntington 1.

Football League Play-offs

(1986–87, 2005–06, 2007–08)

M. Adams 5, M. Aizlewood 5, J. Ashurst 5, N. Aspin 5, I. Baird 5, M. Day 5, J. Douglas 5, B. McDonald 5, B. Ormsby 5, F. Richardson 5, J. Sheridan 5, J. Pearson 4, C. Ankergren 3, J. Beckford 3, S. Derry 3, D. Freedman 3, S. Gregan 3, J. Howson 3, R. Hulse 3, P. Huntington 3, B. Johnson 3, G. Kelly 3, M. Kilgallon 3, N. Kilkenny 3, E. Lewis 3, L. Michalik 3, L. Miller 3, D. Prutton 3, N. Sullivan 3, A. Ritchie 2/1, D. Crainey 2, J. Stiles 2, K. Edwards 1/4, E. Bakke 1/1, D. Healy 1/1, P. Butler 1, B. Taylor 1, R. Blake 0/2, R. Cresswell 0/2, A. Hughes 0/2, T. Kandol 0/2, S. Stone 0/2, S. Carole 0/1.

Goalscorers: Edwards 2, Howson 2, Freedman 1, Hulse 1, Lewis 1, Ormsby 1, Richardson 1, Sheridan 1.

CITY CAREER RECORDS 1905–19

Below are the career records (League and FA Cup) of every City first-team player since the club's first League match in 1905. The years given are the first years of seasons. Thus, 1906 means 1906–07. The 1904–05 FA Cup first preliminary-round tie versus Rockingham Colliery (lost 3–1) is not included below. The team on 17 September 1904 was W.H. Mallinson, Skeldon, H. Dixon, R. Morris, J. Morris, T. Tennant, P. Heffron, Page, Musgrave (scorer), Cummings, Simpson. Both R. Morris and J. Morris played for City in the following season but their totals below are not credited with this game.

Player	Played	LEAGUE		FA CUP		TOTAL	
		App	Gls	App	Gls	App	Gls
ACKERLEY G.	1909	2	0	0	0	2	0
AFFLECK G.	1909–19	182	1	9	0	191	1
ALLAN J.	1912–14	14	0	1	0	15	0
ASTILL T.	1908–11	1	0	0	0	1	0
BAINBRIDGE S.	1912–19	64	15	5	0	69	15
BATES W.E.	1907–09	15	0	0	0	15	0
BEREN H.G.	1909–10	3	0	0	0	3	0
BLACKMAN F.E.	1914–19	44	0	2	0	46	0
BOWMAN A.	1908–09	15	6	1	1	16	7
BRIDGETT H.	1909–13	13	2	1	0	14	2
BROMAGE H.	1905–11	143	0	9	0	152	0
BROUGHTON T.W.	1912–13	4	0	0	0	4	0
BURNETT J.J.	1908–10	20	2	4	1	24	3
CAMPBELL A.	1911	1	0	0	0	1	0
CLARK A.	1906	24	0	0	0	24	0
CLARKIN J.	1911	1	0	0	0	1	0
CLAY W.E.	1905	0	0	1	0	1	0
COPELAND C.W.	1912–14	44	0	1	0	45	0
COWEN R.W.	1914	2	0	0	0	2	0
CREIGHTON A.	1910–11	66	0	3	0	69	0
CROOT F.R.	1907–14	218	38	9	0	227	38
CUBBERLEY S.M.	1906–12	181	6	7	0	188	6
CUNNINGHAM G.P.	1910	3	0	0	0	3	0
CUNNINGHAM T.	1908	1	0	0	0	1	0
DOUGAL D.W.	1908–09	25	2	0	0	25	2
DOUGHERTY J.	1913	1	0	0	0	1	0
DRAIN T.	1905	9	3	1	0	10	3
EDMONDSON J.	1914–19	11	6	0	0	11	6
ENRIGHT J.	1910–12	77	23	3	0	80	23
FENWICK G.	1912	5	3	0	0	5	3
FERGUSON J.	1912	17	0	0	0	17	0
FOLEY M.	1910–19	127	6	6	1	133	7
FORTUNE J.J.	1911	1	0	0	0	1	0
FREEBOROUGH J.	1905–07	24	0	0	0	24	0
GEMMELL J.	1907–09	67	14	6	0	73	14
GEORGE J.S.	1905–06	8	0	0	0	8	0
GIBSON A.	1912	5	0	0	0	5	0
GILLESPIE W.B.	1910–11	24	10	0	0	24	10
GOODWIN E.W.	1914–19	20	3	0	0	20	3
GREEN J.	1914	·1	0	0	0	1	0
GUY R.W.	1908	18	3	4	1	22	4
HALLIGAN W.	1909	24	12	1	0	25	12
HAMILTON E.M.	1909	3	0	0	0	3	0
HAMILTON J.	1908	21	0	4	0	25	0
HAMPSON J.	1913–19	71	8	3	0	74	8
HARGRAVES J.F.	1905–07	63	12	7	7	70	19
HARKINS J.A.	1910–11	63	0	3	0	66	0
HARWOOD A.	1906	1	1	0	0	1	1
HEANEY F.	1911	2	0	0	0	2	0
HENDERSON J.T.	1905–07	75	0	5	0	80	0

Player	Played	LEAGUE		FA CUP		TOTAL	
		App	Gls	App	Gls	App	Gls
HOGG A.	1909	96	0	5	0	101	0
HOPKINS W.	1919	7	0	0	0	7	0
HORSLEY J.E.	1909–10	29	0	1	0	30	0
HOWARD G.	1905	1	0	0	0	1	0
HYNDS T.	1907	37	0	1	0	38	0
JACKSON J.B.	1913–14	54	10	4	2	58	12
JEFFERSON R.W.	1906–07	17	5	1	0	18	5
JOHNSON G.J.W.	1906	1	0	0	0	1	0
JOHNSON J.T.	1913	1	0	0	0	1	0
JOHNSON S.	1911	7	1	0	0	7	1
JOYNES R.A.	1908–09	22	1	1	0	23	1
KAY H.	1907	31	0	1	0	32	0
KELLY C.	1910–11	4	0	0	0	4	0
KENNEDY J.J.	1906–08	58	1	2	0	60	1
KIRK G.	1906	8	1	1	0	9	1
KIRTON W.J.	1919	1	0	0	0	1	0
LAMPH T.	1913–19	11	1	0	0	11	1
LAVERY J.	1905–07	56	20	1	0	57	20
LAW G.	1912–14	105	1	5	1	110	2
LAWRENCE V.	1914	6	0	0	0	6	0
LINTOTT E.H.	1912–13	43	1	2	0	45	1
LOUNDS H.E.	1919	8	0	0	0	8	0
McALLISTER T.	1908–09	53	0	5	0	58	0
McDANIEL E.	1911	1	0	0	0	1	0
McDONALD J.	1905	25	0	6	0	31	0
McDONALD W.	1908	14	0	0	0	14	0
McLEOD W.	1906–19	289	171	12	6	301	177
McQUILLAN J.	1914	20	0	0	0	20	0
MILLERSHIP H.	1919	8	0	0	0	8	0
MORAN J.	1911–12	25	0	2	0	27	0
MORGAN C.	1905	41	1	6	0	47	1
MORRIS J.	1905	10	0	0	0	10	0
MORRIS R.	1905	25	5	6	5	31	10
MORRIS T.H.	1908–11	106	3	3	0	109	3
MULHOLLAND T.S.	1909–11	78	21	3	0	81	21
MURPHY L.A.	1911	18	0	1	0	19	0
MURRAY D.B.	1905–08	83	7	2	0	85	7
MURRAY W.B.	1906	8	0	0	0	8	0
NAISBY T.H.	1907–09	63	0	5	0	68	0
PAGE G.	1906	4	0	0	0	4	0
PARNELL G.F.	1905	104	15	7	4	111	19
PEART H.	1913–14	7	0	1	0	8	0
PICKARD H.	1906–09	8	0	0	0	8	0
PRICE A.	1912–19	78	25	0	0	78	25
PRICE I. H.	1909	8	0	0	0	8	0
RAY R.	1905–06	38	0	6	0	44	0
REINHARDT C.G.	1911	12	0	1	0	13	0
RICHARDSON W.F.	1914	2	0	0	0	2	0
ROBERTS H.P.	1909–12	108	13	4	2	112	15
ROBERTSON J.	1912	27	7	1	0	28	7
RODGER T.	1908	25	4	0	0	25	4
ROTHWELL A.	1914	1	0	0	0	1	0
SCOTT W.	1912–13	26	0	0	0	26	0
SHARPE I.G.	1913–14	61	16	4	1	65	17
SHORT W.	1919	5	0	0	0	5	0
SINGLETON H.B.	1905–06	45	7	6	0	51	7
SPEIRS J.H.	1912–14	73	32	5	0	78	32
STOCKTON C.M.	1909	3	0	0	0	3	0
STRINGFELLOW H.T.	1905	13	1	3	0	16	1
SWIFT G.H.	1905	1	0	0	0	1	0
THOMAS W.	1907	9	2	1	0	10	2
THORPE J.	1907	9	0	0	0	9	0
TILDESLEY J.	1909	6	0	1	0	7	0
TOMPKINS T.	1907	11	0	0	0	11	0
TURNER N.M.	1913	4	2	0	0	4	2
WAINWRIGHT W.	1914	2	0	0	0	2	0
WALKER F.	1905	26	0	3	0	29	0

Player	Played	LEAGUE		FA CUP		TOTAL	
		App	Gls	App	Gls	App	Gls
WALKER W.	1914–19	22	0	0	0	22	0
WATSON J.	1908	45	0	4	0	49	0
WATSON R.	1905–07	83	21	7	3	90	24
WHITE J.W.	1908–10	60	0	4	0	64	0
WHITLEY J.	1905–06	7	0	0	0	7	0
WILSON D.	1905–06	21	13	0	0	21	13
WILSON T.C.	1906	20	2	1	0	21	2
Own-goals			6		0		6

UNITED CAREER RECORDS
1920–2008

Below are the career records (League, FA Cup, and League Cup) of every United first-team player since the club's first FA Cup match in 1920. The years given are the first years of seasons. Thus, 1946 means 1946–47. FA Premiership and Football League appearances are classified together under League. In the 'Others' list are all competitions not accounted for in the rest of the table. This contains figures for the Charity Shield, European Cup, European Cup-Winners' Cup, UEFA Cup, Inter-Cities Fairs Cup (including the 1971 Play-off), Full Members' Cup, Football League Trophy and League Play-off games. Substitute appearances are given to the right of full appearances. (eg 26/2).

Player	Played	LEAGUE App	Gls	FA CUP App	Gls	FL CUP App	Gls	OTHERS App	Gls	TOTAL App	Gls
ABEL C.R.	1934	1	0	0	0	0	0	0	0	1	0
ADAMS M.R,	1986–88	72/1	2	6	1	4	0	6	0	88/1	3
ADDY M.	1962	2	0	0	0	2	0	0	0	4	0
AGANA P.A.O	1991	1/1	0	0	0	0	0	0	0	1/1	0
AINSLEY G.E.	1936–47	91	30	6	3	0	0	0	0	97	33
AIZLEWOOD M	1986–88	65/5	3	1	0	3	0	7	1	76/5	4
ALDERSON T.	1930	4	2	0	0	0	0	0	0	4	2
ALLAN J	1925–27	70	0	4	0	0	0	0	0	74	0
ALLEN J.W.A.	1923	2	0	0	0	0	0	0	0	2	0
AMEOBI T.	2007	0	0	0	0	1	0	0/1	0	1/1	0
ANDREWS I.E.	1988	1	0	0	0	0	0	0	0	1	0
ANDREWS W.M.H.	2007	1	0	0	0	0	0	1	0	2	0
ANKERGREN C.	2006–07	57	0	2	0	2	0	3	0	64	0
ARINS A.F.	1981	0/1	0	0	0	0	0	0	0	0/1	0
ARMAND J.E.	1922–28	74	23	5	1	0	0	0	0	79	24
ARMES S.	1935–38	79	8	3	1	0	0	0	0	82	9
ARMITAGE L.	1920–22	48	11	5	3	0	0	0	0	53	14
ASHALL J.	1958–60	89	0	2	0	0	0	0	0	91	0
ASHURST J.	1986–88	88/1	1	6	0	6	0	8	0	108/1	1
ASPIN N.	1982–89	203/4	5	17	0	9	1	11	0	240/4	6
ATKINSON J.W.	1924–27	52	0	1	0	0	0	0	0	53	0
BAIRD H.	1957–58	46	22	0	0	0	0	0	0	46	22
BAIRD I.J.	1984–86/1988–90	160/2	50	8	6	9	1	13	0	190/2	57
BAKER A.	1927	2	0	0	0	0	0	0	0	2	0
BAKER J.W.	1920–25	200	2	8	0	0	0	0	0	208	2
BAKER L.H.	1923–24	11	0	0	0	0	0	0	0	11	0
BAKKE E.	1999–2005	116/27	8	9/1	6	7	2	32/4	5	164/32	21
BALCOMBE S.W.	1981	1	1	0	0	1	0	0	0	2	1
BANNISTER E.	1946–49	44	1	0	0	0	0	0	0	44	1
BARMBY N.J.	2002–03	17/8	4	0/2	0	1	0	3	1	21/10	5
BARNES P.S.	1981–83	56/2	5	1	0	5	1	0	0	62/2	6
BARRITT R.	1951	6	1	0	0	0	0	0	0	6	1
BATES M.J.	1966–75	106/16	4	10/4	1	9/8	1	26/9	3	151/37	9
BATEY N.R.	1946	8	0	0	0	0	0	0	0	8	0
BATTY D.	1987–93/1998–2003	280/21	4	16	0	21	0	33/2	0	350/23	4
BAYLY R	2006–07	1	0	0	0	0/1	0	0	0	1/1	0
BECKFORD J.P	2006–07	41/9	20	2	0	1/2	0	3	0	47/11	20
BEENEY M.R.	1992–98	38	0	4/1	0	3	0	0	0	45/1	0
BEESLEY P	1995–96	19/3	0	7	0	5/1	0	2/2	0	33/6	0
BEGLIN J.M.	1989–90	18/1	0	0	0	0	0	2	0	20/1	0
BELFITT R.M.	1964–71	57/16	17	6/1	3	17/2	5	24/3	8	104/22	33
BELL A.	1923	1	0	0	0	0	0	0	0	1	0
BELL T.G.	1922	1	0	0	0	0	0	0	0	1	0
BELL W.J.	1960–67	204	15	24	1	15	1	17	1	260	18
BENNETT I.M.	2005	4	0	0	0	0	0	0	0	4	0
BENNETT W.	1931	10	4	1	0	0	0	0	0	11	4
BEST J.	1920	11	1	0	0	0	0	0	0	11	1
BLAKE N.A	2004	2	0	0	0	0	0	0	0	2	0
BLAKE N.L.G.	1988–89	51	4	0	0	4/1	0	4	0	59/1	4

Player	Played	LEAGUE		FA CUP		FL CUP		OTHERS		TOTAL	
		App	Gls	App	Gls	App	Gls	App	Gls	App	Gls
BLAKE R.J.	2005–06	59/19	20	3/1	0	3/2	1	0/2	0	65/24	21
BLUNT J.J.	1995	2/2	0	0	0	0/1	0	0	0	2/3	0
BOARDMAN W.	1920	4	0	0	0	0	0	0	0	4	0
BOWMAN R.	1992–96	4/3	0	0	0	0/1	0	1	0	5/4	0
BOWYER L.D.	1996–2002	196/7	38	16	3	7/1	1	38	13	257/8	55
BOYLE W.S.	1996–2001	0/1	0	0	0	0	0	0	0	0/1	0
BRAVO R.S.	2002	5	0	1	0	0	0	0	0	6	0
BREMNER W.J.	1959–76	586/1	90	69	6	38	3	79	16	772/1	115
BRIDGES M	1999–2003	40/16	19	1/1	0	3/2	0	17/2	2	61/21	21
BROCK J.R.E.	1920	6	0	0	0	0	0	0	0	6	0
BROCKIE V.	1987	2	0	0	0	0	0	0	0	2	0
BROLIN P.T.	1995–97	17/2	4	1/1	0	2/2	0	0	0	20/5	4
BROOK H.	1954–57	102	46	4	1	0	0	0	0	106	47
BROWN A.J.	1982–84	24	1	0	0	0	0	0	0	24	1
BROWN G.	1935–36	37	19	4	2	0	0	0	0	41	21
BROWN V.C.	1931	1	0	0	0	0	0	0	0	1	0
BROWNE R.J.	1935–46	110	0	4	0	0	0	0	0	114	0
BROWNING L.J.	1946–51	97	42	8	4	0	0	0	0	105	46
BUCK T.	1928	8	0	0	0	0	0	0	0	8	0
BUCKLEY A.	1936–39	83	20	3	2	0	0	0	0	86	22
BUCKLEY J.W.	1986–87	6/4	1	0/1	0	0	0	1	0	7/5	1
BULLIONS J.L.	1947–49	35	0	2	0	0	0	0	0	37	0
BURBANKS W.E.	1953	13	1	0	0	0	0	0	0	13	1
BURDEN T.D.	1948–54	243	13	16	0	0	0	0	0	259	13
BURGIN E.	1958–60	58	0	0	0	1	0	0	0	59	0
BURNS J.G.	2000–02	2/1	0	0	0	1	0	3/1	0	6/2	0
BURNS K.	1981–83	54/2	2	3	0	7	2	0	0	64/2	4
BUTLER P.J.	2004–06	99	4	2	0	4	0	1	0	106	4
BUTLER W.J.	1920	1	0	2	3	0	0	0	0	3	3
BUTTERWORTH A.J.	1981–83	54/10	15	6	1	4	1	0	0	64/10	17
BUTTERWORTH F.C.	1945	0	0	2	0	0	0	0	0	2	0
CADAMARTERI D.L	2004	0	0	0	0	0/1	0	0	0	0/1	0
CALDWELL S.	2003	13	1	0	0	0	0	0	0	13	1
CALDWELL T.	1959–60	20	0	0	0	2	0	0	0	22	0
CAMARA Z.	2003	13	1	0	0	2	0	0	0	15	1
CAMERON R.	1959–61	57	9	2	0	4	2	0	0	63	11
CANTONA E.D.P.	1991–92	18/10	9	0	0	1	0	6	5	25/10	14
CARLING T.P.	1960–61	5	0	0	0	1	0	0	0	6	0
CARLISLE C.J.	2004	29/6	4	0	0	3	0	0	0	32/6	4
CAROLE S.	2006–07	24/21	3	2	0	3	0	1/1	0	30/22	3
CARR J.P.	1935	2	0	0	0	0	0	0	0	2	0
CARSON S.P.	2003–04	2/1	0	0	0	0	0	0	0	2/1	0
CASEY T.D.	1961	3	0	0	0	1	0	0	0	4	0
CASEY T.	1949	4	0	0	0	0	0	0	0	4	0
CASWELL B.L.	1985	9	0	0	0	0	0	0	0	9	0
CHADWICK W.	1925–26	16	3	0	0	0	0	0	0	16	3
CHANDLER J.G.	1979–80	21/5	2	1	0	1	0	0	0	23/5	2
CHAPMAN L.R.	1989–92/1995	135/4	62	11	4	15	8	10	4	171/4	78
CHAPUIS C.S.T.	2003	0/1	0	0	0	1/1	0	0	0	1/2	0
CHARLES W.J.	1948–62	308	153	19	4	0	0	0	0	327	157
CHARLTON J.	1952–72	629	70	52	8	35	7	57	11	773	96
CHERRY T.J.	1972–82	393/6	24	28/1	1	35	4	21/1	3	477/8	32
CHISHOLM K.M.	1947–48	40	17	0	0	0	0	0	0	40	17
CLAPHAM J.R.	2007	12/1	0	0/1	0	0	0	0/1	0	12/3	0
CLARK J.R.	1924	3	0	0	0	0	0	0	0	3	0
CLARK W.	1921–22	13	0	0	0	0	0	0	0	13	0
CLARKE A.J.	1969–77	270/3	110	43/2	25	13	2	35	14	361/5	151
CLARKE J.H.	1946	14	1	0	0	0	0	0	0	14	1
COATES W.A.	1921–22	47	3	3	1	0	0	0	0	50	4
COCHRANE D.A.	1937–50	175	28	10	4	0	0	0	0	185	32
COCHRANE T.	1928–36	244	23	15	4	0	0	0	0	259	27
COLLINS R.Y.	1962–66	149	24	13	0	2	1	3	0	167	25
CONNOR T.F.	1979–82	83/13	19	6	2	4/2	1	0	0	93/15	22
CONSTANTINE L.	2007	1/3	1	0/2	0	0	0	1	1	2/5	2
COOPE D.	1920	0	0	2	0	0	0	0	0	2	0
COOPER G.F.	1920	0	0	2	0	0	0	0	0	2	0
COOPER T.	1963–74	240/10	7	30/1	0	21	2	49	2	340/11	11

Player	Played	LEAGUE		FA CUP		FL CUP		OTHERS		TOTAL	
		App	Gls	App	Gls	App	Gls	App	Gls	App	Gls
COPPING W.	1930–39	174	4	9	0	0	0	0	0	183	4
COUTTS T.	1927	1	0	0	0	0	0	0	0	1	0
COUZENS A.	1993–96	17/8	1	0	0	4/1	1	0/2	0	21/11	2
COYNE C.	1945	0	0	2	0	0	0	0	0	2	0
CRAINEY S.D.	2004–06	51	0	2	0	6	0	0	0	61	0
CRESSWELL R.P.W.	2005–06	30/8	9	0/2	0	1/1	2	0/2	0	31/13	11
CROWE C.	1956–59	97	27	3	0	0	0	0	0	100	27
CURRIE A.W.	1976–78	102	11	9	0	13	5	0	0	124	16
CURTIS A.T.	1979–80	28	5	1	0	2	0	4	1	35	6
CUSH W.	1957–59	89	9	3	0	0	0	0	0	92	9
DA COSTA G.P.M.	2007	0/4	0	0/1	0	0	0	1/1	0	1/6	0
DACOURT O.N.A.	2000–02	53/4	3	1	0	2	0	22	0	78/4	3
DANIELS J.F.C.	1934	1	0	0	0	0	0	0	0	1	0
DANSKIN R.	1930–31	5	1	1	0	0	0	0	0	6	1
DARK A.J.	1922	3	0	0	0	0	0	0	0	3	0
DAVEY N.G.	1967–70	13/1	0	1	0	2	0	4/2	0	20/3	0
DAVIES B.	1953	1	0	0	0	0	0	0	0	1	0
DAVISON R.	1987–91	79/12	31	2/4	1	4	1	7/2	3	92/18	36
DAWSON R.	1953	1	0	0	0	0	0	0	0	1	0
DAY M.R.	1984–92	227	0	11	0	14	0	11	0	268	0
DE MANGE K.J.P.P.	1987	14/1	1	0	0	3	0	2	0	19/1	1
DEANE B.C.	1993–96/2004	154/15	38	13/3	4	9/4	3	3	0	179/22	45
DELPH F.	2006–07	0/2	0	0	0	0/1	0	0	0	0/3	0
DEPEAR E.R.	1948	4	0	1	0	0	0	0	0	5	0
DERRY S.P.	2003–07	71	3	1/1	0	0/2	0	0	0	75/3	3
DE VRIES M.	2007	1/5	1	0	0	0	0	2	0	3/5	1
DICKINSON M.J.	1979–85	100/2	2	6	0	10	0	0	0	116/2	2
DOIG R.	1986–87	3/3	0	1	0	1/2	0	0	0	5/5	0
DOMI D.	2003	9/3	0	0	0	0/2	0	0	0	9/5	0
DONNELLY J.	1982–84	36/4	4	1	0	3	0	0	0	40/4	4
DORIGO A.R.	1991–96	168/3	5	16	0	12/1	0	9	1	205/4	6
DOWN W.	1920–24	96	0	5	0	0	0	0	0	101	0
DOUGLAS J.	2005–07	88/11	9	3	0	6/1	0	3/1	0	102/13	9
DUBERRY M.W.	1999–2004	54/4	4	4/2	0	0/4	0	9/1	0	67/11	4
DUDLEY F.E.	1949–50	64	23	7	4	0	0	0	0	71	27
DUFFIELD A.	1920–25	203	0	8	0	0	0	0	0	211	0
DUGGAN H.A.	1926–36	187	45	9	4	0	0	0	0	196	49
DUNDERDALE W.L.	1938–39	4	0	0	0	0	0	0	0	4	0
DUNN J.	1947–58	422	1	21	0	0	0	0	0	443	1
DUTHOIT J.	1945	0	0	2	0	0	0	0	0	2	0
DUXBURY T.	1924	3	0	0	0	0	0	0	0	3	0
EDWARDS K	1986	28/10	6	2/3	1	2	0	2/4	2	34/17	9
EDWARDS M.K.	1971	0/1	0	0	0	0	0	0	0	0/1	0
EDWARDS N.R.	1989	0	0	0	0	0	0	1	0	1	0
EDWARDS W.	1948	2	0	0	0	0	0	0	0	2	0
EDWARDS W.	1924–39	417	6	27	0	0	0	0	0	444	6
EHIOGU U.	2006	6	1	0	0	0	0	0	0	6	1
EINARSSON G.	2004–06	12/9	1	0/1	0	3	0	0	0	15/10	1
ELDING A.L.	2007	4/5	1	0	0	0	0	0	0	4/5	1
ELI R.	1984–85	1/1	0	0	0	0	0	0	0	1/1	0
ELLAM R.	1972–73	9/2	0	2	0	2	0	6	0	19/2	0
ELLIOTT R.J.	2006	5/2	0	1	0	0	0	0	0	6/2	0
ELLIOTT T.	2006–07	0/3	0	0	0	1	0	0	0	1/3	0
ELLSON M.F.	1920–21	37	8	0	0	0	0	0	0	37	8
ENTWISTLE W.P.	1979	7/4	2	0/1	0	0	0	0	0	7/5	2
EVANS G.J.	2000	0/1	0	0	0	0	0	0/1	0	0/2	0
FAIRCLOUGH C.H.	1988–94	187/6	21	14/1	0	17/2	2	14	0	232/9	23
FAULKNER J.G.	1969	2	0	0	0	0	0	2	0	4	0
FEARNLEY H.L.	1946–48	28	0	1	0	0	0	0	0	29	0
FELL J.W.	1925–26	13	1	0	0	0	0	0	0	13	1
FERDINAND R.G.	2000–01	54	2	3	0	2	0	14	1	73	3
FIDLER F.	1951–52	22	8	1	0	0	0	0	0	23	8
FINLAY J.	1951	1	0	0	0	0	0	0	0	1	0
FIRM N.J.	1979–81	11/1	0	0	0	0	0	0	0	11/1	0
FIRTH J.	1928–34	72	25	3	0	0	0	0	0	75	25
FITZGERALD P.J.	1960	8	0	0	0	0	0	0	0	8	0
FLO T.A.	2006–07	5/18	4	0/1	0	0	0	0	0	5/19	4

Player	Played	LEAGUE App	Gls	FA CUP App	Gls	FL CUP App	Gls	OTHERS App	Gls	TOTAL App	Gls
FLYNN B.	1977–82	152/2	11	6/1	0	12/1	0	4	0	174/4	11
FLYNN P.	1953	1	0	0	0	0	0	0	0	1	0
FORD M.S.	1993–96	27/2	1	5	0	7	0	0/1	0	39/3	1
FORREST J.R.	1952–58	119	36	2	1	0	0	0	0	121	37
FORRESTER J.M.	1992–94	7/2	0	1	2	0	0	0	0	8/2	2
FOWLER A.	1932–33	15	8	0	0	0	0	0	0	15	8
FOWLER R.B.	2001–02	24/6	14	1/1	0	0	0	0/1	0	25/8	14
FOXE H.V.	2006	12/6	1	1	0	2	0	0	0	15/6	1
FRANCIS C.T.	1937	1	0	0	0	0	0	0	0	1	0
FRANCIS G.	1959–61	46	9	1	0	3	0	0	0	50	9
FREEDMAN D.A.	2007	9/2	5	0	0	0	0	3	1	12/2	6
FREW J.H.	1920–23	96	0	3	0	0	0	0	0	99	0
FROST D.	1949–50	10	2	0	0	0	0	0	0	10	2
FULLAM R.	1923	7	2	0	0	0	0	0	0	7	2
FURNESS W.I.	1929–36	243	62	14	4	0	0	0	0	257	66
GADSBY K.J.	1936–47	81	0	6	0	0	0	0	0	87	0
GALVIN C.	1969–72	6/1	1	0/2	0	1	0	4/2	1	11/5	2
GARDNER S.	2007	1	0	0	0	1	0	0	0	2	0
GASCOIGNE T.C.	1921–23	20	0	0	0	0	0	0	0	20	0
GAVIN M.W.	1982–84	20/10	3	0	0	4/1	1	0	0	24/11	4
GIBSON A.	1954–59	165	5	5	0	0	0	0	0	170	5
GILES M.J.	1963–74	380/3	88	61	15	19	1	63/1	11	523/4	115
GOLDBERG L.	1938–46	33	0	0	0	0	0	0	0	33	0
GOLDTHORPE E.H.	1920	6	2	0	0	0	0	0	0	6	2
GOODWIN F.	1959–63	107	2	4	0	9	0	0	0	120	2
GRAHAM A.	1977–82	222/1	37	12	3	22	4	3	3	259/1	47
GRAHAM D.A.W.	2005	1/2	0	0	0	0	0	0	0	1/2	0
GRAINGER C.	1960	33	5	1	0	3	1	0	0	37	6
GRAINGER D.	1945–47	37	5	3	1	0	0	0	0	40	6
GRANVILLE D.P.	1998	7/2	0	3	0	1	0	0/1	0	11/3	0
GRAVER F.	1924	3	0	0	0	0	0	0	0	3	0
GRAY A.D.	1995–97	13/9	0	0/2	0	3/1	0	0	0	16/12	0
GRAY E.	1965–83	441/13	52	46/1	5	33/2	6	41/2	6	561/18	69
GRAY F.T.	1972–84	327/5	27	27/1	3	30/1	4	12/2	1	396/9	35
GRAY M.	2005–06	16	0	0	0	0	0	0	0	16	0
GRAYSON S.N.	1988–91	2	0	0	0	0	0	1/1	0	3/1	0
GREEN H.	1930–33	19	4	0	0	0	0	0	0	19	4
GREENHOFF B.	1979–81	68/4	1	1	0	5	0	0	0	74/4	1
GREENHOFF J.	1962–68	88/6	21	10/1	2	12	4	18/1	6	128/8	33
GREGAN S.M.	2004–06	63/1	0	1	0	6	0	0	0	73/1	0
GRIBBEN W.H.	1928	3	0	0	0	0	0	0	0	3	0
GRIFFIT L.	2004	0/1	0	0	0	0	0	0	0	0/1	0
GRIFFITHS J.M.	2005	0/2	0	0	0	0	0	0	0	0/2	0
GUPPY S.A.	2004	1/2	1	0	0	1	0	0	0	2/2	1
HAALAND A.R.	1997–99	57/17	8	5/1	0	3	0	7/2	0	72/20	8
HACKWORTH A.	1999–2000	0	0	0	0	0/1	0	0/2	0	0/3	0
HADDOCK P.M.	1986–91	106/12	1	6/2	0	9/2	0	9/1	0	130/17	1
HAIR K.G.A	1950–63	443	1	21	1	10	0	0	0	474	2
HALLE G.	1996–98	65/5	4	8/1	0	3/1	0	2	0	78/7	4
HALLETT T.	1962	0	0	0	0	1	0	0	0	1	0
HAMPSON T.	1938	2	0	0	0	0	0	0	0	2	0
HAMPTON P.J.	1972–79	63/5	2	5	1	5/1	0	3/1	0	76/7	3
HAMSON G.	1979–85	126/8	3	10/1	1	4	0	2/1	0	142/10	4
HANKIN R.	1976–79	82/1	32	1	0	15	3	4	1	102/1	36
HARDING D.A.	2005	20	0	0	0	1	0	0	0	21	0
HARGREAVES J.	1935–39	46	10	2	1	0	0	0	0	48	11
HARLE D.	1985	3	0	0	0	0	0	0	0	3	0
HARRIS C.S.	1974–81	123/30	26	5	2	7/7	1	1/3	0	136/40	29
HARRIS J.	1922–25	126	14	8	0	0	0	0	0	134	14
HARRISON P.	1949–51	65	9	2	0	0	0	0	0	67	9
HARRISON R.	1949	2	0	0	0	0	0	0	0	2	0
HART E.A.	1920–35	447	14	25	1	0	0	0	0	472	15
HART P.A.	1977–82	191	16	11	1	17	1	4	2	223	20
HARTE I.P.	1995–2003	199/12	28	16/2	3	10/2	2	45	6	270/16	39
HARVEY D.	1965–84	350	0	31	0	38	0	26/3	0	445/3	0
HASSELBAINK J.F.	1997–98	66/3	34	9	5	5	2	4	1	84/3	42
HASTIE J.K.G.	1952	4	2	0	0	0	0	0	0	4	2

Player	Played	LEAGUE		FA CUP		FL CUP		OTHERS		TOTAL	
		App	Gls	App	Gls	App	Gls	App	Gls	App	Gls
HATELEY M.W.	1996	5/1	0	0	0	0	0	0	0	5/1	0
HAWKINS D.R.	1966–67	2	0	0	0	2	0	0	0	4	0
HAWKSBY J.F.	1960–62	37	2	1	0	7	0	0	0	45	2
HAWLEY J.E.	1978–79	30/3	16	3	0	6	1	0	0	39/3	17
HAY D.J.	1999–2001	2/2	0	0	0	1	0	0/1	0	3/3	0
HEALY D.J.	2004–06	81/29	29	3/1	2	3/1	0	0/1	0	88/32	31
HEATH M.P.	2006–07	51/1	4	3	0	2	0	1/1	0	57/2	4
HEATON W.H.	1946–48	59	6	1	0	0	0	0	0	60	6
HENDERSON J.S.P.	1954–55	15	4	0	0	0	0	0	0	15	4
HENDERSON T.W.	1962–63	24	2	6	0	4	0	0	0	34	2
HENDRIE J.G.	1989	22/5	5	1	0	1	0	2	0	26/5	5
HENRY G.R.	1938–46	44	4	3	1	0	0	0	0	47	5
HIBBITT T.A.	1965–70	32/15	9	1	0	5	0	8/2	2	46/17	11
HIDEN M.	1997–99	25/1	0	1	0	1	0	4	0	31/1	0
HILAIRE V.M.	1988–89	42/4	6	2	0	3	1	2	0	49/4	7
HILL G.	1920	7	0	1	0	0	0	0	0	8	0
HILTON J.	1949	1	0	0	0	0	0	0	0	1	0
HINDLE T.	1945–48	43	2	3	0	0	0	0	0	46	2
HIRD K.	1978–83	165/16	19	6/2	2	7/1	0	3	0	181/19	21
HODGE S.B.	1991–93	28/26	10	2/1	0	4/3	0	0/3	0	34/33	10
HODGKINSON E.S.	1946–47	2	0	0	0	0	0	0	0	2	0
HODGSON G.	1936–39	82	51	4	2	0	0	0	0	86	53
HODGSON J.P.	1945–47	20	0	2	0	0	0	0	0	22	0
HOLLEY T.	1936–48	164	1	5	0	0	0	0	0	169	1
HOPKIN D.	1997–99	64/9	6	6	0	7	0	6/1	0	83/10	6
HORNBY C.F.	1930–35	88	5	1	0	0	0	0	0	89	5
HORSFIELD G.M.	2006	11/3	2	0	0	1	0	0	0	12/3	2
HOWARTH J.T.	1921	45	19	1	0	0	0	0	0	46	19
HOWSON J.	2006–07	27/8	4	3	0	2/1	0	5	2	37/9	6
HUCKERBY D.C.	1999–2000	11/29	2	1/2	0	1/1	2	1/10	2	14/42	6
HUDSON W.A.	1951	4	0	0	0	0	0	0	0	4	0
HUGHES A.J.	2007	32/8	1	1	0	0	0	0/2	0	33/10	1
HUGHES C.	1950–51	21	2	2	0	0	0	0	0	23	2
HUGHES P.A.	1983–84	6	0	1	0	0	0	0	0	7	0
HULSE R.W.	2004–05	45/7	18	2	1	1/1	0	3	1	51/8	20
HUMPHREYS A.	1959–61	40	0	1	0	3	0	0	0	44	0
HUMPHRIES W.M.	1958–59	25	2	1	0	0	0	0	0	26	2
HUNTER N.	1962–76	540	18	65/1	1	39	1	80/1	1	724/2	21
HUNTINGTON P.D.	2007	12/5	1	2	0	0	0	5	1	19/5	2
HUTCHINSON G.H.	1955	11	5	0	0	0	0	0	0	11	5
HYDES A.	1930–36	127	74	10	8	0	0	0	0	137	82
IGGLEDEN H.	1948–54	169	47	12	3	0	0	0	0	181	50
INGHAM A.	1947–49	3	0	0	0	0	0	0	0	3	0
IRWIN D.J.	1983–85	72	1	3	0	5	0	2	0	82	1
JACKLIN H.	1921	3	0	2	0	0	0	0	0	5	0
JACKSON M.G.	1995–99	11/8	0	4	0	0	0	0	0	15/8	0
JACKSON W.	1925–26	38	2	1	0	0	0	0	0	39	2
JENNINGS T.H.O.	1924–30	167	112	7	5	0	0	0	0	174	117
JOACHIM J.K.	2004	10/17	2	0/1	0	3	0	0	0	13/18	2
JOBSON R.	1995–97	22	1	1	0	3	0	0	0	26	1
JOHANNESON A.L.	1960–69	170/2	48	14	5	8	6	5/1	8	197/3	67
JOHNSON A.	2006	4/1	0	0	0	0	0	0	0	4/1	0
JOHNSON B.P.	2007	18/3	3	0	0	0	0	3	0	21/3	3
JOHNSON J.P.	2006	3/2	0	0	0	0	0	0	0	3/2	0
JOHNSON R.	1964–67	18/4	4	1	1	6/1	1	0	0	25/5	6
JOHNSON S.A.M.	2001–04	43/11	4	3/1	0	1	0	0	0	47/12	4
JOHNSON S.A.	2000–04	3/8	0	0	0	1	0	0	0	4/8	0
JOHNSON W.	1923–27	72	0	1	0	0	0	0	0	73	0
JONES A.	1960–61	25	0	1	0	3	0	0	0	29	0
JONES M.G.	1997–2000	11/12	0	0/2	0	1/1	0	4/2	0	16/17	0
JONES M.D.	1967–73	216/4	77	36	12	13/1	5	43	17	308/5	111
JONES V.P.	1989	44/2	5	1	0	2	0	4	0	51/2	5
JORDAN J.	1971–77	139/30	35	16/3	4	9/1	3	19/4	6	183/38	48
KAMARA C.	1989–91	15/5	1	0	0	1/2	0	1	0	17/7	1
KANDOL T.O.	2006–07	43/16	12	2	0	2	0	0/3	0	47/19	12
KANE R.	1935–46	58	0	3	0	0	0	0	0	61	0
KEANE R.D.	2000–01	28/18	13	2	0	2	3	6	3	38/18	19

Player	Played	LEAGUE App	LEAGUE Gls	FA CUP App	FA CUP Gls	FL CUP App	FL CUP Gls	OTHERS App	OTHERS Gls	TOTAL App	TOTAL Gls
KEETLEY C.F.	1927–34	160	108	9	2	0	0	0	0	169	110
KELLY D.	1937	4	0	0	0	0	0	0	0	4	0
KELLY G.O.	1991–2006	419/11	2	31/1	2	28/2	0	38/1	0	516/15	4
KELLY J.	1934–37	59	17	5	1	0	0	0	0	64	18
KELLY J. 'Mick'	1934–35	4	0	0	0	0	0	0	0	4	0
KEMP J.	1958	1	0	0	0	0	0	0	0	1	0
KENNEDY D.	1969	2	1	0	0	0	0	1	0	3	1
KENTON D.E.	2007	16	0	0	0	0	0	0	0	16	0
KEOGH A.D.	2003	0	0	0	0	0/1	0	0	0	0/1	0
KERFOOT E.	1949–58	336	9	13	1	0	0	0	0	349	10
KERR D.	1988–90	6/7	0	1	0	2	0	0/4	0	9/11	0
KERSLAKE D.	1992	8	0	0	0	0	0	0	0	8	0
KEWELL H.	1995–2002	169/12	45	16	6	8	4	34/3	8	227/15	63
KILFORD J.D.	1958–61	21	0	0	0	2	0	0	0	23	0
KILGALLON M.S.	2003–06	73/7	3	4	0	6/1	0	3/1	0	86/9	3
KILKENNY N.M.	2007	16	1	0	0	0	0	3	0	19	1
KING M.F.	2004	4/5	0	0	0	0	0	0	0	4/5	0
KIRBY D.	1947	8	0	0	0	0	0	0	0	8	0
KIRK R.	1950–51	34	1	5	3	0	0	0	0	39	4
KIRKPATRICK J.M.	1925–26	10	0	0	0	0	0	0	0	10	0
KISHISHEV R.P.	2006–07	15/2	0	0	0	0	0	0	0	15/2	0
KNARVIK T.	1997–99	0	0	0/1	0	0	0	0	0	0/1	0
KORSTEN W.	1997–98	4/3	2	2/1	0	0	0	0	0	6/4	2
LAMBERT J.	1923	1	0	0	0	0	0	0	0	1	0
LAMPH T.	1920	6	0	0	0	0	0	0	0	6	0
LANGLEY E.J.	1952	9	3	0	0	0	0	0	0	9	3
LAURENT P.	1996–97	2/2	0	0	0	0	0	0	0	2/2	0
LAWSON F.I.	1961–64	44	17	3	1	4	3	0	0	51	21
LENNON A.J.	2003–04	19/19	1	1/1	0	1/2	0	0	0	21/22	1
LETHERAN G.	1974	1	0	0	0	0	0	0/1	0	1/1	0
LEWIS E.J.	2005–07	82/2	8	3	0	4/1	0	3	1	92/3	9
LIDDELL G.	1972–74	2/1	0	0	0	1	0	1/1	1	4/2	1
LILLEY D.S.	1996–98	4/17	1	0/1	0	0/3	0	0/1	0	4/22	1
LINIGHAN A.	1984–85	66	3	2	0	6	1	2	0	76	4
LOMAS A.	1948	1	0	0	0	0	0	0	0	1	0
LONGDEN E.	1928–30	28	7	0	0	0	0	0	0	28	7
LORIMER P.P.	1962–85	503/22	168	56/3	20	41/1	19	77/2	31	677/28	238
LUCAS D.A.	2007	3	0	0/1	0	0	0	2	0	5/1	0
LUCIC T.	2002	16/1	1	2/1	0	1	0	0	0	19/2	1
LUKIC J.	1978–82/90–95	355	0	28	0	30	0	18	0	431	0
LUMSDEN J.	1966–69	3/1	0	0	0	0	0	0	0	3/1	0
LYDON G.M.	1954	4	1	0	0	0	0	0	0	4	1
LYON J.	1920	33	3	0	0	0	0	0	0	33	3
McADAM D.F.	1948–49	24	0	0	0	0	0	0	0	24	0
McADAMS W.J.	1961	11	3	2	1	0	0	0	0	13	4
McALLISTER G.	1990–95	230/1	31	24	6	26	4	14	4	294/1	45
McCABE J.J.	1947–53	152	0	9	0	0	0	0	0	161	0
McCALL A.	1952–54	62	8	2	0	0	0	0	0	64	8
McCLELLAND J.	1988–89	22/2	0	2	0	2/1	0	0	0	26/3	0
McCLUSKEY G.M.C.	1983–85	57/16	16	4	0	5/3	1	1	0	67/19	17
McCOLE J.	1959–61	78	45	2	1	5	7	0	0	85	53
McCONNELL P.	1958–61	49	4	2	0	3	1	0	0	54	5
McDONALD R.W.	1986–87	18	1	0	0	1	0	5	0	24	1
McDOUGALL J.	1934–36	52	0	7	1	0	0	0	0	59	1
McGEE J.	1920	0	0	1	0	0	0	0	0	1	0
McGHIE W.L.	1976	2	1	0	0	0	0	0	0	2	1
McGINLEY W.D.	1972	0/1	0	0	0	0	0	0/1	0	0/2	0
McGOLDRICK J.	1983	7	0	3	0	2	0	0	0	12	0
McGOVERN J.P.	1974	4	0	0	0	0	0	0	0	4	0
McGREGOR J.R.	1985	5	0	0	0	0	0	0	0	5	0
McGUGAN J.H.	1960	1	0	0	0	0	0	0	0	1	0
McINROY A.	1935–36	67	0	4	0	0	0	0	0	71	0
McKENNA F.	1956	6	4	0	0	0	0	0	0	6	4
McKENZIE D.	1974–75	64/2	27	6/3	2	5	1	1/1	0	76/6	30
McMASTER J.	1999–2004	0/11	0	0	0	1/1	0	0	0	1/12	0
McMORRAN E.J.	1948–49	38	6	2	0	0	0	0	0	40	6
McNAB N.	1982	5	0	1	0	0	0	0	0	6	0

Player	Played	LEAGUE		FA CUP		FL CUP		OTHERS		TOTAL	
		App	Gls	App	Gls	App	Gls	App	Gls	App	Gls
McNEISH S.	1950	1	0	0	0	0	0	0	0	1	0
McNESTRY G.	1928	3	0	0	0	0	0	0	0	3	0
McNIVEN D.S.	1975–77	15/7	6	0	0	1	0	0	0	16/7	6
McPHAIL S.J.P.	1996–2003	52/26	3	3	0	2/4	0	15/4	0	72/34	3
McQUEEN G.	1972–77	140	15	13	1	5	0	13/1	3	171/1	19
MADDEN S.	2007	0	0	0	0	0	0	1	0	1	0
MADELEY P.E.	1963–80	528/8	25	64/3	2	49/1	3	71/1	4	712/13	34
MAGUIRE P.J.	1987	2	0	0	0	0	0	0	0	2	0
MAHON J.	1931–35	78	20	6	3	0	0	0	0	84	23
MAKINSON J.	1935–39	68	0	2	0	0	0	0	0	70	0
MANGNALL D.	1929	9	6	0	0	0	0	0	0	9	6
MANN J.A.	1971–72	2	0	0	0	0/1	0	2	0	4/1	0
MARQUES R.M.	2005–07	48/5	3	2	0	2	0	1	0	53/5	3
MARSDEN J.	1952–58	71	0	4	0	0	0	0	0	75	0
MARSH C.	1948	4	1	1	0	0	0	0	0	5	1
MARTIN C.J.	1946–48	47	1	2	0	0	0	0	0	49	1
MARTIN G.	1960	0	0	0	0	1	0	0	0	1	0
MARTIN J.	1924	2	0	0	0	0	0	0	0	2	0
MARTYN A.N.	1996–2002	207	0	18	0	12	0	36	0	273	0
MASINGA P.R.	1994–95	20/11	5	3/2	4	3	2	0	0	26/13	11
MASON C.E.	1961–62	31	0	0	0	2	0	0	0	33	0
MASON G.	1920–22	65	5	1	0	0	0	0	0	66	5
MASON R.	1923–24	15	0	0	0	0	0	0	0	15	0
MATTEO D.	2000–03	115	2	7	0	2	0	23	2	147	4
MATTHEWS L.J.	1995–97	0/3	0	0	0	0	0	0	0	0/3	0
MAYBURY A.P.	1995–2001	10/4	0	2	0	1	0	1	0	14/4	0
MAYERS D.	1961	20	5	2	0	2	0	0	0	24	5
MEARS F.	1925–26	2	0	1	0	0	0	0	0	3	0
MEEK G.	1952–59	196	19	4	0	0	0	0	0	200	19
MELROSE J.M.	1987	3/1	0	0/1	0	0/1	0	0	0	3/3	0
MENZIES W.J.	1923–31	248	1	10	1	0	0	0	0	258	2
MICHALIK L.	2006–07	24	1	0	0	0	0	3	0	27	1
MILBURN G.W.	1928–36	157	1	9	0	0	0	0	0	166	1
MILBURN Jack	1929–38	386	28	22	2	0	0	0	0	408	30
MILBURN Jim	1939–51	208	15	12	2	0	0	0	0	220	17
MILLER E.G.	1950–51	13	1	1	0	0	0	0	0	14	1
MILLER L.W.P.	2005	26/2	1	2	0	0	0	3	0	31/2	1
MILLS D.J.	1999–2003	96/5	3	6/1	0	4	1	27/2	0	133/8	4
MILLS D.G.	1951–52	34	9	3	1	0	0	0	0	37	10
MILLS F.	1934–38	67	2	3	0	0	0	0	0	70	2
MILNER J.P.	2002–03	28/20	5	1/4	0	1	0	0	0	30/24	5
MITCHELL R.G.	1958	4	0	0	0	0	0	0	0	4	0
MITCHELL T.M.	1926–30	142	19	10	2	0	0	0	0	152	21
MOLENAAR R.	1996–2000	47/4	5	5	1	4/1	0	4	0	60/5	6
MOLLATT R.V.	1951–54	17	0	0	0	0	0	0	0	17	0
MOORE I.R.	2004–06	21/39	2	1	0	3/3	3	0	0	25/42	5
MOORE J.	1921	27	4	1	0	0	0	0	0	28	4
MOORE S.	1931–34	78	0	5	0	0	0	0	0	83	0
MOORE W.R.	1924	6	0	0	0	0	0	0	0	6	0
MORRIS J.S.	2003	11/1	0	0	0	0	0	0	0	11/1	0
MORTON N.	1947	1	0	0	0	0	0	0	0	1	0
MOSS J.	1948–50	23	2	0	0	0	0	0	0	23	2
MUMBY P.	1987–88	3/3	0	0	0	0/2	1	0	0	3/5	1
MURRAY T.	1960	7	2	0	0	0	0	0	0	7	2
MUSGROVE R.	1920	36	2	0	0	0	0	0	0	36	2
NEAL T.W.	1931–35	20	0	3	0	0	0	0	0	23	0
NEWSOME J.	1991–93	62/14	3	3/1	0	3	0	5	0	73/15	3
NICHOLLS K.J.R.	2006	12/1	0	1	0	1	0	0	0	14/1	0
NIGHTINGALE A.	1952–56	130	48	5	0	0	0	0	0	135	48
NIMMO W.B.	1957	1	0	0	0	0	0	0	0	1	0
NOBLE A.H.	1922–24	60	4	3	0	0	0	0	0	63	4
NOTEMAN K.S.	1988–89	0/1	0	0	0	0	0	1	1	1/1	1
O'BRIEN G.	1956–58	43	6	0	0	0	0	0	0	43	6
O'DOHERTY E.F.J.	1920	0	0	2	4	0	0	0	0	2	4
O'DONNELL C.	1989–90	0/1	0	0	0	0	0	0	0	0/1	0
O'GRADY H.	1932	8	2	1	0	0	0	0	0	9	2
O'GRADY M.	1965–69	90/1	12	5	1	5	0	20	3	120/1	16

Player	Played	LEAGUE		FA CUP		FL CUP		OTHERS		TOTAL	
		App	Gls	App	Gls	App	Gls	App	Gls	App	Gls
O'HARE J.	1974	6	1	0	0	1	0	0	0	7	1
OKON P.M.	2002	15	0	5	0	0	0	1	0	21	0
O'LEARY D.A.	1993–95	10	0	0	0	0	0	0	0	10	0
OLEMBE S.R.	2003	8/4	0	0	0	2	0	0	0	10/4	0
O'NEILL J.	1973	0	0	0	0	0/1	0	0/2	0	0/3	0
ORMEROD B.R.	2004	6	0	0	0	0	0	0	0	6	0
ORMSBY B.T.C.	1985– 89	46	5	4	1	1	0	6	1	57	7
OSTER J.M.	2004	8	1	0	0	0	0	0	0	8	1
OVERFIELD J.	1955–59	159	20	4	0	0	0	0	0	163	20
PALMER C.L.	1994–96	100/2	5	12	1	12	0	4	1	128/2	7
PARKER B.B.C.	2007	6/3	0	2	0	2	0	2	0	12/3	0
PARKER N.	1977	0/1	0	0	0	0	0	0	0	0/1	0
PARKINSON K.J.	1977–80	25/6	0	1	0	4	0	2	0	32/6	0
PARLANE D.J.	1979–82	45/5	10	2	0	1	0	0	0	48/5	10
PARRY W.	1938	6	0	2	0	0	0	0	0	8	0
PEACOCK A.	1963–66	54	27	6	2	2	1	3	1	65	31
PEARSON J.S.	1986–90	51/48	12	5/5	0	5/4	0	6/3	0	67/60	12
PEMBERTON J.M.	1993–96	44/9	0	5/2	0	3/1	0	4	0	56/12	0
PENNANT J.L.	2003–04	34/2	2	0	0	0	0	0	0	34/2	2
PETERSON P.W.	1969	3/1	0	0	0	0	0	0	0	3/1	0
PEYTON N.	1957–62	104	17	3	1	9	2	0	0	116	20
PHELAN T.M.	1985	12/2	0	0	0	3	0	2	0	17/2	0
POTTS J.F.	1925–32	247	0	15	0	0	0	0	0	262	0
POTTS J.	1921–22	10	0	0	0	0	0	0	0	10	0
POWELL A.	1936–47	114	25	5	0	0	0	0	0	119	25
POWELL S.	1920–24	28	7	0	0	0	0	0	0	28	7
POYNTZ W.I.	1921–22	29	7	0	0	0	0	0	0	29	7
PRICE A.	1945–46	6	0	1	0	0	0	0	0	7	0
PRUTTON D.T.M.	2007	38/5	4	0	0	2	0	4	0	44/5	4
PUGH D.A.	2004–05	34/16	5	0/1	0	6	1	0	0	40/17	6
RADEBE L.V.	1994–2004	180/20	0	19/2	1	9/5	0	27	2	235/27	3
REANEY P.	1962–77	549/8	6	72/1	3	39	0	76/3	0	736/12	9
REED G.	1925–29	141	2	9	1	0	0	0	0	150	3
RENNIE D.	1985–88	95/6	5	7	1	7	0	4	1	113/6	7
REVIE D.G.	1958–61	77	11	1	0	3	1	0	0	81	12
RIBEIRO B.M.F.	1997–99	35/7	4	4	1	3/1	1	1/1	0	43/9	6
RICHARDSON F.	1999–2007	101/25	3	3	0	8	1	6/1	1	118/26	5
RICHMOND J.	1922–24	56	19	4	0	0	0	0	0	60	19
RICKETTS M.B.	2004–05	10/15	0	0	0	3/1	2	0	0	13/16	2
RILEY V.	1926	0	0	1	0	0	0	0	0	1	0
RIPLEY S. K.	1954–57	68	15	2	0	0	0	0	0	70	15
RITCHIE A.T.	1982–86	127/9	40	9	1	11	3	2/1	0	149/10	44
ROBERTS H.	1925–30	84	2	3	0	0	0	0	0	87	2
ROBERTSON D.	1997–2000	24/2	0	1	0	4	0	0	0	29/2	0
ROBINSON D.	1926–27	5	0	0	0	0	0	0	0	5	0
ROBINSON P.W.	1997–2003	93/2	0	7	0	5	1	12	0	117/2	1
ROBINSON R.	1985–86	27	0	0	0	0	0	0	0	27	0
ROBSON C.	1924	17	4	0	0	0	0	0	0	17	4
ROBSON W.	1921–22	10	0	1	0	0	0	0	0	11	0
ROCASTLE D.C.	1992–93	17/8	2	0/3	0	0/3	0	2/1	0	19/15	2
RODGERSON R.	1920–21	27	0	1	0	0	0	0	0	28	0
ROPER H.	1932–34	18	3	0	0	0	0	0	0	18	3
ROQUE JUNIOR J.V.	2003	5	0	0	0	2	2	0	0	7	2
ROSS R.A.	1951	5	0	0	0	0	0	0	0	5	0
RUDD J.J	1948–49	18	1	0	0	0	0	0	0	18	1
RUSH I.J.	1996	34/2	3	2/2	0	2	0	0	0	38/4	3
RUSSELL D.P.	1924	9	0	0	0	0	0	0	0	9	0
SA A. de M.C.	2006	6/5	0	0/1	0	0	0	0	0	6/6	0
SABELLA A.	1980	22/1	2	2	0	2	0	0	0	26/1	2
SAKHO L.	2003–04	9/8	1	0/1	0	1	0	0	0	10/9	1
SAVAGE R.	1934–38	79	0	5	0	0	0	0	0	84	0
SCAIFE G.	1938	9	0	0	0	0	0	0	0	9	0
SCOTT J.A.	1950–54	111	0	3	0	0	0	0	0	114	0
SEARSON H.V.	1948–51	104	0	12	0	0	0	0	0	116	0
SELLARS S.	1982–86/1992–93	78/5	12	4	0	5/1	1	3	1	90/6	14
SHACKLETON A.	1958–59	30	16	1	1	0	0	0	0	31	17
SHARP K.P.	1992–94	11/6	0	0	0	0	0	0/1	0	11/7	0

Player	Played	LEAGUE		FA CUP		FL CUP		OTHERS		TOTAL	
		App	Gls	App	Gls	App	Gls	App	Gls	App	Gls
SHARPE I.G.	1920	1	0	0	0	0	0	0	0	1	0
SHARPE L.S.	1996–98	28/2	5	0/1	0	3	1	1/2	0	32/5	6
SHEEHAN A.M.A.	2007	10	1	0	0	0	0	0	0	10	1
SHAW J.	1971–73	0	0	0	0	0	0	2	0	2	0
SHEPHERD P.D	1996	1	0	0	0	0	0	0	0	1	0
SHERIDAN J.J.	1982–88	225/5	47	11/1	1	14	3	11	1	261/6	52
SHERWIN H.	1921–24	98	2	9	0	0	0	0	0	107	2
SHORT J.D.	1946–48	60	18	3	1	0	0	0	0	63	19
SHUTT C.S.	1988–92	46/34	17	10	1	6/2	2	4/5	4	66/41	24
SIBBALD R.L.	1966–67	1/1	0	0	0	0	0	0	0	1/1	0
SIMMONDS R.L.	1984–86	6/3	3	0	0	0	0	1/1	0	7/4	3
SINCLAIR R.M.	1985–88	8	0	0	0	1	0	0	0	9	0
SISSONS A.E.	1925–27	30	1	1	0	0	0	0	0	31	1
SMELT A.	1920	1	0	1	0	0	0	0	0	2	0
SMITH A.	1998–2003	148/24	38	11/4	4	4/2	0	28/7	14	191/37	56
SMITH J.E.	1960–62	65	3	3	0	4	0	0	0	72	3
SMITH J.B.	1952	2	1	0	0	0	0	0	0	2	1
SMITH L.	1922–25	32	0	1	0	0	0	0	0	33	0
SNODIN G.	1987–91	83/11	10	5/2	0	9/1	3	5	0	102/14	13
SNODIN I.	1985–86	51	6	1	0	3	2	0	0	55	8
SPEAK G.	1923–24	28	0	4	0	0	0	0	0	32	0
SPEED G.A.	1988–95	231/16	39	21	5	25/1	11	14/3	2	291/20	57
SPRAKE G.	1961–72	380	0	45	0	22	0	58/2	0	505/2	0
SPRING M.J.	2004	4/9	1	0	0	2	0	0	0	6/9	1
SPROSTON B.	1933–37	130	1	10	0	0	0	0	0	140	1
STACEY A.	1927–33	51	0	0	0	0	0	0	0	51	0
STACK G.C.	2006	12	0	0	0	0	0	0	0	12	0
STEPHENSON J.E.	1934–39	111	21	4	1	0	0	0	0	115	22
STERLAND M.	1989–93	111/3	16	10	1	13	1	9	2	143/3	20
STEVENSON E.	1950–51	16	5	0	0	0	0	0	0	16	5
STEVENSON W.B.	1974–81	88/7	4	5	0	7/1	1	2	0	102/8	5
STEWART D.S.	1973–78	55	0	8	0	6	0	5	0	74	0
STEWART J.G.	1951–52	9	2	2	0	0	0	0	0	11	2
STILES J.C.	1984–88	49/16	2	5	1	4/2	0	3/2	0	61/20	3
STONE S.B.	2005–06	6/6	1	0	0	1	0	0/2	0	7/8	1
STORRIE J.	1962–66	123/3	58	12	3	8	5	10	1	153/3	67
STRACHAN G.D.	1988–94	188/9	37	14	2	18	3	14/1	3	234/10	45
STRANDLI F.	1992–93	5/9	2	1	0	0/1	0	0	0	6/10	2
STUART G.E.	1920	1	0	2	0	0	0	0	0	3	0
SULLIVAN N.	2003–06	95	0	4	0	8	0	3	0	110	0
SUTHERLAND H.R.	1938	3	1	0	0	0	0	0	0	3	1
SWAN J.	1921–24	108	47	8	3	0	0	0	0	116	50
SWAN P.H.	1985–88	43/6	11	3	0	3	2	1/2	0	50/8	13
SWEENEY P.H.	2007	6/3	0	0	0	0	0	0	0	6/3	0
SWINBURNE T	1985	2	0	0	0	0	0	0	0	2	0
TAYLOR F.G.	1949	3	0	0	0	0	0	0	0	3	0
TAYLOR J.B.	1951	11	0	0	0	0	0	0	0	11	0
TAYLOR J.R.	1985–88	33/9	9	1	0	5/1	3	4/1	1	43/11	13
THOM J.	1924	7	3	0	0	0	0	0	0	7	3
THOMAS D.G.	1979–83	79/10	3	4/1	0	9	0	0	0	92/11	3
THOMAS M.R.	1989	3	0	0	0	0	0	0	0	3	0
THOMPSON A.	2006–07	18/6	5	0	0	0	0	1	0	19/6	5
THOMPSON N.D.	1983–86	6/1	0	0	0	2	0	1/1	0	9/2	0
THOMPSON R.	1920	23	11	2	1	0	0	0	0	25	12
THOMSON J.	1936–38	41	11	0	0	0	0	0	0	41	11
THORNTON R.G.	1925	1	0	0	0	0	0	0	0	1	0
TILLOTSON A.	1920	2	0	0	0	0	0	0	0	2	0
TINKLER M.R.	1991–96	14/11	0	0	0	1	0	0/1	0	15/12	0
TONER J.	1954	7	1	0	0	0	0	0	0	7	1
TOWNSLEY T.	1925–30	159	2	8	0	0	0	0	0	167	2
TRAINOR J.	1936	3	0	1	0	0	0	0	0	4	0
TURNBULL R.	1925–31	204	45	11	1	0	0	0	0	215	46
TURNER C.J.	1933–34	13	0	0	0	0	0	0	0	13	0
TURNER C.R.	1989	2	0	0	0	0	0	0	0	2	0
TURNER J.K.	1935–37	14	0	0	0	0	0	0	0	14	0
TWOMEY J.F.	1937–48	109	0	2	0	0	0	0	0	111	0
TYRER A.S.	1951–53	39	4	3	0	0	0	0	0	42	4

Player	Played	LEAGUE		FA CUP		FL CUP		OTHERS		TOTAL	
		App	Gls	App	Gls	App	Gls	App	Gls	App	Gls
UNDERWOOD B.R.	1928–30	6	0	0	0	0	0	0	0	6	0
VARADI I.	1989–92	21/5	5	0	0	1	0	1/1	1	23/6	6
VICKERS P.	1950–55	20	4	1	0	0	0	0	0	21	4
VIDUKA M.A.	2000–03	126/4	59	8	5	3	1	25	7	162/4	72
WAINSCOAT W.R.	1925–31	215	87	11	6	0	0	0	0	226	93
WAKEFIELD A.J.	1947–48	49	23	1	0	0	0	0	0	50	23
WALLACE R.G.	1991–93	5/2	0	0	0	0	0	0	0	5/2	0
WALLACE R.S.	1991–97	187/25	53	16/5	4	18/1	8	1/4	1	222/35	66
WALTON J.	1920–22	69	4	2	0	0	0	0	0	71	4
WALTON S.W.	2004–05	26/8	3	2	0	1/1	0	0	0	29/9	3
WARNER A.R.	2006	13	0	0	0	1	0	0	0	14	0
WATERHOUSE F.	1920	0	0	2	1	0	0	0	0	2	1
WATSON A.	1983–84	37/1	7	1	0	4	0	0	0	42/1	7
WEBB R.	1953–54	3	0	0	0	0	0	0	0	3	0
WESTLAKE I.J.	2006–07	29/18	1	1	0	2/1	1	1	0	33/19	2
WESTON C.J.	2007	1/6	1	1/1	0	0/1	0	1	0	3/8	1
WESTON D.P.	1962–65	68	24	7	1	3	1	0	0	78	26
WETHERALL D.	1991–98	188/14	12	21/3	4	19/1	2	4	0	232/18	18
WHALLEY F.H.	1921–23	87	0	4	0	0	0	0	0	91	0
WHARTON C.N.	1939	2	0	0	0	0	0	0	0	2	0
WHEATLEY T.	1953	6	0	0	0	0	0	0	0	6	0
WHELAN N.D.	1993–95	28/20	7	2	0	3/2	1	3	0	36/22	8
WHIPP P.L.	1922–26	145	44	9	3	0	0	0	0	154	47
WHITE D.	1993–95	28/14	9	6	2	2	0	1/1	0	37/15	11
WHITE J.	1926–29	102	36	6	2	0	0	0	0	108	38
WHITLOW M.W.	1988–91	62/15	4	0/4	0	4/1	0	9	0	75/20	4
WHYTE C.A.	1990–92	113	5	8	0	14/1	1	11	0	146/1	6
WHYTE D.	1976	1/1	0	0	0	0	0	0	0	1/1	0
WIJNHARD C.	1998	11/7	3	1/1	1	1	0	1/3	0	14/11	4
WILCOCKSON E.S.	1934	4	0	0	0	0	0	0	0	4	0
WILCOX J.M.	1999–2003	52/29	4	5/1	0	3	0	9/6	2	69/36	6
WILKINS E.G.	1949	3	0	0	0	0	0	0	0	3	0
WILKINSON C.E.	1931	3	0	0	0	0	0	0	0	3	0
WILLIAMS A.	1988–91	25/21	3	2	0	3/3	0	5/2	2	35/26	5
WILLIAMS G.	1987–89	39	3	1/1	0	4	0	0	0	44/1	3
WILLIAMS H.	1949–55	211	32	17	3	0	0	0	0	228	35
WILLIAMS J.	1948	1	0	0	0	0	0	0	0	1	0
WILLIAMSON B.W.	1962	5	0	1	0	2	0	0	0	8	0
WILLINGHAM C.K.	1946	35	0	1	0	0	0	0	0	36	0
WILLIS J.G.	1953	3	0	0	0	0	0	0	0	3	0
WILSON G.M.	1928	3	0	0	0	0	0	0	0	3	0
WILSON J.	1928	3	0	1	0	0	0	0	0	4	0
WINDLE W.H.	1947	2	0	0	0	0	0	0	0	2	0
WOOD B.	1920–21	56	2	0	0	0	0	0	0	56	2
WOOD R.	1953–59	196	0	7	0	0	0	0	0	203	0
WOODGATE J.S.	1997–2002	100/4	4	11	0	7	0	20	0	138/4	4
WOODS M.P.	2002–03	0/1	0	0	0	0	0	0	0	0/1	0
WORSLEY H.	1934	3	0	0	0	0	0	0	0	3	0
WORTHINGTON F.S.	1981–82	32	14	0	0	3	1	0	0	35	15
WORTHINGTON N.	1994–95	33/10	1	6/1	0	4/1	0	0	0	43/12	1
WRIGHT A.G.	2006	1	0	0	0	0	0	0	0	1	0
WRIGHT B.	1962–63	5	0	0	0	3	0	0	0	8	0
WRIGHT J.M.	2004–05	36/2	3	1	0	1	0	0	0	38/2	3
WRIGHT R.W.	1960	1	0	0	0	1	0	0	0	2	0
WRIGHT T.E.	1982–86	73/8	24	4	3	3/3	1	0/1	0	80/12	28
YEBOAH A.	1994–96	44/3	24	6/2	2	7	3	4	3	61/5	32
YORATH T.C.	1967–76	121/21	10	14/3	1	10/1	0	20/7	1	165/32	12
YOUNGER T.	1961–62	37	0	2	0	3	0	0	0	42	0
Own-goals			100		12		5		1		118

ND - #0227 - 270225 - C0 - 260/195/11 - PB - 9781780914343 - Gloss Lamination